Music All The Way

Brian Astell

Pen Press

First published in Great Britain by Pen Press

All paper used in the printing of this book has been made from wood grown in managed, sustainable forests.

ISBN13: 978-1-78003-085-2

Printed and bound in the UK
Pen Press is an imprint of
Indepenpress Publishing Limited
25 Eastern Place
Brighton
BN2 1GJ

A catalogue record of this book is available from the British Library

Cover design by Jacqueline Abromeit

ACKNOWLEDGEMENTS

Usually the author thanks his wife and family for their patience and longsuffering, but I have none of these. I do want to thank my youngest brother, Allen Astell, my cousin, Paul Astell, and a friend and former colleague, Diana Newlands for reading the manuscript and encouraging me to keep writing. Jim Inch of Bugbrook came up with the splendid "Piano on a Cart" drawing, for which I give thanks. Thanks are due to the Dean and Chapter of Hereford for permission to use the photograph of the cathedral choir.Maybe I should thank my dog Badger, who often sat waiting patiently by my desk long after her "walkies" time was due, while I insisted on finishing a chapter.

This book is dedicated to the memory of my Mum and Dad, who sacrificed so much for us and our future

(Roosky, Ireland,March, 2011)

INTRODUCTION

"Sir, you must be a VERY old man," said a quiet little girl at the front of the class, who had been watching me with great concern. This was April, 2003, I was 66, and realised that to this group I could be a hundred, but was indeed part of their history.

One of the teachers in the school next to my house had called one day to ask whether I would give a talk about life in the war as a young child. Her class were doing the Second World War as a project and a talk from me about life as a small boy at that time would give it greater clarity and reality. I agreed, and so was faced with a class of 10-year-olds, eager to learn and bursting with questions. "Was I frightened?" asked one boy; "Did you really see the bombs"? asked another; " Did you have to wear your gas mask?" and so on. I suppose I had to accept that I was part of history, and made up my mind to write about these early years in my life as a kind of therapy, but somehow… having got to 1945 I couldn't leave it alone, and decided to write the whole story.

I have tried to show how music became a dominant feature of my life. Even in the poverty stricken post-war years I overcame obstacles, both financial and parental, to train as a music teacher. First the rude awakening of serving in the Army, playing clarinet in the Band of the Coldstream Guards; university and a teaching career followed and many other interesting jobs came up in my long "retirement". So, whether you are part of that history, or curious about teachers and musicians, I hope you enjoy these ramblings of 'a VERY old man'.

CHAPTER ONE

HUMBLE BEGINNINGS

Well, it all began in Islington – an area of North London which these days is very upmarket – home of the yuppies, television producers, film stars and politicians from ex Prime Minister Tony Blair downwards or upwards, depending upon your point of view; folk, with the most up-to-date four-track or sports cars, all with their ubiquitous personalised number plates, so that everyone may know that they have made it! But in the 1920s through to the 60s, Islington was a very poor area. To his dying day (1979) my father was bewildered by advertisements in the Sunday newspapers, in which a "des. res." was advertised at £1,000,000, with "The added attraction of delectable basements and the Grand Union Canal running at the end of the small garden." My dad would exclaim, "But these were the bloody slums – we used to swim in the canal and watch the rats running in and out of the basements! The very same houses, now tarted-up and suddenly sought-after. These rich people have more money than sense!" This was the gist of his statement, for having lived in Islington all his life he had learned some of the rich, cockney language of the people around him.

This isn't really the type of book where one delves into family history until a disreputable character is found, at which point interest in genealogy is suddenly lost, but I must give some background to our family. Our maternal grandmother, Ellen, married Jack Shepherd, who worked as a French polisher by trade – interestingly two of my uncles later followed the same trade. Obviously it was quite an important job in the days when quality furniture was hand-made and lovingly cared for.

The Shepherds lived in the Clerkenwell area of London, and from Mother's birth certificate I have gathered that they were living at 34 Henry Street Buildings at the time of her birth in 1908. Her father Jack was a very quiet man, rather shy, but also fond of a few drinks – even more than a few when they were available. They had six girls: Mary, Minnie (Min), Rebecca (Beck) who was our mother, Ellen (Nell), Emily (Em), and Elizabeth (Lizzie), and one son called 'Jacky Boy', born around 1902. The names are witness to the predilection for Londoners to shorten as many long words as possible; as a small boy I could never understand why my bald-headed uncle could be 'Uncle Hen', *and his surname was 'Bullock!'* At some point they were living at 16 Rising Hill Street, but by 1922, when my mother left school for her first job the family had moved to 37 Albert Street, as it was known then[1].

Life must have been difficult. Jack, the father, died quite suddenly, and the only son, Jacky Boy – everyone seems to have given him this familiar name – also died of TB in his early twenties. He had just got engaged, and his early death was a tragedy for all. One of the sisters, known as Lizzie, was very backward, although in these more enlightened times she would have simply been put in a special class in an ordinary school; Emily suffered badly from polio, and throughout her life had to use callipers, and when my own mother was about 20 Ellen, her mother, died. The girls were now orphans, but the eldest sister Mary had married, and took on the role of guardian to them all so that the family could stay together – quite a responsibility! I mentioned the fact of Mother getting her first job, but The Factory And Workshop Act, 1901, required a certificate with a copy of entry of birth for young people under 16 to be able to seek employment. Mother's certificate, needed for her first job (probably at King's Cross working in a laundry as a Hoffman presser) was dated 21st October, 1922, just a few months after her 14th birthday. Interestingly enough we can see a discrepancy between Mother's name on her birth certificate and the name copied on the employment certificate: in the former she is definitely Rebecca Shepherd, but the registrar completing the employment certificate called her Rosina Shepherd. No one seems to have noticed, but this is hardly surprising when you realise that Ellen could only make her mark with a cross on both certificates – she had not learned to read and write.

We leave Mother's family working away at 37 Albert Street and look briefly into Father's background.

---

1   Later this became Culpeper Street, N1

Charles William Astell was born on 10th February, 1880 at Grays Inn Road, Holborn and married my Grandma –Emma Georgina Partridge at St.Alban's Church, the local parish church on April 15th, 1900. His occupation in the 1901 census is listed as 'Carman'. Certainly we know he worked for a coal merchant at some point. At this time they occupied a flat at 110 Cromer St, St. Pancras, along with five others – the landlord, single and four widows.

They had a family of six children: Alice, Ellen, Emily, Jessie, Albert and my father Charles, and appeared to move around the Islington area of London, certainly at addresses in Pemberton Road, and Finsbury Park.

Information about how my parents actually met is very scanty, but it seems that he took pity on her. As we've seen already, Mother and her sisters were living in Albert Street, and apart from their own jobs they would all have domestic tasks to do in the house. I have heard that my father saw my mother cleaning the steps to the front door, felt sorry for her, and decided that they might as well marry and she could then clean his front door steps! I just hope it was a little more romantic than that. On Saturday evenings father would 'splash out' to take mother to the Finsbury Park Astoria, the 'posh' local cinema where the great Wurlitzer organ would rise up during the interval to play the latest hits, the audience would be invited to join in –words appearing on the screen by magic, and they could look high up to the ceiling, made to appear as though it had stars twinkling there. Sometimes they would go to Collins Music Hall on Islington Green, and hear Marie Lloyd, Harry Lauder, and other great stars of the old-time music hall. They were married on Christmas Day, 1935, at quite a fashionable large church, St Mary's in Upper Street, by a young curate called Donald Coggan, who, of course, was eventually to become the Archbishop of Canterbury. Not many couples could claim to have been married by a future Archbishop, and I always enjoyed reminding my mother of this famous connection. Donald Coggan had himself only been married for two months before he conducted the service for mother and father. There was a pattern of marriages being held on Christmas Day –it happened at least four times in the family – probably because it would otherwise be difficult for all concerned to have time off from work. At least Christmas Day and Boxing Day were paid holidays.

I was their first child, born on September 30, 1936, (exactly two years to the day on which Dr. Coggan had been ordained) but I very nearly died within three years of birth. At some point in 1939 I developed meningitis and pneumonia; the former was certainly a killer, and not many children recovered from pneumonia. The only information I have gleaned was that I ended up in the Royal Northern Hospital, Islington, and that my parents had given me up for dead, for they had asked the priest to come in and say a final prayer over me. At this point the doctor said he wanted to try one more thing, and I miraculously recovered within days. Discussing this with at least one doctor, we think that somehow he managed to get hold of a new drug, probably still on trial, for it had only been licensed a year before. Almost certainly he was trying me out on a new M&B product called sulfapyridine, and it obviously worked and has given me over 70 years lease of life. I have tried to discover who saved my life, but so far drawn a blank.

As a family we first lived in Hungerford Road, which is close by Camden Road and the famous Nags Head public house. These had been 'posh' houses, large rooms and high ceilings which in their glory days had probably been home to one family with a couple of servants on the top floor. But now this house, like many others, was divided into at least three flats. My parents had the top floor (servants quarters) and Dad's parents occupied the ground floor, while the first floor was occupied by yet another family. We would all have shared one indoor lavatory and bath. I can still remember two things about the flat: a view of Holloway Prison from the front-room window and an awful smell of boiled fish and cats which always pervaded the atmosphere, and even today the smell of boiled fish takes me back to Nan and Hungerford Road.

After this Father moved to Lothair Road in Haringey. It was a squalid, damp, terraced house which also ran close by the canal, and just yards from the main King's Cross railway line. Perhaps my love of trains stems from this time, but the house was found to have water seeping into the floor at an alarming rate– we were sinking, and I wonder whether the level of the canal was also dropping at the same time! On various occasions as I have passed in the train bound for King's Cross, I have noticed that the street and the house are still there, and maybe still as damp as in 1939. These memories are mingled with visits to public houses, where I seemed to be left outside in a pram and given an occasional large biscuit to munch. Pubs in those days were quite strict about having young children in the bar – one assumes that the adults had enough to contend with having the children at home, and they wanted some peace and relaxation. Of course the pub was a very important place in which to meet; grandparents on my father's side were particularly partial to drink, and one of the few stories of the past which both my father and his brother related, was of them having to meet their dad on a Saturday night when he had his pay packet on him, and wrestle the money from him somehow before he reached the pub and spent it all in one evening! There seemed to have been many occasions when my father and his brother had to share the one pair of shoes for school, so the one without the shoes had to stay at home. Because grandpa was a coalman there would be little work for him during the summer months, so that he would be "on the labour" – looking for work at the Labour Exchange with just a small benefit payment for the family. Occasionally the family would get a "charabanc", as coaches were called, and have a day out at the seaside. I have a vague memory, with photos to prove it, of being pushed along the front, possibly at Southend or Margate – very popular destinations for working class Londoners.

Of course these people lived in real poverty, had no possibility of saving, and lived from one week to the next. They would have very strong memories of the Great Depression of the Twenties, with the loss of many jobs, and dozens of applicants for those which were available. You worked hard to maintain your job, never even thought about asking for "a rise", for you were just fortunate to get a pay packet at the end of the week. Coupled with this situation were the evils of alcohol. The men worked very hard for very little, and the night at the pub was one way of escaping from this drudgery. Unfortunately many people could not control their drinking. Gin, always known as 'Mother's ruin', was cheap, and so was beer. For the family who did not want to drink in the pub, one of the youngsters would be sent with a large jug to buy it from a small window at the entrance. I believe this fear of uncontrolled drinking stayed with my father all through his life; when the family came along he had very strong views about our own drinking, and hardly ever had drink in the house. On special occasions or when relations visited us he would send one of us to the off-licence for ale or stout. I can remember one or two

Christmas times when we had the luxury of VP fruit wine, and then only a small glass each. And yet with this hard life people seem to have been content, with strong family ties, and perhaps a feeling that this was as good as it got. All was to change in September 1939 when Mr Hitler became greedy for more territory – maybe he decided he wanted Islington for himself – and started a war.

CHAPTER TWO

LIFE DURING THE WAR

There are many accounts of the effects of the 1939-45 war on individuals, and I can only add my own memories of it as a young boy. As a family we were thrown all over the place during the evacuation phase, but I seemed to be in London for the worst parts of the war. One early memory occurred on September 7th, 1940. My mother had taken us to visit relations who lived in Paddington, near the Royal Oak tube station, and we had travelled home by tube to King's Cross station. Because of an air raid we had to leave the train and found there were no buses running, it was of course a time of blackout with no lights allowed in the streets, and buses and the few cars would have small lights which no one could see. I think there were more traffic accidents with people run over at this period of the war than people dying of bombs – but it was all to change. With no buses around we walked up the steep hill of Pentonville Road. Bombs were falling as we hurried along, and at one point we sheltered in a shop doorway; there was a tremendous whistle as one bomb came very close, my mother just threw me in the air and I was caught by a policeman, who held me up and pointed out the bright glow burning in the east of London. "Look at that son, London is burning". It was the bright glow of the docks. Incendiary bombs were falling on the Canning Town and docks area of London at about 5 o'clock, and were to continue to pound that area for 12 hours and with factories full of spirits, tyres, wood, and pepper along with the huge Tate and Lyle sugar works, there was certainly plenty to burn.

At some point around the beginning of the war my parents moved to Kier Hardie House, part of a block of flats at the top of another steep hill called Hazelville Road. This was just within Islington; the flats bordered on Hornsey Lane which was the northern boundary of Islington. Hornsey Lane consisted of the largest houses I had ever seen, where I saw for the first time the 'Tradesmen's entrance' signs on gates at the side, and other large notices saying "no tradesmen, hawkers, or circulars", whatever that meant. I knew nothing about the man after whom our flats had been named; that he had been the first Labour Party Member of Parliament, and I reckon most of the other occupants also lived there in blissful ignorance. The flat was on the ground floor, with two bedrooms, kitchen, quite a modern bathroom, and a living room (lounge would be too posh a name). From the time we lived there this living room was considered damp; some of the furniture began to go green, and various attempts were made to dig up the floor and find the source of the damp, but this was all to no avail, and in the winter it was most unhealthy. Many years after we moved from the flat, one of my brothers returned to find that it had been boarded up – 'Health and Safety' had at last arrived on the scene. Finally the whole block was demolished to provide a car park for the remainder of the flats – another sign of the times.

So this was the second damp, unhealthy house I lived in. My brother John was born in 1939, just before the outbreak of war, and very soon we were involved in evacuation. I understand that we were evacuated to both Oxford and Cambridge for very short periods at the beginning of the war, and I believe mother had quite a row with the people who had taken us in, who thought they were getting an unpaid housekeeper – as if she didn't have enough to do with a three-year-old and a baby, so we returned home. John was then evacuated to Sevenoaks, in Kent, at some sort of school, I don't think my mother even knew his address. This was just one of the curious anomalies of evacuation, where individuals seemed to be moved around with very little thought about keeping the family together. Mothers were often unaware of the exact location of their own children.

The blitz continued for months. Air raids were frequent; darkness always made one doubly fearful, and sleeping at home was almost impossible. Night after night the siren would sound, and we would rush to the shelter –remember we lived on the ground floor of a five-storey block of flats so I was always petrified of being smothered by the falling buildings. As the shelters were in the middle of the courtyard with flats on three sides it would have been disastrous if they had received a direct hit. Apparently my job on all these occasions was to look after

Mum's old handbag which contained the family insurance documents! Sometimes we walked to Archway, the nearest tube station, to spend the night underground, but so did hundreds of other people. Authorities had tried to prevent the public from sleeping on the station, but had been forced to change their mind after the huge losses of life and palpable fear which was shown by the whole community. On several occasions I saw the results of incendiary bombs which had destroyed shops and houses nearby. Hours after the fire one could still smell the burnt wood, and in the case of bombed houses see where walls had been blown away, the wallpaper, sinks, even furniture open to the sky. Somehow it seemed an obscene intrusion into people's privacy, you felt you should not be looking at somebody's bedroom wallpaper complete with remains of a bed precariously hanging on the sloping floorboards, but, almost certainly the occupants were beyond worrying about such delicate matters. This came home to me in a special way when we went down to visit relations at Culpeper Street and had to walk from the Angel bus stop through the busy market, with stall holders valiantly soldiering on – the policy of " keeping going" was always to the fore, no time for sadness and self-pity to take over. Where several shops had been bombed the night before I saw the blackened timbers, and the still smouldering interiors –realising that only 24 hours before, the occupants would have been about their business, selling carpets or furniture, unaware that it was their last day. That day is still vivid in my mind.

Then while my mother stayed in the flats I was sent off, when I was about six, to a small village near Kettering, in Northamptonshire, called Ringstead. How I missed my mother in the first few days! My new 'carer' was called Mrs Else, had at least 6 boys packed into her small house and neglected us entirely. I think we were there because she could get a very nice allowance from the government for providing us with a home – but it was no home, only a house – a world of difference. I have no memory of the school, except that it was at the bottom of a steep hill – life was full of steep hills – and I spent many hours of spare time helping in the dairy which was at the end of the lane bordering on the fields. Even at six I was quite useful. When the dairy man made deliveries in the village I could transfer the milk, still warm, from the churn into a jug using the pint and a half pint measuring cans. Back at the dairy I learned to use the small machine for putting the cardboard tops on the milk bottles with the small, round section which you had to press – and generally the milk spurted out into your thumb or over clothes!. These have all disappeared now, but some folk will remember them. The dairy farmer and his wife were far more homely and welcoming than Mrs. Else my so-called 'carer'. After about a month I was allowed back to London for a weekend break, but Mother was horrified to discover that I had the dreaded 'nits' in my hair; she washed and scrubbed to get rid of these awful things, and reported the incident to the evacuation authorities and the doctor. She really did feel that she had been responsible, was quite ashamed, and I was soon brought back from my short stay in Ringstead. In the late eighties when I lived in Cambridgeshire, I took mother back to Ringstead and, apart from some extra houses, it had hardly changed from wartime days, though I found I had a strong desire to scratch my head!

Back in London in 1943 life took on a more normal and regulated mode for a few months. I went to Dick Whittington L.C.C. Primary School whenever it was safe – this meant a walk of a mile, crossing Archway Road, the A1 heading north out of London, which was quite a busy main road even then. I can remember nothing of my lessons or the staff, but certainly this was a typical L.C.C. building with classrooms built round a central hall and the essential shelter which we often used – always obeying the strict injunction that one ALWAYS WALKED, NEVER RAN. Apparently the theory was that running would induce panic. I am glad I didn't know about one or two schools in London which received direct hits with terrible casualties, for I would have run at break-neck speed to the shelter regardless of rules. The connection with Dick Whittington is that he is reputed to have sat down on Highgate Hill at the back of our school, to look over London, heard the bells calling him on, and, complete with cat, went on to make his fortune. A stone marks the spot even today. I wonder whether he would have been so eager to return to London in 1943.

We were already well into food rationing: bread units and coupons, with long queues for bread, meat, cheese and butter in quantities so small that people would leave the coupons for a couple of weeks to get an amount that you could at least see. Fresh meat was a luxury, as were eggs, yet a curious package appeared called 'Dried Egg' which we enjoyed. Strange thought that with egg gluts just a few years ago and memories of a certain Edwina Currie come to mind, no one thought of finding the dried egg recipe. We had no real sweets; they were strictly rationed and, like chocolate, were unobtainable for months at a time. We seem to have lived on a diet of cod liver oil and malt, which tasted dreadful, and orange juice – not fresh from a box but in a small bottle. You took the ritual spoonful every day and were grateful! When I spoke to people who had lived in the country they found it hard to imagine all these privations, but any city person will vouch for the truth of these conditions. Of course money could buy anything, and even at the age of seven I knew what the term 'black market' meant. Shopkeepers often went 'under the counter' for certain customers, and this, coupled with the knowledge that in West end hotels one could still get the full works – excellent three course meals at good hotels, with plenty of wine – caused great anger among ordinary people.

Bombing continued, and we spent many nights in the air-raid shelter. It was at this time that I first encountered a wonderful character who became a hero to me. His name was Gregory Hopper, and he was a Baptist minister from the local church. Even during the worst nights of bombing, he would do his rounds on a bicycle with his steel helmet on, calling in at the shelters to chat to the various wives about their husbands and the situation. He would try to help those who had a particular need, and at some point he would ask us all whether we would like to join in a short prayer for all those far away and for God's help during these difficult times. There was always silence while his prayer was offered, no one raised any objections, indeed they seemed glad of a voice that was expressing their hopes and fears on these awful occasions. Dear 'Uncle Greg', for that is what he was affectionately called by everyone, was very much admired by the community. He must have been well on in his sixties, too old to be in the forces but determined to play his part, not only to be involved in the difficulties, but somehow, to show that the Church was concerned. I had no idea then that I would meet up with him again, and be very grateful for his care and concern in my life.

At some point during 1943, when the bombing was really bad, the family was evacuated yet again. My middle brother, John, had returned from Sevenoaks and he and my mother, with the youngest baby, Allen, now aged two, were sent off to Rochdale in Lancashire. They were billeted with an elderly lady who everybody called Nanny Mills, who lived at 8 Birch Road with her daughter, Edna, and the young granddaughter, Margaret, who would be about six. So when three rather bewildered Londoners descended upon them, the tiny house became very full. No room for me, so I was sent to Blackpool. I can still remember sleeping in a school hall for two nights, until strangers began to arrive to look us over. It was rather like being in a cattle market; I remember one man pressing my arm, then telling his wife that I didn't have very strong muscles and wouldn't be much help to them. The whole process was fairly demoralising, but things improved when a couple arrived who were very kind, announced they were Mary and Ralph and would I like to live with them? I thought they were rather 'posh', but, along with another evacuee called Alice – about my age – I was taken back to their house at 87 Grasmere Road. This was definitely posh! It had stained glass windows in the front door, a large back garden, and I had never lived in a house with such large rooms. There was a lounge complete with carpet, a dining room, kitchen and a study downstairs. It all seemed very grand, though I suppose nowadays it would just be considered a fairly typical semi-detached residence. Mr and Mrs Darvill, (Ralph and Mary) told me that I had to share a bedroom with their son David who must have been about a year older than me, and I don't think he was very pleased at the intrusion into his privacy. The other evacuee had to share with the daughter, Gillian. Much later I realised how much of a sacrifice that family were making, to open their home to two completely unknown children, but at that stage I was terribly homesick, I wanted my mum. The other girl from London couldn't stand the separation and only stayed a few days, her parents came to collect her and took her home, where, I discovered later, she and her family had almost certainly been killed by a direct hit on their house about a fortnight after their return.

When I had explored my new home, I noticed that Mr Darvill wore his collar back to front just like my 'Uncle Greg' back home in Islington – yes, he also was a Baptist minister. The Darvills did their very best to make me feel at home. They told me that Sunday was a very busy day for them; the family went to the services in the morning and evening, but if I didn't want to go they would make arrangements for me to be looked after. Of course I wanted to go. I'd already had enough of meeting new people, and longed for the security of staying with them as much as possible. Inwardly I was scared that they would disappear, and that I would be put into yet another billet. I was also very curious about what happened at church. I remember my first experience at the morning service. Suddenly there was *MY* Mr Darvill standing in the pulpit , speaking to everyone in the congregation, *and I was living in his house.* I felt so proud. For the very first time I heard the strains of a pipe organ, a great big monster with shiny long pipes, and a man who seemed to be all lit up playing at the keyboard. I went out with the rest of the children for the Sunday school, but it wasn't half as good. In the hall there was only a piano, and I couldn't wait to get back into that huge church and listen to the organ. After the final prayers Mrs Darvill told me that they had to say goodbye to people, and I was to be patient until they were ready to go home. Within two minutes I had found the door leading up to the gallery where the organ was perched, and there I watched, fascinated, as the organist played with hands and feet. After that, the family always knew where to find me, and it became rather a joke "Looking for Brian? He'll be with Mr. Brammer [the organist]." Dear Arthur Brammer would invariably walk into church on Sunday morning and extinguish his pipe, but retain it in his mouth until the moment he sat down to play, then the pipe would be stowed below the organ stops. I suppose you could say that he was simply exchanging one pipe for different pipes! Of course I had no idea that this was really the beginning of my own life in music, my ambition to play the organ, and a lifelong occupation as an organist in various churches; nearly 70 years on I am still playing the organ at church services.

That family did their very best for me, and life took on a regularity and routine for a short time. I must have gone to the local junior school, probably the one with the hall in which we had slept awaiting allocation, but can remember nothing about it, not even the name of one of the teachers. Sometimes on Saturdays I would go to the Pleasure Beach where there were many entertainments. I used to stand for hours mesmerised by the laughing sailor in his glass box rolling around helpless with laughter, I watched the big dipper, vowing that I would never go on it, and I never did! There were halls of mirrors, and funny moving cottages, and ghost trains. Just beyond the Pleasure Beach were the golden sands where the donkeys placidly walked along with young children on their back. Looking down over the

13

scene was the Tower. If only I'd known then that there was a famous Wurlitzer organ in the ballroom, I would have gone to see it. I noticed many soldiers and airmen enjoying themselves in Blackpool, but their uniform was different, and they spoke with a funny accent. They were members of the US forces from the aerodromes and barracks outside Blackpool, having a good time while they could before they went off at the time of D-Day in June 1944 –most of them never to return to England or their homeland.

On one occasion Gillian Darvill and I both got chickenpox. Rapid changes had to be made because David had not yet contracted the disease, so I was put in bed with Gillian, and I believe we did a little mutual exploration to pass away the time. We were to meet up years later, in 1987, when I was music director at a Baptist church in Cambridge – see chapter 16. I was playing the congregation out after a Sunday morning service when a quiet voice at my elbow said, "Hullo, we haven't met for 44 years, but you *DID* share a bed with me then." Gillian Darvill, the daughter, now with her husband, had recognised my name from the church notices, and come forward to renew acquaintance. On an earlier occasion, when I was going to Holland in 1958 to enjoy a Summer school with the BMS (Baptist Missionary Society), I met the summer school president and his wife at a London railway station –it was Ralph and Mary Darvill, and we were to share a fortnight's holiday. The Baptist world is indeed a small one.

Going back to evacuation time, it seems incredible today to realise that at weekends, every two or three weeks I was put on a train to Rochdale, via Manchester, to visit my mother and brothers. I was only seven years old, but appeared to have no trouble with the journeys. There are hazy memories of smoky, noisy stations, and my being met by someone on the platform. The Mills family welcomed me into their small home. The back garden seemed to lead straight on to the hills and open country of Lancashire. There are vague recollections of us taking pies and peas to the baker's, where they were pushed into a huge oven using a pallet attached to a long handle; then at lunchtime going back to collect our cooked food, covered with a cloth, and hurrying home before it got cold. This seemed to be Saturday's main meal. I can also vividly remember Nanny Mills, who seemed positively ancient, and still wore clogs when she went out of doors, seating us by her side, and taking down a large meat plate on which there was the familiar blue willow pattern. She proceeded to tell us the little rhyme which described the pattern, and all in her gentle Lancashire accent:

These two birds are flying high, while the boat is passing by,
These three men going to Dover, with the willow hanging over.
China church is standing near, twice a week we worship here,
Apple trees with apples on and plaited rails to walk upon.

Obviously no example of great poetry, and yet whenever I get out my soup plates, if there are guests around, I still find myself reciting this simple rhyme. Sometimes in the evening Nanny Mills, with eyes twinkling, would make us laugh with another simple poem –complete with Lancashire brogue – which went as follows:

Let's get to bed, says Sleepyhead,
Tarry a-while, says Slow,
Put on the pan, says Greedy Nan – let's sup before we go!

Despite her busy life, and the fact that she hated writing, mum always tried to write a few lines to me during the weeks when I couldn't get over to Rochdale, but on one occasion I remember a letter arriving for the adults, obviously from my mother, but with no note for me. This seemed very strange, and I made up my mind to have a surreptitious glance at their letter. What I read confirmed my worst fears; my mother was going back to London to meet my father who was on leave, but wanted to keep it from me because she knew I was always worried about the bombs raining down on the flats where we lived. From the daily newspapers I knew that the bombing was still very bad, and I made up my mind that somehow I had to get back to London to see her. I counted up my money the next day, which came to about one shilling (5p) and decided to set off late at night when the family were in bed. Having forced myself to stay awake, I crept downstairs, fully clothed, and clutching my precious money, quietly opened the front door, and set forth on my London journey. I had walked all of 20 yards, when I felt a hand on my shoulder, and a voice gently said, "Come on Brian, it's a bit late to be going out now." I immediately collapsed in tears, as Mr Darvill put an arm round me and walked me back home. He realised how anxious I was for my mother's welfare, and promised to telephone someone the next day and arrange for me to hear my mother's voice. This was in the days when only very rich people had telephones, but because of his job, Mr Darvill did have a shiny, black instrument in his study. This must have been the first time I had used the phone.

We returned home in time for the V1 bombs. The great D-day invasion of Europe had begun on 6th June, and as people explained that the army were now in France, I expected that victory would follow within hours – I had no idea of distances, or of the extraordinary operation which was under way; I just knew that France was next to Germany so we were going to beat the Germans. Then one week later the first V1 bombs fell. Once again we were forced to spend many hours in the air raid shelters, both night and day, for these weapons were being sent over at all times. They were miniature rockets, un-manned, which had a "pop-pop" noise rather like a lawnmower, hence their name "doodlebug". They flew very fast – in the early days our own ack-ack guns were not able to intercept them as they came in over the south of England – and when the engine cut out everyone held their breath until the explosion a few seconds later. Often in the shelter the door would be left open, and we would listen for these rockets. On one or two occasions the engine seemed very close and during the following silence I almost wet myself with fear. Some bombs did fall close by. One raid happened on Christmas Eve; mother was going to take us to the family on Christmas Day for dinner and presents, but as we set off in the number 14 bus from Hornsey Rise I noticed that we were diverted from our usual route, and we drove very slowly passed Thorpedale Road. I could see the smoke, smelt all the dust and fumes, and then saw a huge crater where at least four of the houses had stood. One of my school friends lived in one of those houses, and I never saw him again; Hitler had certainly sent a bizarre Christmas present to those families, all wiped out in a few seconds. Of course these situations were happening all over London, Kent and Essex; it seems that these dreadful rockets hadn't enough fuel to go much further north...oh, why hadn't we stayed in Blackpool and Rochdale? I never will know the answer.

16

Dear Adolf then gave us the 'nsew, improved' version, the V2. This travelled so fast that one never heard the bomb until it exploded. The destructive capabilities of these weapons was frightening. When four of the V2 bombs fell on Croydon, over 2,000 houses were destroyed or damaged. They were sent over from early September, and I had two experiences of these frightening bombs during the day. I was going home from school and the siren went, but before I could take cover I saw a huge flash and then heard the explosion. The bomb had fallen miles away, but the violent explosion made it always seem as though it was close by. In these situations no one stood a chance, and if these raids had continued for much longer, I believe we would have had to surrender. London was being slowly but surely brought to its knees.

When I returned to London from evacuation it seems that Mr Darvill had not let me go. He had contacted the minister of the nearest Baptist church at home, and, sure enough, one Sunday afternoon Uncle Greg himself knocked at the door and said he was taking my brothers and me to Sunday school. This was the same Uncle Greg who I had seen earlier during our time in the shelters, the Uncle Greg who had come to admire for his loving care for all the wives and mothers in those shelters, and now he looking out for me. Mother was quite happy to have a bit of peace on Sunday afternoon, and we used to go down the hill to the church in our best clothes. I remember harvest festival, when mother gave each of us a lovely rosy apple, all polished, as our contribution to the harvest; unfortunately temptation overcame John, and he ate his apple on the way! When the time came for us to take up our contributions he was quite prepared to offer the core, until I told him that this wasn't a good idea. I began to go to the services in the morning and evening, and remember occasions when we prayed for husbands and sons who were away fighting in the war; at the end of the prayer we often sang a hymn from the Baptist hymn book – I even remember the number, 487, which was "Holy Father, in thy mercy, hear our anxious prayer; keep our loved ones now far distant in thy care."

I was interested in the organ, and became one of the organ blowers. Although we had electric lighting in the church, the organ still had to be pumped by hand, and it was very hard work. When Uncle Greg's wife played the organ she only used two or three stops, so that I could keep up with the pumping fairly easily,

17

but on some occasions a visiting organist would come along and play loudly all the time so that it was very hard work to keep the blower full. The minister could see me from his pulpit although I was hidden from the congregation, and on one occasion when he noticed that I was tiring, he came down from the pulpit and took over. Another time he came down and told me to stop pumping at the end of verse three; when I tried to point out that there were two more verses he just winked at me and told me to sit down and take a rest. The organist crashed down the keys for the next verse, but within a few seconds, with a depressing moan, the organ stopped. Uncle Greg stepped out from the back of the organ and tactfully reminded organist and congregation that even the best player was useless without the co-operation of the pumper. Everyone smiled, including the organist and I felt very proud of my job. At least I can claim as an organist today that I started at the bottom, or to be more accurate, at the pump. It was during the sermon at one evening service that I felt that the minister was just speaking to me personally. I cannot remember the details, but I know that I wanted to be associated with this Christian life. I told Uncle Greg at the door, and he put his arms round me, telling me that he had been praying for me for a long time, then he took me to the vestry to meet the other deacons, and we prayed together. He then arranged for me to meet one of the deacons each week at his home to get to know the Bible better; for some reason this arrangement only lasted for a few weeks, but I know that at nine I was quite sincere in wanting to follow the Christian way of life. Even today I can remember Uncle Greg's words after that vestry prayer, when he warned me that life was not a bed of roses. I may not have understood his meaning then, but within a couple of years I knew exactly what the dear old fellow meant. The Christian way of life is really tough.

Eventually father was to return, demobbed from the army, but not before signs of strain had appeared with Mum. I remember the only time when she walked out on us. It was a Sunday and, as usual, she had cooked a good meal for us three boys and herself. During dinner we began arguing -we were constantly bickering and scrabbling – this time it was about who should have the skin on the top of the Birds custard. How banal and trivial could we get! In the middle of the argument Mother just threw the basin on the table, grabbed her coat and walked out, telling us that she wouldn't be coming back, then slammed the front door. Of course we carried on fairly normally, cleared the table so that we could play our games, but I don't recall that we even thought of doing the washing up. It was only by about 6p.m. – getting hungry for tea – that we began to get worried; perhaps she didn't love us any more and had gone away for good. Allen, the youngest began to cry when he heard John and I discussing this possibility, for we had taken her for granted every single hour of our waking life, and had never even begun to appreciate the terrible difficulties under which she coped. There was great relief when the key turned in the front door, and Mum came in – but relief was short-lived for she was accompanied by Uncle Charlie – her brother-in-law, the patriarch, indeed the 'Godfather' of the family and, as he was so strict, a source of fear to us children. We were all told off and Uncle made it quite clear that I had particularly let him down, as he was relying on me as the eldest, to help Mum and take Dad's place …at nine years of age! Many tears were shed that evening, and I later gathered that mother had gone straight to her sister's home, back to 37, Albert Street where she had grown up. After shedding a few tears and recharging her emotional batteries, she was ready to come home and be our mum once more.

* * * *

Before the war ended we were able to enjoy one of the great luxuries – Saturday morning pictures. We caught the 210 single decker bus to Finsbury Park and queued with a grubby sixpence (2½ p) in our hands ready for the great rush when the doors opened. We enjoyed Roy Rogers, Gene Autrey, Abbott and Costello and many others. During the cowboy chases we would all stand on the seats and cheer like mad, and as the curtain came down there was a massive rush for the door – no waiting for the national anthem – and on the bus back to Hornsey Rise we would recount the adventures. I can remember the words and tune of the Saturday morning club song:

"We come along on Saturday morning greeting everybody with a smile,

We come along on Saturday morning knowing it's all worthwhile.

As members of the GB[1] club we all intend to be

good citizens when we grow up, and champions of the free.

We come along on Saturday morning, greeting everybody with a smile, smile, smile – greeting everybody with a smile."

With wall-to-wall TV available these days, it must be hard to understand what a treat these morning pictures were to us. We kept this up when we moved to Dagenham in 1947 and went to the Grange Cinema (the flea pit, as it was known to us) still clutching our 6d.

By the end of the war the dreaded V2 bombs had done terrible damage and killed and maimed so many. Eventually peace came on May 7th, 1945 and I vividly remember the declaration of peace announced on the radio. That afternoon I had gone to visit Aunt Nell and Uncle Charlie in their three storey plus basement house off Essex Road, just a stone's throw from Islington Green. There the statue of Hugh Myddleton stood, who had brought clean water and a sewage system to this part of London – and behind the Green stood the Collins Music Hall, soon to open again for its old-time variety shows.

Around 4 o'clock there was an announcement on the radio –very solemn and serious; Uncle told us all to be quiet, and the announcer, almost certainly Alvar Liddell, a top BBC announcer who I was to meet in the 60s, proclaimed the message that the war in Europe was over. I believe he ended with the phrase: "God save the King" and the national anthem was played. Auntie and the family were in tears, perhaps tears of thankfulness that they had been spared, and certainly tears for those who had not survived those awful five years. There was a tremendous ease of tension and the 'family telepath' began. None of the relatives had a telephone but within hours a party was being planned for the next night in Culpeper Street, and WHAT A PARTY! Bonfires were lit on the roofs of the air raid shelters, the radiogram was set up, with speakers playing out of the windows of the first floor and the whole street was packed with people dancing, and singing. Beer, shandy for the women, lemonade for the children all flowed freely. Complete strangers poured into the street and joined in; there must have been hundreds of people during the night. I can still recall the two local Catholic priests crawling upstairs from the basement at about 4am, well inebriated and

---

1   Gaumon British – a chain of cinemas in the UK

muttering that they had to go across to church to say the early morning Mass. Of course the men in the forces were still absent, but at least we knew they were safe.

I fully expected to be able to go to the shops next day and buy as much chocolate, sweets and fruit as I wanted, but this was not to be. Rationing was to go on for years, but we learned quickly that whenever a queue formed at the local greengrocers or confectioners one joined it – often with no idea what would be offered at the end; the queues were long, but people were patient, and Mother and I would take turns in the long wait for perhaps a couple of bananas or oranges, or three small penny bars of chocolate. When I did get my first banana, I caused a laugh as I tried to eat it with the skin on; having never seen one before. How was I to know that it had to be peeled?

I was attending Romilly Lodge School at this time, although immediately after our return from evacuation we had returned to Dick Whittington School, off Archway Road. Perhaps the main road was considered dangerous for young children to cross – no 'lollipop' people on patrol then – or, as it was at least three-quarters of a mile away, it was thought too far to walk, especially when air-raid warnings were frequent during the day time. Certainly Romilly Lodge was nearer and a good school. I can remember several of the teachers, along with Mr Hobbs the caretaker and gardener. The school itself was a large dilapidated house with a huge garden area at the back, and we all had some gardening lessons and jobs to do in the garden. Miss Smalley was the headmistress, Miss Blacklock – complete with moustache – was a forbidding character; tall, deep-voiced Miss Harrison, gentle and petite Miss Philips who took us for English, and, above all, Miss Rawlins – later to become head when the school moved to new premises in Hornsey Lane. She gave us music lessons and was the first person to inspire me in music. From a plastic Tipperary flute (cost 4/11 or 25p) I had just progressed to a plastic Descant Recorder (10/-or 50p), thanks to a generous Christmas present from my uncle John. I used to learn one or two tunes each day and play them to Miss Rawlins when she was on playground duty. What a creep I must have been; but she obviously had a prophetic nature for she introduced me to the clarinet long before I knew anything about instruments of the orchestra. A group of us were taken to a concert at the polytechnic in Holloway Road at which Frederick Thurston was the soloist. At the last moment Miss Rawlins insisted that I bring along the dreaded recorder, and at the end of a delightful demonstration and recital by the great man I was firmly grasped by the hand. "Come along Brian, There's someone I want you to meet." Having arrived at the green room, the teacher said: "Mr. Thurston, this is the young man I mentioned to you; I think he would take to a wind instrument easily." Mr. Thurston then insisted that I play something to him, and gave me three clarinet reeds, which he said might be useful when I took up the clarinet. It was only much later that I realised both that he was a famous musician –principal clarinet in the BBC symphony orchestra – and that clarinet reeds were extremely scarce, for the Germans had destroyed all the reed beds in France where these things were grown. There was a veritable black market in reeds for quite a few years after the war. How I wished I had saved those clarinet reeds for posterity!

In my last year at the school (1946-7) we performed a short version of Humperdinck's *Hansel and Gretel*, in which I was cast as Hansel and a lovely girl named Mary Howard was my 'sister' Gretel. She teaches her clumsy-footed brother to dance – obviously an apt choice of casting; I remember the dance duet words:

"Brother, come and dance with me, both my hands I offer thee,
Right foot first, left foot then, roundabout and back again."

Later in the forest we both sang our lullaby, having committed ourselves to the guardian angels for the night: "When at night I go to sleep, 14 angels watch do keep, etc." I did enjoy that duet as I snuggled under the blanket with my Gretel. Unfortunately at one of the performances there was a disaster, when halfway through one of the dances I realised that, slowly but surely, my trousers were coming down. All was well for a few steps because I could hold on to the trousers with one hand, but as the dance reaches its climax Hansel offers both his hands to Gretel, and my trousers dropped to my ankles and the audience had a good view of my rather grubby underpants! But, like a true pro, I knew that the show must go on!

During these school days I had one or two friends. Through Roy Thomson I got to know his family, who seemed to keep 'open house' for me after school – a courtesy that I must have abused, for I seemed to go round there every day. It was Roy's mother who helped me with the piano, and suggested that I should call in and practise during the week. She was so helpful and encouraging, especially bearing in mind that she had a meal to cook for her husband and mother, as well as coping with her young daughter Jean, Roy and myself. Mr. Thomson was a tall, well-built policeman from Scotland, who had kept his rich accent; maybe he was disappointed in Roy, for he often made comparisons between his son and me: "Brian's got hobbies, and gets on with them, but you do nothing…" I found this all very embarrassing for it was driving a wedge between our friendship; I did NOT want to be set up as some 'goody-goody' or paragon of virtue. But I'm sure that Roy's father meant well, and longed for his son to achieve something. I can remember their large house with enormous rooms – the lounge was about as large as our whole flat – but it must have been expensive to heat in the post-war days of fuel shortages; somehow they seemed 'posh' and I longed to live in a house like that. Thirty years ago all those houses were demolished and ugly blocks of flats were hastily erected, even their road has disappeared in new developments.

Our nearest relations were an uncle and aunt who lived in a block of flats near by, with three children – our cousins – Harry, Minnie and Frank. Harry, the eldest son was in the navy, away in the USA at the time, but Frank was in his last year at school and he had joined the scouts; he was very keen on this movement, and when the scoutmaster decided to form a cub pack, I joined as part of the original group of cubs. Our Akela, George Mumford, was a super guy who genuinely cared for each one of us, and put a great deal of time and effort into leading. Almost every weekend he would take us out on trips, using train or bus, and although we paid some money towards our expenses, I know that he subsidised the trips himself to a great extent. We had some great times on our days out, and also in the Cub HQ, which was a small hut situated behind some very large advertising hoardings on the Archway Road, just below the bridge, which carried Hornsey Lane high above the busy road below. Sadly I upset Frank's mother, Aunt Min rather badly. It was my 9th birthday, and a few friends and relations had come to tea, with some having to stay the night. I sat and listened as my mother went over the arrangements as to who was to sleep where, and then Aunt Min thought she had better ideas. "Why can't you let mum get on with it, instead of interfering?" I asked. That did it. Auntie said I was very rude, picked up her things and walked out before my mother could pacify her. I was thoroughly ticked off, and made to go over to their house the next morning and apologise. I really had not meant my remark to sound rude, I thought I was just being helpful, but this cut no ice with my mother. So I duly went around on Sunday morning, timidly knocked at the door, but when Aunt opened the door she wouldn't let me in, and closed the door firmly. I just knew I had to do the apology, so I knocked again, and this time when she opened the door I stumbled out at top speed that I was very sorry that I had upset her, and that I would never do it again, then drew breath. It was then that I first heard the phrase that is used so often in these situations, when Auntie said, "Well I may be able to forgive you but I can never forget it." I realised later, that the whole point of forgiveness is to put the transgression behind one completely, so that no grudge remains, but at the age of nine and one day I was not ready with this philosophic point of view. It did take three or four weeks but in due time I was allowed to go back into their rather nice flat. I often seemed to be there around midday on Sundays, when I could smell their lunch cooking while Forces Family Favourites was played on the radio. Right up to the present day the sound of the signature tune, *With a Song in My Heart* played by André Kostalanez makes my taste buds work overtime as I think of roast lamb and potatoes.

Summers seemed to be very hot in those days. Mother was generally glad to get rid of us for a few hours, and I would take my brothers to the local outdoor swimming pool in Hornsey; I remember one hot day when the three of us just sunbathed for hours, and found walking home rather difficult as our skin seemed to be stretched, and we certainly suffered for the next couple of days. Mum was constantly pouring on calamine lotion to red hot skin, each movement was painful, and we could hardly sleep. Occasionally we would wander towards Alexandra Palace, which stood out on top of a hill, always visible with its television transmitter aerial. Most of the palace had been neglected, but a small wing was used to send out television programmes to the lucky few who had sets in their homes. We had no idea this was going on, for television was something completely unknown to us, but we did explore the beautiful grounds around the palace. In its heyday it must have been a wonderful sight. Often we would go to Shepherds Hill, a local park, from which one had a perfect view of Alexandra Palace, and on a couple of occasions our neighbour's daughter came along. Yvonne was just a few months older than me, and she was eager to send my brothers off to play while she practised 'doctors and nurses' with me. She always wanted to be the 'doctor' and found all sort of excuses to examine me. Soon the game became very interesting as I cottoned on to the situation. I hadn't really a clue what we were doing, but Yvonne certainly took charge and I know I enjoyed it, and was always ready when Yvonne suggested a return trip to the gardens!

CHAPTER THREE

HARD TIMES

Eventually Father returned from East Africa, and gave us a big surprise one night when he just appeared on the doorstep. We had been put to bed, but, as the eldest, I had been allowed to stay up a little longer, so was still awake when I heard whispers in the front room. Knowing that we just NEVER had visitors at night, and heeding Uncle Charlie's earlier warning, as head of the family it was my duty to see that all was well. Peeping through the door frame I saw Mum sitting on Dad's lap and rushed in to greet him, then despite the whispers, my brothers woke up and came in. Allen had never seen his father, and immediately told Dad to "Leave my Mum alone!" I realise now how much this must have hurt Dad, indeed it had an influence on his harsh treatment of Allen – amounting to bullying – which went on for many years, and was noticed by all of us. Presents were given out, some beautiful cloth for mother, an elephant tusk and real leather wallets hand-made by the Africans for us; and photos of lions, elephants, Dad's black servant, the house in Mombasa where he had lived made us all quite envious for we were convinced that he had been having a good time while we were putting up with the bombs. He had been offered a chance to remain in the army and suggested that it was possible for us all to go to live in Africa and see the sights for ourselves, and we were ready to pack and go off immediately, but Mother wanted to know about the snakes and wild animals, and the creepy-crawlies at night. Dad explained that one was quite safe with the mosquito net over the bed, but this put Mother quite off the idea, and though in later days Dad asked her to take the idea seriously, she was firmly against moving to Africa. After all the excitement it was time for bed, but again Allen was adamant that he wasn't going to bed until "That man leaves my Mum alone and goes home!"

The food situation at this time worsened , and as children we could not understand why, with the war over, everything hadn't gone back to normal; it was especially annoying having to queue for hours just for a small bar of milk chocolate, or a couple of bananas. The winter of 1947 was one of the worst on record, with thick snow and freezing temperatures for days on end. There were often power cuts and fuel was very scarce. We queued in bitterly cold weather for a sack of coal in what was certainly the longest queue I had ever seen. It must have been about three hours before the coal man shovelled a few pieces into our sack, and then came the job of carrying it home, a distance of a couple of miles. About three quarters of the way along the sack began to split, and my brothers and I had to carry some of the coal in our arms, while mother dragged the sack along – she was absolutely determined that not one piece would be lost after all the trouble we had gone through. Come to think of it I can't understand where father was in this situation. There was a great shortage of flour, which led to bread being extremely scarce, and even with our bread units we had to join long queues to buy a loaf – as for cakes, forget it. The intense cold and damp resulted in chilblains for my brothers and me, and there were many nights when we would cry with the pain; all sorts of remedies were tried, and I remember one, I think it was called Chillproof, a sort of green lump which you rubbed on your feet. It had a nice smell, but didn't seem to do the job. Another remedy was to pee into a chamber pot, and put the feet in that; it seemed a revolting thing to do and yet it seemed to work, and the pain went away for some time.

Dad returned to his post-war job, that of a telephonist at Chilton Court Hotel, a large building built above Baker Street underground station and owned by London Transport. He always did night work, leaving home at around 8:30pm and returning in the morning at around 8:30am; he had one night off every 14 days! He never liked the flats where we lived, and I believe wanted to go a little more up market, so in 1947 we got a council exchange to Dagenham, to live in a two-bedroom house which the rent book quaintly described as a cottage. It seemed even smaller than our flat in Islington, but "was in the country", according to Father. What a laugh! Our so-called 'cottage' was in the middle of the largest Council Estate in Europe at that time. Dagenham had been earmarked just before the war as the new L.C.C.

overspill from London, built on reclaimed marshland by the banks of the river Thames, and was home to many hundreds of workers at the Ford factory near the river. Every house seemed to be built in the same way, with the same type of brick, and the whole pattern of the streets was fairly dull. However plenty of parks had been allocated and the whole sprawl was bisected by the railway line, with District Line underground trains which surfaced after Bow in East London, and ran above ground through to Upminster; main line steam trains going to Southend-on-Sea from Fenchurch Street station ran alongside the tube trains. In an earlier chapter I hinted at people's reactions when I gave them my address as "Keir Hardie" house, but nothing had changed. Eyebrows were distinctly raised when people knew that I lived in Dagenham. When one talked to 'the upper classes', as I thought many people were at that time, the mention of Dagenham raised comments such as, "Oh, how quaint," followed by an embarrassed silence while they scoured their brain for some comment on Dagenham which might be appropriate; I would be asked whether I knew the Dagenham Girl Pipers. I was always tempted to reply that I regularly slept with half a dozen of them, and watch the effect! The plain fact was that I generally felt ashamed to admit that I lived in a council house in Dagenham; it made my developing inferior complex even more acute.

In May of that year I had taken and somehow passed the Eleven Plus examination and was able to go to a grammar school. Miss Smalley at Romilly Lodge suggested that it would be better for me to start at a London school rather than go off to Dagenham. Either she was trying to delay my seemingly downward path to perdition, or she was anxious that at least I would get one year's decent start in a good London grammar school. So it was arranged that I stay each week with one of Mother's nieces, Mary and her husband John. I always knew that they loved children but, it seemed, were unable to have a family of their own; when I asked Mum about this, she just hinted that Auntie had "something wrong with her insides", but I couldn't for the life of me see what that had to do with having a family of their own. At eleven I knew nothing about the 'facts of life', as they were euphemistically termed, although I was beginning to do some research when I went to the local library, where I would furtively look in the Biology section – when no library assistants or readers were around. Somehow this kind of information seemed rude. I also felt in my bones that the 'doctors and nurses' games I had played with Yvonne a year before had something to do with this 'Facts of Life' business. There was certainly nothing wrong with her insides. Even at seventeen I was not very street-wise. When I had my first – and only – suit made to measure the assistant asked, "Which side do you dress on?" and I replied, "Usually by the window, especially in summer". No wonder he went away with a 'What a plonker' look on his face.

Aunt Mary and Uncle John always treated me like the son they never had; he taught me to take a pride in my appearance – we always polished our shoes each morning, and I had to see that my tie was knotted properly.

They made considerable sacrifice when they took me in. Their second-floor flat in Liverpool Road, Islington, almost opposite the great Agricultural Hall (itself steeped in royal tradition, but by this time had become a sorting office for the G.P.O.) only had one bedroom so my bed was fitted up in the corner of their living room. We had meals in the kitchen so that I could spread out my books for homework in the living room and work without interruption. My shirts and pants were rather the worse for wear, and Auntie bought new ones so that I looked smart at the new school –Highbury County High, quite close to Highbury Corner, and the old Arsenal football stadium.

Uncle John was particularly generous and keen to help me musically. Having demonstrated my ability on the Tipperary flute, I had told him that what I really needed was a Descant Recorder – it had a nicer sound, could play more notes and was a *real* instrument. He promised to buy me one for Christmas, and duly kept his promise despite the fact that the recorder cost 10/- (50p), and there were many other relatives' children to buy presents for. In fact he played a wicked trick on me. When the presents were given out at the party I was given a square shaped parcel, duly wrapped in Christmas paper, uncle saw my face fall as I realised it wasn't "recorder shaped", and he pointed out that recorders were rather expensive. Then when I opened the box there was a recorder lying in a bed of protective material, and I thanked him most sincerely – he had kept his promise. I quickly mastered the new instrument, and realised that now I had to learn real musical notation – for the Tipperary flute one just had a fingering system with a rudimentary scheme for the rhythm.

The usual plan was to stay from Monday to Friday in Islington, and then to take the train down to the 'cottage' for the weekend. I soon realised one important difference between our families: Uncle John and Aunt Mary got on well with each other and shared all the domestic chores – after all they both had full-time jobs – and lived in a happy atmosphere, but in our house father was very demanding, rarely helped with any domestic jobs, leaving everything to mother. She usually had to cook a separate meal for him, for he would only eat steak, or an expensive chop, while we would have to make do on sausages, or liver, etc. He rarely took any interest in what we were doing, and on the few occasions when we all sat down to a meal together there would be arguments and shouting matches. Looking back I have tried to be sympathetic and to understand that he was probably very tired for much of the time – it was tough to be on night work always – and perhaps the country cottage experience, his Eldorado, had disappointed him as he realised that even here there were neighbours and other people living in close proximity; not that he ever went anywhere in Dagenham, for other people always did his shopping, and he never joined any club or organisation during the 11 years that we lived there. This was a rather harsh judgement when I realised that his job and its unsocial hours almost precluded any opportunity to join in social groups or activities. Later I came to accept that he had a real inferiority complex but it has to be said that he was a bully to us all.

This came home to me as I compared my life during the week at Islington with the unhappy atmosphere when I was home at the weekend. It all became too much on one Sunday night when I had travelled back to Islington. After a welcome, and general chat about what we had done at the weekend, I prepared my clothes and books ready for school the next morning, had a hot drink and went to bed. However I could not sleep, and kept thinking about Mum, how miserable she was, and what rough conditions she had to put up with; then I was sobbing at the thought that I could do nothing about it. The door opened and Auntie came in – either she had a premonition that I was not very happy, or she had heard me crying, but she listened to my explanation between sobs, and said that she and Uncle knew that Mum was having a difficult time, but there was very little they could do about it. Just being able to talk about it had helped me, and I went off to sleep peacefully.

I have very few memories of my year at Highbury County High School. I caught a 19 bus every morning at the Angel public house in Upper Street and came back promptly every afternoon. There seemed to be no clubs or societies after school, I can't even remember a school choir. The headmaster was a Mr. Marsh – the only name I can remember – and I suppose most of the staff were ex-servicemen, there were certainly no women teachers that I can recall. A more illustrious headmaster took over years later, a certain Dr. Rhodes-Boyson, before he went into politics. I found the work hard, and used to spend hours puzzling over homework, with Uncle and Auntie doing their best to help me, but when it came to French I was on my own, for their elementary school education had never stretched to foreign languages! This was really the only time in my school years when I was able to find the time, space and peace to concentrate on homework; once I had moved to Dagenham permanently it was out of the question. I think I must have passed the eleven plus by the skin of my teeth and always found the academic work difficult. At the end of the summer term I finally left Highbury County and the kindness and security of my Aunt and Uncle in Liverpool Road to head off to the country life in our 'L.C.C cottage' in rural Dagenham!

CHAPTER FOUR

THE LEAFY LANES OF DAGENHAM

I moved to 38 Walfrey Gardens, Dagenham early in July, 1948, ready to start at my new school, Dagenham County High in September. Mother must have noticed a certain apprehension about living in this 'cottage', as if she had to try to defend the move we had made, for, when it was dark, she took me up to the front bedroom window to point out the red lights high in the sky opposite, and told me these were lights of the ships' funnels in Dagenham Dock. I became very puzzled because I never saw any sign of funnels during the day; did they ALL depart before daylight and only dock at night? Were these illegal ships carrying illegal cargo? All very mysterious. Then it dawned on me that the red lights in the sky were actually high electric pylons which carried power across the Thames. This was mum's effort to convince me that we were in a desirable part of the countryside –it was a good try.

We had a tiny living room – I could never even think of using the word lounge to describe it – an even smaller kitchen with a stone floor and painted brick walls, and a copper in the corner for the weekly wash, and for bath water. On bath night you lit the gas to heat the copper, and then manually pumped the water up to the bathroom with a contraption fixed to the wall. After all this expense and trouble the water had to be well-used, so the first one to bath had the luxury of the clean water, the second person got into the grey, luke-warm water and bathed as quickly as possible, and then the third person at least had the extra bucket of hot water from the copper (the pump did not reach to the bottom of the copper) to add to the rather cold, dirty water. By the time my sister had arrived, this became quite a complicated procedure. A larder and 'butler' sink with cold water tap completed the kitchen equipment,

Below the stairs was a cupboard which served as a coal cellar during the first years we lived there, and so one can imagine the dust and dirt created whenever the coalman delivered his sacks; eventually even Dad must have realised the mess which Mum had to clear up every time coal was delivered and when we had to fill the coal bucket, so we had a concrete bunker fitted in the back garden. At the bend in the stairs the council had left a cupboard painted in the same dark green as the rest of the fittings (I reckon they had a job lot left over from decorating one of HM prisons), but had run out of money, for the cupboard had no back! There were many occasions when plates and cups fell through the gap and smashed on the floor. Upstairs we had just two bedrooms, the front one for us three boys, and a smaller backroom for mother and my sister, and, of course, on every second Saturday it would be occupied by Dad, so sister would have to sleep down in the living room on the settee. How on earth did we live like that?

The bathroom was primitive – with the dreaded bath and a cold water tap, and toilet, complete with chain. In those days none of the working class houses possessed any central heating; there were small fireplaces in the two bedrooms, but I can only recall a fire being lit when any of us were ill; during the winter it was incredibly cold, and many a time I had to scratch the frost from *inside* the window to see out. The whole place was overcrowded, there was never anywhere to put things, and we were always in each other's way and with no kind of privacy at all – it makes me smile when I hear people insisting these days, "I need my space."

Just as dear Uncle Greg, the Baptist minister, had followed up my link with Blackpool and the Church, so he had made sure that I did not slip through the net, for one Sunday afternoon Rev C.S. Lower called, and invited my brothers and me to join the Sunday school. So began my happy years at Chaplin Road Baptist Church – indeed it became almost my first home, much to the annoyance of my father. I can remember meeting Mr James, the Bible class leader, and later founder of the Junior Voice choir – more about that later; I also made friends with other members of the Sunday school and church. My first Sunday school teacher was Mr Scott, an elderly gentleman, extremely well-dressed, who was a member of a prosperous large church in Ilford where he lived; he travelled over to Dagenham each Sunday – to do his bit for the poor? – no, much too unkind – to go where he felt he was of more use than in his own thriving church. He seemed very old to us and very rich, with expensive clothes and bowler hat with rolled up umbrella; we *did* rather play him up, and later I came to regret being party to our bad behaviour when I realised what a sacrifice he was making – after all, he could have stayed at home and had a nice after-lunch nap in his favourite armchair, and yet here he was, trying to interest 10 fairly unruly, uninterested boys in stories of the Bible.

One Saturday afternoon soon after joining, we went for an anniversary at a neighbouring Baptist church; these invitations I always accepted, for one was invited "to share in the service and have tea and fellowship later". I always looked forward to this because fellowship meant a good tea, with sandwiches and cakes, on a white tablecloth with lovely crockery; I used to wonder why they didn't just announce tea and cakes instead of tea and fellowship, but came to realise that in Baptist circles fellowship nearly always implied something good to eat! So, with my hearty appetite, I could never have enough fellowship! At this meal I was put at a table with a girl called Megan, who was rather lovely. As I sat wondering whether she even noticed me, and wishing I had some better clothes to wear, rather wicked thoughts of the 'gardens experience' with Yvonne crept in. Her mother was Welsh, very strict and very proud of her only child; years later she married Rob, one of our group, who was a great heart-throb to all the girls, and they went to live in the USA.

I soon had my first music 'gig', at a talent competition held in one of the local cinemas. The Grange was the local fleapit, standing at the corner of the busiest junction in Dagenham, with traffic from the A12 bisected by traffic heading to and from Fords and Dagenham dock. There was a talent competition one Saturday morning and some of my friends from the church were involved in displaying their talents in various song and dance routines, and I was persuaded to play the clarinet; I must explain that I had been given an ancient simple system instrument in C by Uncle Albert – the same uncle who used to let me play his records – which he had discovered tucked away in the loft. I had been trying to teach myself, but cannot remember what I played to the audience on that Saturday morning. I do remember an attractive girl called Barbara who dressed up in Carmen Miranda costume and sang "Ay, Ay,Ay, Ay,Ay, I like you very much"; which brought the house down, as they say, and I fell for her that day. Unfortunately the inferiority bit took over and I was always scared to tell her of my feelings; about three years later the tables were turned, and she came after me, but for some reason I had grown quite cool towards her. My brothers and I continued to attend the Saturday morning pictures for a short time, still sixpence (2½p), until we all took on various jobs, and Saturdays became busy days.

I quickly settled down at the new school, and was put back in the first year. It was certainly a more modern building, with plenty of playing fields around, and it was mixed. We had a young form mistress – probably her first teaching post – called Miss Mann, who was extremely thin and displayed none of the attractive features that us boys looked for in the female staff. She was completely flat-chested, and left the school a year later, though I don't think the two were connected. Our French master was Mr Watson, always called 'Slugger' because he had a tendency to throw chalk at the pupils, and even the board cleaner on some occasions. He was very strict, and would creep up behind you and tweak your hair in a very painful way if you could not answer his question. He did this with the girls as well, so I suppose these days he would end up in prison or at least sacked. However he was a very good teacher, and I learned a great deal of German and French under him; he was always complaining about our ignorance in English grammar, and, indeed, I learned more about the functions of pronouns, adverbs, adjectives and the like from him than from the English department. The music teacher was Miss Cootes, who was a very good pianist but fairly dull teacher who seemed to hate junior forms and boys especially. She sported a fine, dark moustache, which always fascinated me. The headmistress at the time was Miss Williams, who was interested in promoting music within the school, whereas the deputy head, Mr Grainger, whom we all feared, was only interested in sports, especially cricket, and as I was to discover, if you weren't good at these things, he wasn't interested in you. But I was now settling into the school at which I was to spend the next seven years, but always finding the work hard, sometimes the whole thing seemed beyond my capabilities.

In 1949 grandmother came to spend a few days with us, and mother went into hospital. When I asked Nan why mother had to go away, she just told me rather sharply that she wasn't well, but even I knew that you didn't go to hospital unless you were very ill! Dad seemed unusually quiet, but he visited the hospital – we were not allowed to go. However a few days later Nan announced that we could go to visit mother, because we now had a baby sister. How naïve I was. I hadn't the first idea that my mother had been expecting a baby – in my defence it must be said that mother was always fairly small – but even when we arrived at the hospital in Brentwood I still hadn't worked out how our new baby sister had got there as well. I understand now that Nan would not consider it her job to tell me about the facts of life – these were intimate topics, best left well alone – and she probably thought that we learned all this at school; well we did, but not at the age of 13.

Mum brought the new baby home, but had been advised to rest during the afternoons because she was suffering from anaemia; how on earth did anyone rest with four children to look after, and in a tiny two-bed roomed house – sorry, cottage? She took iron tablets, and milk stout or Guinness at night, but it was still obvious that having a baby at 41 had weakened her considerably. I had never seen my father as happy as those first few weeks with baby June in the house, and I tried to share the happiness, but I kept wondering how we were going to manage both financially and spatially. We were desperately poor already, and now there was another mouth to feed, and baby clothes, pram, cot and a multitude of other things that had to be provided.

Well, all the necessary things did seem to arrive, and my brothers and I realised quite early on that this sister was going to be spoilt. I don't think we felt particularly envious about it, except that Dad seemed to have far more time for June than he'd ever shown us. The small passage leading from the kitchen to the living room now had to house a pram, soon to be joined by two bicycles, so that whenever we moved around we had to squash ourselves into the wall, where our coats were hung, to get by, and usually banged an ankle or leg in the process. Friday night was for the weekly shopping, which we had to help carry . There would be a trip to the Co-op stores at Becontree where there was always quite a long queue to be served; Mum would have worked out everything she needed, and there were very few luxuries in her shopping list. We still needed ration books, and even if we'd had the money, the coupon system limited our purchases quite a lot. But whatever the privations, Sunday always had its own ritual of a roast dinner, complete with roast potatoes, Yorkshire pudding and cabbage with lashings of gravy; this was also the day when we had 'afters' – generally fruit pie with custard, although in the later, more affluent days, we even had tinned fruit and evaporated milk, which, poured into a jug, looked like cream. In the evening we would have a proper tea, with a clean tablecloth. During the afternoon one of the street traders would have appeared with his usual call; "Winkles, cockles, shrimps," and one of us would have been sent out to buy a half pint of each. This was real luxury, followed by one of mother's excellent Victoria sponges, which she was always proud of. We had a cat – not to eat I hasten to say, for times were never quite as bad as that – who loved eating the shellfish; before tea I would take the dish of winkles to the kitchen door, and with one rattle the cat would run from miles away to take her place at Sunday tea, and perched on Dad's lap, Ginger would pull the winkle from the shell with his paws, much to our amusement. It also brings to mind the various other street traders on whom one depended, in days when no one had a car, and the shops were a good distance away. There was always Bill the greengrocer, whose call of "Potatoes, cabbage," shouted in a cockney voice, was always recognised immediately. He came round with a horse and cart, and as soon as he had moved to the next street the lady next door would appear with a bucket and shovel to remove anything the horse had 'dropped'. Sometimes in a hurry she would forget her bucket and shovel and pick this mess up with her bare hands and pop it into her apron – but then one could tell many amusing stories about the trio who lived next door, who all seemed to live to a ripe old age. About once a week a positively ancient man with a beard would come round pushing a pram, with his call of "Salt, soda, vinegaaaar!" Then there was the 'library', which consisted of one man on a motorbike with a large sidecar in which dozens of books were kept. For a penny a week you could borrow one of these well-read, scruffy volumes with food stains of every description on each page – usually detective stories or romances. Come to think of it, my brothers and I had joined the local library, but we never seemed to consider that Mum might find the time to read a book, so this visit from Mr O'Neill and his motorbike was the only literary material she read, and probably the only romance she would experience.

Later, when June went to school, mother looked round for part-time work – much against the will of my father, but it was she who looked after the finances, and knew that we were not really making ends meet; not that we ever borrowed money or got into debt. On Friday mornings Dad would put down his unopened pay packet, and after mother had given him back his pocket money there would be the job of sorting out the insurances, with a penny a week for the Prudential, and 'tuppence' a week for the Co-op, something for the Provident Mutual, and a few coppers towards the Christmas club which one of my uncles ran; the rent was counted out, and all these amounts would be set aside in little piles on the mantelpiece. Anything left over was for food and living. Even with the full-time job of running a home with four children she was always looking for work to bring in a little extra to keep us going. Her first job was working at the primary school at the top of the road, which Allen and June were attending, where she became a dinner lady, serving the food to the children, washing up and doing all the other jobs needed to keep the dinner service going at the school. Several of the other women who worked there were neighbours, and she enjoyed meeting up with them. One of the perks was being able to share out the food that was left over, and bring it home. Strictly speaking this was not allowed, but the supervisor turned a blind eye, taking the sensible view that it was better for the food to be eaten by humans than to be put out for pig swill. How we agreed! The evening meal became much more attractive, as we ate our way through the cold meat, salad, and some of the excellent puddings. Just once Allen complained that he was eating the same meal that he had been given at school that day (John and I were sworn to silence not to give away the secret that the food came from the school, otherwise everyone was in trouble), but he was given a quiet kick under the table, and he became silent. Sadly this wonderful scheme came to an end when one of the women, who always considered her family as being superior to the rest of us, was promoted, and blew the whistle on her colleagues to a senior officer, who came to the school, instantly put an end to the whole thing, sacked the supervisor and appointed the whistle blower in her place. Mother was furious as she watched good food being thrown into the dustbin, and was convinced that the very woman who had stopped the scheme was still taking food home herself. It may seem pathetic nowadays to think of people getting worked up over scraps of left-over food, but none of us had much, and waste of good food was considered a crime, and rightly so.

Soon we were all old enough to look for Saturday part time jobs. I began working for Prices, the local bread delivery man. He seemed to have a colossal round of roads and callers but I soon learned the tricks of the trade: which houses to be particularly polite at, if one wanted a tip; always making sure that such customers got the newest loaves, and if one was delivering to a really poor house – usually with many mouths to feed, which needed three or four loaves – then you shoved in the occasional stale loaf, or one that was mis-shaped, hoping they would never notice. Just a few customers would regularly order cakes or tarts for the weekend, and I considered them very rich people. How those iced buns used to make my mouth water at midday when I was desperately waiting to go home for some lunch. On the two Christmas Eves when I worked for him and people needed to stock up for extra days we were delivering bread until 1 o'clock in the morning, and on one occasion when I had been promoted away from bread deliveries, we were all woken up at about three in the morning, looked outside to what we thought was an ambulance, and discovered that it was Prices bread van still delivering the customer's bread in the middle of the night! After discussion with some mates I realised that I could earn the same money but for less hours if I worked for the Co-op bakery. This delivery man was very pleasant, and when my legs ached I could sit in the electric cart and have a ride. After a couple of weeks he allowed me to take charge of the cart – it was run from batteries, and one walked in front holding on to the power handle with its combined brake and accelerator. It was slightly embarrassing the first time I helped him on the bread round when we came across my previous employer, who was rather sarcastic, but I think he was just upset because his round was taking longer with the new boy he was training. Later on I took on a paper round, which required getting up at the crack of dawn and rushing off to Martin's the newsagent. We shoved all the papers and magazines into a large rather dirty, coarse, canvas bag which always cut one's fingers on a freezing cold morning, and then delivered the papers to the four or five roads on one's pitch. One grew to hate particular days – Fridays when it seemed the whole world wanted *Radio Times*, and Wednesdays when the *Dagenham Post* would double the weight of the bag. On the other hand Monday was always a treat, for there were very few magazines published on that day – just *Mothers' Weekly, Picture Post* and *Tit-Bits*, and one always found time for a surreptitious glance at some of the scantily clad blondes pictured within. On Sundays you had a double round, for the newspapers were too large to take out in one batch. I suppose one could tell the type of people who lived in Dagenham from the newspapers and magazines they read: about 97 % were the *News of the World* Brigade, and *Daily Mirror* during the week; just a small handful of *Observer*, or *Sunday Times*, and just one house on my round, in Reed road which took the *Church of England Newspaper*. I had no idea then that I was delivering to the house of a future Archbishop of Canterbury – yes, George Carey lived in that house and was about the same age as myself. His parents went to the local Anglican church, and George left his secondary school early, and got many of his later qualifications through the RAF. When one compares his background with other archbishops who always seemed to come from rich homes, on to Eton or Harrow, thence to Oxbridge, and are seen in various books clad in black from top to bottom, with their gaiters and tall top hats, I think this man did extremely well, and deserved to get to the top. I am just glad I didn't make any mistake and push *Tit-Bits* through their letterbox!

Within a few months I was given an added Saturday job of collecting the paper money for all customers who did not pay at the shop. These were often people running up huge arrears, and they did not take kindly to my knocking on the door and asking them to pay at least something off the debt. Time after time I would be told, "We've been in and paid it already." or very often, "Yes I'll be going into the shop this week to pay." At least I wasn't paid on commission, but the paperwork had to agree with the cash in my bag at the end of the morning. Most of the paper boys came from our school, and one senior prefect, called Farmer, was in charge and I always thought of him as incredibly efficient, so I was astonished when he told me that he wanted to concentrate on his A level work in the Upper Sixth, would be leaving the shop and had recommended me to take on his job.

This was quite an honour and so began the job I was to keep until I left school in 1955. The routine involved being at the shop by 6am, helping to carry in the papers and magazines, checking that we had the correct number or 'quires' of papers, and marking them up at top speed for the boys to take out for delivery, then serving customers while the manager went off to make his cup of tea; one prayed that all the boys would turn up for work otherwise yours truly had to do his paper round as well, which always meant being late for school. Usually I would not be home until 8.15 and had to leave within 15 minutes to dash off to school. On Saturdays I would be working in the shop from 9.30 until it closed at 6pm, with a break for lunch, which was often not ready if Mum was running late. Sunday morning brought an extra hour in bed, as I did not have to be at the shop until 7am, then it was work until 12.30 when the shop closed – breakfast was just a sandwich or biscuits which I had grabbed as I left the house, and ate while I served. The manager would go off upstairs to his flat for most of the morning, leaving me to pay the paper-boys and run the shop single-handed. We sold cigarettes, tobacco and snuff, newspapers and magazines, naturally, cards for birthday, wedding, sympathy, Valentines, and confectionery. I used to help myself to Quality Street and Roses chocolates when the manager wasn't around, looking upon this as perks to make up for the miserable pay and long hours. The hours and work were far more than I should have taken on, and soon I realised that my school work was being affected, but with no pocket money, and the ultimatum that if I wanted to stay on into the 6th form some financial contribution had to be forthcoming, I stuck it out. There were times in the sixth form lessons when I had to fight to stay awake, and on a few occasions I did fall asleep –only to be reprimanded by an irate teacher, after all, it's hard to go un-noticed in a class of five students! Frankly, I was dog-tired all the time and began to hate the shop work. I came across an old school report, dated February 1954, in which my form mistress had made the following comments under the heading of 'Industry': "Brian has worked conscientiously, and has made some progress... but seems often to be struggling and working against time." If only she had realised what a typical week entailed in my life at that time, I think she might have had some sympathy.

CHAPTER FIVE

DISCOVERING MUSIC

In the middle of working in the shop and trying to fit in the odd school lesson, not to mention homework – did we EVER do any home work in our house? – music became important.

As I dictate these notes sitting on the balcony of a Croatian hotel on an autumn day in 2003, watching the last rays of the Adriatic sun go down into the sea, I know that guests are waiting in the hotel for me to play the piano and, after dinner, to continue nine sessions on the music of Czechoslovakia. Music has become a dominant part of my life, from school teacher, to orchestral work, experience in an army band, church organist and choirmaster, accompanist for choral societies, piano and clarinet teacher, repetiteur for opera group, and, for the last 23 years, as a music lecturer for music holidays and work for the WEA, the list is endless, so how did it all begin? It is very hard to think back to the start. No sudden decision, it wasn't even a realisation that there was a little bit of talent there, it was more the fact that I knew that I was not very good at anything else, so it had to be music. I didn't feel that I had any particular ability , or was even that passionate about it, but as I describe how I discovered the clarinet, piano and organ, I am more than ever aware that this is a gift which came mysteriously and I have just prayed all my life that it would never be taken away .

Some time in 1951 our wonderful Bible class leader, Mr. James, of whom more will be said later, decided to start a choir for the young people in the church, to be called the Junior Voice. We did a certain amount of part singing and numbered about 30 at one point. Our pianist was Geoffrey Dunn, who suddenly had a serious row with his girlfriend, a member of the choir , and left the choir and the church immediately. This caused a real headache for we were preparing for a concert at a local church in two weeks time, but I was completely astounded when Mr. James came up with a pile of music and suggested that I practise it for the concert; I tried to explain that I played a recorder and was teaching myself the clarinet, and was only a one finger pianist, but he still believed I could help the choir out. He lent me a small portable harmonium which we carried through the house up to our bedroom, while my father was calling out that it looked like a bleedin' coffin. His annoyance increased when he heard me practising on this wheezy instrument, but, nevertheless, I was able to accompany the choir for rehearsals and concert, and, to this day, *I don't know how it happened!* More music was thrust into my hands, and more practice was done on the wheezy harmonium – in short, I became the choir's accompanist. I was soon asked to play the organ occasionally for the church services – no pipe organ with pedals, but another harmonium, yet much more sophisticated than the primitive instrument installed in the bedroom. When the official organist left to be married, I became the church organist, and this all happened within a few months.

My mother had a good deal of sympathy, and even tried to encourage me, because she bought our first piano, no Steinway, or Bechstein this, but an awful cheap Victorian instrument, complete with candlesticks, fretwork front and decorated feet, which belonged to one of the neighbours and was being sold for 10/- (50 p); we pushed it down the street to the delight of all the other children, and somehow got it into an already overcrowded living room. It was terribly out of tune, and, not having the money to have it properly tuned, I set about doing the job with a pair of pliers. Within a few days it was hopelessly out of tune again, and ended up as the only piano to my knowledge where the sound went lower as the fingers went higher; practice was almost impossible, for father would be in bed most of the day, and when he got up in the evening my baby sister was being put to bed; I couldn't even play in the mornings, as I was busy doing the paper round. Within the year Mr James realised that I needed a decent instrument to play, and he gave me his own piano, saying that his wife wanted more space in their lounge, but I think he was sacrificing an instrument which he loved – after all he did play the piano himself. So one Saturday afternoon, after he had finished his deliveries, Bill, the vegetable man, complete with horse and cart, brought a piano from North

Romford down to Dagenham. I wonder what the rather posh neighbours in Erith Crescent thought as they looked through their lace curtains at the sight of a piano being loaded on to a greengrocer's cart.

It was around 1953 that my life's interest in gramophone records began. James Wright, a friend at the church, bought himself one of the new Dansette portable record players which could play long-playing discs as well as the old 78s we had grown up with. One of his first LPs was the *Planets Suite* by Gustav Holst – a Nixa recording, conducted by Adrian Boult. We played it over and over again, and then James managed to get tickets for the Prom concert at the Albert Hall when the work was being played. That performance was magical to me, for I had no idea that instruments together could make such sounds, from delicate celeste with muted violins in *Venus* through to the powerful full orchestra of *Jupiter*. I then used all my savings to buy my own record-player, a rather lovely HMV model, complete with the famous 'Nipper' sign, and began to collect my own records. I went up to HMV in Oxford Street to spend £3 and had to make a difficult decision: whether to buy two LPs, or just one, leaving enough to buy three 78s. How I wish I had opted for the first choice. I remember buying Anthony Collins conducting Elgar/Vaughan Williams – with *Introduction and Allegro,* and the *Serenade for Strings*, coupled with *Fantasia on Thomas Tallis*, and *Greensleeves Fantasia* on LP, and a couple of 78s one of Gigli, and an organ disc containing *Solemn Melody* by Walford Davies. I couldn't get home fast enough from the West End and through the rush-hour traffic, clutching my precious parcel until I reached the gate of our house, when I promptly dropped the bag smashing the 78s. As mother opened the door I almost burst into tears I was so angry at what had happened. But I still had the LP, and soon it was joined by *Mozart Symphony No. 40 in G Minor* which I was studying at school for O level. No more 78s from that day on. Incidentally James, who was always a very extravagant chap, and never did things by half, booked a complete box at the Albert Hall for the performance of *Messiah* under Malcolm Sargent which took place every Good Friday. Several of us went up – it was the only time I was ever to sit in a box – but it didn't work out very expensive after we had all paid our share and the box was full. Collecting records then became a lifelong hobby, from mono LPs to stereo, in about 1958, and then moving to the compact disc in 1983. At each change it meant swapping most of the large collection I had acquired, always losing money in the process, so that I think altogether I must have bought well over 10,000 records during my life. They have always fascinated me, and the very thought that at the touch of a button one can have the London Symphony Orchestra with a world-famous conductor playing in the lounge always makes me marvel.

At the beginning of 1955 I was encouraged to take piano lessons with a teacher who lived on the Rush Green Road, near Romford. Miss Molyneaux was a very good teacher, and I looked longingly at the grand piano in the lounge; it was made clear that normally one played the upright piano, and only on special occasions were pupils given the privilege of playing the grand piano. The lessons were half a crown a time (12½p), but after a couple of fascinating half hours I had to tell her I could not afford any more. She was very upset, and told me I was already entered in a music competition, indeed she had selected the music I was to play – the slow movement of an early Beethoven sonata, and she would give me two lessons free, and a free lesson with her own teacher. I'll never forget meeting her teacher, because she seemed the oldest person I'd ever seen, and I wondered how on earth she would help me. How much I had to learn about people! Her arthritic hands prevented her from playing, but from the moment I played the first chord of the Beethoven she took over, and made me consider every single note I was playing; she insisted upon correct dynamics, position of my hands and wrists, and made me think about what lay behind the music. At the end of one hour I was exhausted, but exhilarated by all that she had tried to teach me. Now I had to agree to go in for the competition. I duly presented myself on the evening of 15th April, 1955 at Harold Wood Methodist Church, already feeling very nervous, but this was doubled when the teacher admitted that I was taking part in a section open for pianists from any age. Here I was with just half a dozen lessons under my belt against adults who had been playing for years. That wonderful old lady had done her work, because I enjoyed playing that movement to the audience, and just forgot all about the competitive element and was given second place with 84 marks out of 100 – and still have the certificate to prove it. Miss Molyneux pleaded with me to go back and make more progress, and was very sad when I gave up lessons. There were only three months to my A level GCEs, and I was getting in quite a panic about those. From that time on I played as often as I could, getting hold of music as fast as I could lay my hands on it. I have always enjoyed sight-reading, and, as army life was to prove, found I could do this quite well. Even these days, in between gardening, and doing music holidays I enjoy playing my beautiful brand new grand piano for at least an hour a day, in glorious silence, with just the cat as audience – what luxury compared to those teenage years.

I still had this old clarinet which I played occasionally at school. I had taught myself to quite a reasonable standard; now I had come to the headmistress's attention through this and my recorder playing. She had instituted a new scheme whereby for one lesson each week the first years could choose from a number of 'leisure' classes –one being the opportunity to learn the descant recorder, which she would teach. I'm sure she was quite musical but she had lost a finger on the right hand at some point in her life, was unable to cover all the holes, but could still get a rudimentary tune out of the thing. We used to snigger when she was addressing the class and telling us our options, perhaps 1-4, using her fingers –when she came to option 3 her other hand used to flip through the air past the missing finger –sounds complicated? Perhaps I should draw a diagram!

To return to recorders. After about three weeks of lessons she was too busy to take the class and, discovering that I had a games afternoon, she asked me to take over her class. Well, you do not refuse a request/order from the head, and, though I pretended to be unhappy at having to give up games – when I was actually delighted to give up such a waste of time – I took on the job. About 15 pupils attended, mostly girls, we waded through the *School Recorder Book*, learning to read music and some of the notes at the same time. Fairly soon I was taking these classes every Monday, much to the annoyance of the sports teacher. If I had felt even slightly that it was educational, I would have gone out to football, but games lessons consisted of two teams of good players, generally those in the school teams, while the rest of us were given a football, sent into a corner of the field where there was a goal post, and warned not be a nuisance. No one ever came near to help or encourage us. Have conditions changed, I wonder?

The head may have felt that she owed me a favour, because the music master –Peter Cork, more details later – told me that the school was going to buy two clarinets, appoint a teacher, and I was to be given first choice to have lessons at 6d (2½p) a time. I jumped at the chance, and met Mr. John Gunn, the teacher, who worked at Fords Motor Company and played the instrument in his spare time. I believe he was rather nervous at the idea of teaching in a grammar school initially, but he was strict and insisted on practice between lessons. He would always dress very smartly in a suit, white shirt and tie, though I believe he wore rough clothes at Fords; I came to respect him for his disciplined approach, he was an 'ordinary bloke' who lived in a council house nearby, and had no snobbishness or arrogance about him. Yes, he was one of us!

Soon an order came from the head that I was to perform at speech day. Mr. Gunn took this matter very seriously, and we began preparations. I needed to have grade five on an instrument to qualify for A level music at GCE, and he decided that I would take grade seven, so he must have had some confidence in my ability. This meant I could play a movement from a Brahms sonata, with an encore which was to be *The Swan* from *Carnival of Animals* by Saint-Saëns. At this point enter my accompanist, Dudley Moore; he was a great friend and a music student one year above me. Dudley was quite brilliant, and had no problems with the accompaniments, indeed, he rather provoked the teacher by yawning and pulling faces while playing to make me laugh – and it is fatal to laugh while blowing the clarinet. In truth Dudley could have played these accompaniments with one hand tied behind his back. The great day arrived, my first real performance in a packed school hall, and in front of many of my classmates, but I did not feel unduly nervous – just a few butterflies moments before I played – I put this down to the meticulous work of Mr Gunn and his insistence upon attention to detail.

Our fame went before us, and we were soon performing at Christmas, Easter and summer concerts with the school choir, both in our school hall and in a nearby church called Kingsley Hall; this was a Christian socialist establishment, with many weekday activities for people of all ages, and its greatest claim to fame was the fact that Mahatma Gandhi had visited it in 1931 on his last visit to England. Indeed he stayed at a Kingsley Hall establishment in the East End of London, which still flourishes today and, apart from its social work for the poor of that area, it is always preaching for peace and against war.

Kingsley Hall celebrated the 21st anniversary of their warden, Sidney Russell, in September 1953, and as he was the chairman of the school governors, we were required to play on Tuesday 8th September when two famous people were coming as guests of honour; Dudley and I were to perform on our instruments, and then take tea with them . When I discovered that the famous pair were Dame Sybil Thorndike and her husband Sir Lewis Casson I became very nervous indeed, not from the idea of performing, but it was the "taking tea" which scared me. I had visions of upsetting my tea in the saucer, or dropping a sandwich on the floor (rather like the poor neighbour of Mrs 'Bouquet' in the TV programme *Keeping Up Appearances*) but Dudley told me not to worry, he would take care of the situation. When the big day came, I accompanied Dudley as he played the violin, I think it was music by Fritz Kreisler, and I played a couple of movements from some *Bagatelles* by Gerald Finzi with him accompanying, and then we had to gather at a small table. In the event Sir Lewis Casson couldn't come, but there was the great lady waiting at table for Dudley and me to join her. I was so nervous I could hardly hold the tiny, expensive teacup, but he took command of the situation, picked up a plate of food, leaned over to the important personage and in his typical 'Dud' voice with face contorted, he said, "May I press you to a cucumber sandwich, Dame Sybil?" We both roared with laughter, and relaxed considerably for the next half-an-hour; I even enjoyed the food, though I could not understand why the crusts on the sandwiches had been removed. Looking back at the programme they were to have in the evening, I see Donald Soper down as their speaker – how I wish I had stayed on to hear that great man.

I did once compete against Dudley in a house music festival. He was playing violin for Valence, his house, and I did my usual stuff on the clarinet for my house Jenkins, and, wonder of wonders, I actually beat him into first place. I don't think the clarinet teacher or I had any inkling of the future which lay in store for Dudley, and will be mentioning him later in the book. During our last year at school Dudley was competing for an organ scholarship to Magdalene College, Oxford, and practising at least twice a week at a church nearby. I often went to turn over the pages for him, and realised how hard he had to work, for people often forget that he had a 'club foot' as a result of the polio of his childhood, so he wore special shoes with a thick heel and sole to negotiate the pedals. It was a fantastic day when the head announced that Dudley had won the scholarship, and I was extremely chuffed when he gave me his copy of the Bach organ book he had used at Oxford – I still have it along with his own registration and markings for the organ at Magdalene.

Life at the church took up more and more of my time. Apart from playing for the choir, and Sunday services, I often went off during the week with Mr James, the Bible class leader, to other churches where he would speak at women's meetings, or men's clubs or midweek gatherings – the pattern was the same, for he would speak and I would play the hymns and choruses; occasionally another young person would come along to sing a solo or two. We would travel perhaps to the Wembley area, to Walthamstow, to Stoke Newington – all over London, where he had various contacts and was greatly loved by all the congregations. We would have planning evenings for these meetings, usually at his house in Romford. This meant a journey of three-quarters of an hour on the bus for me, and usually, we were so taken up with our preparations and the music, that I would have to rush to catch one of the last buses back to Dagenham. Eventually we formed ourselves into a small team so that we could do music in four parts, and take over some of the commitments that Mr James had in his diary. This meant even more preparation, as we worked our way through various American gospel music books. Some of the individuals did not read music, so the rehearsals involved a lot of 'note bashing', as we call it in the trade. They were very happy times, although my school work was badly neglected, and I was going without sleep, because often I would not get to bed until midnight, and had to get up for the paper shop at six the next morning. Mr James became almost a second father to me, and I could confide in him and converse with him in a way which was totally impossible with my own father. I admired him for his tremendous Christian witness. He had come from a very poor home, but with Christian parents, and had gradually worked his way in life until he owned his own small gentleman's outfitters in Dagenham. Then he employed two young men – Fred Garner and Mr Jeffreys, who had both been converted at church through the example of Mr James. But he felt that he wasn't "getting his hands dirty" in the world, and took steps to get involved with working men. The shop was sold and he took on a job at Liverpool Street Station where he was responsible for the maintenance of the huge electric batteries which were used on the luggage trolleys in those days. The batteries had to be charged on a regular basis, and replaced on the trolleys. This was a dirty and dangerous job, involving handling acid, and it all took place in a tiny, dimly-lit corner of the station. Here Mr James would get to know other railway men, his Bible was always left on his little table, and he would often be found reading it and preparing his talks while eating his sandwiches over lunch. At first the men ridiculed him, pulled out his shirt, called him Holy Joe, and were extremely unpleasant; he never retaliated, seemed to have the patience of Job, and I now know that he prayed for them at home individually. I often went up to Liverpool Street to have tea with Mr James before we travelled off to the meeting. We would generally eat at a super Lyons Corner House, where the food always tasted marvellous, and he would never let me pay for anything. I would always arrange to meet him at his little den, and, by the time I came on the scene in 1953, the men were pleasant, courteous to me, and asked about the meetings we were going to, and if ever one of them swore accidentally, he would always apologise to both of us. If a man had personal problems he would go to Mr James and pour out his troubles to him. This picture of Mr James makes him sound rather like a plaster saint, but he was great fun, always interested in everyone and everything, and I came to realise that this man really did put his Christianity into action. All the young people admired him and looked to follow his example.

It was in March 1954 that Billy Graham came to London, with his team, to conduct the Greater London crusade. Meetings were held from March to May at Haringay arena, and a whole group of us from church were keen to be involved. Some became stewards and helped with the seating arrangements, distribution of hymn books, and the collection, while others were counsellors, who had to be ready to speak and help new converts as they came forward, sometimes in hundreds, at the end of each service. I joined the choir and went along to at least three meetings a week. As this involved the journey of at least an hour on the train, I was giving up a great deal of time which should have been spent doing my A level homework but, like my friends, I was so impressed by the efficiency of the organisation. The Americans really did have something to show us about running an event smoothly; there were hundreds of Christians involved in this crusade and yet it seemed to run like clockwork. The Americans also gave you the impression that you were an important part of a team –your contribution counted. Some critics called it 'slick ', but I think it was efficient and streamlined. We had a big preliminary meeting at the arena on the opening Saturday afternoon, we had already been sent our choir book [I have it before me now] and there were other books we would need ready on the chairs… in fact everything was in place. I found it so moving to see people night after night who, after listening to this great man of God, were willing to come down from their places – and in some instances it required a long journey – and begin a new life there and then. Of course the critics were out in force, just waiting for an opportunity to find some fault with Billy Graham himself, to try to discover that he had his hand 'in the till', and indeed they were always asking him about how much he was being paid for the crusade. The plain fact is that he was always beyond reproach – he was as clean as a whistle in his dealings both financially, politically and in every other way, and despite their best efforts the media could not find any dirt on him. When the crusade ended I still went up occasionally to the London crusade headquarters in Tottenham Court Road to help as a volunteer in dispatching letters, licking stamps and doing anything to be a tiny cog in this great well-oiled machine. Over the years I have met many people whose lives were changed by this crusade. Of course there were failures, there were people who never kept their promise, some who never joined the churches which invited them, or left soon after; there were some vicars who were opposed to the crusade and did very little to encourage people to join the Church, but it was still considered a great success.

One personal story is worth retelling. As a group of young, keen Christians we often sang hymns in the underground train going from Manor House down to King's Cross. This may seem crazy and rather selfish, but we were young and full of enthusiasm at this great event. One night somebody told us in no uncertain manner to shut up or move into another compartment, and Rob, the young man I referred to in an earlier chapter, feeling quite courageous, had a word with him. When the chap began running down Billy Graham and the whole business, Rob asked whether he'd actually been to hear him, and eventually challenged him – Charlie Brown – to go with us on the following night. Sure enough Charlie was waiting for us the next evening at King's Cross, in a much quieter frame of mind, and seeming almost frightened with 20 or so young people around him. Robert was a counsellor but he had arranged to stay seated with Charlie during the meeting. I think he was concerned that Charlie might shout some abuse from his seat, but Charlie sat quietly and seemed to be taking every word in. The last hymn, *Just as I am, Without One Plea* was sung, and, as usual, people began to come from their seats to stand at the front; I was amazed from my seat in the choir to see Charlie slowly moving forward, crying, to make his way below Dr Graham and the rostrum. Rob told me later that Charlie had stood there hesitating all through that hymn determined not to go down, but finally he had turned to Rob, and with tears in his eyes, said, "I must go down to the front. I've got to change". It was certainly a different Charlie who came on the train back to King's Cross that night. He joined our church, became a member, married one of our girls, and he and Jean trained with the Baptist Missionary Society and went out as missionaries to Africa!

Nearer to home, I had joined my first orchestra. Mr Gunn, my clarinet teacher, was first clarinet in the South East Essex Technical College Orchestra, and in 1952 he gave me the chance to play second clarinet. This was such a revelation, to be in the middle of an orchestra and part of this wonderful music-making. Naturally, with my teacher sitting next to me, I had to count bars very carefully and not make any mistakes. The conductor was Alfred Jones, but he had a very strong foreign accent and I think he came from Russia. Looking at the programme I notice that we played Haydn's *Surprise Symphony* and the piano concerto by Greig. At the March concert the soloist was a young violinist of 14 named Ralph Holmes. He attended the Royal Liberty School in Romford (his father was a member of staff) and was a brilliant performer. He played the Mendelssohn *Violin Concerto* with the most beautiful tone and perfect articulation. I didn't know whether to feel inspired to go on with my playing, or break the clarinet in two and give up, having heard this young genius. I still have his youthful autograph on my programme of 1st march, 1953. Ralph went on to become a professor at the Royal Academy of Music, but he died of a brain haemorrhage, while still just a young man. What a sad loss for the musical world. For these concerts I had to wear a DJ and bow tie, and was lucky enough to be given a second-hand suit by the conductor of another orchestra where I sometimes played. I bought tickets as a present for my parents, but my father would not come even though he could not put forward the usual excuse that he had to go to night work, for the concert took place in the afternoon. I suppose my mother was too embarrassed to come alone. How I would have loved to have had somebody in the audience that I knew, but it wasn't to be. I was getting used to the idea of going it alone on these occasions.

Around this time I had bought my first real bicycle. My father had generously let me use his bicycle up to this time, and it was in quite good condition, but I wanted my own machine, a Raleigh Lenton, with Sturmey-Archer gears, a modern hub dynamo and all the accessories available on a modern bike in 1953. Dad was even persuaded to let me buy it on a hire purchase agreement, much against his will, though I paid for it very quickly, and broke my heart when it was stolen outside a shop about 15 months later. Come to think of it, we didn't even try to claim any insurance money for the loss. Anyhow this new machine opened the way to days out during the holidays. I would cycle down to Tilbury, use the ferry to Gravesend and go on to Rochester, where I would enjoy my sandwiches and lemonade before cycling back to Dagenham; sometimes I went off to Southend, using the 'new' dual-carriageway via Rainham, Stanford-le-Hope and Benfleet, and coming back on the old route through Rayleigh and Basildon (then a very small, pleasant town) to Romford and home. Along with a couple of school friends I did some youth hostelling around southern England in the summer of 1953. We stayed at Streatley – glorious still evening with a slight mist over the River Thames – on to Winchester, where the hostel was situated in the watermill, just a stone's throw from the great cathedral – then across country to Marlborough, and I still have a photo of us standing as a group in the middle of the A4 at 10 in the morning with not a vehicle in sight. We crossed the River Severn to stay for a night at St. Briavels Castle, and then began retracing our steps via a lovely old hostel at Stow-on-the-Wold in the Cotswolds, then on to Oxford, and returned to Dagenham. I realised then how important the countryside was to me, and what wonderful and varied scenery England had to offer.

The following year we decided to be more adventurous with a trip to France during the summer holidays. France wasn't as well organised as England in respect of youth hostels, so we were unable to book ahead; we soon realised that at most hostels one had to get the key from someone in the village to even get into the place, no meals would be provided so you had to make your own or eat out. From an old passport I discovered that we were away for 16 days, and I took £8 in Thomas Cook travellers cheques to cover the cost of food, accommodation and spending money(!) – we really were having a cheap holiday in every sense. But there were some glorious moments. We had to completely modify our original itinerary, having planned to cycle right down to the south of France and back, but then we met cyclists who told us that it was far too hot to cycle during the day, and one just cycled a few miles in the cool of the evening or during the night, so we realised that our plans were too ambitious. We had no real conception of the huge size of the country, and obviously hadn't taken into account the climate in midsummer. It was completely impossible to get into any hostel in Paris but we found a sports arena which seemed to be owned by the Communists, and one paid for a few feet of space in which to sleep. There was no question of ever leaving anything at the hostel during the day, it would have been stolen. We even slept with our passports and wallets under our pillows. I intended somehow to get to an opera in Paris, and although the great Opéra itself was too expensive, if I cut down on all nonessentials, like food, I could just about afford to go in the gods at L'Opéra Comique, just around the corner, where *Carmen* was being performed in its original theatre. No chance of dressing up for the occasion, I just turned up in my rather dirty shorts and none too clean shirt and pushed my way in with all the other poor Paris music lovers. It was an occasion I will never forget, and at the end I was in no hurry to retrace my steps to bed in the noisy, crowded arena, so I sat in the gallery letting all the other people go. Then I noticed in the corner a poor old man who seemed to be sobbing his heart out; thinking someone had hurt him or stolen his money I went over and spoke, but he reassured me that he was

"Très heureux –c'est la musique". I agreed, and we slowly made our way arm in arm down the stairs to the exit, said our 'aux revoirs' and separated into the Paris streets, both feeling our sense of poverty yet happy beyond measure. At the end of the holiday we arrived back at Montreuil to spend the last night at the hostel with just enough French money for a boiled egg and roll for breakfast before our flight from Le Touquet. We still had quite a lot of English money and had made up our minds to have a good slap up meal at Lyons Corner House in Maidstone, but then thought we would have a drink on the way. Sadly, the pint of good old English cider did not go very well on an empty stomach, and though we set off from the pub valiantly, within a couple of miles we just had to sleep it off for a while at the roadside. But the meal at Maidstone tempted us on, and soon we were pedalling away to our lunch. That was one of the occasions when I realised the power of alcohol.

June 1955 was getting very near, and panic was setting in at the thought of taking the A level examinations, and working out what I was going to do with myself on leaving school. A few lucky students had already been accepted by their respective universities, and were going to be allowed to complete their courses before doing national service, but for most of us it would be two years in the forces before we could make other plans. I had seen so many friends who had wasted their time doing national service; if you expressed an interest in electrical work they seemed to make you a pay clerk, and if you showed ability in clerical work, you would probably be trained as an electrician, I kid you not – I saw this happen frequently. Mr James, the wonderful Bible class leader I referred to earlier had two sons, David and Michael, who went to our school though they were older than me. David had joined the Royal Artillery as a musician, playing in the band and in the famous artillery orchestra as a double bass player. I was quite interested in doing something musical in the forces and my teacher suggested that I have an audition with Major Willcocks, conductor of the Ford Motor Works band, who had formerly been the director of music of the Irish Guards. I still have the testimonial he gave me – 10th May, 1955 – which closes with "Given these two factors [experience and practice] he has the enthusiasm and ability to become a leading clarinet in a first-class band." Now I had to prove it!

During my last year in the 6th form I made my work even more difficult by taking up the cello. It had been suggested that a second instrument was very useful for entry into college, and I suppose the teacher didn't count the piano as a proper second instrument. Mr Stroob had a remarkable resemblance to James Mason the film star, and the hearts of the girls were given quite a flutter in the individual lessons as he leaned over to show them how to cope with second position! Sadly, I neglected the cello; you may realise that the instrument takes up a lot of room – both to store and even more when being played. There was literally no space in our tiny LCC cottage where I could sit with cello, music stand and find space for the bow, so practice at home was impossible. The lessons were given during lunch-hour on Fridays, and I badly wanted to spend that with a certain young lady who was my heart-throb. This was Anne, who had come to the school in 1952 as part of a form which were called 'late developers' – a very misleading title, for many of the girls were anything but that! It actually referred to a group who had passed the entrance exam for grammar-school at 13 instead of 11 years of age. It made a lot of sense for pupils to be given a second chance to join our worthy establishment. Most of them came from the Ilford area and from fairly well-off homes, where parents had probably worked hard to support them in their grammar-school bid. I remember Anne as she came into lunch on the first day of the new school year, and took the chance immediately of finding out her name from one of the boys in her class, who was sitting at my table. There was something about her I just found completely entrancing, and from that day until I left school I worshipped her, generally from a distance. I was too scared to ask her out, and took to leaving notes in her desk at various times. Gradually I got to the happy position where I could sit with her and her friends on the playing field at break and lunchtimes. My own classmates thought I was crazy to bother about someone who was two years younger than me, and who they thought was completely plain, but I really was in love up to my ears. At Easter 1953 she went off with a group to Paris – including the infamous Dudley Moore – and I missed her so much I stood at the bedroom window at night trying to work out the direction of Paris so that I could concentrate on it and wish her well. At school I sent Valentine cards, birthday cards, Christmas cards and even a box of chocolates – all left in her desk when no one was in the class. I got into trouble about the chocolates, for somehow the deputy head heard about it, and I was wheeled in to explain why I had gone into somebody else's desk – someone who was NOT EVEN IN MY YEAR, *and* was one of the late developers, said the master with a sneer; despite my explanation that I was putting something into the desk not taking anything out, I was still reprimanded. But it all seemed worth it. Three months before I left school I took my Clarinet grade 7 exam for the Associated Board; you had to pass grade 5 in order to qualify for advanced level music entrance, but my clarinet teacher had made it quite clear that he wasn't messing about with grade 5, we were going for the big one. So Dudley, my accompanist, and I made our way to Seymour Gardens in Ilford where the examination was being held, and just as we reached the front door, out came my Anne, who had just taken her piano exam. I felt this was a good omen, and in fact, I got a distinction in Grade 7.

An S.C.M. (Student Christian Movement) group had been started that year, and we had some very lively discussions and speakers, particularly on the two absorbing topics of the time -- apartheid in South Africa and the question of Christian pacifism. During the Easter holiday a number of us went up to Church House, Westminster for a two-day conference on Colour Conflict in Africa and we were addressed by someone who had returned from the region called Trevor Huddleston. He became a very important figure later on, and I was moved when I read his book *Naught for Your Comfort*. Our divinity lesson each week in the sixth form usually consisted of a discussion around a topical subject. Our teacher was Mr Martin Dakin, a very well-read, intellectual figure who went on to become the first 'Brain of Britain' on the BBC programme. Martin was a Quaker and very anti-war. Most of us were going to have to do our National Service and so there was always a lively debate between him and one or two sympathisers versus the rest of us.

The school choir must have been really quite ambitious, for our main work in the last concert I took part in was *Sons of Light*, a cantata by Ralph Vaughan Williams which had only been written in 1951 as a commission from the Schools Music Association. In the school magazine Peter Cork our music master described it thus: "Probably no other music that the choir has performed has caused quite so much controversy as this cantata. At first choir members were frankly puzzled by the work. Gradually, however, the music began to take hold of the singers and by the end of the year everyone was enthusiastic about this strange new music."

However in his book on RVW James Day describes it as "direct and uncomplicated, lively and cheerful – as a piece written for children should be, and as music written by a man of 78 might well not be." I can certainly remember it as a difficult work for our school choir to tackle.

After my application to join the Band of the Coldstream Guards had been received, I was asked to go for an audition at the Duke of York's HQ in King's Road, Chelsea. I played my set piece – don't remember there being any piano around or pianist – and then had to sight read a number of marches and other concert repertoire. Major Douglas Pope seemed very irritable and muttered various remarks under his breath, and then promptly got up and walked away leaving me with the sergeant in charge. Later on I came to accept this as typical army behaviour, but was put off by it at the time. Within a couple of days I received the news that I had been accepted into the band…medicals, eye-tests and swearing-in would all come later, but my career for the next three years had opened up. When I told Mr Dakin that I had solved the problem of pacifism v. conscription by joining the band, which meant that I would not have to do any weapons training, would never have to handle a gun, he was not very impressed. "Brian, you will be the army's shop window. You will go off on a recruiting tour in some northern city, march through the streets while the recruiting sergeants are doing a good business in the rear getting young men to sign up. So really you don't help the pacifist cause at all." I felt deflated, and discovered some months later that Mr Dakin was absolutely right, we DID go recruiting, we DID find many new soldiers that way, and I WAS part of the machine.

Suddenly the exams were upon us, and the last month of my school life rushed by. I did badly in my A levels, partly because I had never found time or peace to do my homework properly, partly because I was far too involved in the youth work and choir at church, not to mention being organist and a deacon by this time, and also because I felt that I had over- reached myself in believing I could ever get to university. There was that chip on the shoulder again!

With the examinations over, we lounged around on the field in glorious sunshine while the rest of the school continued lessons and I was able to read some books that I *had chosen* instead of the rather dull set books of the English course. On our final sports day I excelled myself at running. Having borrowed a pair of 'spikes', which I'd never worn before, and which hurt my feet, I came second in the one-mile race for senior boys, and came first in my lap of the relay race, which our house, Jenkins, won. Perhaps I should have got some running spikes with my hard-earned pocket money a little earlier in my school career. On the last day we had our final assembly, with all the school leavers duly lining up to shake hands with the headmistress, Miss Williams, who, as I see from the current school magazine, was also retiring after 19 years; then it was off to Joe's Café at Martin's Corner, not with Miss Williams, I hasten to add, for our last tea and cake and a chance to swap addresses and wish each other all the best for the future. A lucky few who had got deferment, went off to university, but for the rest, it was off to National Service and a completely new way of life. I was booked to join the Coldstream Guards at the end of August for three years, and I went home with the words of our school hymn echoing in my mind;

"Rise in the strength of God and face life's uphill way,

The steps which other feet have trod, you tread today."

Suddenly I wanted the comfort and safety of school to go on for ever – but now I had to make my own way in a grown-up world.

CHAPTER SIX

SERVING QUEEN & COUNTRY

"You – looking round that f****** corner – get yur' bl**** self 'ere, at the double!"
That was the welcoming shout from a Coldstream Guards sergeant inviting me to
join the great British Army!

The month of August, 1955 had been a very enjoyable time. I had been working
in the newsagents shop full-time for about five weeks, and earned quite a lot of
money, so was off on holiday for two weeks before joining the army. We had
never had a holiday away – in the affluent days Dad would take us to the seaside
or up to London for the day, with his Privilege tickets (PT); these PTs were always
a source of annoyance because though he was able to get very generous reductions
– like 80% off the regular ticket price for any member of the family –he had a free
pass – it meant completing a form and getting a senior member of staff to sign, and
he hated doing this. I believe he thought it was condescending to use PTs. When
I talked to other people who worked on the railway, I realised that they used the
PT for travel all the time – just for a couple of stops down the underground line.
But this was not the way for my Dad. So this was my first real holiday, though I
had been on YHA cycling trips. I went on the first of many holidays to a Baptist
Missionary Society (BMS) summer school at Bexhill in Sussex. About 80 young
people came together at a girls' public school – the girls were sadly on holiday –
where we met missionary couples who were on furlough, listened to talks about
the Missionary Society, and in between enjoyed excursions, played tennis, swam
in the icy waters of the sea, and generally had a lot of fun. I spied the grand piano
in the main hall, and was given permission to play it in my spare time, in fact, I
became the official pianist for the second week of the holiday, playing the hymns
for all the sessions and services. Beside the fun and games, it was good to meet

real missionaries, off-duty and enjoying a holiday with their children, who would be at boarding schools in England while their parents were working overseas. I had many interesting talks with such people. Of course I had to fall in love, and Barbara from Sittingbourne and I went round everywhere, hand in hand or arm-in-arm. Even on the formal group photograph, I notice that I still had my arm round her – how protective I was. Uncle Webb, as we called him, then in his 80s, was the husband of the cook at the school – a Baptist couple who lived in Bristol, where he had been quite a famous tennis player in his day; he had served in the forces for many years, and took me aside and gave me the advice that I had to start in the army as I meant to go on – that I should be proud of my Christian faith, and this meant kneeling down at the side of my bed at night in front of the other men, and being prepared to put up with the consequences. In many ways he was right, for one needed to 'nail one's colours to the mast' and show people who one served, but I never did get the courage to put this into practice. It did mean that I made up my mind not to join in with the general swearing. Their bad language took a lot of getting used to – most of the men swore at every third word, but, in fact, I don't think I swore in all my three years in the forces; I was also ready to talk to others about the Christian message, and got one or two opportunities fairly early on.

So on the morning of 30th August, I set off for the army recruiting office at Wanstead, where I took the oath on the Bible to serve Queen and country, was given a travel warrant to Caterham Barracks in Surrey, and told to report there by 1800 hours. My plan was to have a look at the barracks, go out for a quiet lunch, take in some of the lovely Surrey countryside, and then report at teatime, but all this was changed when I peered round the corner and received the welcome as given at the beginning of the chapter. As for "at the double" – I hadn't a clue what he was on about. So started three years of complete fear, mostly hatred of the army, and general bewilderment, with but one constant aim – to count the days before getting out of this hell. For someone who had just left grammar-school the transition into the Coldstream Guards, and be subjected to a guardsman's training at this depot was just too much.

Having given my details to the duty sergeant in the guardroom I was told to "Follow that man!" – who turned out to be a recruit laden with full kit – steel helmet, large and small pack, greatcoat and rifle (and this was a hot summer's day), who had to march smartly from the guardroom down the drive to the barracks – a distance of about half a mile; this, I later discovered, was one of the punishments meted out. I set off and, having only a small case, easily caught up with him and tried to have a conversation, but was told to in no uncertain manner to shut up and drop well behind him otherwise he would be "on jankers" – whatever that was; I soon found out it meant 'punishment duties'. An army ambulance passed by at speed going out of the barracks, and, when we reached the reception room, his journey being over, the perspiring recruit informed me that it would have been another attempted suicide; it seems that when some soldiers were at the end of their tether, they would stick their rifle, with bayonet attached, into the lavatory pan of the latrine and fall on it. Sadly, this never completely did the trick, and usually the soldier would end up in the ambulance with the bayonet still attached. I was given my army number – is there anyone in the world who forgets that number for the rest of his life? – 23206516 Recruit ASTELL, and told to join the others for tea in the cookhouse. I lined up at the counter for the hot food and a great mug of tea, made my way to a table and noticed that the soldiers were very rude, for they grabbed the thick slices of bread from the basket in the middle instead of passing it round. So I went to a new table, and as others joined me, I politely passed the basket round; of course it came back empty – some thieving tyke had taken my ration of bread. So one lesson had been learned the hard way, when I sat down for my next meal I grabbed my bread along with everyone else, realising that it was the way one survived in this uncouth army world.

For the next few days we seemed to sit around with little to do, and still in our civilian clothes; an elderly sergeant was in charge of us, who, I believe, was being particularly kind knowing that we were heading for a living hell within days, or perhaps he wanted to prove that a sergeant could be a human being, but at any rate, he was the only decent person of rank that I met in my weeks at the Guards' Depot. Some of us read our books, and wrote letters. This happened in the days long before mobile phones, and use of telephones in the barracks was very restricted, so writing was the only real way to communicate. In the early days when I had time to write I must have written the most frightening descriptions, judging from the replies I received from Mum. I have kept two letters from her down the years because I know that she hated writing, and that she would have put pen to paper at about midnight on each occasion, as she was so busy looking after the family. The first letter finishes with the following paragraph: "Well BRIAN, I haven't got any more to say for the present so I will say cheerio and all the best, you haven't got much longer (have you?), love from Mum and Dad and family". Oh, dear Mum –'Haven't got long?' –only another 987 days, for I was counting them already! I soon realised why many of these recruits in the barrack room did not read and did not send letters home, for they were illiterate; a number had to go to education classes to achieve the minimum standard of reading and writing which the army required. They generally were happy with comics and looking at the pictures in magazines.

Soon we were 'squadded' – 24 men who were going to make a new squad in the 13th Company Coldstream Guards. A brisk march down to the quartermaster's building and we were given uniforms, denims, shirts, under wear, pyjamas, beret, cap, steel helmet, greatcoat, cape, socks, mug, cutlery, PE kit, blankets and sheets, and the dreaded two pairs of boots. Then began the whole process of cleaning, polishing and buffing all this gear, which continued for most of the 24 hours in the early days, and later, at any spare moment when we were not involved in drills, PE, army history, etc. I began to realise the significance of the phrase someone had told me: "Join the army and see the world, join the guards and scrub it". Onto the scene comes a Trained Soldier, a peculiar sub-human breed and a rank which only the guards seem to have; these men had passed out as full soldiers, but instead of moving up to do general duties in London or Windsor, they remained in the guards' depot, with one man assigned to each squad under a sergeant , to take charge of them, and particularly to show them how to deal with the boots, belts, brasses, cap badges and all the other paraphernalia. They were usually very lazy, bad tempered, and in the case of our trained soldier, always on the scrounge. I think the truth is that most of them were failed guardsmen, so they were left behind, and certainly took their anger and frustration out on us. The boot business was awful, and I really thought I would burn my hands so much that I would be incapable of playing the clarinet in the band later. This was all so typical, for every day one's hands were ruined with scrubbing, cleaning and polishing the floor, and no one seemed to care that a musician's hands were rather precious. The end of a dessert spoon would be heated over a flame, then dipped in to the boot polish, and pressed on to the boot, to get rid of all the little bumps in the leather. It took hours and hours just to do one pair of boots, and then one had to begin the polishing process until the boots shone like mirrors. Cap badges had to be cleaned and polished until they gleamed, likewise buckles of belts, tunic buttons and so on. It was so boring I could have screamed; if the trained soldier was in a good mood, we would be allowed to go over to the NAAFI for a 15 minute break, to have a cup of tea and bun, or even sausage and beans if the money ran to it. This was only on condition that we all clubbed together so that we could take back some cigarettes, mug of tea and food to the 'dear' trained soldier. The NAAFI became a blessed haven, a place which still showed signs of civilisation amidst the mad house. Soon I got to know one or two members of the Brigade Squad, these were men, generally from public schools, and what we would think of as the upper classes, who were going to become officers. I would join Lord Chelsea, or Viscount Encombe, for they were people with whom one could have a decent conversation, but only in the confines of the NAAFI, for once outside, you never spoke to a member of the Brigade Squad. It must be said that these men were given a very gruelling time, and were bullied relentlessly; the sergeants, corporals and Warrant Officers (WOs) realised that these men were going to be their superiors eventually, so they set out to break them down and give them hell while they had the opportunity. In theory, of course, bullying was not tolerated, but I saw men being beaten to a pulp, sometimes by two or three sergeants at once. Of course the poor chap would never complain officially, because it had to be a case of 'stiff upper lip'.

One morning we were marched down to be allocated rifles, and then started the first of my few attempts to stand up for myself. Most things happened in strict alphabetical order, and at this stage I was number two in line; having marched in, someone gave me a book to sign and attempted to throw over a rifle. I refused to accept the rifle or sign the book, and the sergeant in charge nearly threw a fit. After calling me all the names under the sun he tried again, and again I refused. He threatened to put me "on orders" – which would mean marching before the

Adjutant and being punished for disobeying orders. I quietly retaliated, speaking firmly but trembling in my newly-polished boots: "Sergeant, with respect, I will also ask to go on orders because as a musician, destined for the band, I am not allowed to do weapon training, Sergeant!" at this stage he just laughed and told me to F off. It was one of those cases of trying to wear you down, for he knew from my uniform that I was not one of the guardsmen.

So the training began in earnest. A few trips were taken to the outdoor swimming pool, which was very cold at 8:30 on a frosty October morning. If you could not swim two lengths of the pool you were classed as a non-swimmer. Non-swimmers lined up in alphabetical order, and were pushed in one by one. Every time you attempted to get to the side, a pole appeared, and pushed you under the water; then as you were just about to drown, you were allowed to grasp the pole and be pulled into the side. This was the army's method of teaching you to swim, and it was many years before I plucked up courage to swim voluntarily again. Two of us in the squad had achieved A levels at school, so we did not have to go to the education classes along with the rest. Suddenly, I was glad I had stayed on to do the A levels, although, in this dreadful place school seemed a world apart. The other chap was soon taken off to go on a Warrant Officer's Selection Board (WASBE) course , which was something to do with selection of officer material. He probably became a colonel in the end. I was also, of course, exempted from the weapon training classes, and during this time I stayed in the squad room polishing my boots, badges, the floor… everything. If the trained soldier was around I might be given permission to go to the NAAFI – as long as I paid for some food and tea for him. Come to think of it, by the time I left Caterham he must have owed me many pounds, and when I heard later, that the army has very strict rules about demanding money, borrowing money, and so on, I also realise what serious trouble I could have got him into, if only I'd had the courage, and the desire. But I was having to learn that to survive, you kept your head down, prayed for the strength to keep going until bed-time, and counted off one more day from the chart in my bedside cabinet. We learned to march, quick and slow, to halt, to turn, to come to attention, to salute. How often I was put before a long mirror in a drill shed and told to practice saluting while the others went for "Proper Heducation". We had to learn to dress…oh no, not putting on clothes in a freezing cold squad room at 6am, but in this case learning to be absolutely in line with the man in front and, those on left and right. Even when I had joined the band weeks later the cry would ring through the ranks to "Watch your dressing!", and in those early days in the band it was very difficult to play the clarinet from the march card attached to the bell joint of the instrument, stay in step and keep an eye on both the man in front and to left and right; the band sergeant would be marching close by, ostensibly playing the alto saxophone, but, more often than not, he would be growling at us to "Watch your **** dressing!" Of course, the logical thing at Caterham would have been to let me practice marching with the clarinet, but no one had thought of this.

There were lectures given on regimental history, and the names of the top brass both in our regiment and in the Brigade of Guards, and we were tested on this information at various times. One wrong answer and you were in trouble; many of my fellow recruits had trouble in remembering the diplomas that came after the director of music's name: Major Douglas A. Pope, ARCM, psm. Even I wasn't so sure about the "psm" part. I laughed when I learned the meaning for I gathered that it stood for "Passed School of Music" and didn't even have the courage to announce itself in capital letters – it could have meant that he had driven past in a car or bus, but I suppose it referred to the fact that he had trained and passed out of Kneller Hall.

Everyone just lived for Sunday. It was one day of comparative freedom, you could lie in bed most of the morning, though if you wanted breakfast you had to get up by 8 o'clock; and in between meals you could read the paper, or just sit on the bed and count the days to getting out of Caterham. Of course you weren't allowed out of the barracks at any time, but you could walk around, though this meant dressing up and looking smart. I had put down that I was 'Free Church', and I attended the informal service which was taken by a visiting vicar. I found myself playing the piano for the hymns, and, wonder of wonders, he asked me if I would like to go to play for one or two of his services at church. He obtained permission, collected me and brought me back to the door, but it was one way of getting out of the dreadful place for a short while. I have mentioned before that many of the squad seemed to read comics because they were fairly illiterate. The chap in the bed next to me received a letter from his wife and asked me to read it to him and help with the reply, which I was glad to do. Unfortunately the next letter contained some rather shattering news, for it was from a well-meaning neighbour, who was informing him that his wife was seeing somebody else. Bill was heartbroken, and started talking of jumping over the wall – of going AWOL (absent without leave)! I persuaded him from taking any action, and went to see the vicar about this matter. He urged me to go on company orders to explain the affair, which I did, though with some fear that I was getting into something bigger than I could handle. The result was that Bill was given a 48 hour leave to go back to Birmingham and sort out the whole affair. He came back very happy, feeling sure that the neighbour had got all the wrong information, because it was his brother-in-law who had been going to the house. My letters home must have sounded dreadful, because my mother and father came over to see me on a couple of Sunday afternoons, having been driven over by Uncle Albert and Aunt Nell in their small Morris van. This was quite official, visitors were allowed for a couple of hours to walk around the camp, but not into our billets. I was so scared of being caught marching slowly, that I kept up a terrible speed, with my arms raised shoulder-high (normal for marching in the Guards), and they all had to keep asking me to slow down for they were totally out of breath. Yes, the letters must have sounded very drastic to have got my father out of his chair on a Sunday to travel from Essex to Surrey.

One of the worst experiences in training was the dreaded cookhouse fatigues. Into the kitchen by 6.30am and then being shouted at, sworn at, and ridiculed mercilessly for the next 14 hours. All the dirtiest jobs were found – I discovered that it was true that the cooks spat in the gravy and the custard, and they certainly used the same long poles to stir the contents of each item in the large containers. In the afternoon a nasty sergeant from the Irish Guards shouted at me to clean up the water on the floor, using a bast broom, which was a broom with a long piece of leather at the base to push the water towards the drain. Exit the sergeant. A few minutes later a sergeant from the Scots Guards walked into the kitchen and told me I was using the wrong sort a broom – I must use a hard broom. I duly changed brooms and continued. Exit the sergeant. The first man came in, calling me all the names under the sun because I was using the hard broom, so… I duly changed brooms again, and then, you've guessed, back came the Scots Guards sergeant who told me I was insolent, obstinate, and lazy, because he had definitely told me to use the hard broom. Eventually I was standing in the middle of the kitchen with a broom in each hand, totally perplexed, when they both came in laughing, called me a few more names and disappeared. The important thing was that I had not said a word of argument or complaint at any time. If they had told me to lap the water up with my tongue I would have done so; those two 'gentlemen' were just waiting for me to object, and I would have been punished for insolence. The story would be funny if it wasn't so serious – and was one of the many experiences that made me make up my mind that I would *never* make the army my career.

Kit inspections were another awful nightmare. Everything had to be laid out on the bed: shaving kit, spare bootlaces, utensils, items of uniform, all pressed and folded accurately. The list was endless, and it all had to be measured to the last centimetre. If anything was found wrong by the inspecting officer the sergeant following behind would tip up the bed and most of the contents would go through the open window onto the path and garden below. We would come back from a marching session to find all our things mixed up, being trampled into the ground, if not already stolen, and then would have to lay it all out again for a further inspection. On one occasion I had cut the end of the bootlace obliquely instead off at a slant, and received the wrath of the Almighty for this terrible crime. As well as inspection of our kit, the room would be inspected, so one laid out the kit on the bed the night before and slept on the floor ready for the inspection next morning. There would be a rota of men who had to take it in turns to 'bump' the floor, this would mean attaching a duster or polisher to a long pole, which you would then push around the floor. I don't remember actually whitewashing any coal, but I do know that the coal bucket shone like a mirror – you practically had to put on dark glasses to look at it, and everything that could be was whitewashed over and over again. After about four weeks of this hell I was at a really low-point, and was not alone in often crying myself to sleep on the pillow. The other 23 men had been chosen to be guardsmen for their height and strong physique, but even they were exhausted by the end of the day. They all reminded me daily how puny I looked, and I know I just crawled into bed some nights wondering how I would ever get up next morning.

After some days on the parade ground, I began to get violent pains at the side of my head, and when it got worse I went on to sick parade, which meant getting up extra early to put on best uniform, and reporting to the medical room by 6.30 am where a doctor eventually called me in. The outcome of the visit was a trip to Woolwich, to the army hospital; I was given a railway warrant, and told to report back by 1800 hours. Even with the pains in my head, I still enjoyed this opportunity to find out whether the outside world still existed. The appointment at the hospital was soon over, and, X-rays being taken, and consultation with a specialist, I was free for the rest of the day. Now my home was only about six miles from the hospital, so I risked going home to see Mum and Dad, and to have a decent meal. I had to leave by about 3pm, and was suddenly scared to see a military police van following my bus. I was convinced that the police were watching me, and went through all kinds of agonies wondering how I would explain away my visit home. I got off the bus and went on to the station platform to wait for the train, each moment wondering whether there would be a tramp of heavy feet and someone coming to arrest me, but all was well. I got back to the barracks in time. As it happens no one ever came up with any explanation for the pains, though the doctor at the hospital told me that my belt was far too tight, and was perhaps causing me breathing problems. The next morning on parade the sergeant did his usual test on parade; if he could get any finger between belt and body it was too loose. I was curtly told to fasten the belt tighter – you just couldn't win in the army.

A few days before the end of October my squad sergeant warned me that I might be moving out to take my place in the band at any time. 'Passing out' at Caterham Barracks meant going on various parades where one was marched in with much clattering of boots, halting, right turn, saluting and standing stiffly to attention while the officer said a few words. These parades were called company orders, early in the morning, then adjutant's orders, and finally, commandant's orders – meeting the top man at Caterham, Lieutenant Colonel Bowes-Lyon, who was a brother of the Queen Mother. One of my fellow musicians, Roger Brenner, a trombone player, who later held top jobs in London orchestras, went through this ceremony, and told me all about it, as he packed to go to London. He was joining the band ready for a trip to Copenhagen for a tattoo, and I was warned that I might be needed as well, so my hopes were raised – at last I was getting out of this hellhole. Another Coldstream musician, a violinist, who was to play in the regimental orchestra was also warned to go on these orders. I must explain that one had to be immaculately turned out, with not a button out of place or a crease out of line, particularly when one met the commandant. With all these officers you were warned never to look at them – this was insolence of the worst order – you looked over their heads at a picture of the Queen which was smiling back at you, your actual boss, I suppose. In the case of the violinist called Tony, he was only given a few minutes to get himself down to the commandants orders. He was never a very smart soldier, and on this occasion he didn't have time to lace up his right boot. In he marched, with his toes stuck up to keep the boot firmly on, did his smart right turn, saluted and stood rigidly to attention while the commandant addressed him. Then he had to salute, smart right turn, and march out with a junior officer and sergeant major watching. Unfortunately in his excitement, he had forgotten about the right boot being loose, and as he marched across the room the boot left his foot, and he hobbled through the door with just one boot on. Apparently the commandant went purple with rage, and the warrant officer almost collapsed, and then had to rouse himself to go back and pick up the boot quite close to the commandant's desk. When Tony told me this story weeks later when I was stationed with the band we had a damn good laugh about it. My turn eventually came and I marched into the commandant with both boots firmly laced. He said a few words about my turnout – representing the cream of the British army, and being seen by thousands of people, and mustn't let the side down, etc – then I was dismissed, having just said two words: "Yes, Sir". Back to the barrack-room to pack everything up, for I had to report to London wearing my full pack: greatcoat, a large pack, small pack with tin helmet. I was terribly laden down and could hardly walk with the weight; almost opposite the barracks was a bus stop, but, I was so scared that someone was going to call me back, that I practically ran to the next bus stop. Down to Caterham station and on to the railway train to carry me to the Duke of York's headquarters in King's Road, Chelsea. I duly reported at the office, it was about 4:30pm on a Friday afternoon and only the office staff were still working. The band sergeant asked me whether I could take myself home for the weekend and report back to him on Monday morning, and even gave me permission to leave most of my kit in a corner and to take it home later. I was saluting and banging my feet as I had been trained to do, until he could stand it no longer, and told me I was giving him a headache, and to go home and have a good weekend. Suddenly I realised that there were such things as human beings again!

CHAPTER SEVEN

STILL SERVING QUEEN & COUNTRY

Even as I try to recall some of the events which happened while I was playing in the band of the Coldstream Guards, my memory tries to blot out a great deal of those three years, because they were years of fear and bewilderment for the main part: fear because I was always scared of doing the wrong thing and landing in trouble, and bewilderment because I just wondered why after staying on at school for three extra years, I should be in the position of counting every day, every week, to be free again.

One good thing had happened in moving from the training depot to London on the first weekend in November, 1955, because that weekend was always one of the busiest in the band's calendar – with the Lord Mayor's Show on Saturday morning, the British Legion Festival of Remembrance in the Royal Albert Hall on Saturday evening, followed by an early start for the cenotaph service in Whitehall on Sunday morning – and I was at home enjoying a long weekend leave, so the good Lord was looking down at me from time to time in a kind way. Monday morning saw me reporting back at the Duke of York's headquarters, the band's HQ during my three years' stint in the army. I had to be kitted out with the various uniforms needed for duties, with a trip across to Chelsea Barracks and the quartermaster. Suddenly I realised that these soldiers were fairly human, and equipment wasn't thrown at me, and I wasn't laughed at, though the quartermaster sergeant did make a few jibes about "Bleedin' musicians and their awkward sizes". For the life of me I can never work out how I stored all my uniforms and equipment in our two bedroom house in Dagenham. There was the best uniform, then a second best, my khaki and a set of denims, large and small pack and the steel helmet –these last were items which I never wore or used at all, a blue greatcoat – and I still had to keep my khaki greatcoat – a blue cape and of course, the bear skin. Everything had to be cleaned and polished and kept in order, but the bear skin often caused amusement. At home it lived in a holdall, and frequently became a nice warm home for our cat; on more than one occasion I grabbed the bag to set off to the station – for we never wore the bearskin itself except on parade – only to discover that the cat was still sleeping inside! This was a very expensive piece of army equipment, and I often wonder what Lieutenant Colonel Bowes-Lyon, commandant at Caterham depot, would have said if he had realised that my bearskin provided a home for our cat!

Within three days I was on parade for the first of the guard changing duties. This would happen two or three times a week, depending upon the availability of the five regimental bands, and whether they were all in the country at any one time. You would report to Chelsea or Wellington barracks, by 9am, put your march cards in the correct playing order (see later) and fix them to the clarinet, spend a good few minutes brushing the uniform, combing the bearskin, and making sure that you were smart for inspection. You would then be lined up on parade, and the duty officer would inspect you. If anything was wrong you would be 'put in the book' by the band sergeant who would be following behind. I fell foul of duty officers on two or three occasions, which comes later. After the new guard had been inspected, we would all get into marching order, and would head the procession off to Buckingham Palace; from Wellington Barracks it is only a stone's throw into the courtyard of the palace, but from Chelsea it meant a march of about half-an-hour via Buckingham Palace Road, and then to the palace itself. At the approach to the palace tourists always rush forward to take photographs of the band, especially of the drum major who is leading, and on one occasion I can remember a Japanese gentleman with a very expensive camera who ventured into the road ahead of the band, 'snapping' like mad, and left it rather too late to withdraw – *he* managed to get back to the pavement but dropped his camera, and after about 200 pairs of army boots had trodden on it I don't think it was worth very much. The Japanese man looked heartbroken, both at the loss of his camera and thinking of all the precious photos which he had hoped to take back home to impress all his friends. The band would form a circle in the corner of the palace courtyard and play music for about half-an-hour while the guard changed. The music would of course be accompanied by various commands, shouts and general stamping of feet, and, particularly in the winter when your fingers practically froze to the clarinet – we could only wear standard issue white mittens – you really wondered who you were playing to. The Queen was probably at Sandringham or Windsor, sitting by a nice fire, and all the servants and workers in the palace would be far too busy to listen to our music. But that is part of our wonderful tradition! The old guard would be marched out, with the band in front, to lead them all back to barracks. One or two things did go wrong for me in guard changing. Once I was 'put in the book' for an idle shave; the officer inspecting the band came very close to my chin and quietly declared that I was guilty of an idle shave. For this offence I was marched before the company adjutant, the charge was read out, that I was guilty of an idle shave, and the officer asked whether I had anything to say. In a normal court of law one would admire such evidence of justice and giving the guilty person a chance, but I realised this had nothing to do with justice. You never, ever denied the charge for that would be bringing into question the actions of an officer – of course I had shaved that morning – but, as always, I stared at the picture of the Queen above his head, waited for the sentence, and marched out smartly. The punishment was pronounced: I had to sweep the parade ground for my idle shave.

One cold, February morning, while marching, I dropped all my march cards. For those unfamiliar with the procedure, a small thing called a lyre is fixed to some part of the instrument and A5 sized cards with the march music printed on are fixed in the lyre and read. As one march comes to a close you put the old march at the back of the lyre and the new one is ready for you to play, all the while marching. It has to be done quickly but in a very dignified way, you must keep absolutely in step and watch your dressing while you carry out this process. Everybody was very anxious to get back to Chelsea Barracks to thaw out; even the marching pace seemed to be a little faster than usual, but as I changed march cards the whole pile slipped from my frozen fingers onto the road. Nothing for it but just to carry on, playing the marches from memory, and realising how that poor Japanese man felt when he lost his camera. We reached the barracks, and were duly dismissed, and I thought I had got away with it, that no one in authority had noticed, until a mounted policeman slowly rode over and held up what can only be described as a brown, filthy mess; those cards had been trodden on by many feet, and made firm contact with some horse manure in the process. As I went forward to claim this disgusting mess, the band sergeant came out of the shadows, and I was charged with negligence for letting the cards fall to the road, and for mis-using army property. I suppose I got off lightly, as I had to pay for the new cards and spend an afternoon repairing music in the band library.

The winter season was the quietest part of army life, because on most days, when not involved in guard changing, we would attend band rehearsal. At 9.20am precisely the band sergeant would begin the rehearsal, sometimes the director of music, Major Pope, psm would make an appearance – we would all be brought to attention – and we would plough through some of the music to be played in the various activities of the next few months. There would be race meetings at which the band performed. In between the races, after performing one or two numbers, the band would be free to go off with just enough time to place their own bets; I had no idea about betting, but after watching some of the band pocketing their winnings, I thought I'd have a go and took some advice from a corporal friend. He took me through the process, but, naturally, I never won a penny. We did television appearances, particularly at Christmas and New Year, performing in West End hotels and on the big TV Christmas shows from Shepherd's Bush. During my time in the band I made two LPs, both at Kingsway Hall. One of these records was to go out to Canada, to prepare for the visit we were to make later in the year, and it was in one recording session for RCA that I actually saw a sergeant reduced to tears; we were recording *The March of the Peers* from Gilbert and Sullivan's *Iolanthe*, which has a brass fanfare with very high notes, but every 'take' was being spoiled by a player 'fluffing' a top note. It is generally recognised that brass players lips get very tired, particularly when playing high notes repeatedly, a lot is demanded both of the lip muscles and the lungs, so the longer the high notes are demanded, the more chance there is of 'splitting' them. Finally, the director of music lost his patience, and stood over Sgt. Nicholson – a tall, well-built fellow, defying him to make a wrong note in the next take. Well, he did split a high note, he just became a nervous, trembling heap, tears appeared and he was duly 'put in the book' for being idle on parade. The piece was finished, the record made, and when I occasionally play *The March of the Peers* this incident comes back to me as an example of the stupid attitude shown to music and musicians. All our music-making was done in an atmosphere of fear and dislike: we were scared of making even the slightest mistake, because it would mean sarcastic remarks being made, or being shouted at, or even worse, ending up 'in the book', and the dislike of the music-making was a natural consequence of this ridiculous approach. It wasn't all bad; sometimes the band sergeant would be left to run the whole rehearsal, and he was usually quite decent. He would get out music which we just played through for enjoyment – good transcriptions of classical orchestral pieces, and quite difficult pieces originally written for band.

It wasn't all doom and gloom! Dad had laughed at my claim that I could wear 'civvy' clothes for much of the time and live at home but I was proved right. Civilian clothes could be worn at rehearsals and any duties where we were not required to wear uniform, but they had to be smart – no jumpers and flannels, and no jeans. The rule about jeans wasn't actually written in because they were not part of the fashion scene in the late fifties – people who wore denim material were factory workers or cleaners. In the band you were required to wear a smart suit with tie, and well-polished shoes. I was warned that if I did choose to live at home and arrived on parade late, then the privilege would be taken away, so I urgently looked around for somewhere else to stay, believing that the daily trip backwards and forwards to Dagenham was too much of a liability. Once again Aunt Mary and Uncle John came to the rescue and allowed me to stay during the week in their home. Since I had stayed with them seven years before, when attending Highbury County School, they had moved up-market and now lived in Stoke Newington. They had also adopted a young girl, since they could have no children of their own. The top half of their house was sub-let to another family, so it was a little crowded downstairs for the four of us, and I slept in the front lounge, a room which was hardly ever used by them for social occasions.

One afternoon I set off for the city to buy a couple of books, and spotted a notice in the window of the shop: "Young boy required for full or part-time work – would suit school leaver – apply within". Well, I knew that I wasn't exactly a young boy,

I couldn't even take on regular part-time work, but something made me approach the manager, who gave me one of the shortest interviews in my life, and asked me if I could start the next afternoon on a part-time basis. Of course I had to explain that always the army came first, and there would be times when I would be unable to work, and often at short notice; he was quite happy with this situation, and so began my links with Pickering and Inglis, a Christian publishing firm, which lasted on and off for the next seven years. Most of the members of the band had such part-time posts, often as peripatetic instrument teachers in London schools; when I come to think of it I would have been far better paid as an instrumental teacher than as a packer of books – but I was still 'green behind the ears' and had much to learn. Occasionally panic would set in. If a band rehearsal had gone badly, the music director would turn to the band sergeant, mutter words like "they are bloody lazy! Get them in this afternoon". This would mean a great rush to the telephones, as 40 musicians tried to contact their schools and employers, to explain their absence.

The shop sold religious books, Bibles, cards, stationery, scripture erasers, pens, pencils, and anything which could have a scripture text printed on it. My boss in the packing dept – Ernest Oliver, had worked at P&I all his life, and knew the job and all the stock thoroughly; there would be daily visits by a species known as colporteurs –men and women employed by publishers to go around London purchasing books that were not published by their own company, for mailing –and these people would pop in every other day to "pick Ernie's brains" for information. Ernie would not have called himself a practising Christian, and often jokingly said that he was waiting for the day when we would stock scripture toilet rolls –a helpful text with every wipe! Of equal interest to me was the fact that the shop sold record players, radios, and records; the LP [long playing record] was replacing the shellac 78s and when I found I could get a substantial discount on all the shop products I began to order classical LPs, so that I hardly took any wages, but instead bought lovely, pristine LP records, with appealing covers and extensive notes, and all at trade price. Thus I began the journey of building up a large collection, which was eventually to top the 3,000 mark. Incidentally, when stereo showed its head just a few years later, I set about swapping about two-thirds of my collection, and have had to do the same with compact discs when they appeared in 1983. I referred to this collection mania in an earlier chapter, not realising in 1953 that it would become such a passion, still with me today. In my job, I had to carefully pack, address and post all the items going out by mail, and as Christmas drew near the mail-order department in the basement of the shop became very busy; I was often working until 8 o'clock at night, then taking the train home, having a late meal, then polishing all the equipment and getting my uniform ready for the army job early next morning.

At the beginning of 1956 I became more confident, and decided that I could live at home and make the journey by train each day. It meant an early start, and often anxious moments when the train was held up before it reached Sloane Square Station and our headquarters. If it was just a normal rehearsal at the Duke of York's headquarters, then being late would mean a telling off, but if one was going on to guard changing duty, then there was no question of ever being late. During spring there would often be a recruitment tour, which meant going off to the Midlands or the north of England for about five days to find new recruits for the Coldstream Guards. In the case of the band it would entail a march through the city, usually followed by a good meal in the town hall, and later, a concert in one of the parks followed by 'Beating Retreat'. Overnight we would stay in a local barracks, and there I learned something about marriage. For many of the men, a meal in the mess would be followed by a trip into the city to drink and find women; for the life of me, I could not understand this hypocrisy, that men would ring their wives to check that all was well, to declare their love, and then go off to find some unknown woman for a one-night stand. On the one occasion when I challenged one of the sergeants about this, and boldly asked him what he would do if he discovered his own wife was playing the field, he replied that he would teach her a lesson she would not forget, and anyhow, I was to mind my own so-and-so business. I began to wonder how many young men were influenced to join up, by the sight and sound of the regimental band leading a corps of guardsmen. I remembered our discussions in the sixth form, and Martyn Dakin's words, that once I was in my smart uniform, playing martial music, many young men would follow the band, take the oath, and be given a rifle, so I was responsible for proliferating the army. As I marched through Coventry, Newcastle, Birmingham or Leicester, I would acknowledge that my wily old scripture teacher was so right.

One of the hardest duties in the year was Trooping the Colour. This took place on Horse Guards Parade on a weekday – later, when traffic began to get too heavy, this was changed to a Saturday, and it involved at least four tiring rehearsals before the big day. We had to rehearse the music, and then be instructed by the Regimental Sergeant Major (RSM) in the intricate marching procedure which took place during the parade. It was only years afterwards when I watched the whole thing on television, that I actually realised what happened during the trooping, when the whole band goes round in a circle and comes out in a different formation – or that's what it seemed like! So far as we were concerned, you just followed the man in front, and wherever he went, you went, all the time playing the march and 'watching your dressing' of course. You were shouted at by all and sundry, pushed and shoved, and made to feel a complete idiot, the air would be filled with foul language and colourful descriptions of the musicians. When the great day came, you were on parade from 10 o'clock through to 1pm, then, after the concluding march up the mall, following the Queen to the palace, you took your places in the courtyard and proceeded to give a concert to all the crowds behind the railings outside. It was always boiling hot, and on the one occasion in the parade when I nearly fainted, the band sergeant behind me muttered such terrible warnings of what would happen if I fell to the ground, that I just clenched my buttocks tighter, moved my weight further onto the front of my feet, and just felt the sweat running down my body. This was certainly one occasion which we did not look forward to, and, after being dismissed, there was no question of going in to pack books that day – I felt completely knackered.

The band would be used for broadcasts – I often took part in *Music While You Work*, a radio programme on the Home Service of the BBC, with continuous music – one player at each stand would be responsible to turn the music for the next item to maintain continuity – no quiet serenades, nothing slow, because the object was to keep people working and happy in the factories around the country. Occasionally we went to Hampstead or Shepherd's Bush to appear in *Friday Night Is Music Night*. Television was a remarkable thing, for one spent ages rehearsing march movements on a very small stage, being very careful not to clash with the person in front or his instrument, and then on the actual transmission, it would be cut down to just a few minutes. This also happened on New Year's Eve, when the band played at the Dorchester Hotel – I think we were on stage for all of eight minutes! During the summer season the band would perform at the seaside; I remember being at Folkestone for one week, performing on the bandstand at Leas Cliff Pavilion in the afternoon and evening, and having the mornings free to do sight seeing or to sit on the beach. We also did a broadcast from the Pavilion during the week. Of course, all these extra jobs meant extra pay, sometimes the supplement pay was bigger than our standard army pay, so my dad really had to eat humble pie as he saw me getting quite well-off, with a part-time civilian job thrown in, though it didn't alter the fact that I still crept around in the army in an attitude of fear.

In August, 1956 the band was flown out to Canada, where we were to play for two weeks at the Canadian National Exhibition in Toronto, with trips to Montreal and Quebec for marching ceremonies and some concerts. This was a wonderful experience, and I fell in love with Canada. Toronto seemed so spacious, so clean and everybody was friendly. We were boarded out in private homes, and I shared a room with one of the bass players. The usual routine in Toronto consisted of a free morning, then a performance on the bandstand at about two until four, and a concert at night, sometimes followed by a 'beating retreat' ceremony. Then most of the band headed off to parties or clubs until the early hours. I wasn't the slightest bit interested in drinking at parties, and as I wanted to see as much of Toronto as possible, I would go back to my digs, have a drink with the husband of the family we were with and retire for the night. In this way I was able to see a great deal of the city, and I didn't miss the parties one bit. Near the end of our stay, the Canadian Watch Regiment were hosting a party for the band, and the band sergeant made it quite clear that everyone would go – no exceptions. I did enjoy the drink which I think was malt whisky and ginger – in fact it went down a treat, with waiters taking away half drunk glasses and replacing them with full ones, so I had no idea how many drinks I'd had, I only knew that most of the band were considerably drunker than me. When our director of music replied to the toast, he could barely stand. At some late hour we all got on a coach back to our digs, and Dick Lord, the bass player, and I staggered up to our room as quietly as we could. Now, he always relied on me to wake him up around midday so that he could get some breakfast, and prepare for the afternoon's concerts; on this occasion we both slept very soundly, I woke at about 1 o'clock and we both had a great rush to get ready and head off to the bandstand – and as he was a bass player and had to polish his instrument, it was even more of a rush for him. But we made it by the skin of our teeth. We stayed for a few days in Montreal, where there was a strict rule that no member of the band should go out alone in uniform, for there was a French Canadian group who disliked the British army. I did not know about this rule at first, and on Sunday evening I wanted to make my way to a church. I explored the city, finished up at a service, and afterwards made friends with many people over coffee and cake, and one couple insisted upon giving me a trip in the car round Montreal to see it lit up. They were all such lovely people, and I realised that Christians are really one big family, and our churches should always make outsiders welcome. After a memorable visit to Niagara Falls, and a trip to Quebec to play at the Governor's Palace, we boarded our plane back to England, and 10 days' leave, which we all badly needed. I went off to North Wales on a walking trip, staying at youth hostels.

Looking back on life in the army, at least one could say that no two days were ever absolutely alike, for we never knew what was planned for the following week. On one occasion I was selected to play in a small group at Westminster Abbey for a service in aid of all those who had won the Victoria Cross; the Queen Mother was present and I was thrilled to be sitting in the organ loft, having last seen it on Coronation day on the black and white TV at Uncle John's. The next day the band was at Crufts dog show at the Olympia, so it was all in a day's work.

Then came the black day when I lost army equipment! In the morning I had travelled up as usual on the District Line tube to Sloane Square Station, and was walking along King's Road with another musician when I suddenly realised…..
I HAD LEFT MY ARMY CLARINET UNDER MY SEAT ON THE TRAIN.
This was REALLY serious and I just wanted to run away to the end of the world.

I went into the HQ and told the band sergeant what had happened, expecting him to hit the ceiling, and hit me on the way down; instead he was very calm and quiet – this was ominous. He just told me to go back to the underground, and get off at every station, find the station master and ask whether the clarinet had been handed in. "Don't come up to the surface until you've found it." he said. So I spent all that day going on and off trains, but to no avail. The clarinet had gone. As I was wearing my 'blues' uniform, with peaked cap, many Japanese and German tourists thought I was employed by London Transport, and kept asking me which trains they needed. Well, I couldn't just stay down there indefinitely, and I really needed to see daylight if only to find out whether the world still existed, and so at 5 o'clock I went back to headquarters and reported to the sergeant. He told me to do exactly the same thing the next day. This went on for three days until I reported in and was told that my clarinet had been found, and handed in to the lost property office at Baker Street; I would go there and pay the required fee. This I did, and it was very expensive, about three weeks' army pay, and I reported back thinking this was the end of the matter. How wrong I was. The sergeant told me that I would go before the adjutant, and be charged with wilful misuse of HM equipment. This all sounded very serious, and a few days later I was marched in before a captain and the charge was read out. The great personage informed me that this was a *very* serious matter – it could have been a gun or a bomb (I was dying to tell him that I would hardly carry a bomb on a District Line underground train, but I thought better of it) and this lazy attitude would not be tolerated. I was given the task of cleaning and scrubbing the steps to the sergeants and officers' mess. I duly had to draw one bucket – steel, one bar of soap -carbolic, one mop, one scrubbing brush; 'drawing' in this case didn't mean sitting down to make a picture of these implements, but one drew them from the quartermaster's stores, signed for them and was responsible for returning them. I did the job, it took two hours and my hands were worn away by the time I'd finished. A sergeant came to inspect, shuffled his boots in a puddle on the parade ground, walked up the steps and declared that they were "Bloody filthy, you are bone bloody idle, and you'll come back and do them again tomorrow!" Of course I agreed to this arrangement, did the job a the second time, handed back the implements with a signature (probably in triplicate), and made a quiet promise that I would never let the wretched army clarinet out of my sight in future.

Going on leave was always a pleasure to look forward to, and in 1957 I returned to Bexhill for another BMS summer school and stayed for two great weeks. I remember the extravagant James Wright- last mentioned in Chapter 5 –deciding that he and I would travel down on a special express which had Pullman carriages. So we took tea in fine style as we left the London suburbs and headed for the coast –even though we had very little spending money for the holiday. But that was the way of James. Incidentally, and I have photos to prove it – he used to be the only person on the beach always clad in white shirt, tie and blazer. It had to be VERY hot for him to remove just the blazer. During the second week a small group arrived from a church at Elm Park – quite close to us at Dagenham. The Elm Park Christian Endeavour had taken one of our meetings on a joint exchange which frequently took place, and I had gazed longingly at one girl who did a reading. Couldn't remember anything of the meeting when it was over, except that I longed to meet that girl again. As ever, I had been too shy to approach her on the night. Lo and behold, Pat, the girl in question arrived on holiday – trouble was, she seemed to be one of a foursome and I did not want to compete. So again, I worshipped from afar until the Thursday afternoon. I was quietly playing the piano in one of the school practice rooms when this Pat rushed in and asked if she could hide; this was quite a problem as there was only one chair, the piano and a small cupboard in the room. Almost on her heels came the boyfriend armed with a water pistol, and he aimed the contents at her; I had leaned forward to try to protect not her, but the piano, so I got a real soaking while he went off laughing. Pat showed great concern in helping to dry me out, then asked if she might listen to the music; selecting something which would impress her, I began to play, and then suggested that she ought to join her boyfriend. "Boyfriend?" she exclaimed, "He is nothing of the kind. I just palled up with him for the sake of Dorothy, my friend, who has come with her boyfriend." So, the way was opened. The last two days of the holiday were fantastic. We went everywhere together, swam, walked and enjoyed our ice creams at Fortes Parlour, in town, with another opportunity to impress, as I bought two of the most expensive knicker-bocker glories on the menu, and we dabbed our hankies over each other to wipe away the last of the ice cream from our mouths. Some bits remained, and we were almost glued to each other as we kissed each other goodnight. Pat O'Connor and I travelled back home and we went out together for a little time. She would often come over to my church for the evening service – very hard for me to get an evening off, as I was the organist. She was also the only girl who ever met my parents –not at home, for I was far too ashamed to let her near 38, Walfrey Gardens, but at the home of an aunt and uncle. Pat and I had been to a matinee performance of *South Pacific* in the West End and we went back to Tufnell Park for tea. They all loved Pat, and Uncle Albert told me to hang on to her. Unfortunately I never did. She made an effort by sending me a beautiful Parker pen for my 21st birthday – most of which I spent in bed, having had to play at a London hotel the previous night – and even sent a reminder card charging me with neglect. I was so stupid, but somehow fear took over, even as I grew to love her. If I had married, I'm sure it would have been to Pat. Brian, you complete idiot!!

At last the time drew near for me to leave the band and consider my next job, but before this came the occasion when I was giving orders to the sergeants and corporals, and that doesn't happen very often in the army. For a long while the musicians had been campaigning to take trade tests which were normal in the rest of the British Army, and benefit from the subsequent rise in pay. Everybody was very pleased when the band sergeant informed us that tests had been devised and we could try for the three tests. The written examination involved simple harmony exercises, and two-part writing. I realised that I had done much more complicated exercises for my A level at school, but many of the NCOs hadn't done anything like this, so they came to me for help, and for a few afternoons I became the teacher and they became the students. I found the exam very easy, and because I had finished long before time I decided to write two versions of each exercise – not knowing that this was to be my undoing. The practical part of the test consisted of conducting the band in a prepared piece, rehearsing them and correcting wrong notes, and then being given a piece to conduct at sight. While one candidate was conducting on the rostrum, the rest of us would play, and occasionally, the band sergeant would give someone a message telling him to play "a wrong 'un" to find whether the conductor could tell. This isn't always easy when 60 people are playing. The final part of the test was on the parade ground: the band lined up in marching formation, the exam candidate took the place of the drum major, at the head of the band, to bring the band to a halt while playing, do right and left turns and an about turn. It is quite a frightening moment when 60 men and instruments are behind you waiting your instructions, done with the movement of a mace – the long gold stick which the drum major holds. One candidate came to grief. Musician Carter played the flute and piccolo and was very small, rather like his piccolo. He marched ahead of the band towards the boundary wall, but failed to give instruction to the trombones to right about-turn, with the consequence that we all marched straight into the wall with a clash of instruments and men doubled up with laughter. When I spoke to Brian Carter later he told me that he had just panicked, missed the moment when he had to give the signal, eight paces from the wall, then told himself it would be the next pace, and so on, until it was too late. Well, the trade tests were a great leveller, those of us who had come from A level at school did rather well, and many of the musicians who had been in the army since they were band boys had to do the tests again.

I applied to Goldsmiths College to train as a teacher when I left the army – see next chapter – and so began to count down the days in the band with great impatience. A month before my demob I was called into the band sergeant's office, where he was sitting at his table with a number of forms and pen in hand. An awful coldness gripped my stomach – surely I hadn't lost something valuable from the army, a bomb, a lorry, a regiment? "Right, Ali, I just want you to sign these 'ere forms; there's a good chap". Now I know I was green about the gills, and as naive as they come, but at least I had learned after three years in the forces that you don't sign anything without reading it first. The sergeant seemed annoyed that I wanted to know what I was signing, and asked me whether I trusted him – I was very tempted with a suitable reply, but I overcame my feelings and remained polite. It transpired that because I had done so well in the trade tests I had been selected as the guards candidate to go to Kneller Hall and join the band master's course for 1958. When I replied that I wasn't interested, and had no intention of staying in the army one day longer than necessary the sergeant began to get very annoyed.

"But you have been chosen; it's a great honour to be selected to go to Kneller Hall; you can't say no, because we have already decided." I replied quite firmly that I had my own plans and still wasn't interested. I did however feel that it was polite to ask a few questions, and was told that when I passed out I would have my own band, in Singapore, Bombay, Gibraltar or some other outpost of the empire GB still possessed then, that I would be an officer – with the rank of at least captain. It was sounding quite encouraging, and then in a quiet voice, he muttered, "It only means signing on for nine years." I asked him to repeat that sentence again, and he said it even more quietly, but I had heard enough. I was NOT going to stay in the army. He informed me that as he was in a generous mood he would allow me 24 hours to come to my senses, and report back in the office ready to sign the forms the next day. Suddenly I had never been more certain of my intentions, and the next day I refused point blank to sign the forms. He called me dreadful names, told me I was a complete bloody fool, and dismissed me. Life in the band became rather difficult for the next two or three weeks, but then they all went off on a recruiting tour; the last I saw of the band was when I waved the coach off from Chelsea one August morning. They hadn't taken me on this tour because I was to be demobbed in the middle of it.

In the regular army you were given the choice of choosing demob clothes or taking the equivalent in money. Another wrong choice – how I wish I had taken the money, but I decided otherwise; one morning I was given a railway warrant to go down to a large barracks 'somewhere in Surrey' to get my demob outfit. We were still living in the days of utility clothes and without doubt these were very utility. The suit did not seem to fit, one leg of the trousers seemed longer than the other, shirts and tie, shoes and socks, even a hat and mac. At least the outfit was useful when I started as a student at college two months later. I had to do a few more days tidying and repairing music in the band office, until the great day came to leave, and after my final ordeal of going on commandants orders, and being told by the lieutenant colonel that it appeared that I hadn't been such a bad soldier after all, he wished me luck in my future career; with a smart salute, right turn, and a crashing left foot stamp, I marched out of the Wellington barracks office, changed clothes, handed in every item of War Department property I possessed, and marched out of the army for good.

I thought it was all behind me, but for years afterwards I would have awful dreams that I had deserted, and that the military police were looking for me – that was the effect of three years in the army.

CHAPTER EIGHT

BECOMING A TEACHER

During the late fifties the motor scooter had taken over. Everyone was dashing about on their Italian Lambretta or Vespa, so I decided to save up and become one of that growing circle of scooter owners. Not for me the Lambretta which had to be kick-started, but a German NSU Prima, complete with splendid windscreen above the handlebars, and an electric starter; you sat astride, and with one press of the starter, you were away! Very dignified! Once I had learned to ride this new machine life took on a new dimension, for I was able to ride everywhere, and very cheaply. Fill the tank with a gallon of fuel for about 4/6 (20p) and you could drive about 300 miles. Those were the days!

With the prospects of going up to college in late September, I decided that I would have a good holiday in two parts. It was back to BMS summer schools again, but the first one was to be in Holland. I met the group at Waterloo Station to travel down to the ferry, and discovered that the resident of the summer school was to be my old friend Ralph Darvill, the minister that I had been evacuated with at Blackpool during the war. He was coming with his wife, and their daughter was there to wave goodbye – three people that I had not seen for at least 14 years. Holland proved to be a wonderful country, and we had visits to the World Exhibition which was held in Brussels, and a trip to view one of the polders, these man-made barriers which were built to dry out the sea water, and reclaim a great deal of badly needed land. This project was taking a number of years, and I'm very proud of two black-and-white photographs which I took at the time, showing vast amounts of water with just reeds growing through, these reeds were chosen because they helped to dry out the land. It was so interesting to return to Holland in 1993, alone, and using a railway season ticket for a week, I realised that I was travelling over whole tracts of land which had been part of the sea in 1958.

Naturally, I had to meet another girl. This was Enid, a rather shy young lady of 18, who, I discovered came from Woldingham in Surrey, and from a rather posh home. This put paid to the friendship at the end of the holiday, for I realised again that if I visited her, then she would want to come to our tiny council home in Dagenham. It wasn't that I was ever ashamed of my parents – well, of mother, at least, for I was always proud of her and all that she tried to do to keep our home clean and cosy – but it all seemed so hopeless to bring anyone else in to it. So, dear reader, you are beginning to realise why marriage has passed me by, because I was stupid enough to think that someone who was fond of me would judge me by my circumstances.

For the last two weeks of August, I went to Barton on Sea, yet another BMS summer school, and this time I travelled with a number of friends from our church. Jim Wright, who had been to Bexhill with me the year before, always fancied himself; he, who never appeared on a beach on the hottest day without his white shirt, tie and blazer on, decided that we would both travel in style on the Pullman train. So at 3 o'clock on a Saturday afternoon, we glided out of Victoria in our reserved seats, and took tea very graciously in the restaurant car. It cost a fortune, and I did keep grumbling that we could have had a whole dinner at a Bournemouth restaurant for the price of the Pullman tea, and some left over.

I had been accepted at Goldsmiths College, part of London University, way back in July. I had chosen this college because my own music master had trained there, and it had a good reputation. People said that if you could teach in the schools around Goldsmiths, in New Cross, south-east London, then you could cope with anything. The first interview was with the vice-principal, who put me at ease immediately. He asked me what I thought of the army, and I feared my reply would let me down – for when I got outside and looked at his credentials, I realised that he had been an officer serving in the war. Early on in the interview I informed him that we were probably both wasting our time, since my father would refuse to sign any application for a grant, without which I could not afford the two-year course. Yes, my Dad had done it again. Having called me a complete fool in 1955 for making the decision to go into the band, and thus the regular army, in 1958 he had told me I was quite stupid to be giving that up when I could have made a career in the army. It was when he muttered that all his family had been quite content to have ordinary jobs and not go to college, that I realised how bitter and class-ridden he was. His attitude made me more determined than ever to complete the course and become a teacher. I did not mention any of these things of course during the interview, but Mr Wheeler then told me that I was over 21, would complete my own application and be considered financially on my own merits. Things began to improve. I realised I was a person in my own right – no dependence on father. In between having the two holidays I kept up my work at the bookshop in Ludgate Hill, where the manager was very happy for me to work full-time, and I was able to get some of the required books needed for my course straight from the press at trade price.

At the beginning of October I began my course at Goldsmiths, studying music as a main subject, with divinity and art/craft as subsidiary subjects. The first two made sense, but anyone who knows me would realise that I can hardly a draw a straight line without spoiling it, that at school, in the woodwork lessons, I could not even make a straight edge with my plane – the wood just gradually disappeared into shavings. Unfortunately the choice of subsidiary subjects was quite limited, as I was already doing music; there seemed to be only PE or this art/craft left. I had taken one look at the enormous gymnasium, and the ultra-fit PE lecturer and decided immediately that it would have to be art/craft! Our craft tutor Mr Morgan was quite upset when we first met him; after he suggested that there were two types of student following his subject: those who wished to teach the subject, and those who were just pursuing it for their own enjoyment. I piped up that, "With respect, sir, I'm part of a third group, that seems to have no choice in the matter."

"Yes, I'm sure you're right – and what is your name please?" he went on in his wonderful Welsh accent. I knew I was a marked man, though we did become firm friends when he discovered that I played the clarinet, and performed some lovely Mozart at a concert which he attended. More about Mr Morgan when I eventually get to my finals. The first few days at uni are given over to clubs and societies, when everybody tries to persuade you to join their particular pursuit. We had been advised not to join more than two or three, and even then I wondered how we would ever find time to do any academic work and attend lectures. I joined the Christian Union, and was to make many friends in that group; as a musician it was expected that I would be in the choral society, and I was selected for the assembly choir – a small group of students who could read the music fairly quickly and perform rather more difficult works than the larger choir. I got involved in the madrigal group and in a recorder consort. The clarinet was to be put to good use in the College Orchestra, which was made up partly of full-time day students, and members of the evening department. Goldsmiths was very proud of its successful evening courses, and people came from all over London to spend their evenings both getting the education that they had been denied as children, and enjoying themselves in hobbies and pursuits. Playing standards in this orchestra varied from year to year, as I will illustrate later.

Head of the music department, Dr Lesley Orrey, was enjoying a sabbatical year in the USA, at Santa Barbara University, and so we had a substitute part-time lecturer called Ewan Reece-Davies. He came in to do aural training and keyboard harmony with our group, and most of us found him useless. It was obvious he prepared nothing before he arrived, and used to try to get by with charm and a handful of chords that he used to harmonise all his music. There seemed to be no plan, and every lecture seemed the same; we only continued to attend so that we could maintain a clean sheet in our college portfolio. On the other hand, Elizabeth Barnard (she used her maiden name, although married to a Spaniard, Manuel Lazareno) was an indefatigable worker. She did so much to prepare us for work in schools, and was not afraid to work 'at the chalk face'. On several Mondays in that first term she would take us out to a local school – and they were all fairly tough schools in that area – seat the students on benches around the room, and then have a class wheeled in to be taught by her; we would watch and when the class was dismissed, we were allowed to ask questions and make our own contributions. Miss Barnard was quite small but she certainly packed a punch, metaphorically speaking; she was quite able to deal with quite enormous lads with an acid tongue or withering look and conveying the feeling that they had let her down personally. All this was of course an act, but then I have always believed that most of teaching involves acting and drama. We all came to admire her, especially for her willingness to put herself in the firing line; most of the lecturers were very good at the theory side, and recommending books to read, but we often wondered how they would cope in the classroom. There was always a feeling that some of them were there because they had promoted themselves from the classroom having realised they were not very good at teaching and didn't enjoy it. Miss Barnard carried a large black handbag, which had seen better days, and from it she could produce almost anything. If a student had no chalk, it would be produced in seconds, likewise board rubber, tissues, in fact anything connected with class work seemed to be contained in that large black bag. Often in lectures we would be given a topic that we had to teach to the other students, who had to adopt the age required and act in like manner. For example, David might be asked to teach quavers to a class of eight-year-olds; we would pretend to be the eight year-olds, and Miss Barnard was always naughty Eleanor who tended to ask awkward questions. On one occasion Trevor was teaching a topic, and 'Naughty Eleanor' was causing him considerable embarrassment, until he turned and told her that if she didn't keep quiet he would ask her to leave the room – but at that point she became Miss Barnard again! Dr.Paul Steinitz (Uncle Paul to all the students) lectured at the Royal Academy, was organist and choir master of St. Bartholomews' church in Smithfield and was the founder of the London Bach Society. We really were so fortunate to have him in the music department. What a tremendous character he was, and what a first-rate musician, but above all, what a great sense of humour he had. Within five minutes of any lecture which Uncle Paul gave, students would be clutching their sides with laughter, and yet we learned so much from him. I've a feeling he didn't do much preparation for our weekly music lecture, but then he didn't need to, every sentence was helpful and full of a lifetime of musical experience. One could learn so easily from him. I took part in the first concert of the term which he organised, and played a movement from the Mozart clarinet trio, which went down very well, and the vice principal made mention of it when I went for my end of term review.

Life suddenly became serious as we realised that within six weeks of starting at college we would be on our first teaching practice – stuck in a classroom in front of real pupils who would answer back. My education tutor was Mr Betts (Dickie), who went on to be one of Her Majesty's Inspectors (HMI) and talked a great deal of sense. I vividly recall the opening of his lecture just a few days before we were going into schools. He suddenly turned on a very quiet young lady in the front and barked at her, "So how are you going to start your first lesson?" She nearly jumped out of her skin, and while she paused for breath he went on, "In five days' time you're all going into the school thinking that you are God's gift to education. Let me tell you now that this will really be a damage limitation exercise – we just hope that it doesn't take the school too long to get back to normal when you return to college!" He turned to someone else and asked them how they would start the lesson – every time a suggestion was made he gave a reason why that would be an opportunity for the class to play up. Then he asked us to write down a few basic points about beginning lessons with the minimum of fuss; seemingly obvious things like finding out whether the class was used to lining up outside the room – always the best thing – getting them quiet before they actually go in, with explicit instructions that they are to remain standing at their desks, at which point you told them very clearly what they were to do when they sat down, etc. Mr Betts was right, for if you had an obedient class at the beginning, and you had asserted yourself from the outset, then there was always a chance of a successful lesson. When we discussed points over coffee with other groups, their education tutors had given them lists of books to read, but I found Mr Betts' straight talking very useful. Northumberland Heath was a fairly good school, at Erith in Kent, incidentally, only a matter of half-a-mile from where my sister has lived for the last 30 years, though the school has changed. The pupils were tidy, wearing obligatory school uniform, and the school was well disciplined and had a real sense of community. Oh that there were more schools like it today. I can remember nothing at all of the lessons I took, only that I had to do a great deal of lesson preparation and writing up of results with an honest assessment of my own successes and failures each day. So life went on until the end of that first term, with a very happy weekend in November when the Christian Union group went on a retreat to the Isle of Wight. This was an excellent way of getting to know people and make friends as well as being given some excellent Christian advice. We were already finding that being away from one's church and friends at Goldsmiths College could be quite a challenge to faith.

Christmas term ended with various parties and dances in the women's halls of residence, with carol singing, mulled wine and mince pies. At the end of the first term the choral society were going to perform extracts from Haydn's *Creation*, and yours truly was singing Raphael the solo bass; the work begins with a brilliant orchestral introduction – very modern for its time and quite difficult to play – which is called *Representation of Chaos*. This incident illustrates the varying standard of the orchestra which only gathered together for the dress rehearsal. Our marvellous conductor, Dr Paul Steinitz, began the proceedings and I watched his brow become more furrowed, and his expression darken as the orchestra ploughed on; at the end he quietly put down his stick, and said, "Ladies and Gentlemen of the orchestra, that is the most lifelike *Representation of Chaos* I have ever heard. Tonight we will leave it out!" This meant that I had to stand up and begin the whole work alone with a recitative, "In the beginning God created the heaven and the earth". When the actual performance came I went quite cold as I realised that there was no one to give me my opening G, for the orchestra only came in one bar later. As the orchestra lifted their instruments and the choir stood up, Uncle Paul, as we always called him, with a twinkle in his eye whispered to me, "How much will you give me for a true G?" He knew that my perfect pitch was not perfect, and, very softly, he hummed the first note. At the same concert I played a movement from the Mozart clarinet trio, which seemed to go down very well with the audience, and I loved this opportunity to play chamber music.

I was called in for my end of term review with the vice principal, who seemed pleased with my progress, he made some flattering comments about the Mozart and my part in the *Creation* performance, and this did no end of good for my own self-confidence. It was at the end of the interview that I asked him whether the college library would be open during the vacation; I was assured that, apart from the public holiday, the library would be open during the day, but he chuckled as he replied that very few students would be interested in the library during the Christmas holiday, and I let out that this was the only place where I would get any serious study done as it was completely impossible to work at home in such crowded conditions. I got up from my seat, apologising for this remark, as it was nothing to do with him, but he became quite serious as he told me that if conditions at home reflected my work then it was very much his responsibility. He advised me to get in touch with my local MP. This I did, writing to John Parker, the Labour member who had represented Dagenham for many years in the House of Commons, and received a note by reply, to meet him at the House the following evening. We enjoyed our coffee, and I told him something of the conditions at home; he made a few notes and said that he would get on the phone to Bill Fiske (I realised later that he was referring to Sir William Fiske, leader of the London County Council). Within a couple of weeks we were given an opportunity to look over a new house at Abbey Wood, part of an estate being built on the other side of the Thames, just beyond Woolwich.

Things seemed to happen so quickly. After visiting the house, trudging through mud, where roads had still not been made up, we found 13, Stanbrook Road – the road names all linked with abbeys and castles of England – very posh, and we took to the house straight away. By mid-March we had moved from Dagenham to Abbey Wood; my sister and I each had bedrooms of our own, my brothers shared a large bedroom, we actually had a dining area in the kitchen, a side entrance, a downstairs toilet, and above all, a modern bathroom. Suddenly we all had some space, and some privacy. My mother fell in love with the place, at last she could take a pride in keeping her house clean and tidy. Within months we had a telephone, although father gave strict instructions that we were never to use it, only to accept incoming calls! As I recall this move, I realise that it took place far too late; my brother John was just completing his time in the forces, and both he and Alan would be married and moving out of the house within three years, and I was at college, only coming home at weekends.

Changes would take place in and around the Abbey Wood estate later. There was a an electric sub-station behind our garden, and beyond, a 20 foot high bank, in concrete and with bushes and grass which had grown on to it over the years. This bank contained pipes with all the sewerage and drainage from south London, leading to the Southern Outfall pumping station at Crossness, on the banks of the Thames, and from here barges would take the waste to be discharged in the estuary. The pumping station is actually quite a famous London landmark from the 1860s, when Sir Joseph Bazalgette , a forward thinking gentleman, decided to try and clean up the capital...On some summer days we would be reminded of the bank, with a strong smell which pervaded the area. Beyond this bank were vast acres of dilapidated land which had belonged to Woolwich Arsenal; grass and trees had fought their way on to the site so that it resembled the nearest thing to open country for a few miles around. I took one or two girlfriends there in my courting days, and was astonished to read that when they cleared the site to build HM Prison Belmarsh For Serious Offenders, quantities of unexploded bombs, grenades and batches of ammunition were collected up. It puts new light in the phrase, "Was it like an explosion for you, Gladys?" I hate to think now what the uncomfortable objects beneath my outspread coat actually were! Next to the housing estate of Abbey Wood some architects were given a field day in the late 1960s designing another vast estate to be called Thamesmead. At the time I had a neglected allotment on what is now a six storey block, and would like compensation for my potatoes and sprouts which were buried in the foundations. These houses and flats were designed with cul-de-sacs, covered walkways and underpasses which soon became ideal trading ground for drug dealers and a quick getaway for criminals, but were hated and feared by the residents. However this 'mess' called Thamesmead won several international awards. I am just so glad that this development began as I was making plans to move away from the area in 1969.

During my first year, I was put into 'digs', as it was considered that I lived too far from college; sadly, there were only two halls of residence for the men, and one of those was miles away from the college – I would have liked to have gone into a hall of residence to at least feel that I was at university. At the beginning of the first term I met Mr and Mrs Ross in their home at Lee Green, quite close to Lewisham, and moved into my bedsitter, which I shared with a piano and three-piece suite for this was their lounge. Mr Ross worked at Courage's brewery in London during the day, and spent most evenings 'Moonlighting' at the local pub.

I soon came to the conclusion that I was there so that Mrs Ross had some company during the evenings. The general plan was that as soon as the two children had been put to bed, there would be a knock on the door and an invitation to go and have a cup of tea with her, and apart from general chat I would be obliged to watch the recommended programme on television which she was about to see; this seemed to drag on until about 10:30pm when Mr Ross would arrive home slightly the worse for wear, and insist that we all have a drink before going to bed. I would return to my room tired out and frustrated that all my work was still lying there after yet another wasted evening, and realised that at this rate I would never get any study done at all. The young girl seemed to be having piano lessons, and the piano was in my room, so there was an understanding that she could come in to practice after her tea; this also resulted in half an hour of work not done. After the first term I got into the habit of having my evening meal in college and going back to the digs when the library closed at 9pm. I also began to go back home each weekend, partly so that I could be involved in the church and its services. This is yet another example that seemed to show that I could not cut the ties of living at home.

I missed the lively church at Dagenham very much, and looked around for a church nearer the new home. I went to a small church in Abbey Wood, but it was rather pathetic, with just a handful of worshippers and about three young people. The church secretary was very keen to get me 'on board', but I then went a little further afield to the East Plumstead Baptist Church. Amazingly the minister there, Arthur Hallworth, had been the minister at our church in Dagenham some years before I had joined, and here I was following him to his new church. He was nearing retirement, and eventually settled with his wife in the lovely village of Eynsford – which had been famous in the late twenties as the home of Peter Warlock, who chose it because there were 27 pubs within a 4 mile radius, it had its main line to London, and he did like to ride naked through the ford and the streets on his motorbike late at night. He also gathered around him a number of musical friends who were into drink and drugs in quite a big way. But all this was in the '30s and had ceased when Arthur Hallworth went to live there.

I was received into membership in July 1959 and soon made many friends and had some very happy occasions. The church had a real organ – 2 manuals, full pedal-board, and I longed to get an opportunity to play. I was asked to play for three or four weddings and youth services, but generally I deputised for the official organist, Mr Williams, who seemed to be so dreary and uninteresting as an organist. The organ was smack in the centre of the back wall, behind the minister's pulpit with its usual curtain to prevent the rest of the congregation from watching; on a few occasions Mr Williams went right off to sleep during the sermon, and the secretary would have to go and wake him up when the next hymn was announced. One of my friends was Alan Butler, whose wedding I did play at; we seemed to have the same sense of humour and fun, and I remember buying several LPs of Spike Milligan and Peter Sellers, and playing them at his parents home, where we just cried with laughter, rolled around on the floor, and ached with the pain of laughing. Some years later Alan and his wife went off as BMS missionaries, and I lost touch with them.

Back at college we prepared for our second school practice, and I discovered I was to be at Penge Secondary Boys' School – well *somebody* had to go to Penge! It was really a large collection of shabby houses and shops, close to Croydon in South London, which sprawled on either side of the main line to Victoria. The school was a typical old LCC building which stood immediately beside this busy railway line; during the morning rush-hour, with trains going by every minute, it was almost impossible to make oneself heard in the classroom, for one needed the windows open as it was the middle of June and there was no air-conditioning, so the class had the option of either suffocating with heat, or putting up with the noise. I remember meeting several elderly male staff who seemed to be counting the time to retirement, showing little interest in the lessons they taught; they welcomed the chance to retire to the staff room when I took over their classes and I felt that they were thinking that one day my youthful enthusiasm would be taken over by boredom. I certainly realised that the lethargic attitude of many of the boys wasn't just due to the hot classrooms, but to the boring lessons which they had to endure. With my grand schemes of work and plans I was going to revolutionise the teaching!

Well, I don't know whether I succeeded in making the lessons more interesting, but I came away from Penge having had a challenging but successful school practice. On the journeys back to college after school, whether by train or bus, I would look out on a dismal picture of dingy, terraced houses with hardly any gardens, appearing even more gloomy in the bright sunlight of the summer afternoon. Years later I was to go on the Eurostar train from Waterloo, and it always seemed to pick up speed through Penge Station, as though it couldn't wait to get out of London to the green fields and bright colours of the Kent countryside.

During the last two weeks of June with the sun beaming down, it was time for end of year exams, and I wondered very seriously whether I would still be at Goldsmiths in a year's time to take my final exams. Results went up very quickly, I had passed, and with a sigh of relief looked forward to the summer vacation; though it wasn't to be all holiday, and among the assignments I had to do a case study. From a local school the headmaster and I selected a pupil whom I would 'shadow' in lessons for a couple of days, meet his parents, visit his house, and generally get to know the boy. I don't know what he made of all this, but I did explain my reasons, and he co-operated in all the questions I asked him. He had been adopted at an early age by parents who could not have children. I was able to see how he had become a member of the family, indeed, their own child. The boy wasn't particularly brilliant, and certainly no angel, but I was able to produce a suitable essay on him, with many charts and IQ results, tests, and graphs which the tutors at college would be able to gloat over. The Health Education Department also made us study the local council's activities with regard to drainage, sewerage, hospital facilities, and this meant a great deal of work both in the local library and making appointments to meet representatives of the various departments in Woolwich town Hall. I suppose one would argue that all this is rather irrelevant to the training of an individual for school teaching, but it was interesting and it helped me to see the local community from a new angle – after all, the health of the community is directly linked to its education, both for pupils and parents. For the music department we had to write a sizeable volume showing research and study on a topic we had chosen. With advice from the music tutor I chose to write about the clarinet, its history, its repertoire, place in the orchestra, etc. Along with most of my friends, I got behind in this project, and had to 'burn the midnight oil' just days before returning for the new college year

At the very beginning of the holidays I travelled up to Keswick on my motor scooter, to attend the Keswick convention. This is an inter-denominational gathering which fills the lovely village for a week or so each year. Meetings were held in the big tent, with well-known church speakers conducting morning Bible studies, various fringe meetings and the main evening service. The whole atmosphere there was quite unique, with so many Christians of different churches taking over the town and all its accommodation. It was delightful to go through the streets late in the evening and hear people singing hymns and songs in their various boarding houses. I was camping outside Keswick as part of the IVF (Inter-Varsity Fellowship) group. It was great fun in the camp, although it was run on fairly strict, rather military lines, with a commandant, padre and various other officials to see that we towed the line. I'm quite amused looking at the official photograph, with all the students looking quite smart -- many with ties and college blazers on – taken in a formal setting, the officials seated at the front with arms folded. Of course the girls were kept in another camp at least half a mile away, but we were allowed to see them, and indeed various functions were arranged to bring us together, UNDER SUPERVISION. Naturally I had to fall for one of the girls, who was Jennifer Morley. She was musical, we seemed to have very much in common, she was pretty, just a shade taller than me, but I could live with that, and her home was in Romford, just a few miles from the Dagenham I had moved from earlier that year! I was invited to her home, met her parents and brother, and got on with them splendidly. Her father was a classics teacher at the Liberty Grammar School, and had taught the very clever violinist, Ralph Holmes, who I mentioned in a previous chapter. Sadly, the inferiority complex won the day, and I was too embarrassed to even think of inviting Jennifer back to meet my parents – not the first nor the last time this was to happen, and another budding romance hit the dust.

Dear "Uncle Paul" Steinitz came up trumps again. A couple of weeks before the end of term he invited me to Canford School for the music course which took place there in August. He would be doing a course on Bach, with many of the members of his London Bach Society taking part, and I was invited to sing bass in the choir. This sounded a wonderful opportunity, but I realised that it was extremely expensive and completely out of my pocket – my aim in the vacation was to *earn* money for next term, not to spend what little I had – but with a twinkle in his eye he told me that he was sure that the college would pay all my expenses, and sure enough they did. Five of us from college went down to Canford and had a marvellous time. Apart from singing in the choir I was able to play the clarinet in one or two chamber music groups, and join in singing madrigals down by the river late at night, with just torches to read the music. It was a very romantic setting, and always very enjoyable to walk back through the fields in the dark, arm in arm with one's favourite soprano or alto. Suddenly madrigals and all those 'fa-la-la' refrains took on a new meaning!

I found it a bit disconcerting to discover that most of the young people on the course were from public or independent schools, often with very 'plummy' voices to match, and in the first couple of days my inferiority complex nearly took over, until I realised that in the realms of music making we were together with the aim of working to reach a higher standard of performance, enjoying the music – the background and the posh family were quite irrelevant. I also met several young students who were to be well-known professional conductors and musicians within a few years. Canford School itself was like another world, with acres of well-kept grounds, beautiful old buildings and very close to the sea, and I did compare all this with the awful conditions which prevailed around Goldsmiths College, the noise, the smells and the squat, dull terraced houses – in particular the dull school buildings at Penge. Why couldn't those people have an opportunity to enjoy these surroundings? I suppose a little bit of my left-wing conscience was coming to the fore, as it did from time to time. Somehow during the holidays and while getting through the workload which I have just mentioned, there was still time for me to earn some money back at Pickering and Inglis, in Ludgate hill. Mr Gray the manager was very considerate, and allowed me to do some full-time employment. Most of the time I was working down in the basement, along with the rats, packing books and records, but quite often I would be asked to serve in the shop, particularly in the music section. Most of the customers wanted to hear the gospel music of the day, including George Beverley Shea, who had been the main vocalist in the Billy Graham crusades, a group which sang in broadcasts in the USA called the Old-Fashioned Revival Hour, the Emmanuel choir, conducted by Edwin Shepherd, and using a British soloist , very sincere, but who had the most awful voice, he sounded about 90. All this music was rather too sweet for me, and after two or three hours it was like standing in a vocal syrup pudding! I did not enjoy being cooped up in the shop and the basement, with no daylight, and so looked forward to the lunch breaks, taking my sandwiches and coffee to St. Paul's churchyard, where I could sit in the gardens and get the benefit of the sun and a few flowers which tried to brighten up that crowded area, with all its pollution and noise. Of course, I still spent most of my hard earned cash on classical CDs, which left me almost penniless at the time, but was opening up my mind more and more to the great treasures of music.

At the end of September 1959 I returned to Goldsmiths for the second year. This time I was living at home, travelling in and out from Abbey Wood to New Cross on the scooter, and able to give my mother a good slice of the grant money which the Ministry of Education bestowed upon me. Leslie Orrey, the head of music department had returned from the USA, and we soon realised what a splendid musician he was – an excellent pianist, and a brilliant exponent of harmony, especially keyboard harmony and improvisation. With his bow tie and a little quiff in his hair, he always reminded me of a photo of Chopin taken in his last years. At the Christmas concert in December I was asked to play two movements from the Mozart clarinet quintet. This meant buying a clarinet in A, which I also needed for orchestral work. If you don't understand why the clarinettist needs two clarinets, then I recommend that you look up clarinet in Grove' s dictionary. Many musicians don't understand, including my own teacher at school, who had written a piece for clarinet and piano, and when we came to rehearse it sounded absolutely ghastly, until we realised that he had transposed the clarinet part the wrong way. A lecturer in the French department, M. Lequét played the cello, and Mary Hunt, a degree student played the viola – I believe she went on to play in the Israel Symphony Orchestra later in her career, Father Aucoin, one of our own music group was the second violinist; he was one of a number of Roman Catholic priests and nuns who were training at the college before going off to Africa as teachers. Within 10 years the awful regime of Idi Amin took over in Uganda, and

I think many of these splendid people must have been put to death. Father Aucoin was bound for Rhodesia, so he was able to continue with his teaching career. He had his own personal problem in that he became very fond of one of the girls in our music group, and I'm fairly sure that he had to make the most difficult decision between Valerie and his calling as a priest. He chose to follow the call, and a very tearful Valerie had to accept that decision. What a pity that the Catholic Church is so strict about celibate priests, for the pair of them would have made a wonderful couple working and teaching in Africa. The first violinist in our quintet was one of the college lecturers, Honor Matthews, a delightful lady but rather eccentric. We only had two rehearsals for this performance, and Miss Matthews would either arrive late with her music and no violin, or the other one way round. When the time came for our performance all was fine and we were well into the movement when I realised that she had lost her place in the music, but then I heard her whisper, "Don't worry I'll catch you up!" she did catch us up very quickly, in fact hardly anyone in the audience realised that the first violin was slightly astray, while the rest of us were struggling not to roar with laughter and give up the whole thing. I did enjoy these opportunities to play, learning about the music intimately, and making decisions as a group, with no boss, no heavy-handed commands, just five happy people making music together – and an audience of 1,000 that just happened to be listening in.

For our first Christmas at Abbey Wood we stayed at home and had members of the family to stay with us. It was very crowded, and I cannot remember how we all managed to find beds or places to sleep, but it was a very happy occasion. Mum was greatly overworked but she enjoyed showing off her house to the relations who came.

In January, 1960 I was asked to sing in a performance of Handel's *Messiah* which was being given by a choir in Dagenham , complete with orchestra and four professional soloists . The tenor soloist was Kenneth Bowen, who later became a professor at the Royal Academy, and whose son I was to meet up with in Hereford at the cathedral over 30 years later. It was good to find one or two young people from my church at Chaplin Road. This really signalled the end of Dagenham links apart from an occasion later when the church asked me to go back and preach at an evening service, when they were without a regular minister. Back at college, the choir gave a performance of Brahms *German Requiem* at the University Church in Bloomsbury at the beginning of April, conducted by Leslie Orrey. I still had memories of one particular number which we had done in the school choir during the 50s, when I was head and shoulders in love with Anne, one of the sopranos. Ever since that time the opening bars of *How Lovely Are Thy Dwellings* always reminded me of her.

During the next few months it was a case of getting down to real serious work, ready for the finals, including final school practice. I was sent to Charlton secondary school, which was really in two buildings, the senior school for the third-fifth year children, housed in a very old, typical LCC building on the Woolwich Road. When I reported there, and saw some of the 'raw material', and met the headmaster, I was quite relieved to discover that I was going to be working mostly in the annex building, at least a mile away, in Foss Road, Charlton, which was even older and served for the first and second year pupils. The building was a series of small square classrooms, with glass doors, built around a central hall. There was no music room, of course; my music teaching was to take place in that central hall – with no privacy, but all the noise and prying eyes from the classrooms around. These were hopeless conditions in which to teach, but then I met the deputy headmaster who was in charge of the Foss Road Lower School, Mr Milanophie. This gentleman was a larger-than-life character, very Irish, and ruled the school with a rod of iron. He sported a large reddish blue nose, which I later realised was the result of some heavy drinking. With his laid-back attitude, he helped me to relax a little, and informed me that he would see that I had no trouble from the boys while I was working in his school. There was no record player to be found, so I made arrangements to bring my own portable machine in for lessons, and he suggested that I might use it also in the staff room after lunch, to give him and the staff a little Irish music – jigs and reels and ballads. On these occasions when the bell went for registration, he would just tell everybody to hang on until we reached the end of the piece, for the children could wait.

Halfway through the teaching practice we all had a day back in college, to compare notes, and commiserate with each other and that's when one found

104

people in even worse situations. My tutor informed me that an inspector would be coming down to watch me teach, and at first I was rather alarmed. HMIs, as we called them, only came down to watch students who were either borderline/failure cases, or those who might be in the distinction category, but my anxiety was put to rest when the tutor said that I was one of the latter group. I could teach any topic, to any particular class, with the inspector and tutor watching from the back. Mr Milanophie was quite brilliant. The lesson was fixed just before lunch, and he had asked the rest of the staff to be considerate about noise in their classrooms; he also said that he would have a word with the boys before the start of the lesson. Standing outside the hall I overheard his words, and quite frankly, he put the fear of God into them, telling them that if anyone dared to play up or be awkward in any way, then they would get the strap at lunchtime. I think I can say that this caused quite an artificial atmosphere, for I certainly had no problems. I had chosen to demonstrate the clarinet, to let them have a look at the instrument – most of them had never seen one in their lives, for this was before the days of peripatetic lessons and encouragement at playing instruments. I also played part of the Mozart clarinet concerto, having given them some background about Mozart's last days in Vienna. The lesson seemed to go well, and they all went off to lunch; the inspector shook my hands and thanked me for letting him and the tutor watch me in action, and I returned to the staff room to get myself back on an even keel, for I had been so nervous teaching in front of the HMI. Mr Milanophie informed me that he had been listening, he thought I'd done very well, and asked if I would join him in his room after lunch. This I did, discovering that he was already pouring the Irish whiskey in celebration, and with some more jigs and reels playing from my record player, we enjoyed a very pleasant drink. The bell went and I instinctively went to move. "Oh, just stay a while, let the little buggers wait." he said, in his strong Irish accent. He then persuaded me to do the whole lesson again the next morning, in the hall, in front of the whole school. How could I refuse? Looking back these many years later, I realise that under present conditions we both would have been given the sack for drinking during working hours, indeed, he would have been locked in prison for the times he had punished the boys; yet he ran a very good school, the boys respected him, they knew what would happen if they misbehaved, and the school was able to get on with teaching, albeit in a rather authoritarian atmosphere. God bless Mr Milanophie, he helped me to get that vital distinction in teaching which went on my certificate; I heard later that he had died suddenly, and I presume this was from alcoholism.

There was a great deal of midnight oil to be burned as the time for finals grew nearer; everyone wondered whether they were going to pass, and have the assurance that the last two years hard work was going to pay off. Finals day dawned, and we all took our places in the great hall, it seemed like hundreds of people, and looking through the 1960 pass list I've counted 308 students who were sitting various courses during the end of June and into July. There were just so many papers: three in the main subject, and aural and practical tests in the case of music, papers in the subsidiary subjects, then health education, history of education and theory of education. Looking at these papers again after 45 years, I see that the latter was subdivided into papers on principles of education, educational psychology and social background – seeing the questions now I wouldn't know where to begin – did it really help to make me a good teacher? For practical music we had to prepare pieces on each instrument we could play, and to be prepared to sing; this meant that I played the clarinet, piano, the organ, and sang a couple of English songs by Vaughan Williams. We were given a little help and advice from the staff, and Paul Steinitz heard the organ piece I was preparing, and then tactfully suggested that I choose something far more simple, and so I went for two contrasted choral preludes by Bach. I believe the external examiner for the practical music was Eric Thiman, a well-known composer in his time. I really dreaded the craft practical, for we had to display all our work, for all to see, including the external examiner. I was rushed into finishing my work; I hadn't time to do lovely printing for the titles of the books I had covered, so I just typed the details on paper and stuck them on the front cover. Having bound volume 1 of the *48* (preludes and fugues) by Bach, I wanted to impress with some flowery writing, but at the last moment I just wrote the name on the front of the spine, and found that I couldn't stick the endpapers together. Apparently when the examiner saw my work he took particular interest in the Bach and went to examine it in more detail – the book fell apart, and my tutor just wanted the earth to open at that point. I know this because Mr Morgan, the tutor, relayed this information to me later. In his wonderful Welsh accent he said, "I can only forgive you because you have given me great pleasure in your clarinet playing, but please take my advice, and don't offer yourself to teach craft in a school situation." I was only too quick to re-assure him that I would teach any other subject rather than craft, I was so bad at it.

Suddenly the two-year course was over, and I remember thinking how much of an anti-climax it all was, and people drifted away as their exams finished, while others stayed on to take the last papers. We had already had our farewell assemblies, when the warden had read to us and wished us well in our teaching careers, but somehow this 'dribbling away' just didn't seem right. A few days into the vacation, and the results came through; there I was in class one, with a distinction in music and practical education – only two of us achieved this in music, and only eight of us out of 250 got distinctions in practical education. I even passed in craft and was told I could offer this as a subject for teaching. This result was an incredible boost to my morale, to be followed by a letter from the Ministry of Education confirming that I had reached the status of Qualified Teacher.

During the long, lazy vacation, just about the first two months that I could remember when I didn't have assignments to prepare or book lists to wade through, I worked and had holidays. Yet again Paul Steinitz at the college pulled a few strings; he had approached me about returning to Canford to sing with his choir, and once more I pleaded that I couldn't afford it, and there was no way Goldsmith's would foot the bill for a second time. With the usual twinkle of the eyes Paul told me he would do what he could, and within a couple of days a note arrived from the warden telling me that the college were pleased to pay for all my expenses for the week. This time I went with great confidence, after all I was a qualified teacher now, and felt on equal terms with everyone. If anything it was even more enjoyable than the holiday in 1959, and I did fall madly in love with a student who was not really there for the music. I even gave up the late-night madrigals to spend a few late nights with her. Sadly nothing ever came of it.

From Canford I drove my scooter onto Bexhill to have a couple of weeks back at the BMS summer school. I supposed I showed a lazy attitude in going back to the same places time after time for holidays. My answer would be that in the case of Canford it was a free holiday, and I needed to go to places where I was certain to be accepted. Having changed address from Dagenham to Abbey Wood, I found that people were much more ready to befriend someone who came from south London, but maybe this was just my imagination! At the beginning of September I was on a student campaign with the Baptist Student Federation, when we were based as a team at Teddington Baptist Church in Middlesex. I was part of a student team of 21, just two of us from Goldsmiths College, others from Oxford, Cardiff and Birmingham; our job was to speak at the various functions in the church, to take part in services, visit houses in the area and join in the house groups. We were billeted out with members of the church, and I can just remember being with a young man who lived in a very large, comfortable house quite a long way from Teddington, somewhere near Sunbury, which backed onto the golf course. I had not just a room of my own but a whole suite. He was very kind and did his best to make me feel at home with the family, who did not seem to be particularly interested in Christianity or the campaign in which we were involved. With their fine house they rarely seemed to eat as a family or spend evenings together.

I was going to work at Pickering and Inglis again during the holiday, and was asked to go up to Keswick, this time helping to man their large stall at the convention, so I was seeing Keswick from a different angle, selling books, Bibles, music, records during the morning and early afternoon, and then able to attend the big main meeting in the evening. This time I had the luxury of staying in a boarding house in the town instead of living under canvas, as I had the year before, and I was being paid quite well by the firm. I still did have my share of living in a tent, however. David Iliff, my best pal at college, was a Crusader, and he told me of the shortage of suitable tent officers at the various camps which were held throughout the country during the summer. I offered my services and found myself in Cornwall at Polzeath. This camp was also run on rather military lines, with a commandant (he even gave me a lift all the way there and back), adjutant and padre, in this case it was Dick Rees, brother of Tom Rees the evangelist, and an excellent speaker – the boys took to him immediately. I was one of 10 tent officers, looking after seven boys, sleeping in the tent with them, organising them for tent inspections, joining in their games and expeditions, and doing the late-night Bible reading slot before lights out. The Crusader boys were mostly sons of professional people, fairly upper-class, many went to public schools as boarders, but were great fun and were a delight to be with. The surfing was also rather good down at the beach and this was another first for me. Once the results had come out, I felt quite proud to tell people that I was a teacher, when they asked me about my occupation; but, as I will explain in the next chapter, I was a teacher now without a job.

CHAPTER NINE

TEACHER WITHOUT A JOB

At the time I was preparing for finals I had been called to meet the head of department and the warden who offered me a one-year supplementary course in music. The college must have had great faith in my ability to have offered such a place before I had even taken my exams. The supplementary course was offered to a select few of the current students, in this case four of us, while another five practising teachers returned to college for the year. We were allocated a small room in a very old house in Lewisham Way, already condemned, and to be demolished along with several others, as part of the college extension program; here we were able to leave our books, drink coffee, occasionally work, and here we got to know each other quite well as a group. One teacher, I'll call her Ruby, certainly wouldn't see 50 again, and we did have some fun with her, often at her expense, but she was always a good sport. I believe she was also looking for a man, because one day Derek, one of our own Cornish students, rushed into the refectory where we were drinking coffee, looking in quite a state, and red in the face. It appeared that Ruby, the mature lady referred to above, had come into our room when he was there alone; Derek was looking for a piece of music, and in a frustrated tone said, "Oh dear, I don't know what I'm looking for!" whereupon Ruby softly put her hand on his shoulder and said in a very quiet but romantic voice, "But Derek, I know what *I'm* looking for!" Poor Derek, he swore he would never go into the room alone again.

At the beginning of the term I was elected chairman of the college music society, which was quite a privilege, and also meant some work at organising lunch-time recitals and getting new members during Freshers week at the beginning of October. After a few weeks on the course we realised that there was actually very little to do – a handful of lectures to attend, one afternoon of teaching during the first two terms, but otherwise we were left to practice our instruments and do general reading. David Iliff and I sat in the library one day and decided that we would each try for an external diploma. As we looked through the prospectus from each college, we thought it would be good fun to go for one which awarded a gown and hood. I made plans to work for a diploma in school music teaching at Trinity College, London, though I didn't eventually sit this diploma until July 1962. During the first term I was offered a chance to have a few consultation clarinet lessons with one of the greatest clarinettists in the country, the famous Jack Brymer. He had been a Goldsmiths' student some years before, incidentally, training as a PE teacher, and, moving from his North country home to Croydon, he married and played for a time in amateur orchestras while teaching. It was Sir Thomas Beecham who gave him a tremendous boost by offering him the principal clarinet post in his new Royal Philharmonic Orchestra. I got in touch with Mr. Brymer and received a letter on the 28th of October 1960, and I notice that my first lesson was on 5th November at 11am. He was a brilliant teacher and a great all-round musician, he could play the piano accompaniments for most of the clarinet repertoire, and he had a great fund of stories about life in the music world. I was actually having a lesson with him on the day in March, 1961, when Sir Thomas Beecham died. Jack's wife Anne interrupted the lesson, which was very unusual, and whispered something to him, and his expression changed. When he told me the sad news I immediately began to put away my instruments thinking that he would rather not carry on the lesson, but then he asked Anne to make some coffee, and invited me to sit down while he talked about Tommy Beecham and all the wonderful experiences he had had in the orchestra. I think my one-hour lesson that day went on for over 2½ hours, but that was typical of Jack Brymer. In the event, we both decided that I should sit my LRAM on the clarinet, and I began to study the very difficult pieces. My only regret about these lessons is that I did not practise more in between, and that the instruments I had were really rather poor; I was still using a clarinet which I had bought second-hand in 1956 while playing in the band. Come to think of it, I'm still playing the same instrument today, in 2011. Working on these diplomas became a discipline which was good for me, for I had many moments when I regretted not going straight out into a school where I would have been paid rather more than the government grant. With the three years in the army and now another three years of training I began to wonder whether I would be an old man before I actually started on my chosen career – I even wondered whether there would be any jobs left.

Christmas concert time arrived again – we were becoming 'old hands' by this time. Miss Barnard gave me the chance to rehearse and conduct a suite of Christmas carols written by my old school music master, Peter Cork; these were for four-part choir and a small orchestra, and I got down to rehearsals, and practised my conducting technique. I had never even been a conductor on a bus let alone an orchestra, but once again, she helped me enormously. What Miss Barnard didn't tell me until just two days before the concert, was that Peter Cork was going to be in the audience, and these were a first performance. This really did make me sweat, for I did not want to let everyone down by giving a bad performance in front of the composer. In the event he was very pleased with our performance, came to take a bow on the platform, shook my hand, and I felt that this was all part of that long chain of events that had started back at the little junior school and the Tipperary flute, about 15 years before. Very little stands out about our work at college during that year. I had to do one afternoon a week in a junior school, to get some experience of younger children, and this had quite a funny side to it. I was trying to teach a very young class in the school gymnasium, no music room of course, and trying to get them to feel the rhythm of the music by stepping to the beat. Miss Barnard was observing from the back of the gym, as I tried to help the few pupils who didn't seem to have any sense of rhythm. I put the music on, and holding hands with two of them, we set off around the gym, with me trying to emphasise the beat with my own steps; somehow, the children didn't seem to keep up with me. Miss Barnard quietly intervened and whispered to me, "How can they walk with you, Mr Astell, when you take such giant steps? You appear like a great elephant to these young children!"

On another occasion the children were moving to rather faster music, and I made it quite clear that I was looking for the last one to obey my command that when the music stopped, everyone stood still immediately. Well, eventually I stopped the music and watched expectantly, but a few characters decided to continue walking, then running round and round the gym. The rest of the class thought that this was huge fun, and they joined in. With 36 young children of seven years of age tearing around the gym making a noise, what was I to do? Miss Barnard was lurking once again, and she quietly moved to tell me to stand back, and let them tire themselves out. By the end of the term we had come to an agreement that junior school work was not for me – but I could have told her that at the beginning of term, and saved everyone a great deal of bother!

The last part of this year seemed to fly by, for in the middle of preparations for my clarinet performance LRAM at the academy, I had to cope with some more final exams at Goldsmiths. Then the college had an open day, on 10th of June, with a concert in the afternoon at which we were expected to perform. Well, I had played chamber music, I had conducted the madrigal group, and the music society choir and orchestra, and now I was to make my debut as an opera singer. Looking back college must have been very short of singers that year to have selected me to sing Figaro, in excerpts from *The Marriage of Figaro*. We only had one or two individual rehearsals, and then came the dress rehearsal. At one point Figaro's intended, Susanna, has to give him a slap round the face, but Pat, my Susanna, was very timid and didn't want to hurt me. Miss Barnard made it quite clear that the audience wanted to see something happen, and that she was to make it real. "At this point Ms Hannaford, you just hate him." said Miss Barnard, "Just remember that at the performance." Well, when the performance did come around, Ms Hannaford obviously remembered the advice, and gave me a smack around the cheek which almost knocked me to the floor -- people said they could see the red mark for hours afterwards. I was so taken aback that I wanted to hit her in return, instead of continuing with our duet. I don't know whether the audience enjoyed it, and once again, it was in the great hall, with about 800 people in the audience, but we certainly had a good time. When I hear just a few bars of Figaro music today it brings it all back.

Then followed four weeks of sheer grind as I took all these examinations. Maybe I was getting too confident about exams, because the LRAM brought me up in my tracks. I had engaged a professional pianist to accompany me in my three prepared pieces for the practical part of the exam. She was very good, and very expensive, and we duly arrived at the academy to be examined by John Davies, who I did not realise at the time, was the professor of clarinet at that institution. We were first in, at 10 o'clock, and he was like a bear with a sore head, at one point swearing at me, and generally behaving in a very unhelpful way. My accompanist stood up at one point and told him she had never heard anyone treated in such an unprofessional manner, and that she would report him. He ignored this completely. I just stood there completely dismayed by his attitude. One of the pieces was the second clarinet concerto by Weber, which has some very hairy running scale passages, which are extremely difficult to play. Instead of letting me start at the beginning of the movement, to work myself into the movement, he snatched the music away, muttering, "Any bloody fool can play that, try starting from here," indicating the bar when the nasty scale passages commenced. This was all so unfair. When the results eventually came out, it was obvious that someone had tinkered with the mark list, altered the mark for performance, so that I failed the diploma by four marks. I was so angry I took the mark list to Dr Steinitz, who was on the staff of the Royal Academy, and he took up my case, but warned me that the academy would never ever change their mind. I was later offered an opportunity to be re-examined, but, quite frankly, I'd had enough of the wonderful Royal Academy of Music, and vowed never to darken its doors again. Jack Brymer was very sympathetic, and had warned me that the standard was very high; but it also appeared that some of the people taking the examination would have been John Davies's own pupils at the academy, and as only a fixed proportion were ever allowed to pass, I really didn't stand much chance as an external candidate. Shouldn't there have been some rule forbidding an examiner to examine his own pupils? How could he do this objectively? I made up my mind there and then that I would take another clarinet exam, but at a later date and with a different college. By the end of July 1961, as my studies at Goldsmiths finally came to an end I'd had more than enough of examinations. Looking back at the pass list of Goldsmiths for 1961, I noticed that David Iliffe and I both completed the course with distinction, so self-confidence was restored for the time being.

From the middle of April we had been studying the sits. vacant columns in the Times educational supplement. There was a great shortage of specialist music teachers in the secondary schools, and we were almost able to pick our own school. Was I to move well away from London and set up a life of my own, or hang around living with my parents at Abbey Wood for even longer? The answer came when Miss Barnard asked me whether I was interested in a teaching post at Maidstone, Kent. A headmaster had approached her, asking for a keen young musician, and she thought I might be interested. I went down to Maidstone by coach to attend the interview, after four of us had been shortlisted for the job. In the event it was offered to another candidate, but he later changed his mind, for in the middle of a lecture a few days later somebody arrived with a telegram, from the headmaster, asking me to return to Maidstone the next day and be prepared to teach a class in front of the head and the County Music Adviser. Books available were included in the telegram, and I was asked to telephone immediately. I realised later that this was the way Mr Norman Evans, my future boss, always worked – everything was done at speed, with not a moment to be wasted. Well, I did my lesson in front of the audience, the children were cooperative – they could hardly be anything else with their headmaster sitting behind them – and the lesson went off quite well. I was subsequently offered the post of music master at Senacre secondary school, to start in September. The head was very friendly, wanted to put me at ease, and suggested that I should go down to meet him and the staff, to discuss music in the school, at the end of our college term. The staff never forgot the moment when he took me into the staff room and introduced me to them all. First I met the head of science, shaking hands with Frank Barker, "Good afternoon Mr Barker," I said; then it was off to the deputy head.

"Come and meet Gordon Hawkins, Brian, my deputy," and I duly shook hands, saying,

"I'm pleased to meet you Mr Hawkins."

Onto the head of maths – "…and this is Dan Lloyd, Brian, in charge of maths." so I shook his hand and said I was pleased to meet Mr Lloyd. At this the head turned to me, and said, in a very laid-back manner, "Oh we are all on Christian name terms here, Brian."

In my completely naïve way I then drew silence from the whole staff as I replied, "Oh, right, Norman".

The staff didn't know where to look, as Norman quietly said, through gritted teeth, "But not when you're addressing *ME*." When I finally joined the staff in September they constantly reminded me of my induction, for they thought a really bolshie music master was coming into their midst. The head of music, who was moving on to another school, did seem rather cynical at this introductory meeting, as he took me aside and said, "Well, I just hope you've got a good religion, you're going to need it".

I do remember having a holiday at Bexhill . I met up with some great people, including the president of the school, the Rev Tom Rogers. He was a minister at Sittingbourne in Kent, and with his charming wife Wendy, their twin boys, and young daughter, Pauline, they were a great family. The secretary was the Rev Bernard Wilson, who had a great sense of humour, and two of the group leaders were students from Spurgeon's College in London who were training to be ministers. It was a very memorable holiday, and all these people were going to appear again later. I'm sure I must have worked hard up at the bookshop in Ludgate hill to get some much-needed money for my new job; Mr Gray the manager always seemed to be able to find work for me, and this time I was mainly in the shop, standing in for a couple of their permanent staff who were on holiday. The days flashed by but I couldn't wait until the beginning of September to show the children at Senacre school what music was all about!

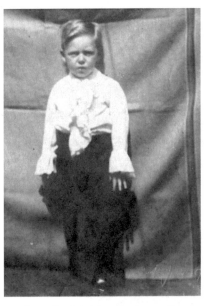

Angelic Pageboy minus silver-topped cane

Into uniform at an early age. That cane has been found

The first car – my pride and joy

Parents' wedding: Nan, Mum, Dad, Pa, Aunt Mary

Wedding of Mary And John:
L to R. unknown , Nellie, John, Mary, Gladys Front: BA, Peggy and Eileen

Dad in the army – Royal Artillery

Uncle Albert – Royal Artillery

Aunt Nell and Uncle Charlie's Golden Wedding. One of many happy family parties at Goswell Road Everyone laughing despite the tough post-war conditions.

"Uncle Greg" who cared for us all in the blitz

Rev. Ralph Darvill and Mary (extreme right) who took me into their home in Blackpool

Family picture taken c. 1946
John and Allen on left

1955 Bexhill – first love, Barbara

1953 'Lanky Whitwell and I off to France by plane

Dudley Moore's well-used Bach for his
Oxford audition, 1954

Only photo of me in uniform
– was originally b&w but I
experimented in colour
Note our wonderful cottage
garden at Dagenham

1955 Bexhill Jim WITHOUT jacket – sitting on ME!

April 1952 Hiking on A 417 above Gloucester

A proud father with daughter
Plumstead 1969

Some of the young people
at my Dagenham church
I was sporting my new
bow tie

Frank and Edith James,
who gave all his time
and energy for the young
people at our church – a
wonderful leader

Playing the organ at Goldsmith's
college, 1959

John's wedding day, March,
1963 I was best man

Aunt Nell and Uncle Charlie's Golden Wedding.

BMS Bexhill Jim Wright (in usual formal attire) next to Kath, the girl he jilted at the altar

BA seated on right, next to Ruth Champion,later to hold prominent position in the NHS.

CHAPTER TEN

TEACHING FOR REAL

It wasn't really a long journey from Abbey Wood to Maidstone, one could manage it comfortably in under two hours either on the train or on my scooter; initially I did use the train so that I could carry all my baggage. Through a contact at Goldsmiths I had been put in touch with a family living at Bearsted, just outside Maidstone. Mr and Mrs Salter were very friendly and I knew I would be happy staying with them. They were both of the Brethren persuasion- Mr. Salter was an Elder – quite strict about some things, especially on Sunday activity, and yet they both enjoyed their glass of wine with their TV. I came to the conclusion that it was only the Baptists who tried to avoid alcoholic drinks. I had a very tiny room, not even enough for a table in which to work; they would have been happy for me to work downstairs, but the television was usually on and was quite a distraction. I would have my breakfast, but take lunch at school, and then a light meal in the evening, which Mrs Salter would generally prepare. She did seem to make heavy weather of the slightest job, often complained of poor health, though there was rarely anything wrong with her. Mr Salter was a travelling salesman for Proctor and Gamble, trying to boost sales of Blue Daz, Fairy Liquid and other indispensable domestic products; he set off before 7 in the morning and usually after a hard day's work he would return to find that he was doing the washing-up and other household chores. His overworked wife had just found the whole day so tiring, pondering over the preparation of my light meal. I soon got into the habit of going back home at weekends, so I wasn't too much of a burden on her. Perhaps she thought that as he was working in Fairy Liquid, he ought to have his hands in it each evening. They still had a daughter, Beth, at home, who was a real beauty, but also quite a tough cookie. She was about 20, but still seemed to be going through the teenage growing up phase, flouncing around, often moody -- indeed, at times she just didn't answer when I spoke to her. She and I were never really friends, maybe she didn't like the idea of sharing her family with me.

Day one at Senacre, and after the usual assembly and a period of time in their form rooms, the pupils set off, and lessons began in earnest. The experience of my first lesson showed what I had *not* been taught at Goldsmiths. Class 2C were not very bright. Being enthusiastic, I had them clapping to rhythms, and we worked out on the board the rhythmic notation. Everyone joined in wholeheartedly, and they clapped away until one boy near the back of the class reared up, making a horrible noise; I told him to sit down but then saw the look on his face before he collapsed onto the floor. I just didn't know what to do, but a little girl called Susan immediately took charge. "Donald is having a fit, it's all right, I know what to do." she said. She went straight up and put a cushion under his head and prevented him from swallowing his tongue; at this point I left the class and went to get help from the office, but before I could explain, the secretary told me to sit down for I looked deathly pale. When I stammered out what was going on she took it all in her stride. "Don't worry, Mr Astell, another three epileptic types in that class; you'll get used to it." It seems that excitement, and repetitive rhythms can bring on a fit, so I was very careful not to overdo it in future, but I do take my hat off to little Susan, who must have had quite a low IQ but was so sensible and calm in that emergency. I hope she went in for nursing, but, for sure, I was having to learn all over again!

The headmaster required me to introduce an item of music every morning in assembly, and this was tough at the start. After the religious formalities and notices, I had to leave the piano, mount the stage, tell the assembled company something about the music or the composer to get their interest, and then play an extract which must not exceed five minutes. I didn't mind doing this in front of the whole school, but it was the thought of the head and staff sitting there which put me off. On the whole the staff were very sympathetic and encouraging – they realised that this idea was very much the head's, and I was just obeying orders. Sometimes my remarks about the music would cause great hilarity back in the staff room. On one occasion I was going to play La *Calinda* by Frederick Delius, and told the school all about his poor health – he was blind and paralysed and very weak, needed someone to write the music down for him, but that nobody really knew what had caused it. When I returned to the staff room they were rolling about with laughter. One of them said: "Really Brian, even the first years in the hall would have known that you were describing all the symptoms of VD. They know all about these things, and you obviously don't." Actually I did, and had chosen my description with tact, but perhaps the staff were right, probably most of the pupils knew more about VD than me.

Just after the beginning of term the headmaster held a soirée at his converted farmhouse in the country. This was for new members of staff with just a sprinkling of the old lags to keep conversation going. I was warned that Rachel, his wife, liked to know all about one's background so that she could make a decision as to whether you became part of her little club or not. I was fairly sure I would never be part of her little club, and so it worked out. I was already feeling nervous as I knocked at the door and then literally fell in to the room, for there was a huge step down onto the floor of their converted lounge. The headmaster was standing by the grand piano next to the door, and he greeted me with, "Hallo Brian, glad you could make it," followed by, "roojooblon?" What on earth was he saying? I hadn't a clue. Once again "roojooblon?" He asked.

"Yes." I said, thinking he was referring to the weather. For the third time he asked the same question with the same word, and I replied "Of course."

At this he exploded, "Do you want red or white wine?"

"Whatever you've got handy," I replied, which made things even worse. Eventually I settled for a glass of red wine, and went away wondering why on earth he couldn't have asked me that in the first place. It took me ages to work out that it was '*rouge ou blanc*' wine he was going on about. But why use French? I obviously wasn't used to mixing with the higher classes. Inevitably his wife made her way towards David Owen, a new maths teacher, and me. David had warned me to be careful in my replies, since she was nosy and desperate to find the *right* sort of person, someone with a good, reliable upper-class background. Her opening gambit was to suggest that David was Welsh; this was rather unnecessary, he had a Welsh accent you could cut with a knife. Then she asked what his father had done. "In mining", he replied briefly.

126

"Oh, he was one of the managers, I suppose." she said, enthusiastically.

"No, he was cutting coal down the bloody pit." he retorted, in an even stronger accent.

"But he's happily retired now?" continued Mrs Evans, hopefully.

"No, he's bloody dead, isn't he? He died very slowly of silicosis." At this point Mrs Evans turned on me almost in despair.

"Norman is so pleased to have you join the Senacre team and put our music on the map here in Maidstone; I expect you come from quite a musical family", she said, trying to ferret away at my 'background'.

"No, Mrs Evans, I'm the only one who is musical in my family."

Mrs Evans had another go: "So what does *your* father do?"

I stared her straight in the face and said: "He works for London Transport." noticing immediately that she was perking up, perhaps I might be worth including in 'the club'.

"Ah yes, I know, he'll be one of those managers working at 55 Ealing Broadway."

"No." I replied, "He's working on the underground, helping to dig the new Victoria line at the moment".

Mrs Evans was now at a complete loss. "Oh, how fascinating that must be."

I took great delight in my measured response, "No, it's pretty awful. It's pitch black; in the winter it's freezing, in the summer it's hot and damp, and the men never work in the tunnel on their own, in case they are attacked by the rats, especially if they are carrying lunch." This completely floored Mrs Evans, and she took herself off to pursue someone else's background, leaving David Owen and I chuckling together. The wine, or perhaps I should call it the 'roojooblon' continued to flow, and by the time the food arrived on the scene staff were feeling very relaxed. We could help ourselves to plates with enormous lettuce leaves, on which we put our salad, but no one could find any cutlery. David Owen, in a very relaxed condition, called to her in a loud voice, "Don't you have any knives and forks in your 'ouse, Mrs Evans?"

She must have been wondering what sort of people she had invited to her soirée, and matters were made worse a little later. Admittedly, she had informed us that the banisters were wet as she had just painted them, and there were notices telling us not to touch them, but at one point, Robin, the English master went up to the lavatory – he'd drunk quite a skinful of the 'roojooblon' and leaned heavily on the banisters for support; when he came down the stairs again, after relieving himself, he put his hand on the wall, and left many fingerprints, for there were paint marks all down the staircase. At the end we said our goodbyes, and all piled into one of the cars, and Dave Owen summed it all up, "Well, at least Robin made his mark during the evening; somehow I don't think we will be invited back there for some time"… and we never were.

Apart from a fairly full timetable of teaching, I worked hard to get more people in the choir, I tried to get an orchestra going, and was keen to start a recorder group. Many people regard the recorder as either a toy, or at the most, something that makes a shrill noise out of tune. When taught properly, the recorder player can make a lovely sound, produce a pleasant tone, and it is a great help in learning to read music and in playing together. I often found that successful clarinettists had started their music on the recorder – it gave them very good practice at fingering, and at 'reading the dots', as musicians say, referring to the music. Norman Evans was very keen to promote the music in the school, and he supported me in every way. I was soon in trouble with the school caretaker, Mr Brown, for I used to get into the hall and start the choir before he had cleaned it, and this upset his routine. Why he had to clean the hall first at 4 pm I had no idea. Sometimes we compromised, and I let him go on cleaning and moving chairs while I rehearsed the choir, but on one Monday evening the headmaster poked his head in at the door to listen, and saw Mr Brown moving chairs. Before I went home that evening I saw a note in my pigeonhole, asking me to see the head urgently next morning. So I went back to my digs feeling rather anxious about what I might have done to upset him. I duly called at his room before assembly the next day, and he made inquiries about Brown, as he called him – he never called us Mr or Mrs, as the case may be. I was told that I should never have allowed him to clean or move chairs while I was rehearsing, and that his job was to get in to clean the hall when it was free; the head then asked me to return to his study at break time, and when I did, there was

Mr Brown looking very upset. The head treated him like a child. "I believe you've something to say Brown." The caretaker turned to me and apologised, and said he would never do it again. "No you won't, Brown. The school is here to be used, and you get your cleaning done when the rooms are empty, and now get out." The head told me to refer the matter to him if anything of this nature happened again, and I was free to go. I felt terrible, for Mr Brown was old enough to be my father, and it was humiliating to see him treated in such a way; I wanted to go after him and give *him* an apology, but I began to realise that I was the music master, and he was the caretaker, and class distinction was flourishing in the 1960s. Incidentally, during the following term, Mr Brown dropped dead in the school while cleaning, apparently he had suffered from high blood pressure for some time. The head called the staff together, told us of Brown's death, adding that he would represent the school, along with the head boy and girl, at the funeral. I wonder whether he had any pangs of conscience as he stood at the graveside comforting Mrs Brown, who also cleaned at the school.

At Christmas I put on my first concert, with much hard work and anxiety, for this was the time when parents and visitors would see the results of my efforts. The hall was packed to capacity, and the head brought along many of his own visitors, which made my anxiety even worse, but he seemed pleased with the result, so all was well. We finished the term with the staff party, when, halfway through the evening, some of the young staff asked me to play a few tunes on the piano. The piano was in the music room, but it only took a few minutes for them to wheel it round. All went well until someone spilt some of their 'roojooblon' into the instrument. I tried to mop it up as best I could. Weeks later when the piano was given its usual tuning, the technician told me he would have to write a report, because something had been spilt. He told me he thought it was wine, but that couldn't be, for there would be no wine around during lessons. I kept very quiet at this stage, and we heard no more about it.

When I got back home it wasn't to relax, there were concerts to play at in the church, I was used for the Christmas services, and the usual carol singing. It is always the same for music teachers, they are expected to enjoy taking part in all these Christmas events which are a one-off to the general public, but are a

Busman's Holiday to us. It is very hard to be fresh after playing or singing *Oh Come All Ye Faithful* for the 10th time. Throughout my school career it was always a very busy and hectic season.

Word soon got around that I was a new music master at the school. I attended union meetings in the first term, and met some of the other music staff who worked locally. From this I received an invitation to be a clarinet teacher at the Kent Music Centre in Maidstone; this meant a quick getaway after school, and I taught five or six pupils for an hour. I had also joined the Maidstone Choral Society, and used to grab a quick meal in between these two events. During the summer term Kent Opera gave a production of Rossini's *Barber of Seville* in the town, and I was asked to play second clarinet. This was great fun, and after a whole week of performances I got to know the music very well. Of course I arranged for a party from my school to attend a performance, and the head and his wife duly made their appearance, making a beeline for me during the interval – it seemed I might even be considered for "the club" after all.

One more event stands out in my first year at Senacre. During the summer term Mr Evans was away at Avery Hill College, presumably showing all the students how to teach, and his deputy, Gordon Hawkins, was in charge at school. Gordon had been a Goldsmith's student sometime before me, and I believe had applied for the headship, but did not have a degree, so was turned down. Many of the staff at Senacre would agree with me that Gordon was one of the best teachers in the job; he was efficient, friendly and could deal with the discipline of the school with no difficulty at all. It wasn't long before I found out how helpful he could be. The lowest point of the week for me was taking the fourth-year boys, 4B/C. most of whom would be leaving at the end of the term, and couldn't wait to get away. The head had arranged them into separate boys and girls classes for music because he wanted me to try to do singing with them. By the summer term I had certainly given up on singing with those boys. I could just about keep control of them, keep them seated, quiet and at least looking as though they were learning music, but it was a struggle. On one occasion one John Arnold came in, sat himself down at a desk, putting his feet up on another chair, and resting his greasy head against the wall. Apart from this insolent attitude, I had put a number of my own record sleeves on the wall to try to give a bit of musical atmosphere in the room, and I could see his dirty hair coming into contact with my record sleeves. Twice I told him to put his feet down and sit up, and he completely ignored me; for a third time I told him, and the response was just as though he were deaf. When I raised my voice finally, he told me to "F--- off!" This made me angry, for no one had used this phrase to me since the army days, and I certainly wasn't going to be sworn at by a 15-year-old boy. He was taller than me and probably stronger than me, but in my anger I just swooped on him, got hold of his hair and shirt and dragged him out to the head's study. I just knocked at the door and went straight in, still holding on to Arnold. Gordon was at his desk, and in his usual calm way took control of the situation. He sent Arnold out of the room, and I explained what had happened. He told me that he would deal with Arnold for the time being, but that I ought to return to my class immediately. At lunchtime Gordon had a word with me. "I can understand why you are angry with him, Brian; we will not have that language used to staff in the school, and he must be punished. He must be caned." I agreed wholeheartedly, until he went on: "He swore at you, and you ought to do the caning." I quietened down at this moment, realising what I had to do, but then agreed with Gordon. "But you're not going to cane him today, Brian, while you are still angry; we will let Arnold simmer overnight, and you will cane him at break tomorrow morning." Well, I went back to my digs that evening and couldn't get this out of my mind. In the cold light of day I was to inflict physical punishment on this character, and try to hurt him; this went round and round in my mind, and even Mrs Salter noticed that something was wrong. I explained the situation to them both, and Mr Salter took the line that the boy needed punishment, and I was just carrying out the necessary action. I hardly slept that night, because apart from the moral issue of caning the boy, I had never caned anyone and I wasn't quite sure how to do it. Gordon Hawkins came to the rescue, for he called me in after assembly and told me that Arnold would report for his punishment at break time. He asked me how I felt, and I explained my anxieties. Gordon then placed a couple of cushions on his desk. "This is Arnold's backside." He then took a selection of canes and asked me which one I wanted to use. "None of them," I replied, "this is insane." He turned quietly to me and insisted that I had to cane Arnold, emphasising that the boy had had the cane more times than I'd had hot dinners; if I didn't hurt him I would become a laughing stock with that class, so I had to make it hurt. He would show me how to carry out the punishment, and invited me to cane the cushions! I stood there and feebly slashed at the cushions. "If you hit him like that he will get up and laugh at you," said Gordon. "Let me show you how to do it." Whereupon he moved to the far corner of the study, took a run at the desk and hit the cushions at about 60 miles an hour. I was invited to do the same, and told to work out how many paces I needed to get a good aim. The whole business seemed surreal. What on earth was I doing? Gordon brought me back to reality, emphasising that he was going to bring the boy in. "Just remember, Brian, what happened 24 hours ago, and keep that picture of insolence in your mind." He had arranged to stand behind the desk so that he could see Arnold's face, and when the tears began to flow he would signal for me to stop beating him. Arnold came in, without a care in the world, looking as though this was just a normal part of his daily routine, and bent over the desk without even being told. I found myself trembling from head to toe. "Arnold you know what this is about, I will not have you swearing at staff, and this is what you get for doing so. Take over Mr Astell." I took my run and made contact. There was just a grunt in response. After three more strokes I looked hopefully at Gordon, and he signalled that I should give two more. Arnold straightened himself up, and the tears were there; Gordon then made it clear that there was no going off to the cloakroom to dry the eyes, and he conducted the boy back to his classroom so that the rest of them could see the result of his behaviour. This last act showed especially how Gordon understood the pupils. He returned to the room and said, "In some ways, Brian, I know that it has left its mark more on you than on him, but it had to be done, and it's given you another first in your teaching career." I thought about this a lot in the days that followed; certainly the class behaviour was much better, though in the long run it didn't seem to help Arnold, because shortly after leaving school he was put in Borstal for breaking into an elderly woman's home and threatening her with a rifle. I'm certainly glad that I never had to use the cane again for the rest of my teaching career. Examinations for the whole school took place at the end of the summer term, which gave me hours of marking, as I was the only music teacher, and taught almost the whole school, and then there was stocktaking, which this headmaster took quite seriously; he would do a spot check with various teachers, making sure that the number of books tallied with the entry made in the stock book – all rather tedious.

I was to take my LTCL in class music teaching at Trinity College, London, which I had begun working on in my final year at Goldsmiths. I had been tempted to give up the whole idea while I was so busy working at Senacre, but I decided that if I didn't take the exam then, I would never return to it. At Trinity College it was just hard slog, with papers on psychology of music, aural, methods of music teaching, viva-voce and a very artificial practical exam, in which a class of children were wheeled in from a neighbouring school, and I had to teach them in front of three examiners, using prepared work, and, at one point, an examiner gave me a piece of paper with a topic listed which I had to teach immediately. The children were very cooperative, helped me enormously, and I felt like going out to buy them all an ice cream when the ordeal was over. I gained this diploma, and it was a great boost to my confidence after the dreadful treatment at the Royal Academy the year before. When term came to a close I was more than grateful for the six weeks holiday, but realised that I would also have to earn some money. My take-home pay each month was £59, after tax, and, after paying £36 for my digs, there wasn't much left over to save; at least I had been promised a promotion – a scale 1 allowance – for the following year, so there would be a little more coming in. Yet again I put in some work at the bookshop, and met up with the staff who were keen to know how I had got on in my first year. I also went off to another BMS summer school at Boscombe, staying at a very posh girls' independent school called Wentworth House, but this time I was a group leader on the staff, which earned me a free holiday. The tricks and stunts which we used to play on our group leaders were now reversed – I had to get used to being at the receiving end; I suppose the worst was being thrown fully clothed into the swimming pool, but it was all good fun and this holiday was fantastic.

During the next year at Senacre I went into a bedsit on the top floor of a large, old house in Maidstone. At the end of the previous term Mr Salter had told me that I would have to give up staying with them; it appeared that his wife's health had deteriorated, and she couldn't cope with looking after me. I felt rather sorry about this because in actual fact I only had a meal at the house on three evenings a week so she didn't have that much to do, but I thanked them for taking me in and promised to keep in touch. Sadly I never did go back to see them. From my bedsit window I had a good view over the roofs of Maidstone; the room was sparsely furnished, just a small single bed in the corner, a couple of easy chairs which had seen better days and a tiny, primitive gas ring for cooking. The room was heated with a small gas fire, but on cold nights it was so bad that I would go off to the pub to get warm. David Owen, the maths teacher from Wales, who I have already mentioned, lived in the room opposite. We generally took it in turns to cook a simple evening meal, 'simple' being the operative word; I would manage to do sausage, baked beans and mash on Mondays; on Tuesdays I was out doing my clarinet teaching and singing in the choral society, so he organised his own food. On Wednesdays he was off to rugby training, preparing for the big match at the weekend, and on Thursdays we would perhaps have tinned steak or a prepared meat pie – you see he was lucky – he had a small oven in his room, but then he had been in residence at Bower Mount Road for two years already. On Fridays I tried to get away to Abbey Wood to spend a weekend at home. Years later I looked back on this time and realised how silly I was, trying to keep up with a home life as well; if I had spent a few weekends in Maidstone I might have put down roots and got to know more people and found interesting things to do. When the year came to an end I realised it more than ever.

During the Easter holidays, my brother John got married, the first of the family to leave home. He had left our school at the end of his fifth year and started work for a large firm of solicitors in London, and then had to do his National Service in the army, being stationed in Cyprus for most of his two years. Only recently I discovered that in fact he was put in the Intelligence Corps, but was not allowed to disclose this to anyone, even his family. At some stage he had got to know Jackie, who lived in Deptford with her parents, brother and sister. They were married on the 23rd March at St Johns Church in Lewisham Way, just a stone's throw from Goldsmiths College. I was the best man and tried to do the job as well as I could, but the reception was chaotic. This was to be held over a public house, a pub used by many of her family and friends, so that the Grovers – the bride's family – were well-known, and that's where the troubles began. Instead of a formal meal with set places, there was a buffet, and mingling with the wedding guests seemed to be half the inhabitants of Deptford. When I had finished welcoming guests, organising the telegrams and cards, I turned to the table and discovered that everything had gone. I don't think I had even one sausage roll at that wedding. One uncle and aunt had travelled from Hampton in Middlesex, and Uncle did rather fancy himself as a cut above the rest of us. At one point he went downstairs to the saloon bar, but within a short time he was given a slap round the face and retreated up to the wedding. I think he'd rather fancied a 'bit of rough', but had been firmly put in his place by a local woman. One of the relations was Aunt Ena who entertained on the pub piano, and the wedding was going to be another opportunity for her to play. I always watched in amazement, because she had never learned to read a note of music and seemed to play everything in a key of five flats; when I asked her why she chose such difficult keys, she shrugged her shoulders and informed me that all she knew of flats were that people lived in them and keys were to open their doors!

At the end of the Easter holidays I returned for what was to be my last term at Maidstone. The accompanist at the choral society rehearsals was Mr Grainger, a local school music teacher, who was given a sabbatical year by the Kent Education Committee, and he asked me if I would take his place at the piano; I have some memories of this particular task. I often use to rush in from my clarinet teaching and start the rehearsal, just grabbing a sandwich or a sausage roll while the choir sang. One of the sopranos noticed this and seemed very concerned for my comfort. She spoke to me during our break and said she would arrange to bring some food to each rehearsal which I could eat in the break or take home afterwards. What a kind gesture. I discovered that Mrs Paine was the wife of a local fruit farmer who lived outside Maidstone, and she had a very attractive daughter, also singing soprano in the choir. Right at the end of the summer term I got to know Angela quite well, visited the farmhouse and met her parents, and indeed went down to spend a day on the farm with her in the summer holidays, but it was just my luck that I had left my school and was going to work in London, so the friendship never went any further. Perhaps I should have stayed down at Maidstone and given it more time.

Quite close to my lodgings they were building new bungalows, detached, with three bedrooms, at £850. One would now pay more than that for a garage, but at that time £850 was like a king's ransom to someone who was still earning about £63 a month.

It was in June that I received a letter from Mother to tell me that Dad was seriously ill in Hammersmith Hospital after having an accident at work. It appeared that he fell from a platform when the support gave way on to a pile of rubble which broke his back, then the lead piping he was working on in the tunnel fell on top of him and this broke many of his ribs. Mother was having to visit him nearly every day up in London, and it was months before he was able to come home. He was never the same person again and never really went back to work after that accident. His union took the case to court, and were looking for him to give evidence on the grounds that London Transport had failed to provide adequate protection, and that the accident was made much worse because the railings which should have held him gave way, causing him to fall about 10 feet. One of the union representatives who visited Dad at home spoke to me and admitted that the task for compensation would be hard, not because of London Transport, but because my father was refusing to help the union in making the case, once again he never wanted to put pen to paper, just to be left alone. "Let sleeping dogs lie," would just about sum up my father's philosophy in most things. It took over a year for the case to be settled, and he received a derisory sum of money in compensation.

I was still going back home at weekends so that I could join in the activities with the local church and meet up with my friends; I had one of two girlfriends around that time, but always seemed to choose girls who were much younger than me – in fact that has probably been my trouble throughout life – I've *always* gone for the younger ones, maybe subconsciously because I knew that there would never have to be any serious commitment made, perhaps I was trying to run away from marriage. Who knows?

Back at Senacre School I had my first big tussle with Mr Evans, the headmaster. When I attended a union meeting at another school- I had joined the NUT before leaving college – I met a caretaker who looked at me rather closely when I explained that I was I was music master at Senacre. "You'll be the teacher who is opening up the school and locking it again on Saturdays, I suppose." he said, and went on to explain that Saturday music activities were nearly always held at Senacre because caretakers in other schools would not do the job, the overtime was so badly paid. The head had always been keen to open the school so that the music adviser could use it for rehearsals and workshops. I would find some willing boys to help me on Saturday to put out chairs and arrange refreshments, and then hang around to put everything away and lock-up in the afternoon. I was doing this for nothing, or rather, because Mr Evans thought it was very good for the school. To give him his due he usually put in an appearance at some stage with the wife, met the adviser and then disappeared. On Thursday a note appeared in my pigeon hole informing me that the music adviser would be turning up on Saturday to use the school hall, and I would do the usual 'caretaking' jobs. This time I went in to face Mr. Evans and when I quietly replied that I would be going home for the weekend and someone else would have to do it, he was not amused. I suggested that perhaps some other member of staff might like to do it, but he did say that he thought I was not just letting the school down but not doing myself any favours either. "It's worth getting to know the music adviser." he said. "Someone like that can be very useful." To which I replied that I didn't try to make friends just because they could be useful to me. He regarded that as an impertinent remark, but suddenly lots of things became clear: I was the innocent, naïve new teacher who gave up his Saturdays to open the school so that the headmaster had all the credit for offering Senacre to the musical members of the county. But I'd had enough, let someone else do the job.

Incidentally, I did have some awful journeys on my motor scooter. Often, leaving Abbey Wood late at night on Sunday I would run into dense fog and struggle to see the way ahead. My route took me over the top of Wrotham hill which was one of the highest points in that part of Kent, complete with a communications mast which dominated the scene. On one bitterly cold night I could hardly see a hand in front of my face, was travelling in first gear at about 8 miles an hour but seemed to have wandered all over the road. In desperation I stopped and found a signpost telling me I was on Death Hill! I took this as a serious omen, and practically walked the scooter for the next few miles. There were indeed many journeys like that, and I would arrive back at my digs or in the bedsit numb with cold and vowing to use the train next time.

I did miss London; in a funny old way Goldsmiths College, all the noise of traffic and the bustle of the city seemed to appeal to me. Perhaps, in truth I just wanted to be back home. I had tried to put roots down in the local musical community, where, apart from the choral society, I also played the clarinet in the local orchestra and remember one very enjoyable concert when we played Michael Tippett's *Concerto for Double String Orchestra*, and Shostakovich's *First Symphony*, the latter having quite a difficult second clarinet part. The first clarinet was played by a young professional named Georgina Dobrée who went on to appear in a number of orchestras. Towards the end of the summer term I took part in *Carmina Burana* by Carl Orff. David Cutforth, music director at the boys' grammar school in Maidstone conducted all these concerts, and for this work he used his own boys at the grammar school and the choir from the local girls school, so I was playing in the orchestra while my beloved Angela was singing away in the choir. Many of us had quite a chuckle at rehearsal as the junior boys were singing all kinds of rather steamy expressions about women and love, in Latin. David leaned across to the orchestra and said, "If only they realised what the words really meant." Perhaps this was an occasion when it was best not to explain to the children the story behind the music, but leave them in their ignorance.

I put on one last concert at my school, using the choirs and orchestra, and was very touched when they presented me with leaving presents and a card which they had all signed. Many of the pupils seemed genuinely unhappy that I was leaving the school just as the music was getting going, and if ever I had real second thoughts about leaving Maidstone it was then, for the children were so kind. Mr Evans did give me a glowing testimonial to take for my interview for the next job, and I think he was sorry to let me go. So in the middle of July, 1964, I did my last stock take for the headmaster, we had the inevitable party where many bottles of 'roojooblon' were drunk, I packed up my few things in the bedsit, and left Maidstone to return to Lewisham to a school which was just a couple of miles from Goldsmiths College. Was the college calling me back?

I certainly was to have a new life involving Goldsmiths at a later stage, yet I was also to return to Kent when I bought my first house six years later, though it was rather more expensive than the £850 bungalows I had seen being built at Bearstead.

CHAPTER ELEVEN

LEWISHAM –MUSIC EVERYWHERE

After two years in teaching I looked forward to the long summer holidays; if they had been taken away I don't think I could have coped. It was back to Pickering and Inglis in London for a couple of weeks, to earn some money for my holidays; looking back in the diaries I realise now that I must have decided to splash out before starting at my new school, for I had two holidays which, geographically, couldn't have been further apart. For the first two weeks in August I went down to Penzance, where I was a group leader for another BMS summer school. I enjoyed working with a splendid staff, which included the Rev Tom Rogers, a popular, much loved minister at Gillingham Baptist Church in Kent. He was married to Pauline, and they had a wonderful young family of twin boys and a daughter. He was president, and the secretary was another minister, Rev Bernard Wilson, who took a keen interest in everybody and was a great conversationalist. The third member of the team was Rev Viv Lewis, very Welsh and very funny. With such a team the holiday went like a rocket, and we all felt it a privilege to work with such enjoyable and devoted ministers. I was to be on Tom's team on later occasions at summer schools, and always enjoyed being with him. Sadly both Tom and his wife died of cancer at a very young age, and this despite the active, healthy life they lead, both involved in sports and outdoor activities. They were a great loss to the Baptist denomination and to the rest of us.

We had some wonderful weather in Cornwall; it was still a very unspoiled county and we had good times in the extensive grounds of the school, on the beach, and exploring Cornwall by coach on the outings. I left after two weeks hoping to return at a later date, and this I did. Of course the steam trains were still in action, and I looked forward to the long journey to Scotland, setting out from

Penzance Station at 2.30 in the afternoon, taking in wonderful scenery as the train hugged the coast for many miles before winding its way inland to Exeter. However the train became very crowded, and we seemed to stop and start all through the night, so that I arrived at Glasgow at 8.30 the next morning feeling like a wet rag, having only had a couple of sandwiches and some lemonade for the whole 17 hour trip. Thinking it over, I realised later that I could have gone back to London and caught a night sleeper up to Glasgow, but I had learned the hard way. I continued to Alloa and another BMS summer school, this time as one of the students. The president was Rev Peter Amies, who was currently the young people's secretary of the Baptist Missionary Society. The group only numbered about 40, and they were also a rather older, more serious crowd, and we had great fun and they were good company. We did go on various outings, although my main memory of Scotland was of rain; from the window of the large house where we stayed people were always pointing out that there were mountains in the distance, which were either clouded over or were unrecognisable with sheets of rain pouring down. We visited Edinburgh Castle, bringing back army memories for me, and we went on the lakes, travelling by steamer from Gourock up Loch Long to Arrochar Pier, walked for a couple of miles to another pier and travelled down Loch Lomond, finishing up on another train. For some inexplicable reason I have kept the old brochure produced by the Caledonian Steam Packet Company in association with British Railways, and see that the whole excursion costs 18/9 pence in old money (about 90p today). The ratio of girls to chaps on this holiday was about two to one and, inevitably, I fell in love yet again – did I ever go on holiday without falling in love? This girl was travelling with her friends, and I was soon accepted into their crowd. They came from the King's Cross area of London, and Ann Bryant was the daughter of the Baptist minister at Vernon Chapel, just yards from King's Cross Station. It must have been a tough area both for her family and the church situation. By the second week of the holiday we were going around together everywhere, and I arranged to return to London with them travelling overnight by coach. Sadly, I only met her once more, and then took fright.

Then came the new school term. The school was situated in Lee Green, a part of Lewisham, which had a wealthy area in the 1960s with large private houses, and avenues of trees and parks, and a poorer part, by far the larger, which contained many terraced houses and blocks of flats. I discovered later that this was very much Spike Milligan country, as he was born and brought up in Catford and Lewisham. I'd had my interview back in May with the headmaster, and I looked forward to working in this Church of England school where, apart from the normal teaching, I would run a chapel choir which led the service for the school in the local church, whose vicar was also chairman of governors. I would also play the organ for the services. This was quite a small school of 400 students – about 60 pupils taken in each year, it had a very small sixth form as most of the pupils left at 16. I think at that school I learned that 'small is beautiful', I knew most of the pupils and certainly all the staff, as we shared a rather small staffroom. My music room was on the top of the three floor building, there was no lift, and so at least I was kept healthy going up and down stairs all day. Facilities in the music department were fairly basic, with a piano in the music room and hall, a couple of record players and that was it. I suppose at times I was green with envy as I looked at some of the neighbouring newly-built comprehensive schools which had impressive music blocks with practice rooms and a great deal of space, but the downside to these wonderful facilities was the idea of working in a school with 1200 pupils. I never did try this out, and maybe it works for some teachers, but I would have been completely overwhelmed by sheer numbers. In my whole career I have come to believe that the school should be small enough for pupils to feel that they are part of a caring community, the head should know each child, so that individual problems could be shared with the staff, an example of which we will see in the next chapter.

One or two particular incidents stand out about the school, especially to do with assembly. This was held every day, and on Wednesdays we had house assembly; each house took part on a rota and a house master or mistress would organise readings, prayers, and perhaps some music. On one occasion it was the turn of the art teacher and he had told me a couple of days before that he was not looking forward to it and hadn't really prepared anything. On the appointed day we stood up for a hymn, which I duly played, and then we remained standing in silence as he told the whole school. "Today we will have silent prayer…" Well, the silent prayer went on for ages, with some shuffling and fidgeting, then the head leaned over to the unfortunate master and tried to whisper the words, "Nick, we *must* have some *proper* prayers." but one thing the head did not possess was a soft, gentle voice – he really could *not* whisper.

Nick 'whispered' back, "Then you'll have to say some." The headmaster found one of his usual said prayers in his book, something about Francis Drake then, with the Lord's Prayer added, I suppose God was satisfied, and we all filed out to begin the day. Poor old Nick was hauled up before the headmaster and told that it just wasn't good enough; Nick took the line that he wasn't a Christian so he felt a hypocrite in taking assembly, but the head retorted that Nick shouldn't have come to teach in a Church of England school if he had no Christian beliefs. Nick maintained that he had told the governors this at his interview but they were still willing to appoint him, so the two of them reached stalemate. Having mentioned the headmaster's speaking voice, which was always loud and gravelly, I remember one of his particular habits when conducting assembly. At the front of the hall was a very large window, and before it hung an equally large wooden cross – a great life-sized affair – which the children could not fail to see; sometimes after a prayer or two the head seemed to run out of ideas, or lose his place, and he always had something up his sleeve, for he would call out in a stentorian voice "Look at the Cross!" The first time he did this I nearly dropped dead with fright, and looked up at the cross with open mouth – was it falling to pieces or was someone fastened to it? But it was all another effort to make our devotions as real as possible. Sometimes the head would stop in the middle of a prayer and shout at some unfortunate child, "You, boy, you're not praying!" How he could tell whether the boy was in a prayerful attitude or not I don't know, but it used to make me giggle inside.

The deputy head was quite a character. Mrs K. lived at Bow and spoke with quite a broad Cockney accent. Almost every evening she would stand at the staff room window complaining, "Where's my Jim? 'E's late again -suppose 'e's bin held up in the ruddy Blackwall Tunnel.". A few of the staff were people I had known at Goldsmiths College, and they warned me that she always used new staff to stand in for her at lessons. I thought this was quite irrelevant because I didn't teach maths, but sure enough, within a couple of weeks I was put down to supervise her maths class. Teachers will know that this happens every day of their lives, usually when staff are absent through illness or otherwise engaged. Mrs K. was there large as life in the staffroom while I took her class, and this happened once or twice more, but then the worm turned. Mrs K. had told me, with a very sad face, that she just *had* to meet a parent at 10.30 so I would have to take her fifth year maths class. "But don't worry Brian, they've loads of work to do, and you don't have to help them." I couldn't have helped her class in maths even if I had wanted to! But when the time came I went off to sit with the fifth form. Shortly into the lesson they were busy and quiet and I realised that I had left a book I needed down in the staffroom, so, having warned them that I would leave the door open, and woe betide anyone making a noise when I returned, I went down to retrieve my book, only to discover Mrs K. sprawled in a chair, with the usual fag hanging out of the corner of her mouth, and coffee in her hand. When she saw me her expression changed rapidly, and I immediately asked her where the parent was who had been going to see her at 10.30. "Oh, I got a phone message, he can't come today after all, and it didn't seem worth upsetting the class for the last 25 minutes". I reminded her that 25 minutes of a 40 minute lesson seemed quite a large proportion to me and to her class, who were after all going to sit their GCE within a couple of months; they would not have regarded it as 'upsetting' at all, and, frankly they deserved better treatment. At break time we had quite a set to. "Other staff have warned me that you do this kind of thing frequently and I've had enough." I said. I went on to say that I considered her a poor example of the NUT and that I would forthwith transfer my membership to the NAS. She tried putting on her deputy head attitude, and maintained that she had every right to insist that staff take her lessons, so I suggested that we both go to the headmaster and have the whole matter thrashed out, but she swiftly declined that invitation; we both knew full well that the headmaster was aware of his lazy deputy. So I was beginning to stand up for myself and not be pushed around. In fact after this incident the deputy and I got on very well. She always helped out in the church choir, and encouraged other people to join.

144

The Christmas service was held at the church, and we had a Christmas concert in our own hall, at which the orchestra made their debut. I must admit the sound wasn't wonderful, but also noticed that some of the staff in the audience had their handkerchiefs to their face and were practically crying with laughter. They were a cruel bunch at times. Staff parties were very boozy affairs, when the beer and wine flowed freely, the carpet would be put back, the piano would be wheeled in, and I would do my stuff entertaining staff and visitors, including governors and the vicar. They went on until the early hours of the morning; it was tough having to be back at the 'cutting edge' by 8.30 the next morning, and the area around the staffroom always smelled like a brewery the next day.

I was kept very busy apart from my teaching, as I was doing more work with clarinet; I joined the Lewisham Philharmonic Orchestra, and took part in some excellent concerts under their conductor, Barry Green. Quite soon I realised the well-known saying that "the show has to go on" in a personal way; I had a concert on Saturday night at the town hall, but woke up in the morning with a terrible pain in my side, in fact I could hardly move. The snag was that although I could ring in and they would find someone to deputise for me, I had the only copies of the clarinet music, and somehow I drove my car through the busy traffic to deliver the precious parts to the secretary – and the show could go on. I hardly remember driving back, just awful pain which would not go away. When I eventually met up with a specialist and had a barium meal he thought I had developed trouble with my gall bladder. A strict diet and medication got things back to near normal.

At about the same time that I started at Northbrook School, in September 1963, I saw an advertisement in a Christian magazine: "Evangelical organist required for Eltham Park Baptist Church – please contact the Minister, Rev Kenneth Furlong." I smiled at the wording of this advertisement and wondered what an evangelical organist had that other organists lacked, but I knew what was meant, and in the interview I subsequently had with Ken Furlong it became even clearer he was looking for someone who saw the organ playing and directing the choir as a means of worship, and not just an ego trip to enjoy the music itself along with the choir. I was appointed almost immediately and met the choir, which included Jean, the daughter of the outgoing organist, Mr Scott. He had been a very faithful worker in that church for many years, but after retiring from his work he and his wife had moved down to a very pretty little village in Kent, and I think he found the journey rather too much. He lived in Trottiscliffe, which the locals pronounce as 'Trosley'. My brief in this post was both to maintain the choir, which mainly consisted of elderly people who still felt they had something to give musically, through anthems and leading the hymn singing, and also to encourage the younger people in the church by introducing some of the modern tunes. This 'brief' was almost duplicated in a post I took on in Cambridge 24 years later – but that's jumping the gun.

I soon became part of the church family, the choir were very faithful and encouraging, and made up in enthusiasm for what they might have lacked in singing talent. Everybody remembers what they were doing when the news of J.F. Kennedy's assassination was announced, and for me it was a Friday evening when I heard the news just before I set out for the weekly choir practice. There was talk of little else that night, and one or two of the elderly members were quite tearful about the shooting of the President.

I mentioned Jean, the daughter of the retiring organist, for she innocently played a part in my future – as you will see. Life seemed busy enough, with school music to run and the organist's job at weekends, but in addition I got involved back at Goldsmiths College in the evening department orchestra, which I referred to earlier in the book. Things would get very hectic at Christmas, particularly, for there would be services and concerts at the school to organise, plus the show at the Lewisham concert Hall which usually ran for four nights, and then when term finished at school and the rest of the staff went off to relax I still had to cope with the Christmas carol services at the Baptist church. I was out night after night, but looking back, it was probably the happiest time of my life.

In March 1964 my brother John had his first boy. Tony was born at Biggleswade, a small town in Cambridgeshire where John and his wife were living, and where he worked in a solicitor's office. Mother was called in to help, as indeed she was for all six of the grandchildren who eventually came along. During the summer holiday that year my brother Allen also married, a local Dagenham girl called Brenda. I believe she was the first and only girlfriend Allen ever had. She lived on the other side of Heathway – a long road which ran almost from the Ford motor works through the length of Dagenham, and seemed to bisect the town, and the impression with us was that the rich people lived on the other side of this 'dividing line'. The only two people I knew who lived on the 'other side' both happened to have cars and lived in their own private house, so I suppose that was classed as rich. When we got to know Brenda we realised that her family were the same as us – poor but honest! As we had moved to the other side of the river, courting must have become more complicated, for Allen had to make the journey across the ferry and catch various buses to meet up with her. On many nights he would arrive home in the early hours of the morning, having missed the last bus, but I suppose true love never runs smooth, and after marriage at least he would have one less journey each day. Sad news came on the eve of their wedding day, when we heard that one of our cousins had been killed at work. Billy worked on a building site, and drove one of the large tractors which were called JCVs, and while working on a steep slope it had overturned crushing Billy and killing him outright. It was a hard decision to make, but everyone knew that the right thing was to go ahead with the wedding, though Billy's family did not attend. They were married at a church in Dagenham, quite close to the motor works and just a few yards from the cinema, where I had made my debut as a clarinettist. Inevitably, seeing both my brothers now married and becoming an uncle for the first time made me realise that I should be doing something about my own single status, but I kept putting it off.

I was still doing the journey from Abbey Wood to school each day, but had become friends with several of the staff, so we often went out for a drink in the evenings, and most of the musical activities centred within a mile or two of the school so John, the PE master and friend suggested that I look round for some rooms near the school. At the beginning of the autumn term in 1964 I actually moved away from home – wonder of wonders – taking on the upstairs rooms of a house almost opposite the school. The owner was a very old man who must have been in his 80s, and lived downstairs alone with his dog. The house was in a terrible state, and the upstairs rooms were very damp. The bath was actually in the tiny kitchen, which was on the landing of the stairs, and one had to remove the wooden table top to use it; I took one look at this bath and was nearly sick, for it was absolutely filthy – the dirt was ingrained. The bedroom and living room were at the top of the next flight of stairs. This bedroom was also very damp and cold, remnants of wallpaper just peeling away from the wall revealing a wet, mildewy surface; it was a miracle that I didn't catch pneumonia in those conditions. The main room was more pleasant, and after ordering coal and getting the fire going it began to seem almost like home. Two of the pupils at school heard that I had moved, and volunteered to come and help clean the place up, so after checking that their parents were happy with this, I accepted their offer gladly. I think they were quite taken aback with the conditions they saw, and you could almost sense them feeling sorry for me. They got to work on the bath and scrubbed away, and they tried to make the bedroom brighter, though with peeling wallpaper, filthy curtains and great damp patches everywhere it was not easy. Unfortunately the weather grew very cold, we had snow and hard frosts and I just shivered in that house. I had moved what furniture I possessed from home, including my large collection of records, and the plan was to play my music in the evenings when I wasn't involved in any shows or rehearsals, but I hadn't taken account of the people next door. Within a couple of days they had complained about my music; it seemed that the husband did shift work, so that even in the late afternoon he might still be in bed, and as he was a policeman I didn't care to argue the point. I *could* listen on headphones, but that did not seem a very satisfactory state of affairs. Toilet facilities were sadly lacking in the house, I had to go down the stairs and through the old man's kitchen to get to the outside 'lavvy'. It was quite embarrassing having to knock on the door and go through in the evening, and I always hoped that I wouldn't have to make the journey during the night. On several occasions when I went into the kitchen he would be lying asleep in the chair and appeared to be dead, with the dog quietly whining at his feet, and I was always scared that he was going to die on me, and what would I do? Sometimes I made quite a noise with the door, hoping he might wake up and prove he was still alive, but usually there was no response at all, and I would go to bed seriously wondering whether I had a corpse one floor below. Looking back it seems laughable, but at the time I cannot think what ever made me take on those rooms, I certainly should have looked at

148

more flats. My mother always encouraged me to go back home for Sunday lunch and I must admit that it was great to drive the scooter back home after morning service to enjoy her cooking and be warm. By the end of term I had had enough of those rooms, and mother suggested that I go back to living at home, because I could have two rooms, a bedroom and a smaller room as a living room; it was very generous of her to make this offer for she could have been quite hardhearted and taken the view that I had made my bed (damp and unhealthy), and should lie on it. Certainly it made sense, because I could give her money for housekeeping, and I believe that she was rather bored with just my father and sister at home, so I packed all my stuff yet again and moved back just before Christmas. The old man was very upset, but at least I left him half a ton of coal which was lying in the bunker. This experience of attempting to move away had a positive outcome. One of the girls who had offered to help clean the kitchen was a musical girl, played flute, violin and recorder, and I believe she must have gone home with the most awful tale of the conditions in which I was living, for her parents obviously felt very sorry for me. They invited me for Sunday lunch, and I discovered what a musical family they were; the girls played flute, violin and oboe between them, while their brothers played the clarinet and French horn, in the latter case, Oliver was only about nine at the time, and this was an incredibly difficult instrument to take up. Their father Gordon was an orthopaedic surgeon who worked at two local hospitals and had his own practice in Harley Street; an extremely clever man who was also an accomplished pianist and kept that as his hobby. Their large detached house was just a few doors down from the Baptist church where I played so very often after the evening service I would drop in for an evening of clarinet pieces, piano duets and music for two pianos – they had a Blüthner grand AND a very good upright piano in a lounge which was about the size of our whole house at Abbey Wood. With a glass of 'roojooblon', and puffing away at our pipes, we would play until about 11 o'clock, and by the time I'd had coffee and conversation with Gordon and his wife it was often past midnight when I went home.

The school was planning a skiing holiday to Davos in Switzerland just after Christmas 1964, and I went along as one of the three members of staff, and discovered that Gordon's two daughters were going as well. One of them was very good at needlework and her mother took my measurements and the eldest daughter made me a good waterproof anorak for the skiing holiday. We set off after Boxing Day, travelling across Europe by train, which meant a whole night trying to get comfortable in a fairly crowded compartment, sleep was almost out of the question; when we got to Davos eventually we realised it was worth the discomfort, with a great deal of snow, crisp, cold temperatures but often a bright sun in a cloudless sky. Our hotel was not 'top of the league' by any means, and at first some of the pupils were disappointed that they were sleeping in dormitories, and we had to move over to the restaurant to get our meals, but when it was pointed out to them that we were halfway up the mountain at the very point where the ski runs and chairlift were situated, while people from much more expensive hotels were having to queue for ages to get into the lift to bring them up the mountain, I think they were pacified, and certainly when some of the visitors learned where we were staying they were envious. We had our skiing lessons in the morning, and I picked the basic movements up fairly quickly, and in the afternoon we were free to practise on the slopes, or to have an extra lesson. On one afternoon some of the pupils persuaded me, very much against my will, to go down the toboggan run. I shared a toboggan with one of the girls who screamed all the way down and with very good reason, for it was very steep, unbelievably fast and we had no idea about steering or slowing down the wretched toboggan. We saw other pupils who had fallen off their machines, but it was impossible to stop to see how they were, we just raced on. When I reached the bottom, vowing that I would never do such a thing again I expected the girl on the toboggan to be very tearful and scared, and got the shock of my life when she immediately wanted to go back and do it all again. "Certainly you can have another go, but don't expect me to come with you." I replied, "I've had quite enough for one day." It was only then that I discovered that the run at Davos is internationally famous, and has been used for Winter Olympics. If only I had known that before we set off! It was wonderful after a whole day's skiing on the mountain, to take the path right down to street level, indeed it actually finished by joining the main road, meeting the buses and cars, so that one had to be pretty efficient not to end up under a bus. Then we would take our skis off and have a lovely hot glüwein or Ovaltine in a cosy warm café, with steam condensed on the windows, and one felt healthily tired. The air in Davos was wonderful, and I felt as fit as a flea on that holiday. We did try to take the pupils out in the evening on occasions to find some sort of après ski entertainment, but they were all very expensive; some of the pupils found out themselves when they went into one dance hall where the entrance was free but they discovered each bottle of Coke was about £10 and they were expected to buy at least one bottle.

So 1965 began with me living back at home. School was still as busy as ever and I put on concerts at Easter, and was responsible for providing some items for the school speech day. For this grand occasion staff were asked to wear their academic dress, so I dug out my new gown and Trinity College hood – a very fetching mauve – as did the rest of the staff. Our deputy, the notorious Mrs K. didn't possess any academic dress, for she had no degree, so she used to wear a chiffon scarf which was a hood 'look-a-like'. She had to make the vote of thanks after the guest speaker had addressed the audience, and she made every effort to get all her aitches in the right place and not sound too much like an inhabitant of Bow. I was down at the piano as the staff filed off in silence, looking very intelligent and dignified, but then it happened; Mrs K. caught the sleeve of her gown in the banister of the steps leading down from the stage, and muttered, in true Cockney fashion, "Oh, this bloody gown!" Unfortunately the microphone was very close by and no one had switched it off, so the whole school heard this loud and clear, and when we arrived back in the staff room, staff were almost crying with laughter.

At Easter that year I went to Spain with the school. We were bound for Loret De Mar, which in 1965 was a quiet seaside village near Barcelona, with just a couple of hotels and a few bars, the lager and chips brigade from Great Britain had not yet found it. A great deal of coach travelling was involved on this holiday, we travelled over to Belgium by air, and then picked up a coach which took us through to Spain and stayed with us during the holiday. The headmaster came, and two of us had great fun putting him to bed one night when he had supped rather too much of the vino. It's quite nice when a headmaster puts his arm round you and tells you, "You're a good chap." but we were very discreet and never mentioned the affair the next morning. I was also to suffer from too much drink on a later occasion; the nightly plan was for at least one member of staff to stay behind checking that the pupils were in their rooms, if not in bed, so the rest of us were free to go to the local bar, where I found that liqueurs were five pesetas a glass, which was the equivalent of about a shilling (5p), and one got quite drunk on five bob, which is what happened to me. Having come from a background where a bottle of VP fruit wine or Sanatogen (fortified the over 40s) at Christmas was the nearest I had ever got to strong spirits, I never knew the names of the liqueurs, had certainly never drunk any of them, and used to distinguish them by their colours, but after four or five of these powerful drinks I was quite tipsy. Going back to the hotel I felt fine, in fact on top of the world, but then in bed, everything started to go round and round, and by the morning I was very much the worse for wear. As the pupils went down to the beach to play football I just sat in the shade feeling like death warmed up, and, of course they all knew why, they were just too polite to mention it.

The scooter was now beginning to show its age, and though it had never let me down, I wanted something a little more comfortable, so in June that year I bought my first car – a brand new Morris Minor 1000, with an 1100 engine installed. It was a wonderful car, although I was very lucky not to crash it on my first journey. I had bought a few driving lessons from the BSM (British School of Motoring), passed the driving test, and was assured that I had good road sense – eight years driving the scooter had given me that – but I had no opportunity to practice in between lessons. It was at least a month between passing my driving test and getting the Morris, and because I was getting a discount through my union, I had to travel up to Berkeley Square in the West End of London to collect the car. After just a few minutes' tuition to explain the controls, there I was having to come up a steep slope from the underground garage, execute a hill stop and start and do a right turn straight into the Piccadilly traffic. Of course I had never driven a car on my own, and I had to negotiate buses, Green Line coaches, in fact just about everything, before I got back to the school sweating and shaking. Bless them, one or two of the staff had arranged with some pupils to put out flags and banners for a royal entrance, but when I finally got out of the car I nearly collapsed through nerves. The car made a great difference to life, I was able to arrive at school warm, carrying all the books I needed and my clarinets; I took great pleasure in showing it off to my parents and to other friends, and it certainly made courting far more comfortable than on the scooter.

Two more musical memories stand out during the summer of 1965. The London County Council, who were always good supporters of music in their schools, arranged a residential course for music teachers at a country house which they owned just outside Petworth in Sussex. One speaker stood out from all the others. We had noticed on our timetable that on the second night after dinner a certain Douglas Kennedy was coming down to speak to us about folk music; we all groaned, for we were intending to head for the local pub, after a busy day. Douglas Kennedy was quite an old man, and at the time I had not realised how famous he was – one of the leading authorities on English folk music in the world -- but within half an hour we were all hooked on listening to his stories, for he had a great sense of humour, and then he invited us to join in some dancing; so successful was this that we all pleaded to have another half-hour before we went to bed. I did not realise that within a few years I would get the "folk bug" very much in my system and be playing out with my own band! Tape cassettes were very much in vogue, and I had bought a small portable cassette player, and remember sitting on a bench overlooking the South Downs at sunset listening to Vaughan Williams' *fifth Symphony*. Somehow the music and that beautiful English scene were made for each other, and I wanted the world to stand still at that point, it was so wonderful. That memory still floods back whenever I hear the VW performed; some rather nasty critics have referred to Vaughan Williams as a writer of "cowpat" music, but he always has been one of my favourite composers.

Of course I had travelled down in the new Morris, and enjoyed a leisurely return, back to Goldsmiths College where I was going to play first clarinet for the college production of Smetana's *Bartered Bride*. At the dress rehearsal I was continually losing my part, because I was always staring at the student playing the part of Mařenka; she was quite beautiful, and Leslie Orrey, the conductor, had to remind me to pay more attention to the score and less to the stage!

Parent meetings have always been an essential part of teaching life, and though one realises the importance of contact with the parents, sometimes, having met them, you end up feeling rather sorry for the child. Now, I would be the first to acknowledge that music is not among the most important subjects in the school curriculum; generally it is the parents of children who are good at music, perhaps playing an instrument, or studying it for GCE who make an appointment to see the music teacher. At such a meeting, while waiting for the next parent to arrive, along came Mrs Jones. She asked if she could have a few minutes to discuss her son George, and I asked her to sit down, but quickly made it clear that George showed no interest in music; in point of fact he was a real nuisance, but I wanted to let her down lightly. "Mr Astell, I just wanted to thank you for making George interested in classical music. After you played that *Romeo and Juliet* thing, he came home and said he wanted an LP of it. We bought a record of it when we went shopping on Saturday and he has played it ever since. Are there any other records like that we could buy him as a Christmas present?"

I nearly fell off my chair with astonishment, and asked her whether we were both talking about the same George. "Oh yes, he often comes home and mentions the pieces you have played, and I think he wants to start his own collection of the classics!" That must be one of the most pure, unalloyed moments of joy that a teacher gets in an otherwise uphill struggle – when you realise that among the barren acres of Philistine fields, one of the seeds has gone into good ground.

The long school holiday at last came round, and again I returned to a summer school at Boscombe, just outside Bournemouth where once more I was acting as a group leader. Memories of that holiday are of a distinctly wet time, with very poor weather. There was an occasional dry spell though, for I have a photo which caused great fun among all my friends. Naturally, I had teamed up with a lovely girl, this time called Ruth, who had just started training as a nurse, and lived in Bath. One afternoon we lay together on the beach with a group of our friends, enjoying the sun; I always carried a book with me, and having studied the book stall at the school, I had come away with a very useful, informative paperback and was still clutching it as we lay on the sand. Some kind friend took a photo – the book was called *Sex and Marriage*, and they were all keen to know how I had used the information so far during the holiday! I also managed to be persuaded by the deputy head, our Cockney Mrs. K, to go on one of the adult holidays which she organised each summer for her particular circle of friends. This was an unmitigated disaster. I found I was bored stiff with them, and didn't really enjoy the holiday. We flew over to Ostend and picked up a Belgian coach which took us through to Italy and stayed with us for the 10-day holiday. Our final destination was Chiavari, which lay on the coast between Genoa and La Spezia, but our hotel was outside the town on the busy coastal road at the very top of a steep hill, with an incredible bend before an equally steep descent. I shared what can only be described as a stable with another single man; they had moved out the animals, but bits of hay were still around, and it certainly smelt like a stable. He snored very loudly from the moment his head touched the pillow, while I listened all night long to the lorries as they reached the top of the hill, with loudly clanging gear changes, and squealing of breaks as they negotiated the difficult bend. The window had to be kept open as it was unbearably hot even at night (air conditioning? You must be joking, whenever did they put air conditioning in a stable?) And as we were at basement level, I was just a few feet from this busy road and its fumes. I never had a decent night's rest all the time I was there. We did some excursions, to Pisa and Viaréggio, and at least could climb the steps to the top of the Pisa tower – that became out of bounds some years later – but I was extremely glad when we set off in the coach for the return trip.

A few months later I went with a school party to Paris, which was organised by Mrs Williams, head of French at Northbrook, and this was a delightful few days away. We stayed in a fairly modest hotel right in the heart of Paris, had some wonderful French cuisine, and altogether one felt the atmosphere of being in that great city. I had last visited Paris in 1954, as you may remember from chapter 5, but this time I had some money in my pocket, wasn't saddled with a bike, and enjoyed visits to Notre Dame, the Eiffel Tower – only up to level 2, Sacré Coeur, and a trip down the River Seine. It was a good holiday partly because the leader kept the right balance between the educational side of our visit, and giving students time to relax and enjoy the place, also because the company was good – Len Ferguson, the scripture teacher at Northbrook had come with us, and we all got on well, a situation which doesn't always happen with school parties.

When the summer holiday of 1966 came round our own family went down to Cornwall. My brother John and his wife, with their son Tony, drove down in their rather dilapidated van, while I took my parents in my shiny Morris. It was a long journey, involving many stops to change and feed the two year old, and we arrived at the caravan park just outside Penzance at 10 o'clock at night, in pitch darkness. It had taken us over 12 hours to get from London to Cornwall. Thank goodness we had two caravans, giving Dad, Mum and I a little bit of space, though mother seemed to spend all her time preparing meals, washing up or helping to organise Jackie and her baby. Each day seemed to be organised around the baby and its requirements. We would plan to go down to the beach in the morning, but then the baby had to be fed, and it seemed best to have our lunch in the caravan, everything had to be washed up, so we would be arriving on the beach at about 4 pm when everyone else was going home after the best part of the day. On one or two occasions I broke away from the family to visit Truro Cathedral and on one day took my parents on a boat trip down the wonderful river Fal.

Once again I went down to Bexhill for the two-week BMS summer school, where Tom Rogers, who I described earlier, was president, and Roy Cave and Richard Weir were secretaries. These were three young ministers with their wives and families and they led a fantastic holiday; I can remember particularly fine weather and sitting out for afternoon tea in the spacious grounds of the school, watching the cricket – after my experiences at school no one in the world would persuade me to actually play the game any more.

In September I returned to Northbrook for what was to be my last year there. The headmaster had told me quite candidly that there would be no chance of promotion in such a small school, and he felt that I should be looking around for promotion – a head of department post with more money attached. From the beginning of March, 1967 I began to apply for jobs and had one or two interviews, one at Ashford Grammar School, which I didn't get, and tried for head of department at Prendergast School, a local grammar school in Lewisham. It looked as though the head was going to have to put up with me for yet another school year when along came one of those "coincidences" which change the direction of life completely. I was still organist and choirmaster at Eltham Park Baptist Church, and after one

156

choir practice Jean Featherstone – the daughter of the previous organist, one of my precious sopranos – casually mentioned that they were looking for a head of music at the school where she was secretary. This was Chislehurst and Sidcup Technical High School for Girls – what a mouthful! The school had just completed the process of moving from Sidcup in very cramped conditions, onto a beautiful site behind Chislehurst Common; they had taken over the lovely old house called Coopers with its extensive grounds, complete with lake and a beautiful cedar tree which the headmistress was always referring to, and just above the house a new building had been put up, with science labs, gymnasium, secretarial suite, school hall, kitchens and dining hall, and a music room. September 1967 was to be the first term when the whole school would be in one building, no more commuting for staff or pupils. I had been warned that the headmistress was rather eccentric but very hard-working, and that she lived for the school alone and I came to see how true this was over the years.

Time was running short, the deadline for handing in my notice at Northbrook was just three days away, though to be fair, the headmaster had said he would not stand in my way at all, and would just have to take anyone he could get as a replacement music master. An interview was hastily arranged for Wednesday at noon, and when I arrived I was introduced to the deputy head, Miss Allen. We talked and talked, she became rather anxious and was wringing her hands, but there was no sign of any headmistress. After about 40 minutes the door was flung open and in marched the head, Miss Anderson, followed by a school secretary carrying a tray with a very cold looking school dinner. "Miss Anderson, you really *must* stop for a few minutes and have your meal; we have walked all round the school," said the secretary, who herself looked ready to drop.

"My dear I have a school to run, I have no time to sit and enjoy meals, but leave it on my desk and I'll get round to it at some point" replied the headmistress, while holding the door open to indicate that the secretary must go.

"Ah, I see we have a gentleman, and who *are* you?" She asked, as I stood up politely to be introduced. The deputy made the introduction, and shortly left to continue 'running the school' while the headmistress talked to 'the gentleman'. She took a quick glance at my CV, and noticed that I had been in the band of the Coldstream Guards, and the rest of the interview seemed to be more about my experiences in the army than about my suitability as the music master in her school. She made several references to a book about First World War experiences she had read which seemed to have the title *They Died with Their Boots On*, and her questions and comments almost implied that I had been there fighting and suffering on the Somme in 1916. She was very pleasant to me, indeed gracious, and tried to put me at ease, but inwardly I wondered whether she was crazy. Eventually the interview came to an end – "Mr. Astell, I would so much like to continue asking you about your army experiences, so interesting, but I really must get back to the girls," already getting up and opening the door as if anxious to see the back of me. Her cold dinner was still on the desk!

I drove back to Northbrook, where the headmaster was very anxious to find out what had happened, and whether he needed to set about finding a new music master. I had to admit to him that I had no idea whether I had got the job, the headmistress had muttered something about seeing another applicant that afternoon, and I confided to Mr Cox that it was the strangest interview I'd ever attended. The next morning there was a telegram sent to me at school, offering me the post. As it happened I was able to do the headmaster a favour in return, because I had kept in touch with a younger music student from Goldsmiths, Geoff Seaman, who was working at a secondary school in Woolwich (the very one where I had done my last teaching practice) but was looking for a change. He was interviewed and appointed on Friday, the deadline for handing in one's notice, but at least Northbrook had a good replacement, and the headmaster was saved a lot of worry; meanwhile, I was looking forward to the challenge of a new school, the responsibility of the music department, with an assistant teacher and a reasonable pay rise with the job.

Money must have still been tight at this time, for I spent at least four weeks of the summer holidays working in the classical record department of HMV in Oxford Street. It wasn't just a 9 to 5 job as the store stayed open until late in the evening, so one might be on a shift from 2pm until 9pm. I found it quite expensive to eat out in the lunch hour, and as I was trying to save every penny, I took along sandwiches and fruit with a good book, and sat in some quiet gardens just off

Bond Street. I enjoyed the work, it was great to have classical music going in the background; I can remember a new recording of Arensky's *Variations on Theme of Tchaikovsky* with Barbirolli conducting the London Symphony Orchestra had just been released by HMV, and hearing this played every day meant that I knew it off by heart after four weeks in the store. Many of the customers were fairly sophisticated folk who certainly knew their classics, and you were expected to give advice on good recordings, answer questions and be ready to have intelligent conversation with them. How unlike stores today, where all the merchandise is set out and the only staff to be seen are those taking the money at the checkout; sadly most of them wouldn't have the slightest idea who Arensky, Barbirolli or LSO are – and that's if you can find a shop which stocks classical music. The only phrase they are taught in training is to repeat *ad infinitum* "If it's not on the shelf we haven't got it." Inevitably, as I could get a good staff discount, I spent most of my wages on records.

CHAPTER TWELVE

FOUR YEARS HARD LABOUR

On a beautiful early September afternoon I drove over to my new school for the staff tea party and meeting. The school was situated at the back of Chislehurst common, close by a beautiful old church, a couple of pubs and then down a lane which lead to nowhere, in fact as I drove from the traffic lights off the main road it was like going back two centuries in time.

The school was housed in beautiful grounds, as I've indicated in a previous chapter, with the old manor house called Coopers, complete with Adams ceilings and ornate fireplaces, bow windows and a view from the back past the cedar tree and the pond away into the distant parts of Kent. In fact the very busy main line from the coast through to Victoria and Waterloo ran close by the boundary of the school, but it was all in a deep cutting, and one was hardly aware of the trains. It seemed a pity that children had to come and spoil the peace of this place, but then I remembered that they were my bread and butter. I moved up a covered way to the main, new building to find the staffroom and to meet everyone. The staff tea party was another trip back into a bygone age. Varieties of cakes laid out on expensive cake stands, and sandwiches with crusts removed, and tea poured into beautiful china cups. I quickly moved to join with the only other male teacher, Mr Law, a rather serious Scotsman who looked after the religious education department; just us two men among around 40 women! Everyone was chatting about the holidays, their families, and what a pity the six weeks had gone so quickly. No one was talking shop, indeed no one seemed interested in the new timetable or the new term about to start – that could all wait. I realised that this seemed to sum up the pleasant, relaxed atmosphere of Coopers School. Everyone was to do their job well, to care for the pupils in their charge, but to have a right sense of proportion.

Miss Anderson and her deputy head joined us and the meeting began, though there seemed no real agenda, she just rambled on in an interesting way, but with no idea of time, and increasingly her deputy had to tactfully remind her that term began the next morning and we had many things to decide.

That was the beginning of two years sheer enjoyment at the school, years in which I respected and admired the headmistress. If anything, she worked too hard, because the school was her life; as I came to realise, she had no outside interests or particular friends away from the school. Later that afternoon I went along to inspect my new music room and was shown the large walk-in store which was attached. Unfortunately one could not walk into the walk-in store because books and music which had been transported from the old school in Sidcup had been simply dumped into the store which was packed from top to bottom. It was going to take me a number of weeks of hard work in lunchtimes and after school, with the help of willing pupils, to sort it all out, tidy it up, and make up a stock book. No one at the school knew of any existing stock book.

A whole volume could be written about the life at Coopers, but I must just pick out a few events and personalities. Assembly was like nothing I had ever experienced, either as a schoolboy or a teacher. If the head were in charge, it could go on for two hours, unless the deputy actually intervened by quietly reminding Miss Anderson that the girls should really go to lessons at some point in the day. Occasionally, after about an hour a few brave staff would stand up and move away from the hall, as a silent demonstration that they needed to start lessons. Sometimes, after about 20 minutes Miss Anderson would tell all the staff to return to the staffroom for a cup of tea while she spoke to the girls. If this happened, we could be fairly sure that the first two lessons would go by default. It was all fairly amusing except for the senior classes whose examinations were coming up, and who needed all the teaching they could get. The head would just talk and talk – interesting, often valuable information, but fairly irrelevant for a morning assembly. Woe betide any girl who yawned, coughed or had the temerity to speak to a neighbour. The head had eyes like a hawk. If one dared even whisper to the member of staff next to them, somehow Miss Anderson would indirectly show that she had observed this disrespect by saying to the whole school: "What I'm saying is right isn't it, Mr. X?" with a piercing glance in that direction, or "I'm sure Miss Y agrees with me." This was her oblique way of informing one that she had taken note. No pupil would dare to go to assembly without a hymn book, and when I arrived in the mornings there would be a queue desperately waiting to borrow a spare hymn book before they went into assembly. Come to think of it, I could have had quite a lucrative business in the supply of emergency hymn books at 1/- a time! I must have mentioned to her at some point that at my first school I had been required to introduce music after each assembly, so at Coopers we had a compromise: Friday morning was Music Morning. After the hymn, reading and prayer I would introduce a short piece of music to the school, played on a record or sometimes at the piano, and then everyone would depart to their classes. The other music teacher, Miss O'Shaunessey and I took it in turns to play the piano, and occasionally on Fridays we would play the pupils out with a duet, or I would persuade senior pupils to play the hymn and a piece afterwards. The school came into every assembly to classical music – a keen girl enjoyed organizing this. A lot of music went on there, with junior and senior choirs, madrigal group, orchestra (of sorts), recorder group and fairly soon, a clarinet choir. Moya, my colleague shared all this work with me.

So why have I called this chapter "Four Years' Hard Labour"? Not because of the school work, which I could cope with, and thoroughly enjoyed, but because as I started at the school, I also began a four-year course at Goldsmiths College to obtain my Bachelor of Music degree. This was the first year that London University had allowed part-time students to take this normally full-time degree – we were the guinea pigs. Professor Thurston Dart had really masterminded the syllabus and came up from Cambridge to introduce the course to us. At one stage he warned us that if we intended to maintain a social life during the next four years, then now was the time to give up the degree, and made it clear that this course would take every bit of our spare time. How right he was! Some students giggled at this, but he was quite serious, and I came to realise the truth of his statement. During the term we had at least two lectures to attend each week and harmony exercises and assignments to complete, which meant getting around to libraries for books and music, sometimes travelling up to central London just to consult a book, and all this while trying to do a full-time job.

There were many times when I really wondered whether I was crazy to have ever taken on this mammoth task, after all there were students at Goldsmiths who were doing the same course over three years but with no added burden of earning a living during the day. Students had to pass the first-year exams to be able to continue, so this was a very busy time. Incidentally, at the end of that first year there was a tremendous investigation into those on the full-time course, for the failure rate was high, while in our group of around 30 part-timers there was only one failure. I could have given the investigating authority at least one good reason why the results had panned out in this way. During my full-time years at Goldsmiths,1958-61, we had one tiny bar which opened for about an hour a day, otherwise it meant a trip to the local pub, The Rosemary Arms for a drink. On our meagre grants most of us just had a celebratory drink at the end of term, certainly not every week or every day. I noticed when I went back to start the B. Mus course in 1967 that there was a large bar, run by professionals, which seemed to be open for most of the day and evening, and which was always fairly full. Students seemed to have got into the habit of drinking every day… so much for the poverty which they all claimed to be suffering from. On the plus side, I began to find the chance to dig deep into musical topics, to debate with other students and lecturers, and to attend concerts and operas with members of the group. In chapter 5 I mentioned my lack of confidence in wondering whether I would ever get to university, and here I was at last tackling the degree which my own music master had failed twice. But what a challenge it proved to be. Once this course got underway I realised that I could certainly not continue as organist at Eltham Park Baptist Church, and regrettably resigned, despite pleadings from the choir and congregation.

The music at the school certainly needed expanding. Early in November of my first term I went in to see the head about the school Christmas concert and the following conversation ensued:

Miss Anderson: "Are you sure you can manage to cope with a concert, Mr ASTELL?" She then proceeded to look through the diary for an *afternoon* which was convenient.

BA: "But Miss Anderson, we can't put on a concert in the afternoon, most of the parents couldn't attend because they are working, we must go for an evening."

Miss Anderson: "How exciting, you would really be willing to give up a whole evening for a school concert?"

BA: "I regard it as part of my job to train the girls for concerts, formal and informal, for their parents and friends to attend, every term. This is what it's all about."

Miss Anderson: "That is so generous of you; Mrs D** [my predecessor] was not happy to come out in the evening. I will make sure the girls support you in every way."

She certainly did. When it was announced at assembly that we were to have an *evening* Christmas concert she made it quite clear that the names of any children who did not attend all rehearsals would be passed on to her, and insisted that I keep a register, which she would examine from time to time, only accepting serious illness or death as a legitimate excuse for being absent from choir practice or the orchestral group!

The concert was a great success, albeit rather long because so many pupils wanted to take part, and we went on to produce music for the final Christmas service of the term and a session of Carol singing, and a small band played Christmas music while staff and pupils ate Christmas lunch in the canteen.

There was a pleasant surprise next term when I popped in to see the head on a fairly minor point and she told me how anxious she was about THE CRUISE. It appeared that nearly a third of the girls were going on a schools Mediterranean cruise, to be accompanied by 12 members of staff.

"I can't think why the staff are all so anxious to go on this wretched cruise, for they will be away from their families." she said, and then expressed surprise when I politely disagreed, saying that I would have given anything to go on the cruise. "Really, would you really want to go on that... boat... to all those foreign places? THEN YOU SHALL. We should have one male member of staff and it will be you." This set the cat among the pigeons when she announced it at a staff meeting, for there was already a waiting list of staff wanting to go, and I upset a few ladies by jumping to the head of the queue.

So on 22nd April a convoy of coaches set off for Southampton to join S. S. Nevasa on an educational cruise to North Africa, Spain, Gibraltar and Portugal.

Practically the whole ship had been taken over by the London Borough of Bromley, who had school parties from about 14 schools on board . At the quayside a voice called down from the deck, I recognised Paul Abercrombie, a teacher friend, who had brought a very small party of boys from his school onto the ship, and I realised it was going to be fun all the way. Within 10 minutes of setting our cases in our cabins, Paul and I were in one of the bars being served by an Indian steward – the ship was run by the British India Company. I ordered a large brandy, Paul had a double whisky, the steward brought the bill which came to 2/8 [14p]. I knew the drinks were cheap but not *that* cheap, and so I called out, "Heavens, look at these prices!" The steward immediately took back the bill, apologised and said it should be 2/3 [11p]! As soon as we left port the education officer of Bromley came over the loudspeaker system to inform everyone, teachers and students alike, that the interest from the money that pupils had paid in during the year would give us all an extra £1 each for spending money, and in 1968 a pound was quite a lot. Of course nowadays adult cruises are two a penny, everyone goes on them, but this cruise was an eye-opener to many of us. We saw abject poverty in North Africa as we travelled by coach to Tetuan from Ceuta; I noticed along the coastal road beautiful hotels with swimming pools and balconies, while on the left in amongst the trees were very small huts; I took these to be toilets for the people who had worked in the building of the hotels. The driver informed me that they were African homes!

As part of the entertainments programme we had a couple of concerts at which the schools could show their talent. We had a girl who specialised in ballet. She worked at the Royal Ballet School on Saturdays and was hoping to be a professional dancer. She subsequently won her audition for the Royal Ballet School as a full-time student, later left and went off to work in Germany, where opportunities for ballet were considerably greater than in this country, and then I lost touch with her. Naomi was a perfect student, not the tiniest bit arrogant and with a good sense of humour. I got to know her parents later, and took her to one or two places to accompany her in dancing. On the ship she was going to dance a Sicilienne by Fauré, which we had rehearsed at school . Unfortunately we were ploughing through the Bay of Biscay, the ship was going from one side to the other, the piano was also moving from right to left as I played, and the stage was very unsteady. I just don't know how Naomi managed to carry on dancing and looking so cool and calm. She was a great success. I had to do a little bit of work at sea, like supervising the classes which were arranged before we reached ports, for distributing pocket money, leaflets, maps, and general information. I also had to take my turn at bedtime duty. The pupils slept in dormitories of about 40, and a couple of staff each evening had to make sure they had gone to bed and settled down at lights out. Every time it was my turn the girls refused to settle down until I had gone round and kissed them all good night. This I quite enjoyed doing, it wasn't such a bad duty after all, though I'm glad there was always another female member of staff around. Of course in these days nothing like that would be allowed, and I would end up in jail, but in 1968, in a holiday mood it was just a big giggle for the pupils, who could write cards back home telling their parents that Mr Astell was looking after them and gave them a goodnight kiss – it puts 'in loco parentis' in a new light. The food on board was out of this world, I had never eaten anything like it, with wonderful desserts, gorgeous salads at lunchtime, the most incredible choices to make, so that after a while one took it all for granted. I remember saying to the others at one lunch, "Well I suppose I'd better have turkey salad again."

All good things come to an end, and we disembarked on May 5, took coaches back from Southampton to Chislehurst, were met by parents longing to be reunited with their daughters, and I made my way home to the council house at Abbey Wood – quite a comedown – yet I still think my mother's liver and bacon and bread pudding were better than all the sumptuous meals on board the ship.

Home from the cruise on the May 5th, back to school the next day, and it meant a lot of catching up in my degree work – essays, harmony exercises and preparation for preliminary exams coming up near the end of term – the holiday was certainly over.

During all this time I still played with the Lewisham Philharmonic Orchestra, and over the next two years we did some fantastic concerts. Jack Brymer, my old teacher, came along to do the Mozart clarinet concerto, with Beethoven's *Eroica* Symphony, then we had Peter Katin performing the Rachmaninov *Rhapsody on a theme of Paganini*, along with *William Tell* and Tchaikovsky's *Pathétique*

Symphony. I played in a performance of Elgar's *Dream of Gerontius* and at another concert we did Vaughan Williams' *Sancta Civitas,* along with *The Bells* by Rachmaninov and so on. It was a great opportunity to get to know standard classical works from the inside, and was a good antidote to all the academic studies which I was doing at Goldsmiths College. This was real music brought to life! Many of us in the orchestra played for the Lewisham Operatic Society whose shows were well produced, with good singers, professional stage managing and always enjoyed by all concerned. I remember doing one week of *My Fair Lady*, which had some marvellous orchestration and was a delight to play, even though it was quite technically demanding, and had sudden tempo changes which required keeping a very watchful eye on the conductor. We also did *Bless the Bride* by Vivian Ellis and almost had a disaster just before the opening night, when the leading man lost his voice completely; the original singer in the West end production, Georges Guétary, came down to help out. He sat in the pit to sing while poor, voiceless Gordon Pole did an extremely good job at miming. Gordon's voice was better by the Saturday evening, but even he realised he was no competition against the genuine West End article, and Georges continued to sing the part. I was to bump into Gordon nearly 40 years later, when I was lecturing on a Saga cruise to the Baltic capitals. It's a small world. There was a very colourful production of Ivor Novello's *Glamorous Night*, and though the music may seem sentimental to some, I enjoy these melodies. I took part in a production of *The King and I* in 1968 which I still remember. After rehearsals, and playing for the show night after night the tunes just stay in your head all day going round and round, it's quite hard to think of any other music, and I'm always grateful for the opportunity of playing the clarinet in those shows.

The end of the summer term was certainly a case of burning the candle at both ends, for I was busy preparing a big concert at school, playing the clarinet in at least three orchestral concerts in Lewisham and taking my degree examination at the end of the first year. This was an internal affair, the real preliminary exam would come a year later; Perhaps it was a matter of weeding out any candidates who had not completed satisfactorily, and also to give us a taste of what examination work would be like. Breaking up for the summer holidays took on a real significance, for I was badly needing a break. I decided rather impetuously to take my car off to the Cotswolds without booking any accommodation – the idea was to stay where I wished and for as long as I wished. But, after three days I felt so desperately lonely, and realizing that my brother John didn't live too far away, I rang and asked if I could go and stay with them. So I ended up taking their son out for walks in the pram and having occasional days out, but always with the company of my brother and his wife in the evening. Holidays alone are tough. I think it's the mealtimes that make one feel isolated. When you enter a restaurant, the waiter realises you are alone and you are put somewhere in the corner as though you have a disease, and finish up reading a book while you eat, and between courses, because there's nothing else to do. Matters are made worse when couples and families come in to make their meal a social event, with talk and laughter, and may notice the person in the corner, who is probably branded as 'odd'. I'm sure that anyone who has been on their own and is reading this can identify with the situation. In these circumstances you just want to bolt the food down and get out as fast as possible.

I did yet another year at BMS summer schools. At the pre-holiday conference I met up with one of the secretaries from head office who was to be the summer school secretary. She was very pleasant, and we arranged to go out a couple of times, and I was going to drive her down to Seaford for the holiday. Something went wrong right at the beginning of the holiday; I don't know what it was to this day, but I just went 'off her' and couldn't wait for the end of the holiday to drive her home and part company. What on earth was wrong with me? Christine was a lovely girl, and I know that she married within two or three years and went off to Brazil with her husband as a BMS missionary, so she got the right guy.

I returned to Coopers for what was to be the last year of Miss Anderson's reign as headmistress. The work at school became harder as music developed, with more peripatetic staff popping in to teach various instruments, establishment of the school orchestra and the university work piling up inexorably. I also began to organise evening trips to London, to take pupils to see operas and ballets. There was very little time for any kind of social activity out of school, or perhaps I wasn't interested. I know at this time I also had quite a crush on one of the pupils

– that situation seemed inevitable when teaching over 400 of them. She was a beautiful girl, with a tremendous sense of humour and fun, loved music and was an extremely good pianist. Sometimes our Friday music mornings in assembly would consist of the two of us playing piano duets to the school. I think some of the senior girls must have noticed the look on my face as Audrey's hands touched mine in the course of the music. I seriously considered waiting until she had left school, and marrying her, for I know we would have got on well together. Unfortunately it never turned out that way. Today I think she is the proud mother of five children, and I've no idea whether she still plays the piano.

In April that year I took my preliminary examination for the B.Mus. Course. There were at least four papers plus a very hard aural exam, and the customary viva-voce, when one was expected to talk intelligently on any subject which the examiner chose to throw at the candidate. We took these examinations along with students from the Royal College of Music, King's College and various technical colleges around London, and our numbers at Goldsmiths were whittled down to 15 when the results came out. After that ordeal I was able to go on to the next round of subjects and topics, but was already feeling that I had taken on much more than I could cope with.

In March, 1969 my sister was married. It had been a long courtship, her boyfriend was the brother of one of her best mates at school, and, I believe he was the first person she ever went out with. She had wanted to marry at 18, but my father made her wait for at least two years, presumably to give her time to make sure Jimmy was the right man, and as she had always been the baby daughter, the apple of his eye, I think he wanted to hang onto her as long as possible. I'm certain he didn't take any action to delay the weddings of my brothers, so I assume he credited them with good judgment as far as their girlfriends were concerned.

As July, 1969 drew near we began the celebrations to say farewell to Miss Anderson; these were planned with thought and care, after all she had been head of the school for 20 years, and quite a few of the staff had worked with her all that time. There was a big open day, with sports arranged, recorder groups played, the choirs sang – a very happy Saturday afternoon. A photograph of the whole school was taken, and one of the staff. Then on the 18th July we had the end of term service, singing her favourite hymns, items by the choir, and when she addressed the school I think it was one of the few times when she had to struggle to speak; the tears were very close, but she was a fighter, and would never let the 'gals' see that happen. Stiff upper lip and all that. She spoke the most sensible words as she addressed them, and there were many tears from both senior pupils and staff as she sat down. The school had been her life, 24 hours a day and seven days a week, and now it was going to be taken away. She was certainly the headmistress I most respected and admired in my career. Sadly, after leaving she slowly went to pieces, for she remained living in her tiny flat close by the school – a terrible mistake in my opinion – and used to go up to the school everyday to watch the children as they went home. A number of her close friends and contemporaries had passed away by this time and I think she was desperately lonely. Perhaps that is what is meant when we talk about a "Living sacrifice", for she certainly spent her life caring for Coopers School.

During the holiday I went off to do what was to be my last summer school, I had been involved with them for 14 summers, both as student and member of staff. Things seemed to go wrong on this particular holiday. We had a young man who was obviously trying to be the centre of attraction. He would give away the most expensive cigarettes, buy books for other students, all to give a good impression. Later in the week money went missing from the house as several students reported losses from their wallets, pockets and lockers. On Wednesday night *he* went missing, and as he was in my dormitory I had to report this to the president and secretary. It was 10.30pm. Several of us took out our cars to try to find him, but with no success, so we had to call in the police; we rang the minister of his local church who informed us that the boy was quite a problem at home. There was even mention of suicide –we were only half a mile from Seaford cliffs – and the fear got through to me as I realized what a responsibility we had taken on in looking after these young people .The school president confided in me that he was just praying that he wouldn't have to take news of the boys' death to his parents next day. However the young man was found in the school grounds next morning and was taken home by train to his parents, we had a "whip round" to make good the money which others had lost, but that situation took the edge off what should have been a good holiday. I also found that I was becoming too much of the teacher, I thought some of their pranks were silly and childish and found myself telling them off rather too often, a case of short memory for I had got up to the same tricks 14 years before, as a student. This seemed to be the signal to give up the summer schools and I drove home that weekend in August knowing it would be my last. But what on earth does a single bloke do for holidays? It took a couple of years, but then I found the answer, as we will see in a later chapter.

When the autumn term of 1969 began there were big changes: we had a headmaster, the school began to take in boys for the first time and many of the staff were new, as a number of "old hands" had decided to retire along with Miss Anderson. Mr Gill was quite a different sort of person. To me he seemed laid-back almost to the point of falling over, nothing seemed to excite him and he certainly didn't have the persona and the character of his predecessor. But then she was a very hard act to follow, and I remember on the two occasions when he was introduced to the school in morning assembly she always insisted on referring to him as, "Your headmaster ELECT" – implying, "You're not in charge yet, my friend." Like any new head, he quickly made changes, but life for me went on in the same frenetic way. In addition to my teaching I was taking on piano and clarinet pupils after school and running an evening class once a week. This meant that I was out every weekday evening, dashing to college for lectures, rushing up to London to find books needed for essays and assignments – books which the local library didn't have, then trying to do the degree work at week-ends. I was certainly beginning to equate the B.Mus. degree with 'blood, sweat and tears', and had certainly experienced the last two.

It was the work for the degree which led to buying my first house. At my previous school one of my friends on the staff had married and bought a house using a 'with-profits' endowment insurance as part of the deal, and he had recommended me to take out an insurance in case I ever wanted to get a foot on the property ladder. I took his advice and paid in my monthly premium without thinking much about it. At our council house in Abbey Wood the people next door had moved, and the newcomers were distinctly noisy and getting worse every week, and when one of the teenagers started practicing his drums, and his pop group started rehearsing next door, things just became unbearable. The climax came one evening when I was in my room desperately trying to complete a harmony exercise – trying to think in my head what chords to put on paper, with a background of loud guitar and thudding of drums to help me. It got so bad that I just began punching the wall and went on punching till I thought I would go right through the wall and become part of the band! The noise stopped but I went downstairs and announced to my parents that I'd had enough, I had money in the bank and an insurance policy which would enable me to buy my own house – I was getting out and leaving the nest fast. My father laughed at the whole idea and stated categorically that I would never be able to afford to pay a mortgage. I acted quickly and began to look at houses which might be suitable. Unfortunately I taught in one of the most expensive boroughs in London and soon realised that I would not be able to live anywhere close to the school. Over the next few months I looked at several houses and bungalows which seemed suitable but were too expensive. I had made up my mind to go for a detached house or bungalow so that the neighbour problem would not arise, but it made the task even more difficult. I quickly learnt to interpret some of the house agents' jargon about room size, outward aspects and facilities; often the decorations and alterations which the house owners were so proud of I found quite distasteful. One very lovely bungalow in the village of Kemsing just below the North Downs was going to be my dream home. A little train ran nearby stopping at Kemsing station, this could get me into London within 40 minutes, there was a long, narrow back garden complete with a small stream, and it was detached. Once inside, the proud owners showed me the bar they had set up in their lounge – in the late 60s bars seem to be THE amenity which everyone wanted. This one was made of stone, with flashing lights and mirrors everywhere, and it would have been almost impossible to get rid of it. I kept my opinion of it fairly neutral in conversation with the owner, but decided if I ever got into the bungalow the bar would have to go! In the event I didn't even get the chance, because, having paid for a surveyor's check and report, the couple decided they did not want to sell after all. I looked at properties in Biggin Hill, in Orpington, and Sevenoaks; the property in Sevenoaks was a small bungalow, not far from the centre of a very pleasant town, with easy access both to London and to school at Chislehurst if I was ever without my car, but when I viewed it the place was cold both literally and in a rather spooky way, for everything had been left as if the owner had just died. The agent then informed me that the owner had in fact just died, about four days previously. I picked my way through the rooms very carefully in case I stumbled over a body, but somehow I just didn't warm to the place. It's one thing to see a house with a lived in appearance, but not when bread and butter, teapot and sugar basin are still there on the tablecloth. Perhaps I was still remembering the flat I had lived in close to my previous school, where the old man used to lie in his chair every evening appearing to be dead. So the search continued, and I even persuaded my parents to come with me on one or two occasions; I think my father was secretly a little jealous that he was still stuck in the council house at Abbey Wood. Then I realised I would have to look further afield for a decent affordable house, and went to check out a small three-year-old detached house in East Peckham, a delightful village between Maidstone and Tonbridge which used to be very popular with the hop pickers before and just after the war. Mr and Mrs Bell, the owners, were waiting to move out as soon as possible, to take over a post office at Henley-on-Thames; there was no chain involved, and it looked ideal for me. I quickly set about getting a solicitor, and began filling in all the forms, with my father deriding me all the time. "Why should you be giving these people all your private information and telling them your income? What's it got to do with them how much you earn?"

"Because, Father, if you were going to lend someone £6,000 I think you'd want to know that you had a good chance of getting it back. That's the way things are if you want a mortgage." was my reply. I had partly hit on the reason why he was still stuck in a council house, for he had this crazy idea that nobody should know anything about him, his particulars, his wages, etc. Maybe also he would have been frightened to take on a mortgage; having lived through the Great Depression and into the Second World War when people lost their jobs and their security overnight, perhaps he just wanted to play it safe by paying a weekly rent to the LCC.

The mortgage was eventually granted, and I had to find £500 for the deposit. These figures look ridiculous these days (2006) but my income at this time was only about £250 a month, before tax. So, before the end of summer term the wheels were set in motion for me to move out and into my first house.

Despite my growing feelings about BMS summer school, I returned to Bexhill, which had been the venue for the very first holiday back in 1955. I enjoyed it but after 15 years it really was time to close that chapter of my life. I drove back in the Morris Minor through Kent, doing a detour to East Peckham to check that my little house was still standing; in fact I was getting quite excited with the prospect of moving to my own pad.

It seemed very odd not to be going back to school at the beginning of the new term in 1970. London Borough of Bromley had been quite generous in giving me a sabbatical year in which to complete my degree, and I certainly needed all the time I could get to reach the standard required for finals in 1971. I was still pretty desperate for money and so went in to teach clarinet and piano after school on two evenings a week, but as this was usually combined with attending lectures at Goldsmiths College later, it was no real hardship.

So the course continued, and I completed all the necessary forms and found out about house surveys, mortgage deeds, and so on. I took over the house on the 1st November, and my mother came down to help me get things organised for the move. She had dug out a number of thing she didn't need – tablecloths, pillow cases, cruet set, a teapot and many other little things I had not thought of buying, or couldn't afford. I had been looking around for crockery and cutlery and most of this came from the garages – those were the days when you were offered free knives and forks, or drinking glasses when you bought petrol – I had found a good second hand fridge, bought the cheapest three-piece suite I had ever seen (it didn't last very long) and was given a table and chairs and cupboards by my aunt and uncle. Mum was very pleased with the house, I had bought it complete with carpets and net curtains, so was practically ready to move in my few sticks of furniture. There was a very friendly grocer up the road who lent us a teapot and spoons, which we had forgotten to bring from home; Mum was very impressed with their friendly spirit, and I was to realise that this was the way of life in a country village – people willing to help you and trust you. I couldn't afford professional removers, and didn't really need them. My uncle offered to lend me his van, which meant I had to get up very early on Saturday, drive to Islington, collect the van and drive it back to Abbey Wood where we were going to load my second-hand furniture. I sweated on that journey, for I had never driven anything larger than my Morris Minor, and had to negotiate all the London traffic including a drive through Blackwall Tunnel before I arrived, a nervous wreck, back home. While the family packed everything in the van, I had to go back on the train to North London to collect my own car. My brother-in-law had offered to drive the van down to East Peckham, and I followed behind. So the time came to take possession of 'Tara Devi', East Peckham. Everything was moved in and the family departed, with my father still muttering that he would give me two weeks before I gave in and returned home, Mother worrying whether I could survive on my cooking, and I went to bed that night realising that I only had 10 shillings (50p) to my name. Above my head, in the loft, the tank seemed to be filling in a very noisy way and I went off to sleep wondering what I would do if there was a flood.

I quickly settled in. Someone had offered me a small black and white TV set, which worked except for a large black line going down the middle of the screen, which I could not get rid of, so I had to put up with two small pictures on the screen instead of one. I had made up my mind that I would not neglect my meals or cleaning, I would make the bed first thing in the morning, would do the washing religiously every week, and I did keep to this routine for most of the time I lived there. I must admit that to go through all the motions of cooking a Sunday lunch, complete with roast potatoes, meat, Yorkshire pudding and veg was a chore; it seemed to take about an hour to prepare, and about 10 minutes to eat, but I felt it was important to keep everything clean and shipshape, for perhaps I had the notion that Mum might appear at any time to inspect!. The moving week coincided with half term at college, which was a great help, but then I had to travel up to London almost every day for either lectures or to work in one of the music libraries. It was cheaper not to take the car, but I would pack the usual sandwiches and fruit for lunch and tea – no way could I afford to eat out, every penny was vital. In March of 1971 the nation went decimal, and we all had to remember that 5p equalled a shilling, and 100p made up a pound. The halfpenny was in currency though later it was to be dropped, for it became worthless. The change of currency seemed to make everything more expensive and we took a long time to adapt.

I decided to join the Methodist church in the village, the folk were very friendly and I was able to help them musically. My next-door neighbour, Mrs Acott, was a wonderful old lady who had lived in that area all her life, and was a staunch Methodist. Her husband had been the baker in the village of Yalding, and she had come to live in East Peckham after his death. On about the fourth Sunday when I got home from church the phone rang. "Brian, go and look under the fence outside the back door, and enjoy it." I recognised Mrs. Acott's wonderful Kentish accent and, utterly mystified I did as she asked, and, lo and behold, I found a dish of baked egg custard waiting for me on the floor. This was part of Mrs. Acott's Sunday ritual, she *always* baked an egg custard, and from this time on she baked two, with my little pudding always left under the fence. I must admit that on more than one occasion I forgot to collect it, and wondered why, late in the afternoon, I could hear the squawk of many birds, and on going out I would discover them finishing off my Sunday lunch. She was a good neighbour, and told me many stories about life in the village of Yalding, by the River Medway, where she had grown up. Some of these old people had never even been to London, their lives revolved around their village.

I continued to travel to London for lectures until the end of March when we were left on our own and it was a case of solid revision until finals began in June. In fact, our last lecture was at Kings College in London, and a few of us gathered for a drink as we tried to cheer up and tell ourselves that we WOULD pass our finals although we all felt rather scared at the prospect of the examinations. As I stood on the platform at London Bridge station waiting for the late train back to Paddock Wood I suddenly experienced a terrible fear that I was going to fail, let everybody down, and that the authorities would be less than pleased at the results after giving me a sabbatical year on full pay; for just a fraction of a second I stood on the edge of the platform with a voice telling me to throw myself off and put an end to it all, but just as quickly, thank God, I drew back in alarm – had I spent four years reading, studying, writing essays, harmony exercises and attending countless lectures for nothing? "Oh no," I said to the devil inside me. "Pass or fail, I'm going for this." and quietly told Satan to disappear. It was the only time in my life when I contemplated ending it all. During the Easter holidays Father and Mother came down for a few days, and I was quite proud as I took charge and showed them round, though Mother gradually took over in the kitchen. Even my father admitted it was a lovely little house, and I had done well. What a compliment from him! I took them round the orchards and fields of Kent, where we watched the young lambs and some horses, and Dad was very happy. I took them home after the holiday and then rolled my sleeves up for six weeks of revision.

I prepared a programme of revision and tried to keep to a fairly strict routine, getting down to work by nine o'clock in the morning and going through until lunch, then, after a short break, perhaps a walk or a trip to the shops, I would go back to studies until five. In the evening I would play some of the music which I needed to get into my head, and go to bed wondering how I could keep any of this knowledge in my brain. On April 6th I was busy reading up the life and music of Stravinsky when suddenly the announcer on Radio 3 told the world that Stravinsky had just died. It was uncanny, in my revision notes I had just written his date of birth…. almost as though someone was looking down on me as I worked; I quickly amended my notes to read: STRAVINSKY, Igor (1882-1971) and carried on trying to assimilate all the facts of his life and music, to be ready for the "Music of the 20th Century" paper.

In June came the climax of four years hard grind, when I went up to London University to take finals papers at Birkbeck College. There seemed to be no end of written papers, a gruelling aural test – certainly the hardest I've ever had to take. The examiner used an electronic keyboard and at one stage seemed to drop his elbows down in a random manner resulting in an excruciating sound, and then we had to write down the lowest and highest notes we could hear. It seemed crazy. Just a few days after the written papers I had to return to London for the vive voce – a "live" interview where the examiner may ask some questions in connection with the written papers or put out a subject in which the candidate might display his knowledge, while he sometimes acts as 'devil's advocate' in putting forward an opposite point of view. When I sat down to face the examiner my heart sank on hearing his first words: "Well, you certainly seem to rank Elgar very highly."

I wondered whether he was being slightly sarcastic, for, in fact in one of my written papers there had been an opportunity to go to town on the music of Edward Elgar, and I had certainly taken advantage of it and written pages of script with many themes – Elgar always has been on my list of top composers. Maybe I had overdone it and written too much to the detriment of other questions. I replied that maybe I had 'gone over the top' with my Elgar question, but the examiner replied immediately: "I don't think you need be making excuses for Elgar, Mr Astell, he doesn't need any defending." This reassured me, and I went on to further discourse on Elgar's music and other composers. It is quite a harrowing experience for one can never prepare for the viva, and I came out feeling completely shattered. Tiredness was soon overcome by sheer joy as I realised that the whole business was finally over, except the result. I had promised myself to go and buy a large number of LPs after finals, and I headed off to my favourite shop in Camden Town to collect the many musical treasures I had already ordered from the Greek gentleman owner. He always greeted me by name, and we would have a little chat. There was a slightly amusing incident in the shop, as one young man came in and asked about the "Underground"; I tried to be helpful and pointed out that Camden Town station was just down the road, and he turned round and asked me whether I was trying to be funny, then asked again for the underground. Mr. Greek gentleman intervened and pointed out a selection of records on the left-hand side of the shop, and there I saw the display sign "Underground". It was some type of pop music which many young people seemed to be enjoying at that time; but I was such a square and had been so cocooned in all my B.Mus stuff that I had never heard of it. Mr Greek laughed about the whole thing before I set off home, anxious to listen at last to music just for its own pleasure – no notes to make, no themes to write out, and no nasty composers who I disliked – it was sheer heaven.

I could have stayed off from school until the end of term, but I did go back for three weeks to sort out the music department. A temporary teacher had been put in my place, but everything had to be put back in order again and I did help with the summer concert which had been planned for the end of term. One of the English department commented that I looked as though I needed a holiday, and invited me to join her school party which was going off to Greece in the summer.

178

I jumped at this opportunity, a chance to get away completely from music and to have a holiday with good company, and at a price I could afford. The examination results came out within a few days and I discovered I had achieved a second-class honours degree – I had become a B.Mus (hons), so there was a great time of congratulation and a few drinks in the staff room. I went home on the last day of term very happy, with the prospect of six lovely weeks in which to relax and read whatever I wanted, but equally determined that I would never again take a music examination of any kind.

CHAPTER THIRTEEN

MOVING ON FROM COOPERS

The summer holidays gave me a wonderful chance to relax after the hard labour of the previous four years working for the degree, so I looked forward to joining with staff and pupils on a holiday to Greece at the end of July. It was a pity we chose the hottest month of the year, but we had some very enjoyable times. Sue Ingle, the English mistress, was in charge; she had been to Greece on holiday with her doctor fiancé, John, on a number of occasions, and knew how to handle the Greeks, and to give us sound advice and information before the holiday; her friend, another member of the English department, was Sandy Dorne, who loved the sun and the easy-going life in Mediterranean countries; also travelling was Richard Ely, a young modern languages teacher who also happened to be very interested in music and played the organ – he was not going to stay at Coopers as a teacher for long, destined for better things and a quick climb up the educational ladder, until he became the director of education for Dorset. I made up the foursome. The students were all sixth formers, very attractive and nubile, who realised they were continually admired by all the Italian and Greek men, and at first certainly took advantage of the attraction, though they soon became irritated with all the men hanging around them, especially some who looked old enough to be their granddad; our task was to try to keep them apart, not a very easy process!

We travelled down from Ostend by train to Milan, stopping at the wonderful Central Station which looked more like a palace, one of the examples of Mussolini buildings before the war, and had just a few hours break for food and sightseeing before boarding our next train which was to take us all the way down the east coast to Brindisi. How we needed to get out and stretch our legs after the long haul in the train! From there we waited to catch the ferry across the sea to Patras; the girls soon realised that our traditional British way of queuing and waiting patiently was quite non-existent in this part of the world. When the ferry came in it was every man for himself, and girls were screaming, crushed and pushed as we all tried to get on the boat, while others were pushing to try to get off. Complete chaos, but somehow we all survived, and during the long crossing we found places to lie on the deck and get some sleep. Looking back after 30 or so years, it seems amazing that we didn't just get a plane to Athens, but flights were very expensive then, we were quite poor, especially the staff, and so we did it the hard way. The coach waited for us and took us to Athens – though there was a hold-up when we got a puncture – and we stayed in a hotel for a couple of days so that we could see the sights of the Acropolis, the open-air theatre and museums. Our guide was very keen to talk to us about the Greek way of life and politics, but we had been warned to steer clear of the subject, after all, this was the time of the Greek colonels and one never knew who was listening in on conversations in cafés and on the streets. We visited Delphi to see the site of the Pythian games, which seemed to be a younger brother of the Olympic Games first held at Olympus on the other side of the mainland. One could imagine the shot put, javelin, marathon and all the other events which have come down to the present-day. On one hot evening Richard and I went to the Herod Atticus open air theatre next to the Acropolis for a concert, featuring a Brahms piano concerto. While enjoying the atmosphere I was wondering at all the music and events which had taken place there since it was built around 160 AD ! What a history! After a couple of days we travelled across the Corinthian Canal to the seaside resort of Nàvplion, then a very quiet backwater, though I believe it is teeming with holidaymakers these days. It was a good base from which to explore Epidaurus further round the coast, where there is a huge outdoor theatre, still used. It was amazing to think that 15,000 spectators could hear quite clearly every word from the stage area with no amplification whatsoever. Sue had taken into account the heat and the tiring journey which we had undertaken, so that we only visited one site each day, and had a lovely day off in Nàvplion just to unwind and relax.

Then it was off on another ferry to Crete where we had delightful accommodation in the port of Heraklion with a private family who had a fair sized dormitory for the students and a couple of bedrooms for the staff. I don't remember the owner's name, but I'll call her Mrs Popodopoulos; she couldn't do enough to make our stay pleasant and enjoyable; the meals were fantastic, all home-cooked, lovely concoctions with vine leaves, rice and pasta. I know the staff appreciated this, but students, who I always found to be incredibly conservative about food, may not have appreciated how lucky they were to have well-cooked proper Greek food. Unfortunately Richard went down with a stomach bug, and I didn't enjoy sharing a room where he was throwing up every hour or so. On one evening, with the girls safe in their dormitory and getting ready for bed hopefully, Mrs P promising to keep an eye on things, and Richard still looking like death warmed up, in the bedroom, the three of us ventured into the town for a drink of retsina; as we made our way back to the house it was still very warm and I didn't relish spending yet another night with the invalid, so Sue suggested that as there were a couple of spare beds in the dormitory and the girls would all be asleep, I could 'kip' down there as long as I didn't undress. This seemed like a good idea and I tiptoed into the dorm, found the bed near the door and settled down for the night. Early next morning one girl woke very early, decided to have a wander round and discovered me on a bed. Before she cried out – and she was rather an emotional type – I explained the position quietly and asked her not to wake everybody up. She agreed to this and I slipped on my shoes and crept away. Of course, when the others woke up and Vivien told them I had been sleeping in the dormitory nobody believed her. "Having nightmares again, Vivien; he wouldn't dare sleep in here with us, would he?"

Later in the day I had to come clean and own up for the sake of poor Vivien, and soon 20 girls were writing 20 postcards back to England telling the folk at home what a wonderful adventure they were having, and how the music master cared so much for their protection he had spent the night with them all! We had a chance to spend two or three days lounging on the beach, swimming and thoroughly enjoying the Greek weather, while Richard, still feeling sorry for himself, cut a lonely figure in the deckchair, wide umbrella over his head, four days growth on his chin and a jacket and tie on – the figure of Dirk Bogarde in the film *Death in Venice* came to mind, and even today whenever I watch the film I think back to

Crete and poor, sick Richard. We visited the Palace of Knossos, home of King Minos, on the site which went back to at least 6000BC. It was only a few miles from Heraklion, and we wondered why there were so many coaches coming away from the palace, but when we reached the place at about midday it was just boiling! All the sensible people had gone to visit in the comparative coolness of the morning and were heading back to the port to get out of the sun and have a siesta. But not us, intrepid explorers that we were, we left the bus to walk across a large open space and I've never felt so hot in my life; the sun literally beat one down, and we reached some shade and flopped down until we got our strength back. Later we did the tour of the palace – almost the only people there – returned in the coach, grabbed our swimming things and waded into the sea, ready to cool down after the exhausting temperatures we had experienced.

All good things come to an end, and we had to eventually make our way back to Piraeus by ferry where we were to catch a train on a nightmare journey that was to take us up through the Balkans, through Italy and Austria, terminating in Salzburg. The train just became more and more crowded and for quite a time I was separated from the main party. The order was for the girls to try to stay in their seats otherwise they would be taken over by the locals who were pouring on at every station. Corridors were heaving with people, it was very hot and some of them must have stood for over 24 hours. When we stopped at a station people would get out, or, rather, fall out, and buy watermelons to quench their thirst. We finally reached Salzburg and both us and the engine heaved a sigh of relief, and alighted on to a quiet platform, though in the course of moving through the corridor I came across an old man lying with his hands pressed into half a watermelon – he never moved at all, and I was convinced he had been crushed to death in the cramped conditions; should I tell the authorities about it? I decided it was best to keep 'schtum' because we might have been delayed and missed our connection – yes, yet another train – through to Ostend and the ferry. That long journey through Greece and the Balkans was not so much a journey as an endurance test, and I think the girls were marvellous to put up with the conditions without any serious complaints, and we all laughed about our experiences when we settled down on our cross channel ferry. The main party went off to Victoria, soon to be reunited with their parents and boyfriends, and a chance to tell everyone about their adventures, though I suspect some of the girls left out the stories of the boys they had teamed up with on holiday. I left the party at Dover, and caught a train to Paddock Wood and home to East Peckham, to enjoy the rest of the summer holiday, with no essays to write, deadlines to meet, or set books – it was bliss.

Beginning of September, and it was back to school for the new term. Within a few days of returning I realised that the school had changed during the year I had been away – and not for the better. Discipline in the corridors and in going to and from assembly had deteriorated; children were noisy, often running down the corridor, and walking along in groups, and whereas in the old days pupils would have stepped aside for a member of staff, and even offered to carry books, now, they wouldn't budge – it was a member of staff who had to step aside and get out of the way. No longer did children worry about having their hymn books for assembly, no one seemed to care; under the previous head there would be absolute silence as she entered the hall, but now some of the pupils were still talking as they grudgingly stood for the headmaster while he made his way to the platform. It all came home to me in a rather special way when I was about four weeks into the term; a class of the new first years came into the music room and sat down – I had always insisted that the class stand at the beginning of lessons until I told them to be seated – and one girl immediately leaned her head back and put her feet up on the nearest chair. This was a complete replica of the incident I had gone through at my first school, but this time the pupil in question was only 11. Watched by the others, she treated me to some rich language, and I took exception to being called 'a bloody old fool', so I grabbed her by her black hair and blouse and marched her off to the headmaster's study, having threatened the rest of the class to stay quiet or else… During his first year he had installed an electric sign by his door which told the intending visitor he was either "1.Engaged 2.NOT to be disturbed 3.Free, please knock", and on this occasion the sign proudly told us he was NOT TO BE DISTURBED; I decided to ignore this command, knocked sharply and went straight in, to be greeted by the headmaster reading The Times with *his feet firmly on the desk*. When I told him what had happened, there, in front of the pupil

184

he said, "Mr. Astell, I don't think we can be too harsh about the language they use, you know, it's the homes they come from."

At this reply I told the girl to leave the office, shut the door, go to the other end of the corridor and wait, and then I turned on him and retorted, "With the greatest respect, I don't think you should have said that in front of the pupil, she will probably be laughing all the way back to the classroom; you have taken away the last ounce of respect, and, as it happens, I grew up in a home with bad language from my own father every day. Surely if we are in the business of education we are trying to lift pupils from this situation, show them another way, and not just accept bad behaviour and language as the norm." Phew what a mouthful, but I felt better for saying it. He looked quite mystified and, telling me that the deputy head would deal with the matter, asked me to return to my class, presumably so that he could carry on reading the newspaper and "NOT BE DISTURBED". That was when I realised that the school was no longer for me, and I would begin to look around for another job. In fact, it took over two years and many applications before I moved on.

School continued in the same way, with discipline falling, to my mind, though there had been such a change of staff when the previous headmistress had left that many of the new staff had no perception of this, but the staff who had served under Miss Anderson certainly noticed a difference. I carried on with the usual round of concerts, kept the orchestra and choirs going, but with less enthusiasm.

Life in my village at East Peckham picked up. I had joined the Methodist church and made many friends, including the minister, David Butler, who was in his first church appointment. He and his wife, Fionna, often asked me to a meal as did a number of the members; I recall an intriguing cheese fondu which he served for his guests.

One last reminder of my four years hard slog to get the B. Mus. came in May 1972 when I was invited to go to the Royal Albert Hall to be presented with my degree certificate by the Queen Mother, who was chancellor of London University. My father refused to go so my mother took along my sister's mother-in-law for company. I think we drove up in the Morris Minor, parking at an underground station and getting the train for the final stage, because parking would be impossible at the hall. So, along with several hundred other graduates I lined up, wearing my gown and hood, to be presented to her Majesty. Mother and Mrs Bambrough were very impressed with the whole ceremony – it was the first time that either of them had been in the Royal Albert Hall, so quite an occasion. We did not go off for a celebratory meal as most candidates did, but just drove home and had our normal tea. Like all the big occasions I have experienced, there has never been any fuss or chance to show off. But 10th May, 1972 is the day I will remember as the climax of all the hard work to gain the coveted degree. It was worth it, especially as it helped me to get my next teaching post.

In 1972 my parents moved from Abbey Wood. Ironically, having put up with very overcrowded conditions for many years, they now found themselves in a house that was really too large; we had all 'flown the nest', and they were still living in a four bedroom house. Mother was not rushing to move, for she still loved the house and spent many hours keeping it spotless, but she was now in her sixties and it was pointless cleaning empty bedrooms. Although I had moved to my own home in East Peckham, there were still many occasions when I had been glad to put up at home, especially in the time leading up to my finals. This time my father organised the move in conjunction with the GLC (Greater London Council). They went to live in a first-floor, two bedroom flat in North Chingford, an area which was the constituency of Norman Tebbit, later to become "The Chingford strangler" during the days of Margaret Thatcher's premiership. I never knew whether Father enjoyed being in a Tory stronghold. I was scanning the pages of the TES (Times educational supplement), completing application forms for posts, and wondering why I never got to the interview stage. I applied to Benenden – the prestigious school in Kent which some of the Royal family had attended, and perhaps that was rather a cheeky effort, probably they would only interview people from public schools or the posh end of the state system. I applied for a post at Ashford Grammar School, with no luck, and the Weald of Kent School quite close to home – a job which would have allowed me to stay in my home at East Peckham, I was very disappointed not to get that job.

During the early part of the summer through attending one of the social events in the Methodist church, I had met up with a very nice family who had three children, a girl of 18, her younger sister about 14 and their younger brother who was around seven. The father worked on one of the large estates near Tonbridge and was responsible for the large orchard of apples and pears, and they lived in a cottage on the estate. I was invited to have a meal with them, and my music was a point of contact with the family, particularly the two girls. In short, they invited me to share their holiday at Lands End in Cornwall in a cottage they took over, a place that was less than a mile from Lands End itself. The plan was for me to take the eldest girl in my car so that the rest of the family had more space, and could fit in all the hundred and one holiday things one needs. The parents were very nice and made me so welcome, and I think they had high hopes that the daughter and I would make a couple, but their young boy was an absolute menace. He always behaved like a spoiled brat. Everything we did revolved around the wishes and whims of 'that boy', and he began to get on my nerves. In truth, I realised after a few days that I had no real feelings for the girl, and the holiday became tiresome, for she tried to organise each day so that we were alone, away from the family as often as possible. Cornwall was very pleasant, and I realised years later how lucky I was to stay at Lands End before it became commercially organised. When I went back in the early 90s, I couldn't believe it was the same place; there was a huge car park and you actually had to pay to go on the site to Lands End, with all its tacky cafés, merry-go-rounds, haunted houses, animals, and there tucked away in a dip was the famous landmark with the signs pointing the direction and the mileage to other countries. I was rather surprised they didn't charge people to photograph that landmark, and perhaps these days they have even plugged that loophole. In 1972 I saw it completely unspoilt, with a few animals grazing almost down to the cliff edge, and the chance to watch the sea in its various moods in complete silence – a memory which has been lost forever to present and future generations. The holiday came to an end and I drove the daughter home, I don't think I ever saw her again, and can't even remember her name or the name of the family. Another lost opportunity?

The new term began at Coopers and once again I was again scanning the Teachers Bible – the TES for possible music posts. I had found it strange that in all the applications made, only one had got me through to an interview, so I asked the headmaster for a testimonial. "Quite unnecessary, Brian," he said, "I will give you a reference and am always ready to answer questions on the phone." But I insisted on having a testimonial so that I would see in print what he had to say about me to prospective employers. Reluctantly he did give me a fine testimonial, and I took the attitude that with something written and signed by him, he could hardly go back on his word if any head happened to phone him about my suitability for a post. I noticed a job being advertised at Woodford Green, Essex. It was to head the music department and carried a scale 4 allowance – which in those days was one step below senior teacher and deputy head allowances – a very generous post. After making some enquiries about the school, which had brilliant results each year and a large proportion of pupils going on to study at Oxbridge, I came to the conclusion that I stood very little chance of getting that job, but something made me apply in writing. Just before school broke up at Christmas I received the news that I had been put on the shortlist, would be given an invitation to visit the school at the beginning of term and an interview would be arranged. They were certainly getting organised very early, for the new job would not start until January, 1974, and here they were 12 months before organising interviews.

Early the next term I took a day off from school and visited Woodford, and what I saw and heard made me really determined to get the job. The school was a former bishop's palace, on the A11 going towards Loughton and Epping Forest, set in quite substantial grounds and right opposite Woodford Green itself, complete with cricket pitch, pavilion and a large statue of Winston Churchill, who at one time had been MP for Woodford and Epping Forest. I discovered later that the Labour Prime Minister, Mr Clement Attlee, had also lived in Woodford Green, so it was quite a posh place. I met the head of music, Miss Drybrough who had worked there for 28 years, was very happy and looking forward to retirement. After being taken around the school by her, we went into the hall and I saw not one but two grand pianos – a beautiful Blüthner on the stage, and a Broadwood down in the hall itself. What an opportunity for two-piano works! She seemed rather embarrassed at having to ask me to play the piano, but I accepted it as a natural requirement, and when she produced a volume of Beethoven sonatas I asked her to select one for me to play; this was a bit cheeky, but I did want her to realise

188

that I could bash my way through most of the early and middle period Beethoven. Before I had finished playing two pages, Miss Drybrough stopped me and said that she was more than satisfied.

I have mentioned this in detail because years later when I left the school, my permanent successor could not play the piano at all, and this was a disaster, leading to him being moved to another school in the borough, which he gladly accepted. It seems perfectly obvious to me that to be any sort of music teacher requires keyboard skills of a high standard, after all, you would hardly have an art teacher that couldn't draw or paint, but the sad fact is that school heads often don't set this out as a requirement, and even sadder is the fact that through the years far fewer applicants have been able to offer keyboard skills

Lunchtime was an experience in itself. The staff ate in a beautiful wood-panelled room complete with chandelier and large oak table and were waited on by the pupils, who brought tureens and dishes to the table, poured out the water, and generally treated us like royalty. This was quite different to the usual business of eating with pupils amid all the noise and chaos of a dining hall – lunch at Woodford was an enjoyable, relaxing experience, and the food was great. This made me even more determined to get the job!

Later in the day I went in to meet the headmistress, Miss Joyce Satchell, and her dog, Robbie, a cocker spaniel who lay under the desk, but came out wagging his tail to greet me with a ball; I naturally made friends with the dog, and then was informed that of the six short-listed candidates I was the only one who had taken advantage of the invitation to make a preliminary visit, even though a couple of the applicants lived and worked within the borough of Redbridge. Woodford was the only girls grammar school, and Ilford County High was the boys counterpart. Pupils were selected by the 11+ exam, much to the annoyance of the ten or so comprehensive schools in Redbridge. I am convinced that this preliminary visit helped me to get the job.

As I mentioned earlier, my parents had moved to Chingford, and this was only about ten minutes ride away in the car, so, later in the afternoon, I headed off to see them, and try to do justice to the usual large meal which mother had prepared in spite of the fact that I'd had an enormous meal at lunchtime with the staff – and told them all about the job, a job I really wanted.

So, the day of the interviews came, and I duly presented myself back at Woodford, along with five other short-listed candidates. We sat in a semicircle in the room and were given an introductory talk by the headmistress, who mentioned that I had taken the trouble to visit the school earlier, and then Robbie the dog came from under her desk with his rubber bone and placed it at my feet… was this a magic omen, I wondered? We were then interviewed individually by the head and borough music adviser, and while waiting for our turn some gave the impression that they weren't all that worried if they didn't succeed. The presence of the music adviser made me a little anxious, for I knew that at least two of the candidates worked in local Redbridge schools and he might want to recommend them. Once again there was the added bonus of a superb lunch, and we had the opportunity to meet other members of staff. My turn for the interview eventually came, and I've forgotten everything that took place except that it was impressed upon me that with the large subject allowance which went with the job I was expected to put in plenty of out-of-school time; I nearly burst out that I would willingly devote all the hours God gave if I was appointed. I certainly did express willingness to put my shoulder to the wheel, and keep up the standards of choirs, orchestra and madrigal group which my predecessor had set. Later in the afternoon there was a long, nail-biting recession while the decision was being made; at about 3.30pm the deputy head came to the door and asked me if I would return – I was offered the post and gladly accepted. I was to be the new head of music at Woodford County High school from January, 1974, and I drove back across London to East Peckham with my head in the clouds. This appointment meant that I had nearly ten months to serve out at Coopers, surely a record in school staff appointments, normally it would be about half a term between appointment and taking up the new job. I tried to keep my enthusiasm going, and certainly was not going to reveal my departure to the pupils until much nearer the time.

During this school year, John Buckle, the physics master at Coopers had discovered that I played the piano accordion and I went off to play for him at a couple of folk dances at which he was calling. Later he suggested that I might form a small folk group to play for one or two of his local 'gigs', and I selected a handful of pupils and we set too, practicing a number of reels and jigs. Thinking back, I believe we had Vicky on banjo, certainly a clarinet, for I had to transpose all the music up one tone for Mary our clarinettist, there was a violinist and flautist, and when we went to play in Bromley for a local church hop we were all rather scared – this was a professional job, and we were getting paid. We were skating on thin ice – I can remember that we had just enough tunes for the dances on the programme and if anyone had shouted for an encore or special number we would have been finished. So "The Pitchforks" was launched on an unsuspecting, innocent public. That first dance was quite successful and we went on to do a few more, even after I left the school I fulfilled the engagements we had already taken on. This folk music was a new interest which was to become a more important part of my life for the next 25 years.

At the end of the summer term I was feeling very low, and wished, desperately, that I could have left Coopers to take up my new job in September. I was very fond of someone at the school, but was 'ditched' on May 14th – her birthday, and this hurt a great deal; it is so hard to have to face someone every day when this has happened, and the pain took a long while to go away, indeed perhaps it has never really gone away. It's better not to go into any details, but I was glad to get away down to Kent for the summer holidays, still destined to stay at Coopers for one more term.

Now that I was no longer doing the Baptist summer schools it was hard to find an attractive holiday, and, still hoping to find someone who might become Mrs Astell, I was interested in the 18-30 club which offered holidays in Corfu. I was outside the age range, but they were happy to take my booking and I flew off to Corfu in midsummer looking for a rest, good scenery and perhaps to make friends with some people of my own age. The holiday turned out to be a disaster! We flew into the airport and were transported up to the northwest part of the island. The accommodation was in a fairly old building, with large bedrooms, high ceilings but no air-conditioning or fans, just ever-open windows. I found I was sharing a room with three other blokes, but a different three each day. In my naïveté I did not realise that, in fact, this was like a 'knocking shop', where the object was to find a girl you fancied and spend the night with her, either in her room or yours. This came home to me very quickly when, on the third day I was asked to change rooms so that the others could bring their girls back to our room. Rather unwillingly I moved all my stuff to another room but a couple of days later I was asked to move again; more grudgingly I moved to yet another room, but when, the next day I was asked to move out again I refused and told the other occupants they could do what they liked in the room but I was NOT, definitely NOT, moving any more! Young people were flying in and out of the resort every day so it was hard to make friends. I soon came to understand the shallow attitude of some of the men, watching them plead eternal devotion to a girlfriend, arranging to meet back home... glowing future together, etc. and then 24 hours later when a new 'batch of chicks' had arrived, they were off swearing eternal devotion to someone else. It made me rather sick of the whole process. I did meet up with one girl who was quieter and more reserved than the others and we went on a couple of good excursions together, visiting an island, swimming in a gorgeous warm sea and having a fish lunch, some of the best fish I'd ever eaten. The trouble was when I went to bed at about midnight the others were all just going off to dance the night away at the discos nearby, and so close that with open windows it was impossible to get to sleep. My pattern became one of sleeping during the afternoon when the sun was hot, and I realised why all the Mediterranean people are sensible enough to have a siesta. I was quite daring one day when I hired a moped and took to the hills. In the towns the traffic was pretty chaotic and mopeds were highly dangerous things to ride, but up in the hills it was very peaceful with little traffic but the downside was the dreadful condition of the roads. I stopped in a typical hilltop village for lunch and a drink and tried to have a conversation with the locals, while I ate some beautiful Greek food. They seemed to feel I was very courageous to make the journey on the moped and told me to look out for the wild animals when I made the descent into town. I thought they were joking, but they assured me that there were bears around and wild boar which often came into the road. Then the outing took on a serious side, for when I went to mount the moped I found there was a very flat front tyre – the journey over the dreadful road had caused a bad puncture and had holed the tyre. Somebody rang the moped shop and I was told to wait for someone to come up to the village. Two hours later it was getting dark and I was worried, there were no lights on the moped, and I was very relieved when a small lorry appeared; I expected the driver to shove the moped on the lorry and for me to get a lift back, but, no, he insisted on changing the wheel and left me to ride back in semi-darkness on unlit roads with potholes everywhere, and the fear of one of these wild animals coming out. I was so relieved to get back to the shop in one piece, collect my deposit and leave the wretched moped. But at least it was a day out and a good chance to meet with the local people. I enjoyed the island, and coped quite well with the very high temperatures, but in most respects I was quite glad to get the plane back home to good old England.

I had made no long-lasting friendships on holiday and I wondered how many broken hearts there were back in England as so many of the girls expected their holiday romances to flourish. Out of curiosity, as I am writing, I decided to look at the Club 18-30 website, and read what it has to offer these days: *"And what Kavos hasn't got, you'll never need! Great venues, pumping club nights and tons of bars to suit every taste, mood and pocket! Add go-karts, water sports and restaurants and you're talking holiday heaven!"* Well, it's not my idea of a holiday heaven.

At the Methodist church, David Butler had moved on to another post, part of the quaint Methodist rule that ministers aren't usually allowed to stay longer than three years in any one church. It seems such a pity that after building up the membership, making friends and settling into the place, Methodist rules require you to leave, presumably because Charles Wesley the founder was always moving on, leaving the new church behind, and perhaps the powers that be are frightened that people will become too attached to the minister. Over the years I've seen it thoroughly upset families, especially when the children's education is so irregular – little wonder that so many of the children have nothing to do with the church later on. David and Fiona became great friends. I discovered at one point that they were deeply upset because they found they could not have children; both had been through the interminable tests, and the only choice left was to adopt – which they did later. It affected Fiona especially, living in a village community with a number of young couples who kept producing their bouncing babies; one day she came in for a cup of tea and just burst out in sadness and anger, "If another doting mother insists on showing me her new baby in its new pram I think I shall just scream and run away." I had discovered the problem they had to live with from day-to-day in the village, going through a traumatic experience, but having to keep the stiff upper lip expected of the minister and his wife. He always had to be at the end of the phone, and they never seemed to get any time to themselves. I produced my spare key and told them that on their day off they should regard my house as their little escape nest, no one need know, the phone would not ring and they would have some quality time. On a few Mondays they took me up on the offer, after all I was at school and the house was empty. David and I were to meet up again many years later, as we shall see. In his place came Martin and Ruth Wray, quite different people, but very friendly and eager to settle down to village life and that of the church. At the beginning of the holidays they were both going down to stay with relations in Dorset and kindly invited me to go along with them – it was just what I needed to cheer myself up. They both had a wonderful wicked sense of humour and we had lots of opportunities to laugh together. We were staying in Sturminster Newton in a beautiful part of the Dorset countryside, with meadows and stream running close by the house. On one of our excursions we went into the inevitable second-hand bookshop and I bought a music book; when we got back home I was showing Martin some photographs including the great pianist Arthur Schnabel's hands, and for some reason he found this extremely funny that someone should take a picture of a dead musician's hands – I started laughing at him laughing and we were just reduced to tears. For years afterwards whenever I spoke to him I only had to say, "Arthur Schnabel's hands!" and we would be off again.

September came round all too quickly and I was back for my last term at Coopers. During the holidays I had decided reluctantly to sell the Morris Minor, it had been an excellent car over eight years, never let me down unless we count the two occasions when I was in the middle of a field and the car got bedded down in mud; I had needed help in towing the car out, and faced some embarrassing looks as the helpers wondered what on earth I was doing in the middle of a muddy field. Yes, I was entertaining a girlfriend on each occasion! There was no problem selling the Morris, someone turned up as soon as I advertised, and bought it for his daughter, in fact I think I undersold, but they were willing to hang on until I had collected my new car. I was quite impressed with my new Triumph Toledo, with its lovely finish – walnut fascia, leather seats, excellent radio and a general feeling of comfort and space. I should have learned my lesson; whatever induced me to go back to the same West End show rooms where I had bought the Morris in 1965? In fact it was because I was able to get the union discount at Berkeley Square Motors. Going up to collect the new car was another nightmare; I had become a much more experienced driver during my eight years but the traffic in central London had increased enormously, and a new car does take some getting used to. I got it back to Coopers School without mishap and showed it off to staff friends and pupils.

There was great turmoil during the term in school as workmen were moving into the main hall which meant it was out of action for the whole term, including Christmas time when we would have had our Christmas concerts. I think we made arrangements to perform in the local church, but at no point did the headmaster call me in to discuss an end of term service; I felt I was being taken for granted, annoyed that he assumed everything would happen, so I hardly prepared anything; at the last minute a service was cobbled together, and we managed to get the choir and the madrigal group to take part in a school service at St Nicholas's just across the way from the school. There was the usual staff Christmas party, and I was presented with my leaving present – a set of drinking glasses, and a send-off from the headmaster which I like to think was sincere. We certainly had some happy times at the school, and the headmaster was never given an easy ride. There were the lively staff meetings when he would calmly announce some new proposal – he was ALWAYS looking for new ideas and change – and the scripture master, Mr Law, an elderly , conservative, sober Scotsman – typical member of the 'Kirk', would stand up, glare at the head and say, "What you are proposing, Mr Gill, is utterly preposterous!" And he would sit down to murmurs of agreement from most of the staff. Then there was the Martin Gilbert affair. This happened after I had left the school but whenever I met members of staff we all laughed about it, so it's worth repeating here. The episode has striking similarities with a film made in 1934, for which Prokofiev had written the music, later taking the best parts to make into a suite called *Lieutenant Kijé*. In the story an official of the Russian Tzar is negligent and a mistake is covered up by creating a fictitious officer, Lieutenant Kijé. This 'man' was found a wife, took a journey in a Russian troika which has become the most famous movement of Prokofiev's suite; in fact he became a blessing in disguise; he could shoulder the responsibility for all the stupidities committed by the faithful servants of the Tzar, until the day when the Tzar exiled him to Siberia to atone for his errors. Then, in a burst of clemency the Tzar decided to recall the Lieutenant who by now has become a General and the officials have to quickly announce that sadly Kijé has just died. In our non-musical version one of the staff had to invigilate in a scripture exam, found he had nothing to do, so he decided to pass the time doing the exam and putting a fictitious name at the top of the paper – Martin Gilbert. Mr Thomas, the scripture teacher marked the paper and awarded Gilbert 80%. The pair decided to start a report slip, which went round the staff room, most teachers inventing some marks and words of encouragement or sadness on the report of Martin Gilbert. It went as far as the headmaster's remarks and signature; according to Mr Gill, Martin Gilbert had worked very hard during the year! He only became suspicious at the beginning of the next term when pupils had to return the slips with their parents' signature, confirming that they had seen and read their child's report – why had a slip not arrived from Martin Gilbert's parents? I don't think anyone owned up at that point and it became a mystery. Later on sports day, someone found an old silver cup but could not track down who had donated the cup – the school had had it for years; it was polished and presented by Mr Gill on sports day to one of the winners as the Martin Gilbert Memorial cup – apparently our Martin Gilbert also had died and his parents had wanted to make a contribution to the school. Only at this point was it revealed that there was no Martin Gilbert at all; I'm afraid the headmaster took it very seriously and was furious with the staff for this trick. For years afterward on sports day the teacher who would announce the results would often mention that although so-and-so had performed an excellent long jump, or someone else had run a very fast 100 yards, they had not come up to the record which Martin Gilbert had set some years earlier! The staff used to laugh at these statements, but the head always looked grim. On the last day of term I drove home with mixed feelings, on the whole I had enjoyed my time at Coopers, I had made many friends on the staff, am still in touch with one or two over 30 years later, but I was also looking forward to a whole new chapter working at the new school.

End of term at Woodford was a few days later, and I went over to tie up a few loose ends with the retiring music teacher, and to particularly collect some music scores of works which the A level group were studying, so that I could do some preparation during the holidays. Woodford was having a staff pantomime, and somehow I got dragged in to play the piano for one or two songs which I could rattle off. The pupils thoroughly enjoyed seeing the staff dressed up and making fools of themselves; there seemed to be a few rather attractive sixth form girls taking part with the staff, and it was only when I went to the tea party afterwards that I realised these beauties were actually members of staff!

It was a great atmosphere and an exciting introduction to my new school. I had no idea at the time but my next post at Woodford County High would be my last permanent teaching position – I would retire from teaching just before my 48th birthday – but that's all to come.

CHAPTER FOURTEEN

MOVE TO WOODFORD

At the beginning of January, 1974 I drove up from East Peckham to my parents' flat in Chingford, a journey I was to get to know very well during the next couple of years; although I had put my house on the market, it had not sold, indeed it took another 2½ years before I finally moved out of 'Tara Devi'. This meant that I stayed with my parents during the week and generally drove back home on Friday afternoons for the weekend. The staff meeting on the first day was a very civilised affair, rather like Coopers had been, with plenty to eat, and tea served in rather expensive teacups, and lots of conversation about the holidays. Then it was down to the formal meeting, and Miss Satchell took charge with deputy head, Miss Innes looking on with watchful eye. The latter was a very feisty character, very Scottish and although short in stature, she made up for it in her commanding nature. You didn't argue with Miss Innes. Like most deputies, she was aware that we did like to linger in the staff room at the end of morning break, and she would clap her hands and call out, "Ladies, the girls are ready and waiting, please get to your classes." Reluctantly, coffee was drunk quickly and we all went off to 'the gals': just one person, head of English, Mr Goudie, would answer her back, with a phrase like, "Stop fretting, Mary," or even, "Don't get your knickers in a twist, the girls will make up for the few minutes they are kept waiting!" She would stamp her feet at this point and march out, slamming the door firmly behind her. He was the only member of staff to my knowledge who would address the deputy by her Christian name in public, and I think she had a secret desire to get even with him. The head herself was also fairly short in size, but had an almost regal authority about her – indeed, behind her back we often called her 'the Queen'. Obviously they were well in charge of the school and staff, and I think they realised that they had to keep a certain distance from the rest of us. During the meeting I had a chance to look round and discovered there were just two other men, Brian Wheatley, who was head of French and Richard Goudy, head of English. There we were, surrounded by a couple of dozen women, and I was to discover that this was indeed a women's world; the men had no toilet of their own, we shared with the women, and often I was to go into the cloakroom to see one or two wiping back the tears after some problem with the girls or staff, and sometimes, to my embarrassment, they would still be adjusting their underclothes in the cloakroom. There were one or two who positively delighted in being caught displaying their nether garments! I never felt inclined to take advantage of their exhibitionism, certainly not in the women's cloakroom. After that meeting I returned to the flat, really looking forward to my first week of teaching, and set too, to spend two or three hours preparing lessons so that I was well organised in front of these intelligent girls.

First day of term, and assembly. The pattern was always for the music teacher to play the school in to assembly, they came down the corridors in single file, with complete silence on their part, I would accompany the hymn, and play them off to lessons with something suitable. I soon realised there were girls who had already reached grade 7 or 8 in the associated board exams so I always took great care in my own playing. I had a part-time assistant, Judith Liddell, and we soon established Friday mornings as duet morning, and would send the school off with a Dvorak Slavonic dance or a Schubert march, in a happy mood. I had always believed that one could tell the character of the school by the way assembly was conducted. Here there was always silence when required, a sense of dignity and respect – although staff sat with their forms, at the end of assembly the staff left first, partly to let them get off to meet the class in their respective teaching rooms, but also it gave the staff that special dignity; the rest of the school would dismiss in order of seniority, sixth form with prefects first, going down to the youngest first years at the end. It was all done in an orderly manner, no scrabbling or noise or confusion – an excellent start to the school day. During the first term I was to introduce one or two new tunes for the hymns, and occasionally chide the school for poor singing (actually they sang better than any school I had worked in, but I never let on), and sometimes I would stop the hymn, and with the headmistress's approval, take them to task: "Stand up properly, heads up, open your mouths and let's make a better sound; I want to hear 550 voices all doing their best!" on Tuesdays we had form assembly, when each form would take it in turns to organise and conduct the proceedings – sometimes with some drama thrown in, and on one day a week the deputy head or a volunteer member of staff would lead. There was quite a large Jewish population in the school and on at least one morning each week they would have their own assembly.

My predecessor had informed me that the school was to take part in a BBC Radio Four "Sunday Half Hour" programme at the end of January to be transmitted from All Saints, the local church across the green; our choir was to sing a couple of verses of one of the hymns alone, so I had to put on my skates to get this up to standard. We took the girls to the church for a rehearsal directed by the organist, and on the Sunday afternoon, with the BBC microphones in position we had a run through for the producer and director of the programme. It all went very well, the girls were an absolute credit to the school, and not for the last time I was to feel very proud of them. We had junior and senior choirs organised, Judith Liddell taking the juniors and small madrigal group of hand-picked senior girls, I took senior choir and ran a recorder group where we had the full consort of recorders – bass through to descant – and quite accomplished players, and I tried to lick the orchestra into shape. The orchestra provided the first problem for me, the head and with Redbridge council, via the music adviser, Malcolm Bidgood. The borough of Redbridge had a very good music school which met on Saturdays, giving the pupils some individual tuition and the opportunity to play in an orchestra, wind band or smaller instrumental group. A large number of our girls were in the Redbridge orchestras or bands, but I was rather put out when some of the better players informed me that they would not be playing for our school orchestra. I took the view that their first duty was to use their musical ability in school functions, and told them so. Then one or two girls told their parents, I received letters, and, more to the point, so did the headmistress. She appeared to support me on the matter of loyalty to the school, but when the borough music adviser arrived to discuss the matter with us, she seemed to sit on the fence, and I was left to fight my cause. In the end we had to agree that girls would come to the orchestra if they chose to, and I had to put up with the fact that some of the best string players, particularly, decided to 'keep themselves' for the Redbridge orchestra. At the very time of writing this information, news has just come to me of the death of the headmistress, Miss Satchell, after a long illness, bravely borne. Right to the end she would always put on a dignified face, and not let her pain or suffering be noticed by others. She was almost 90 at the time of her death.

On a cold day in February I went with my colleague, Judith, to a gathering of fellow music teachers from the other schools in the borough. Some were quite interested to see who had got the rather prestigious job as head of music at Woodford, while others gave the impression that they regarded our school and the Ilford Grammar School for Boys with suspicion; the view that a borough could not be completely comprehensive while it maintained its two grammar schools was an attitude which I was to discover very often during my time at Woodford. The meeting was chaired by the music adviser, Malcolm Bidgood, of whom more later. The invited guest was Russell Burgess, who had founded the Wandsworth School boys' choir a few years after joining the staff in 1954 as a young 23-year-old teacher; the choir's breakthrough was in 1967 when Benjamin Britten chose them for the first performance of his *War Requiem* in Coventry Cathedral, and later on his recording from the same venue. This choir had established a great reputation in the country, and all the brainchild of Russell Burgess. He was only 43 and we expected to meet up with an energetic, enthusiastic musician, but we got quite a shock; it was obvious the man was ill, completely worn out, as he himself admitted in his opening remarks. When it came to playing extracts from his recordings his hands were shaking so much that someone else had to put the LP on. I can still remember some of his opening remarks as he told us, "You see before you a broken figure of a man who has literally given his life to this choir. You probably imagine that I'm given all the time off I need to rehearse the choir and take them to recordings and performances, but I can assure you that I have to fight to get any time at all; rehearsals take place just off the dining hall, where we compete with the smells and noise of several hundred children having their meal. Any school time I am allowed I have to make up in my own meagre free periods – I get no privileges at all. The only privileges the boys get is that of going first in the dinner queue so that they can get to rehearsal on time." We were absolutely amazed at these revelations. I know how much the choir meant to the boys of that school, how they worked hard to pass the audition to join; indeed a son of my cousin Margaret was a member of that choir, and it led him onto a life of music. Nigel Spearing, later to become famous in the King's Singers, was a member of the Wandsworth choir. I know that Russell was not guilty of self-pity, he himself said he would do the same all over again, but I think he was partly getting at the comprehensive system. Wandsworth had started as a most successful grammar school for boys before the war, but then in the early 60s it had orders to expand – eventually reaching over 2000. Pictures on the website tell the story, a story similar to our own grammar school in Dagenham. I think most of us came away from the meeting feeling that though we were enthusiastic for the music in our school, we were not going to literally let it take away our life. Russell Burgess died five years later in 1979, at the age of 48. So sad!

Out of curiosity I looked up the website for the replacement school – Wandsworth School had closed in 1985 – and out came the following headline:

"Dog gang admit terrifying school attack"

11:50am Wednesday 22nd October 2008 By Paul Cahalan

"Six teenage gang members have admitted carrying out a terrifying attack in a Wandsworth school, where a pupil was stabbed six times and a snarling pitbull was released into a playground full of children. Teachers and pupils froze in horror as the innocent 16-year-old was knifed in the chest and buttock. The gang, all aged between 14 and 18, "steamed" into the school on April 24 this year just after the home time bell rang at 3.30pm.

An illegal pitbull was let loose, chasing terrifed pupils inside the school building, while other gang members swung the dog's metal chain at youngsters outside. It is believed the gang members had come to the school looking for a pupil who was in a rival gang. However when an innocent boy stepped in to calm them down he was stabbed and had to be airlifted to hospital."

Whoever dreamed up these large, impersonal 'Incomprehensives', as one comedian once described them, has a lot to answer for; excellent schools were destroyed for purely political purposes.

I see from my programme notes that we actually put on a spring concert on Thursday, 28th March in which we included the junior and senior choirs, recorder group, madrigal group, cello duet, items on clarinet, cello, and Judith and I entertained with some items for two pianos – after all, we had the luxury of Bechstein and Blüthner grand pianos in the same hall, and I was determined to use them. A grand finale was the senior orchestra playing *Marche Militaire* by Schubert – not too much difficulty there, followed by the finale of Beethoven's *fifth Symphony*, and that really took some hard work and rehearsing – right up to the wire, as they say. All our concerts were the result of very hard work in addition to all the teaching and extra-curricular activities I was involved in, but then I knew that most of the performers were also very committed and involved in many school activities, and they always looked so smart and professional on the night – they were a real credit to the school.

I was invited to go to Italy with a party from school, and jumped at the opportunity. We stayed at a small hotel right in the centre of Florence; the party consisted of the Italian teacher, Mrs Tracey, her husband and son, Gill Burn from the geography department, and myself. The girls were mainly fourth and fifth year students all waiting to take their Italian at GCE level. Of course we visited all the famous sites in Florence, including the wonderful cathedral and the Uffizi gallery, but also got away from the noise and heat of the city to visit Siena – though, typically, we arrived just as siesta time was beginning, so many places were closed, but we were able to relax with some lovely Chianti in one of the cafes around the piazza. We also made a trip to Pisa, and in those days one was able to go up to the top of the leaning tower. The girls got rather tired of all the men hanging around, and they weren't just young men – all the old lechers of Florence seemed to make a beeline for our hotel and stood around for hours waiting for the girls to appear. We had to keep a very close eye on them, but agreed that they deserved a treat at the end of the holiday, of visiting a nightclub – I don't think they were called discos in the 70s – and we would go along to keep an eye on them. I got tired of the deafening music and paying a king's ransom for each Coca-Cola I drank, and arranged that Mr Tracey would stay on to see the last girls back to the hotel, while the rest came back with his wife and Gill, and I agreed to stay up to let the late comers safely in. The hotel was just about one star in quality, my single room was more like a cupboard, and the staff went off duty at about 11 and the door would be locked for the night. I got back and went to my room to get my pipe and a good book to read, and returned to sit near the door to wait for the late comers. By about one in the morning I was very tired of looking through the window watching the men cleaning the streets, and wondered what on earth was keeping the girls out so late, and by two o'clock I decided I'd had enough, would lock the door and go to bed. Now it so happened that I had to pass the room of Mr and Mrs Tracey, and definitely heard snoring of the masculine type as I walked by... I just couldn't believe it, Mr Tracey was obviously there and in a sound sleep. It never crossed my mind that Mrs Tracey might have invited another man back to her room, who might have dropped off... anyhow, more in anger than surprise, I knocked on the door, went in and discovered that it was Mr Tracey in bed. So I got about four hours sleep that night before we had to set off for the airport and the return home. It transpired that the girls had changed their mind about staying on, and they had all slipped in the front door and up to their rooms in the 10 minutes or so that I had gone to fetch my pipe, book and slippers, so I had been waiting up for three hours for absolutely nothing. Gill Burn, the geography teacher was a very determined traveller, who took all her sightseeing very seriously – she was invariably up by seven each morning to visit places before the crowds arrived, and I subsequently discovered that she went off travelling all over the world during each summer and Easter holiday. She would arrive back at the beginning of term informing us of her adventures trekking through some jungle in Borneo or climbing a mountain in Tibet; she had incredible energy, curiosity and desire to see every part of the world.

During the holiday I got to know three of the girls quite well; they had a happy personality, and a wicked sense of humour and I found them good fun to go around with. They were Helen, Kim and Linda. Kim lived in a beautiful house up on Chingford Green, and I was invited to go and watch the cup final with them on their super large TV screen; I also used to play tennis with them after school; Kim mentioned that her father always got two tickets for her and Linda to go to the Wimbledon final, and she managed to get a third ticket for me to go with them, as long as I was willing to drive them to Wimbledon. This was a fantastic opportunity, and although my seat was towards the back of the stands I looked forward to a marvellous display of tennis. Unfortunately the men's final on 11th of July 1974 was one of the most boring, one-sided matches in history: Jimmy Connors was playing the veteran Ken Rosewall, who had always longed to reach the men's final, but, sadly he went to pieces on the day, and Connors absolutely thrashed him. The result spoke for itself, 6-1, 6-1, 6-4, at one stage Jimmy Connors was calling out to Ken, "Come on mate, let's make a match of it!" and later on, almost in despair, "Come on mate, we've got to give 'em something for their money.". In that final set Jimmy Connors was desperate not so much at winning – he had it in the bag – but realised how bored the spectators were becoming. In fact, the women's singles and the men's doubles were much more exciting. Trust me to choose the wrong year for my only visit to Wimbledon.

Summer holidays were looming up, I was exhausted but had nothing planned. Then the captain of the guide company, Liz Martyn a maths. teacher, asked me to join them on their guide camp down in Devon for the first week of the school holidays. I gave lifts to two of the helpers and we arrived quite late, the girls having gone ahead and put up all the tents and got the camp organised. Of course, the inevitable happened, for, supper over and retiring to my small tent I heard whispers and giggles outside, and slowly my tent collapsed around me to squeals of delight from the guides; this was to happen almost every night, though I soon got used to listening for the first whispers, and carefully left the tent and gave them all a surprise by coming upon them from behind and making frightening noises. But it was all in good fun, and we had some great times including visits to Liz's local church on the outskirts of Plymouth. I had given up the BMS summer schools by now; but several of the staff spoke of happy holidays they had had with a company called HF. This stood for Holiday Fellowship, and I later discovered that its founder had been a Christian minister, Rev. T.A. Leonard. He was in charge of a congregational church in Colne, a Lancashire town which, like many others, had its wakes week when as many as possible would take a well earned break at Blackpool or Morecambe before returning to the drudgery of their jobs in the mill. Leonard wanted to provide healthier holidays with walking and good company. In his own words, "This kind of holiday leads to thoughtless spending of money, inane types of amusement, and unhealthy overcrowding in lodging houses. Moreover it makes for perverse or corrupt conceptions of life and conduct, and produces permanent ill effects on character. Clearly the great majority of our young folk do not know how to get the best out of their holidays." So he formed a rambling club and took 30 people to Ambleside in the summer of 1891. However the rather Spartan, basic arrangement of those days had given way to excellent facilities in many of the HF houses by the 1970s.

I chose the centre at Freshwater Bay on the Isle of Wight – the house stands on the cliff looking towards the sea and the Needles lighthouse – and decided to go for two weeks. It really made sense to go by train and I set off to go via Lymington and the ferry to Yarmouth, then a bus over to Freshwater, and was immediately captivated by the sight of the house. The guests were an excellent crowd and I soon made friends with a particular family who had two daughters, and was invited to go with them whenever they went out exploring in the car. Of course we did the usual walks during the day and in the evening had a mixture of easy dancing, games and entertainment. I enjoyed the formula of the holiday – the staff who had put me onto HF were absolutely right about it being the ideal holiday for the single person. I didn't realise at the time but in a few years time I would be going back to that house and many others as a leader rather than a guest, but that wasn't to happen until 1979. I was also to be very much involved in the folk music festival on the island later, so I got to know the area very well, but my favourite part was always the village of Freshwater where Tennyson had lived, and which still retained a Victorian charm long after the rest of the island had changed. I travelled home at the end of the holiday determined to go HF again. It is interesting that in my diary for that time I had actually written on the day before the new term started: "New term at Woodford, yippee!" Normally I went back to school very reluctantly but I was actually looking forward to my music job at Woodford. Once again we had the 'bun fight' before the staff meeting, and this time I joined in all the conversation about holiday experiences.

During the autumn term, apart from all the usual schoolwork, we rehearsed and took part in EFYMA, which stood for the Epping Forest Youth Music Association and had been running for many years as a means of bringing together the girls of Woodford and Loughton high schools with the boys of Bancrofts school close by. By 1974 EFYMA was on its last legs, mainly because Bancrofts was soon to go coeducational, so they already had their potential sopranos and altos at the school, and because the Redbridge music service was taking up so much time, and giving opportunity for our girls to sing in choirs within the borough. Nevertheless we performed the oratorio *Samson* by Handel, with John Railton, a most energetic conductor and pianist who had no problems despite the fact that he only had one arm! In the following year we did a very exciting performance of Carl Orff's *Carmina Burana*, not with the usual large orchestra but an accompaniment of two pianos and percussion; Mike Hatch, a pupil at Bancroft's played the percussion (more of Mike and his musical talents later in our story) and Chris Dolan, music master at Bancroft's and I did the piano parts, which needed a lot of practice, particularly in the complex rhythms with which this work abounds.

Nora Dryborough, my predecessor had been connected with Ernest Read, probably through the Royal Academy of Music, and had always been invited to take along a small group of senior girls to sing in the Ernest Read Carol concert in the Royal Festival Hall. I discovered this was quite an honour, most of the schools which took part were select, public schools. Naturally I wanted to continue this association, and certainly the girls queued up to take part in such a concert. It needed rehearsals, both at school, and later, two Saturday afternoons at the Royal Academy, with the conductor, who was none other than the John Railton who conducted our school EFYMA concerts. So all in all, Christmas was a busy time both at school and in church life outside, with carol singing and carol services involved. Always by the time Christmas came around I was ready for a rest and a break. I came up from East Peckham to take my parents over to spend Christmas with a cousin, George, his family, including his sister, Ellen and her husband, Albert who was my uncle, and their two children. If you're scratching your head over these relationships, you must go back to chapter 1 and read all about it. George lived at Cherry Hinton, just outside Cambridge, and as we drove on the outskirts of Cambridge the famous King's College concert of nine lessons and carols was just beginning, in fact we could see the spires of the college chapel. I had always made a point of listening to this service – Christmas seemed to really begin as the single chorister announced *"Once in Royal David's City"* – but this was the closest to actually being there. We drove along the Backs, and I thought how grand it would be to actually attend the service, and be in the heart of music in Cambridge, perhaps singing in one of the choirs, for the standard of singing was of the highest and one was always interested in the new carol which would be commissioned each year. Little did I realise that one day I would be working in Cambridge as a music director, and be attending the Kings' Carol Service as a 'special guest'. This may also have been the time when I began to have secret ambitions to sing in a cathedral choir myself – it did happen 22 years later!

George and his wife were so proud to welcome us in their home for the holiday; the wine and beer flowed freely, and George himself became almost legless at one stage. He had to be helped to the toilet, and in throwing up managed to lose his false teeth! I don't know whether anyone was brave enough to attempt to recover them!

Meanwhile my house in East Peckham showed no signs of selling, so, typically, I would leave school promptly on Fridays to drive back to Kent for the weekend, where I continued to play the organ at the Methodist chapel and to lead the little group of recorder players. The village primary school had a very musical headmaster called Mr Lawrence who had an excellent recorder group, a number of this group came to the Methodist chapel and I had been asked to train them for the Sevenoaks Arts Festival in 1973. We achieved honours and took part in the Methodist District Festival that same year, winning our section; for some strange reason I also won a winners certificate for Piano Solo – 19 years and over at the finals at Maidstone. I also received honours in the competition in the 1974 Festival for solo piano, but cannot think why I competed or what I performed on the day. Perhaps it was to show the children that I was also willing to go under the spotlight of competition, as I expected them to. In 1975 we really went for it; the children came to my home for rehearsals, and we worked hard at the music and were ready for the festival at Tunbridge Wells on March 22nd, 1975. We gained first prize in the recorder class and in singing, and so we represented that region of Kent for the finals in Maidstone, which we also went on to win on 26th April. The kids were a marvellous group, and I sometimes regret not having trained to teach primary rather than secondary pupils. Up to the age of 11 they seem to have so much enthusiasm and innocence, it was always the dreaded teenage tantrums which made teaching difficult in the secondary school. How well I remember Lynn, Jill, Alison, Carolyn, and others; looking back over 30 years, almost certainly by now they are not only mothers but grandmothers, and I just hope that they have passed on some of their musical enthusiasm and expertise to their offspring.

The busy but enjoyable life at Woodford continued into 1976, and in March of that year we took a number of singers to the first Redbridge Festival which was held in the Royal Albert Hall. We had practised hard and done our rehearsals at the town hall, and then came the big day in the hall. It was a great success, and all credit to the council and to the visionary music adviser, Malcolm Bidgood, who I was going to get to know later on, but in less than happy circumstances. There were orchestras, concert bands, junior and four-part choirs – a number of us as teachers volunteered to sing as tenors or basses to supplement the boys. There was even an amusing item given by the head teachers which brought the house down – the pupils having a chance to see their head as a human being and funny – a great boost to morale for everyone. The girls talked about the festival for weeks afterwards and this biennial trip to the Albert Hall has continued down to the present time. Our school recorder group also took part in the Stratford Music Festival where we gained first place and a cup.

In the spring of 1976 I found a buyer for my house – a local family – and had to move out in August, putting my furniture in storage. It was sad to say goodbye to all friends in the village; they had a little party for me, presenting me with a picture painted by a local artist, showing a nearby farm and oast house, past which we often walked on summer evenings at the weekends. I still treasure that picture today.

Since 1974 I had been in touch with estate agents to find another house in the area and had viewed several, including, in June, 1975, a detached house in

St Ronan's Crescent, just about half a mile from the school, well within walking distance. The house had everything I wanted and was just the right size, BUT, it had already been sold to another client. I kept ringing the agents in the hope that the new clients would withdraw, for I really wanted that house; sadly the new family moved in and I started house hunting yet again. The good news was that 57, St Ronan's Crescent would be mine two years later.

After starting at Woodford School I seemed to become someone destined to rescue lost musical causes, but without much success. Wanstead and Woodford Choral Society approached me to become their music director and conductor; over the years it had been a very successful choir, with quite large numbers and ambitious programmes, but by 1975 it had fallen on hard times. At our committee meetings – which comprised half the choir – the accompanist and the chairman would reflect, with glazed eyes, on the wonderful past, on the times they had performed *Elijah, St Paul* and, of course, *Messiah*, with at least 50 singers and orchestra. Now they were reduced to one good tenor, a couple of enthusiastic basses, and a *very* small sprinkling of sopranos and altos. We did organise two or three concerts at a local church and I brought in some of my own pupils to give a youthful input to the proceedings; in particular, there was a very talented 12-year-old violinist who was quite happy to come and play to an audience of mainly old people. Madeleine Cuthbert was a talented kid, with bags of energy, but I think she dropped out of music when she left school. By using instrumentalists and a group from our own choirs we did bump up the audience considerably, and I notice from a programme that we actually did most of Haydn's *Creation* in May, 1976, with organ accompaniment; but I felt the choir was never going anywhere, and after about two years I resigned, to the regret of the choir. I also became organist and choirmaster at St Johns Church, Buckhurst Hill, in 1976, mainly through the husband of one of the Woodford staff. Michael Sharpless was in the choir and very keen to keep it going – their new vicar was fairly 'low church' and although he had no strong feelings against the choir, I believe he had firm ideas about the type of music they should sing. A couple of my own pupils were choristers, but, again, numbers had dwindled and we were down to just a handful of children and about four adults. I got on well with the vicar and certainly enjoyed playing the organ in what was a very old and beautiful building. I tried hard to build up the choir and made the repertoire fairly simple so that we could reach a reasonable standard and also satisfy the vicar in our choice of material, but it was an uphill task and I'm afraid I gave that up as well after a couple of years. Looking back now, I realise that I never gave it enough time and probably didn't put in enough effort, but I was running the music department at school, and doing folk gigs and that occupied much of my time, and to be doing music at weekends as well was just too much. Perhaps I was too cynical about the future of such choirs. Parents often wanted to take their children away for weekends or even for the day, so they did not want the commitment of bringing them to Friday choir practice and services on Sunday, and neither did many children. Sunday was already beginning to change its character, and over the next 30 years it was to become just another day of the week, for shopping, eating out, sports, both participating and watching, and a host of other distractions. Regular commitment to a church choir was very low in the list of priorities.

In the summer of 1975 I had returned for another HF holiday – two, in fact – a week at Swanage in Dorset. Close to the beach, it really consisted of two large houses put together, and opposite a convent where one could park the car. Then I moved on in my Triumph Toledo to Lyme Regis; these were enjoyable holidays, and again I got to know one or two families quite well. At Lyme I went for the cheapest option for there were number of small garden house "rooms", just big enough for a bed, chair and small dresser which suited me. Well, one spent so little time in the bedroom with all the activities of walking during the day and social activities in the evening so the bedroom was just somewhere to lay one's head at night. I wasn't looking for anything up market! A year later I decided to go to Lynmouth HF for two weeks where the house was literally on the beach, in a super setting, the steep Lynmouth hill at the back of the house and the beach and sea in front. The house had been full when I booked but I was offered a cabin situated at the side of the house. These cabins were almost literally next to the park and a putting green, so while you sat in the cabin you could hear the people putting their balls just outside the window. The summer of 1976 became very well-known as one of the hottest years on record. The walks from Lynmouth were pretty difficult, with many hills, and many guests opted for the easy walks. Swimming was superb, and every morning and evening I walked the manager's dog along the beach and promenade. An incident occurred towards the end of the holiday which makes Lynmouth '75 stand out. I had made friends with a headmaster, his wife and son and on the second Wednesday we went out together for the day. He was a big, tough chap who excelled in sports, and he had made his way up to the semi-finals of the tennis competition. He and his opponent had to play their match in the early evening of Thursday, and I watched them battling it out as I took the dog for its afternoon walk; when I returned there was an ambulance parked next to the tennis court and I discovered that my headmaster friend had collapsed and died almost instantly on the court. It's not difficult to imagine the atmosphere in the house that evening; the host who ran the social events was in a dilemma, whether to cancel activities that evening or to run a normal programme, he felt that somehow we had to keep the holiday going. In the end he decided to run the evening with a couple of quizzes and party games, no dancing or singing, but it was hard going and we were only really going through the motions. During the night the man's wife and 12-year-old son went back home, later they would have to arrange the funeral and pick up life without husband or father, and a school would return without a headmaster. It would be a holiday marked indelibly on their lives, and an experience I will never forget. Ironically, it was while taking the dog around the tennis court that I told the head I was surprised to see him playing so soon after coming back from the walk, while it was still very hot; he just laughed it off, but that must have been his last occasion to laugh. His opponent was a woman PE teacher – all muscles and 'jolly hockey sticks', but certainly she would never forget that particular tennis match.

On the final Saturday I moved off for the pleasant drive from North Devon through to Somerset to stay at Halsway Manor, a beautiful old country house, some of it dating back to 15th century, which nestled below the Quantock Hills near to Crowcombe. Halsway Manor was a residential centre connected with the English Folk Dance Society (EFDS), and I was going there to spend a week as part of the musicians' workshop, to increase my knowledge of folk dancing and how to play it. Without realising it at the time, this week at Halsway was to be an important development in my musical life. I met the main host, Peter Boyce, an absolutely wizard folk violinist, later to become a great friend. I realised then that playing the violin for folk dancing is a very special art; I knew a number of good classical players who would play folk and get the notes right but couldn't get the idiom of folk playing. I suppose it's like the experiment carried out by Yehudi Menuhin, when he partnered Stephan Grappelli for some jazz CDs and concerts. Dear Yehudi could play all the notes, and in the right order, but just hadn't the sparkle and the magic of Grappelli. Ross Winter, was an expert at the recorder; whose father had been a music teacher in Chingford for many years and had written a number of books about music teaching. Robin Bowman, who, I realised, was not just a brilliant pianist and folk dance player but an all-round musical genius. He went on to lecture in music at Southampton University and then at the Guildhall in London, and retired recently. I was fascinated with Robin's keyboard style and learned so much from him; in the evenings we often played for the dancing, which was great fun, and during the day, after the workshops, we were free to enjoy the countryside or go off to Minehead and the sea. England was in the middle of a severe drought and Halsway Manor got its water from a well at the back which had almost dried up, so we were asked to forego baths and showers and to conserve as much water as possible – this led us to wear small perfumed bags round our neck, but no one smelt *that* bad. I made friends with a local girl who worked at the house, and Janet and I went out in the evening when the dancing had finished, though, having worked all day she was always terribly tired and could hardly stay awake even for a kiss and cuddle in the back of the car. Peter Boyce was senior master at the local Chingford County School, and Ross and Robin were just two of many young people he had encouraged and helped in the folk world; he ran a number of bands in the area, and soon after returning home Peter was in touch with me offering some bookings for folk evenings with a couple of his bands. These folk evenings, or ceilidhs, were very popular in the 70s and early 80s particularly for school functions, parent teacher socials, occasionally weddings and even bar mitzvahs, so within a couple of months Peter had persuaded me to buy an accordion and amplifying equipment and to lead a band on my own. He suggested "Brian's Barnacles" as its name, and that's what it became during the next few years when I ran the band. But this is all jumping ahead, and meanwhile the new term had begun and I was anxiously looking around to buy a suitable house, but with little success.

I got on quite well with the headmistress, Miss Satchell, and she actually invited me to go for a meal at her flat, along with a new geography teacher, John Nivison, and his wife. Some of the staff were quite envious, a few made snide remarks about my being the teacher's pet, and the deputy head was incandescent with rage because during all the years she had worked at the school with the head she had never been across the threshold. I think the headmistress wanted to hear about John Nivison's experiences in Africa, where he had spent some years teaching, and I was just the third one to make the number up. I do remember that the meal was excellent, marvellous food, for she was a good cook and well able to entertain guests, but I let the side down somewhat in two ways. She asked me what it was like living with my parents, and I replied that it was fine for a short time but that I would be glad to have my own house as soon as possible, "You know what it's like, when we sit down after our meal and watch rubbish like *Coronation Street*, which my father never misses."

"But, Mr Astell," she interrupted, "I ALWAYS enjoy *Coronation Street*; it's a great insight into social life in the north and they are such wonderful characters; I look forward to each episode!" So, I was well and truly put down, became a fan of *Coronation Street* from that day on, and still enjoy the episodes to this day. We were given some beautiful fresh raspberries and cream for dessert, and she offered me a second helping, and this is where being truthful leads one into all sorts of problems. "Miss Satchell, I really can't eat any more, I had my meal before I came out; mother always cooks extra food and was so disappointed when I declined her food that I felt I ought to at least have some supper with them." Well, that did it; her feathers were truly ruffled and she muttered words to the effect that she wasn't used to her guests having their meal *before* coming to eat with her, that they usually trusted that they would get good food at her table and didn't need to eat first, etc., etc. The atmosphere was distinctly icy, and John quietly suggested that I take the dog out for a good walk in Epping Forest while he and his wife helped Miss Satchell do the washing-up, and that I should come back when things had calmed down. So, as on so many occasions in life, you can see where honesty and my big mouth got me; I should have either politely declined *without long explanation* or even eaten the blessed raspberries, just to keep the peace!

During the term I began to see light at the end of the tunnel with regard to house purchase, and the opportunity to get away from the parents and *Coronation Street*. Incredibly the house in St Ronan's Crescent which I had previously visited but which had just been sold now came back on the market; I went to view it, taking Mother along for a second opinion and for her to see things which I tended to ignore; I noticed straight away that a lot of work had been done on the house, most of which had spoiled the whole character of the place. It was now one great open space, the walls between dining room and lounge had been knocked down, also the wall between the lounge and the kitchen, and a breakfast bar had been added – 'open plan' taken to extremes. A large extra lounge at the back of the house with big picture frame windows was very impressive but, I was to discover how cold it became in the winter, so it was a mixed blessing. A long cloakroom had been added to replace the side entrance, but upstairs everything had been more or less left. I really wish to that the occupants had not gone mad to make such 'improvements', and would have been quite happy with the rooms as they previously existed. But, there it was, a detached house close to the school in a good area and at a price I could just about afford – £25,000. I was able to get my mortgage organised and in March, 1977 I got my furniture from the warehouse and moved into my Woodford home where I was to stay for the next 10 years. My parents and relations came along for a sort of housewarming, so to create a good impression I went off to Ilford and bought a rather grand G-plan suite, very attractive Ercol table and chairs, and a double bed – the luxury I had wanted for some time, and perhaps hoping still that marriage bells might ring and someone might come to share the new home. Apart from my busy week at school and the organist work at weekends, I was playing in folk bands and leading my own band, so there was precious little time to enjoy the house, but I did need the extra money to pay the mortgage and buy food. The scale 4 post did give me a pretty good income from teaching, and I always counted myself lucky to have landed the job, for such posts were few and far between in subjects like music.

In the summer I went off to Swanage again to the HF guest house, and had some days with the Kilbey family at Ludlow in Shropshire. This latter holiday came about when I was asked to help one of the school pupils to prepare for O level music; Margaret Kilbey –always known as Maggie – was one of these really clever girls who was already doing about 12 subjects and the headmistress was of the belief that 12 was enough. But she was keen to have a go at the music and her parents asked me to give her some coaching, and in getting to know Joan and Leslie Kilbey I found a really happy family and was to have some great holidays with them. They used to rent a cottage at Burrington, a hamlet miles from anywhere – nearest place was Ludlow, and they asked me to join them. The Kilbeys were a brilliant family, Maggie's two sisters were very clever, and Richard, her brother was about to qualify in medicine; it was either on this holiday or a later one that he joined us, and we had some great conversation and lots of laughs together. Joan was brilliant at conjuring up fantastic meals, Leslie was great fun in discussions, we often disagreed over things – he was fairly right-wing; at that time he was senior librarian in the Walthamstow area, and his knowledge of books and subjects was quite phenomenal. Joan was a fantastic person who had been headmistress of a small independent girls' school in Buckhurst Hill – ironically, a school I was to do some part-time teaching at later when my career at Woodford finished. She had a wonderful personality, always cheerful and optimistic. Some time after Maggie had gone off to Oxford they sold up and moved to St.Albans, where Maggie met her first husband; they were married in the abbey. Later, Joan and Leslie moved on to Malvern into a beautiful brand-new house where I stayed on several occasions, and I was able to meet up with them when I moved to Hereford in 1993. It was a tragedy that years later, Joan was to be stricken with cancer in the mouth, and had a very painful and stressful time at the end. Leslie lived on until just short of his 91st birthday, in October, 2008. Needless to say the daughter went on to pass her music GCE along with all the others, with flying colours. Later she was to put the music aside to concentrate on biology, and botany in particular. She went up to Oxford to be the first woman undergraduate at Keble College, Oxford. After graduating she became very interested again in music, especially early music and the instruments of that period. After many years working in early music, making and playing instruments and doing endless research, Maggie published the authoritative book about the curtal – forerunner of the bassoon – in 2002.

I enjoyed my times with Holiday Fellowship (HF); at each centre there would be an opportunity for people to give to the Goodwill Fund. After a talk on Sunday evening, holidaymakers had a chance to make a contribution so that a person who couldn't afford it could receive a free or assisted holiday. I had put my parents forward, and in September, 1977 they had a chance to spend a week at an HF centre on the south coast, at Milford-on-Sea. On Saturday morning I drove them down to Conway Hall, near King's Cross, where they were to meet up with the other guests and join the coach. Mother was looking forward to it, but Dad was very reticent, and as we went in to meet the other people I think he was almost on the verge of giving up and asking to go home again – it was almost the action of a child dealing with the unknown. I waved them off, everybody looking rather tense and uncomfortable, not knowing what was awaiting them at Milford. Exactly a week later I returned to Conway Hall to be met with a crowd of very happy, sunburnt folk. They were all calling each other by their Christian names, swapping addresses and phone numbers, and Dad was as happy as a sandboy. As they got into the car he said that he'd had an enjoyable week. I hadn't seen him look so happy in years; we didn't realise then but it was to be the last holiday he would have, and I like to think that it was a such a memorable week for him. As it happened, the Goodwill Fund was replaced in 1998 by the Pathways Fund; the welfare state had made great inroads and it was becoming hard to find people who needed and deserved such holidays – that was the official line, though I still maintained that there were many in our society who would have benefited from such a good cause, people who were too proud, too quiet to be noticed and nominated. During the 80s and early 90s I did meet up with managers at centres who felt such funds were often misspent; some claimed that these poor guests arrived with their own portable colour TVs, and when the children turned their nose up at a good, wholesome dinner, Mum would give them £5 to go off and buy chips at the local shop. But the Pathways Fund took its place; many of the footpaths which had been trodden by HF members and others over the years were in a bad state, and needed repair, and the fund would help alleviate the situation. In passing, I must mention another short holiday which my parents had in 1976. Dad had always fancied a cruise, but this was way beyond their means, so I helped them to go on a little mini cruise to Norway; I think they were only away for five days but, again, they both came back with wonderful stories and lots of pictures – sadly Dad's hands were so shaky by this time that the photos came out very badly. He talked with enthusiasm of the food all beautifully laid out in the dining room, which would be the Smorgasbord or Norwegian buffet. I think the sea air did them both good and they came back with wonderful sun tans.

Although they had been happy to move to Chingford and their flat, we soon found out that it was a very damp place, and they were both ready to move again by 1978. My brother John had moved to Biggleswade shortly after his marriage, and subsequently bought a larger house in St Neots when the two boys came along, and he found that there was opportunity for my parents to move up to a council estate on the edge of the town. He came down to help arrange the move and had to do a great deal, for I was busy at school and Father was ill in bed; it must have been a horrendous time for them all, but somehow the move went ahead and they took up their abode in Howitts Lane, a two-bedroom end of terrace house complete with cemetery at the side! It did have a small front and back garden and I think father felt he had more freedom and was not isolated as he had been in the Chingford flat; indeed he felt very happy in the new home, though he was to spend less than a year there.

I had remained friends with John Buckle, the physics master at Cooper School during this time, and had actually done several folk gigs for him. Now, as I had got to know the Holiday Fellowship scene, so John had become involved in its counterpart, the Cooperative Holidays Association (CHA). He had already done several holidays as a host, looking after the entertainment side of the holiday week, arranging socials, treasure hunts, dancing and all the events that went to help make these holidays so enjoyable yet unique. In 1977 he invited me to go with him to Barmouth, on the Welsh coast, where he was hosting, and I was a guest. I remember the journey very well because once we had got clear of London he invited me to take over the driving of his wonderful MG sports car. I was scared stiff at first, but got used to the controls and quite enjoyed watching the people give a second glance at the lovely old car. John went off to sleep and all went well until we had to go through a Welsh town and up a steep hill in the evening rush hour with much traffic; at one stage I needed to stop the car on the hill, then do a hill start, couldn't handle the brake and woke John in a panic. He controlled the brake while I did the accelerator, but it was quite a hairy moment with buses in front and behind us. We reached Barmouth very late at night and I realised I had done almost all the driving. The holiday was great fun, the house was in a wonderful position right on the seafront. One of the guests was Irish, who claimed that he was an expert dance caller, but he always had to go and get his fill of Guinness before he could perform, so he usually came back from the pub the worse for wear at about 10.30 each night, and wondered why we were all packing up and going to bed. One of the students working there was a gorgeous girl called Ursula – we christened her Martini, for she wore a Martini pinafore when working. We both fancied her a lot. On one evening we took Martini in the MG and the three of us went off for a drive – bear in mind this was a two seater car! Of course, I would have been no competition in the race for Ursula – John was the holiday host, the big white chief, and _he_ had the MG! The last we heard she had married a man from Iraq, or somewhere in that area, so goodness knows what happened to her. I'm glad we had a week at Barmouth because it closed just a few years later.

I spent Christmas, 1978 with my parents at St Neots, and vividly remember the journey from Woodford, driving through some of the worst fog I've ever experienced. There had been a couple of serious accidents on motorways during fog in the preceding weeks, I was taking no chances and I had to drive very slowly on the motorway, always scared that some idiot driving in blind faith and too fast would run into me. The further I drove from London the worse it became, and at Bishops Stortford it was complicated by motorway construction – the M11 was being extended. But I arrived in one piece and was greeted not only by Mum and Dad but the new member, their small Jack Russell called Jess. She was a bundle of fun, and so small that she could sleep comfortably in an LP size record box. She would sit up to beg without any bidding, and could maintain that position for ages – she was a lovely pet, but unfortunately was thoroughly spoiled by my father. He would insist on giving her sweets and toffees, despite our pleadings; a few years later she had to have all her teeth removed, but father wasn't there to admit to his stupid behaviour, he had already died, 1978 was to be his last Christmas. We went to my brother's house for Christmas Day dinner and for the evening, joining the general chaos, with their boys, Tony aged 14, and Ian aged 9, plus the dogs and the cats. We were to have some memorable times in their home on Cambridge Street, St Neots.

Some events in our lives stand out so clearly they could almost have happened yesterday; one such event was when my father died very suddenly. At Easter time in 1979 I had spent some days with the Kilbey family up in Shropshire, and there we had a great time, not just enjoying the countryside in spring but on Good Friday we went to part of the three-hour service in Ludlow parish church which was very meaningful and moving. On Saturday I left the family, and had arranged to travel over to stay with my parents at St Neots; when I reached the outskirts of Bedford in my cross country journey I pulled in trying to decide whether to have a break and lunch in Bedford or whether to keep going; I remember thinking that it would be good to get there early, and have my lunch with them. Dad had been painting the hallway and with doors and windows closed the place smelt very strongly of paint, and this had some influence on later events. We enjoyed a good meal, and the dog was up to her usual tricks, although Father did complain that he had a slight pain. After the washing-up mum came out to the car to help me carry my things in, and there was Jess sitting on top of the luggage waiting for an outing – she loved the car. As we laughed at this Mum went back indoors to bring Dad out to see the dog, but then came back to say that something had happened and he seemed ill. I went into the front room and realised immediately that he had gone from this world – he was still sitting in his chair, the budgerigar perched on his finger, but with his head down. John, my brother came round as soon as we telephoned him, and we called the ambulance. I know they tried to resuscitate him, but it was all to no avail; within the few minutes of my going from the lounge to the car he had died, it was all unbelievable. Dad was taken away, and my brother and I were left to comfort Mum for whom the shock must have been tremendous – one moment the three of us happy and laughing over a meal, and the next moment her husband had gone from her forever. She always said later that she was so glad that I had been there at the time it had happened, and I remembered that moment when I pulled in at Bedford and made the decision to keep going for home – it was meant to be.

The weekend was a sad time, telephoning to relations and friends, and waiting to register the death and for a post-mortem which had to take place, and being Easter time, everything was put back until normal work began on Tuesday. Although I felt terribly upset to see Mother in such a sad state, inwardly I had very startling thoughts: I was relieved that he hadn't been revived by the ambulance men, for the effect on his brain and body would have been traumatic. I believe he would have been affected mentally and physically, but even more shaming was the fact that I didn't feel very upset at the time. Father and I had never been close until the last couple of years of his life. I could still remember distinctly the way he had bullied my mother and youngest brother Allen in earlier days, and was disturbed that I didn't feel more unhappy – in fact, I knew that Mum would have more freedom and enjoyment in the future.

Obviously I couldn't go back to school at the beginning of term; I telephoned the headmistress, explaining that my father had died suddenly, and listening to her response: "Oh dear, how inconvenient at the start of a new term, I like things to get off to a smooth start, but I suppose you'll need some time off." So, Dad's death was "an inconvenience", I ask you! The funeral was held some days later at Cambridge Crematorium, with a large number of our family and friends coming together. Allen confided in me later in the evening that he also felt awkward about Father's death for he couldn't bring himself to grieve, as he said, "I felt more sadness when our cat died." and although it sounds callous, I understood exactly what he meant. I suppose memory plays peculiar tricks on us, for down through the years I have tried to fathom out why father was 'distant', why he used to be unapproachable and always so negative. Part of the answer lies in our age, for I think we all get more critical, more pessimistic and cynical about life and society as we get older – "It's not like the good old days," is such a familiar cry, but then, the memory is being very selective. I'm also convinced that the war had a great deal to do with it; during four years when we would have been growing together as a family, he was away from us in the army, and I think this affected many, many thousands of families all over the world. There were some great things about Dad: he was always very honest and straight about money, he always laid down his pay packet on the table for mother to take out the household expenses and to leave him his rather meagre pocket money, and he never complained at that. I think experiences of his parents drinking to excess left their mark; I can only think of one occasion when he came home drunk, but very happy, and bearing in mind he was doing some pretty dirty, boring work in the tunnels that were to become the Victoria Line on London Underground, I think he could be excused for 'a few extra' on that occasion. It was Christmas time, he had been out with one or two of his workmates, and one, a well-built black man called Winston went out of his way to bring Dad home right to the front door, and father was very grateful for that action. In his own way I think he always tried to do the right thing for his family but there was always this barrier between us. I had always envied other families who seemed to have fathers who shared their lives, and who wanted to know about their experiences from day-to-day, but it just wasn't to be, in our family.

With the funeral out of the way Mother came to stay with me down at Woodford for a week or two until she felt she could face the home situation on her own, and I made frequent trips to stay with her at weekends.

At Whitsun I took on new responsibilities in the form of two dogs. Chris Potter, the PE teacher at school was lamenting the fact that with her brother going off to the Far East to live and work he had real problems over leaving his dogs behind, as the RSPCA and other bodies could not guarantee that they would be given a home together, and he felt that if the dogs were parted they would pine. I jumped in and said I would be quite happy to take on both dogs as long as they would be used to staying together when I came to school. The upshot was that a couple of days later the dogs arrived on my doorstep; when they saw the back garden and were allowed to roam and enjoy themselves they were very happy. Chris's brother warned me that they might be unhappy when he went, but the dogs just sat on the doorstep with me, watched him go, and then went back into the garden. So came another change in my life, for William and Bonnie, my two West Highland terriers became a very important part of life; I shared everything with them, I took them wherever I could and they really did become part of the family.

I had arranged to return to Halsway Manor, where I had been 'inducted' in folk music three years before, going back as a musician this time, to play for dancing and workshops during the week. Fortunately the manager was willing for me to take the dogs, they could sleep in my room, but, naturally, they were not allowed in the dining room. So at the beginning of the Whitsun week I went off to Halsway, taking the dogs for wonderful long walks into the Quantock Hills; I took them in the car for a special treat at the seaside, and drove to Minehead. We went down to the beach. I proudly showed them the sea as though I had specially arranged for the water to be there, and expected them to swim off, but they just took one look, had a sniff, and turned around to sit on the beach with me. I don't think they were great water lovers.

Summertime came round again. After the Barmouth holiday, where I had watched John Buckle doing his stuff as a holiday host and walking leader, he thought I could do the job as well, so he had recommended me as a CHA host, and I was asked to go to Barton to run two weeks in August, 1979. It seemed rather cruel to put the dogs into kennels so soon after I had taken them on, and Christine, the sister of their previous owner, volunteered to look after them – Christine and her husband Malcolm were keen dog lovers. The two weeks at Barton were a baptism of fire so far as hosting was concerned. The house was very large, on the front, with the sea just yards away, separated by a road, and for both weeks the house was full, about 50 to 60 guests each week. I pulled all the stops out and organised dancing, treasure hunts, games, evening barbecues and lead excursions each day, so by the end I was very tired, but had made many friends, and I felt it was a successful holiday.

My friend John Buckle, still working at Cooper School, had the idea of us sharing together in a special activities holiday which CHA ran. We would do the usual walking program during the day, and then in the evening people would have the choice of folk dancing with him in the main hall, or listening to classical music with me in a side room. We even offered some late-night music for everybody, so that they could wind down before going to bed. We went to Hope, in Derbyshire

– one of the first houses which CHA had purchased at the turn of the century. This combination of holiday went down very well. From that time on many people followed us around the country to book their holidays wherever we were going to be. Many of them became firm friends, and we are still in touch with them nearly 30 years later. The house, Moor Gate, was quaint to say the least. Like many of the old centres there were not many showers, so there was always the mad rush at the end of a walk to jump in the shower first. Bedroom accommodation was mainly dormitories, but the food was excellent, fabulous walks right from the house, and in those days people had not been pampered with ensuite bathrooms and individual bedrooms – in fact, in years to come, the conversion of these houses to provide the latest facilities was to prove their downfall – individual bedrooms with ensuites meant fewer guests, and financially it was to prove a step too far.

I then moved off to Cromer to host another week so CHA must have been happy with my first efforts. They had a spare place, so my mother came along for a much-needed holiday. We left the dogs with my brother Allen, and on arrival I became very busy welcoming the guests, meeting up with the walking leaders – fortunately the walking from the Cromer Centre was reasonably easy, for there aren't many hills around that part of Norfolk, and I would help with C (easy) walks. The manager and his wife, Mr and Mrs Duckering, were a lovely couple who ran a very efficient, happy establishment, with excellent food and plenty of it. The house was only a few yards from the seafront, so after the walk of the day and a shower, I used to often take Mum down to the pier or just to walk along the seafront. I remember on the Wednesday, which is always a free day for guests to do their own thing, a group of us went on the North Norfolk Railway; the weather was delightful and mother perked up a lot. I think that holiday did wonders for her after losing Dad the year before. In the evenings we had games, some dancing, the traditional concert, which the guests organised and participated in, and a treasure hunt; inevitably some guests would want to go off on their own, and I would be left with just a small handful to organise. I can remember one incident clearly. I had got to know a family who came from the Liverpool area. They supported me in all the activities and thoroughly enjoyed themselves. On the Wednesday evening, as I was pinning up some advertisements behind the door I heard the brief conversation on the other side. "Daddy, can we go out tonight to the concert at the pier?" this was the boy, about 10 years of age. There was a low murmur of conversation, but then his mother clearly said: "No, I know you'd like to go out, but we must stay and support Brian in the evenings." At this, I'm afraid I did give the game away and admit to them that I had overheard their private conversation, but I had to insist that they were on holiday to do what *they* wanted, to take the children out as a family, and they were not to worry about supporting me – I would organise something for the handful left behind. A little later, as I went into the room there were just five women left, sitting against the wall, and one spoke up for the others: "Well Brian, here we are, what are you going to do with us tonight?" What a leading question. In all honesty I would have willingly given them a couple of pound each to go to the concert on the pier, but I knew I had to provide some entertainment, and we got by.

At the end of the holiday I was left questioning my suitability and enthusiasm for doing this sort of hosting, somehow, treasure hunts and rather silly games seemed to be out of date, and the very idea of people just taking part because they felt sorry for the host was horrifying. A few weeks later I contacted Derek Browne, who was in charge of the special activity holidays at CHA. I put to him the suggestion that I might run a holiday as a music host, offering a programme of classical music each evening as an alternative to the traditional fun and games. I can still hear his reply and his rather serious northern accent: "OK Brian, perhaps we'll give it a try, and be prepared to lose money for just one week. We will go for the first week of August, 1981, back at Cromer, but I don't think we'll get many customers." What a prophet of doom he sounded, though, during the next few years, it was his special activities department and the enterprise and work he put in that kept the company afloat. CHA should have been very thankful to Derek – in fact they quietly pensioned him off when they didn't need him any more – such gratitude.

I put off contacting Derek about the holiday for as long as possible, because I quite expected to find out no one had booked; eventually, in April I rang him, and received the incredible news that Cromer was fully booked and they had a waiting list for this classical music week – fantastic, even Derek sounded cheerful.

I didn't realise it at the time, but music holidays with adults was to become an important part of life later... and I admit here and now that I don't believe in coincidences; there is a Hand that guides us through our decisions in life, though often we only see it in hindsight.

CHAPTER FIFTEEN

GOODBYE TO TEACHING CAREER

At the end of summer term 1979 there was an exodus of teachers, some of whom had served for a long time at Woodford. The deputy head had retired a year earlier, along with the head of physics, both had been there for at least 20 years; I believe some of these old-timers knew that big changes were coming to the school, in staff, in examinations and intake of pupils, and they really wanted to get out and remember the school as they had known it rather than face new challenges. Perhaps challenges *are* for the young.

1979 was the diamond jubilee of the founding of Woodford, and the school wanted to mark it in a special way. A former pupil and teacher at the school, Diana Newlands came in to organise a grand end of term event, which we called *Kaleidoscope*. Diana always thought big, and took on challenges with great relish; in this instance she was rightly proud of the fact that almost every girl in the school, and indeed most of the staff, played some part in this production, either on stage, backstage or in preparation. How she managed to engender such enthusiasm and commitment I don't know; I do know that her energy and her own enthusiasm were infectious – it was just impossible to say no to her requests. We had to cater for a large audience, and decided to put on three evening performances, which were all sold out weeks before it happened.

Listing just a few of the acts will give some idea of the variety on offer, everything just flowed with no interruptions or pauses, it went like clockwork. The choirs performed, many types of dancers, ballet, one set dressed in armour, a Cossack group and Spanish set; percussionists performed, with xylophone, timpani, marimba, maracas and tambourines; for one item we had at least 15 guitars to accompany a ballet dancer, there was an excerpt from a Shakespeare play, and that was just the first half. I had been training about 30 musicians to play while they marched, to form a marching band. Over many lunch hours in the preceding weeks we lined up on the playground and they learnt all about 'dressing' – to march in step and keep straight lines, to counter march and halt together – but to do all this while still playing and holding heads up. Mrs Taylor and the art department performed wonders by producing black hats and tunics, so that on the night the marching band looked smart and sounded good. The plan was for us to open the second half by marching in from outside the hall playing, then a couple of marches at the halt, then finally leading out of the hall. *Colonel Bogey* was the obvious choice, and everyone began to clap in time with the band. After even more items: gymnastics, circus clowns, complete with man on stilts, more drama, some chamber music, the madrigal group, suitably dressed in Elizabethan costume, the band led the whole cast back into the hall for their well-deserved applause. It was a triumph for Diana as producer, and all the participants, including so many who had worked behind the scenes. This was a tremendous success, and, perhaps the highest moment of my time at Woodford, for it was all down hill from there.

The headmistress had been out to the far east a couple of years earlier for a summer holiday, unfortunately contracted cholera, and was very ill in hospital back in England, so the deputy took charge of the school, and everything went on just as smoothly as before, perhaps to the head's surprise; maybe we all have this feeling inside that we are indispensable, that the world will tumble to the ground without our expertise and leadership. What a fallacy! Having moved from one job to another during my career one of the lessons I learned was that as one person exits through the door, someone else is there to step in one's shoes and prove that life just goes on. The illness had certainly weakened the head, the old deputy had left and the head of maths had been appointed, which was the head's choice all along, and younger staff were coming in with new ideas and attitudes. Miss Satchell, with no fuss quietly announced that she would be retiring at the end of summer term 1980. There were few special events to mark her retirement and she seemed quite ready to go. Her successor was very rapidly chosen, and we were to meet Miss D before summer holidays began. She was 58, and came from Barnsley; was it just a coincidence that Mr. Radcliffe, the retiring chief education officer of London Borough of Redbridge also came from Barnsley? Along with other heads of department I had my allotted time with her, and she asked very few questions about the music at the school but seemed very interested in the fact that a) the department had a full-time assistant, and a comment to this effect was noted, b) I had a scale 4 post – in financial terms this was just one step below senior teacher, and had been openly advertised with the job in 1973. She muttered something to the effect that this was highly unusual, and this was also noted. If only I had realised, there lay the seeds of a determination to get rid of me!

As the autumn term began many of us noticed that things were already changing for the worst. I used to type a list of assembly hymns for the week and give them to the head, and she would invariably lose the list and claim that I had never given it to her; I backed this up by taking the hymn number up to her each morning, and as I waited to go into her room out would come the deputy looking upset and distressed. On one or two occasions in assembly the head would lose her place in the Bible reading, once she dropped the Bible, and, naturally there would be a little giggle from the first years in the front of the hall. This would make her very angry, and once she turned to the whole school and announced, "I just hate Woodford!" Back came the barely audible reply from the senior girls in the gallery, "And we hate you." Sometimes the hymn singing was very poor, and I would stop playing, tell the girls I was very disappointed with their efforts, and we would start the hymn again. After assembly I was sent for and told this was impertinence on my part – she, the head, would determine when the singing was poor. I just couldn't win, and this was just assembly. She just didn't have the charisma, the bearing of a headmistress.

One morning during the term two of the youngsters were hanging around at the end of my lesson, and I went to close the music room door and to send them packing off to break. One girl told me, "We've got to see the dinner lady." and there was an embarrassing giggle.

"Don't be ridiculous, Jane," I replied. "The dinner ladies don't come in until 12 o'clock, now go off to break."

"Shall we tell him?" Jane asked of her friend, and they nudged each other, and one told me, "Sorry, we mean the headmistress". So, the nickname among the juniors was 'the Dinner Lady'. I pretended to be quite angry with these girls, and gave them a good telling off, but inwardly, I knew what they meant.

Within weeks the chairman of governors called an extraordinary staff meeting, asking the head *not* to attend, and opened proceedings by asking us what the hell was going on at Woodford School, he had never had so many complaints from outside, etc. Would we tell him, in confidence, what the trouble was? Five or six of us lifted our heads above the parapet, and told him politely but firmly WHO was the source of the problem; for my part I mentioned assembly, and some of the embarrassing times we had witnessed, reminding him that we were dealing with intelligent girls who were bound to judge the person leading assembly – and this alone had lead to a lack of respect on their part; respect had to be earned whereas obedience could be demanded. At the end of the meeting several other staff came and told us how much they agreed with what had been said, but, despite his promise of confidentiality, within 24 hours the head had a list of the staff who had spoken out and what they had stated. I should have realised that Woodford was no different to any other group of people – there's always the snake, someone who will 'grass' to be noticed; some teachers would sell their own grandmother for a higher scale post, and we had a few such people on our staff. To this day I believe the chairman and his promise, but what could he do when others were ready to step in and drop us in it? Before the end of term we had had an inspection by the borough, and later a report was published. At the end of the school year the head, with the borough's approval had appointed a second deputy head – our original deputy had to cling to her job by her fingernails with the help of her union. The only conclusion we could reach as to why the deputy was so disliked by the head was that she was still friends with the last head –Miss Satchell, who had been informed early on that she was not welcome back at the school! Life went on as before, and once again I trained, and took a small group of girls to sing at the Festival Hall for the Ernest Read Christmas concert, and obtained tickets for the headmistress to attend the concert and the tea party afterwards; I was desperately anxious to try and get on good terms with her, I had to work with her every day of the week. She came with a friend from Barnsley, and at tea the conversation was not easy. I said I hoped the head was proud of her girls and how splendid they looked in their school uniform. "I should hope so." came the reply. Then the friend asked for directions to Covent Garden, and suddenly I knew –THIS was the musical interest, they were both opera lovers, and after explaining the best way to get to Covent Garden, I smiled and said, "Ah, so you're both going off to see an opera."

"No, [in strong Barnsley accent] we're going to buy chocolates at Thorntons!"

Judith Liddell and I worked our socks off to make the school Christmas concert a success, but with no thanks from the top. During the spring term she called me in, did not offer me a seat, and calmly stated: "When are you thinking of leaving?" I was dumbstruck, and replied that I had no intention of leaving Woodford, it was the best school I had ever worked in; I added that I thought it a very strange question –verging on unprofessional, but was told that my reply was impertinent. Apparently one wasn't allowed to answer back. I then suggested that I ask the school secretary to witness the head's question, but she said that she would deny ever saying it. I couldn't win, but asked whether there was something wrong with my work. "No," came the reply, "I just don't like you." The complete bluntness of her answer left me speechless, but then retorted that I may not like her very much, but, professionally I was there to carry out her wishes – she as the head, me as head of music and would continue as such. At that I left the room.

Around this time Judith got married to a music teacher from Forest School, an independent establishment about 5 miles distant. A number of our senior girls, under Judith, had joined together with the Forest boys and Christopher Connett their music teacher, and her husband-to-be, to do concerts and a tour. Chris was a great bloke, very talented, and we got on very well but within months something went wrong. Judith seemed to become very distant, and was organising concerts at the school left right and centre, concerts of a very high standard, but I was left to feel totally outside her work. We had always had an excellent relationship, enjoyed working together and laughing together, and this new distant attitude quite worried me. She became a workaholic, not allowing herself to pause at all. The atmosphere was not good, not helped by the fact that the headmistress began to work on her by convincing her that there might have to be a reduction in staff, and she might have to look for another job. Maybe the pair of them thought they could wear me down, but I could not think that of Judith; I did my level best to assure her that her job was secure, I even got the music adviser to reassure her, but I think from that time on she began to look for another post, and perhaps the concerts and extra work were a means to go off with a handsome reference.

During the summer holiday of 1981 John Buckle and I went up to Ambleside in the Lake District to run a combined week of dancing and classical music – along with some challenging walks during the day. It was a centre I was to return to on several occasions but this week was rather special because Prince Charles and Diana were being married on 29th July. It happened to be a Wednesday which coincided with our day off from walking, and it was fairly obvious that most guests were going to try to watch the ceremony on television. The local cinema was going to show the wedding; we both laughed as guests went off early to see this wedding, but thought that we might amble down to Ambleside at about 11 o'clock and drift in to watch the event. The cinema was packed out – 'House Full' notice outside, so we looked around at the hotels but soon realised you couldn't just walk into the hotel and watch their TV unless you were a guest. The streets were completely empty – everybody in Ambleside was watching the wedding except us, so we beat a hasty retreat back to the house and ended up squinting at the small black-and-white television in the staff quarters. That evening over dinner everyone was talking about the wedding, and, as events were to prove, the couple never stopped being an item of interest from that day forward.

Back at school for the new term once again Redbridge Festival at the Royal Albert Hall came up in 1982, and again we prepared the girls for this. There were problems over the sale of tickets, and the head became very awkward over this. All parents wanted the best, most expensive tickets, and there were never enough to go round so we would have a draw for the expensive seats on the understanding that the 'losers' would take the cheaper seats; this took time, but money had to be paid very quickly, so I would send a cheque from the school fund and collect money from the pupils later. On this occasion Miss D had refused to let me use a school fund cheque, so I sent a personal cheque. A few days later a number of girls came back not with money but with their cheap tickets returned to me – they had been offered better seats when they went to their Saturday lessons at the music school, so, in fact I was left with the cheaper tickets and was over £50 out of pocket, and in 1982 this was getting on for half my week's pay which I could not afford. I have gone into details in this matter because the whole thing came back to haunt me two years later. The atmosphere in the school was bad; staff were suspicious of others, the discipline became harder and some staff became quite ill. Within one year both the head of English and a member of the maths department developed multiple sclerosis and I'm convinced that the stress and unhappiness in the school was a factor in this situation. Rosemary Batten, head of English, went downhill very fast, was quickly given early retirement but soon was hardly able to walk. Some of us used to go to her house at Epping at lunchtime to eat our fish and chips with her and keep her company, but she died within a few months of retiring, being found dead in her home quite alone. Janet Stock in the maths department lost the use of her legs very quickly, was compelled to use sticks, and also was awarded early retirement on health grounds. She soon became completely immobile, had to take to a wheelchair, and was nursed by her mother, and sister. It must have been most unusual for two people in one establishment to get the disease almost at the same time.

I used to long for the holidays, and the chance to get away from school. In 1981 I returned to Cromer to present my music programme. During term time the weekends became a precious oasis. On most Saturday afternoons I would take the dogs off to Epping Forest for a good two-hour walk, which they always looked forward to. Bless them, they had to spend so much time during the week on their own, just lying in their basket waiting for 'Sir' to return. In July, 1982 Judith left Woodford for another post and I knew I would never be given a full-time assistant again. She was very fortunate in obtaining the job of running the chapel choir at Wycombe Abbey, one of the most prestigious public schools in the country, and within a few years she had become the head of music at the school. I tried to contact her on various occasions but she never returned to Woodford or had anything to do with the staff, except one close friend, who informed me that Judith wanted the chapter of her life in Woodford to be closed for good.

In 1982 JB (John Buckle) and I travelled up to Kinfauns Castle near Perth to lead a CHA holiday, where John had a magnificent hall for dancing, and I was allocated a grand wood-panelled room with large open fireplace. Sadly, the castle was in a rather shaky state of repair, and this came home to me during the week. Two of my greatest fans were Christine, a blind girl, about 20 at the time, who came away with her mother and guide dog. I'm afraid I was always guilty of feeding the dog surreptitiously under the table with bacon rind at breakfast, and was eventually told off by Christine and Mum, who assured me that the dog was already well fed, that, like all Labradors, she would just keep eating, and Christine would be 'ticked off ' by her guide dog inspector if the dog grew too fat. We were all sitting in silence listening to some rather haunting Tchaikovsky when the dog got up and moved away from Christine, who tried to get it back under her chair. The dog just would not go back, and when we stopped the music and looked, we discovered all that area was crawling with ants, some moving up the chair legs to attack Christine – no wonder the dog was anxious to move away. We got the manager to deal with the ants, but the next night one of the guests was stung by a wasp, and on examination, we found hundreds of them in the fireplace and at the foot of the chimney, and at that point I insisted that we move to another room. The dog always made us laugh, for when it considered that I had gone on long enough with my wretched classical music, she would stretch, sit up and have a good shake of the harness to remind me that it was time to wind up. You could set your watch by the dog's antics – and this little threesome used to come on almost every holiday for years on end. The manager and his wife were Macphersons, very Scottish, generous in talk and rather mean with the food. On our arrival after a long journey in the car, we were invited in to a cup of tea and sandwich, and it really was one sandwich each, but after our preliminary talk about the week's holiday, as John and I left the room, I noticed that Mrs MacPherson quietly produced another plate of sandwiches for her and her husband to plough through. Mr MacPherson told us he always "Liked to give the guests a wee haggis," so Thursday night was to be the great haggis meal, but what an anti-climax it turned out to be. McPherson insisted that it would have to be ceremonially brought in at the appropriate moment, with silence on the part of the guests; no piper was available so I agreed to play a suitable Scottish air to precede the entry of the haggis. I assumed that he would be dressed up in his kilt, to carry in the great haggis; I went to the door of the dining room, asked for silence from the guests, and peeped round to tell Mrs MacPherson we were ready. I then began playing on the recorder and doing a suitable slow march, but after about 32 bars, I quietly turned and saw, to my dismay, that the cook was just wandering in, still wearing her not too clean apron, the haggis boringly wrapped in silver foil – I think it had been bought at the local supermarket – and just proceeded to dole it out at the first table. So *this* was "Giving the guests a wee haggis." I know we laughed for days afterwards. The walking part of the holiday was quite strenuous, and after dancing for over two hours in the evening, some dancers would finish the day listening to music with my group, and would apologise to me if they nodded off to sleep. I just don't know how they had the strength to do all this, but there was never a dull moment, always something to be involved in and guests thoroughly enjoyed these activities. A few years later we were to return to Kinfauns under another manager.

Derek Brown, the CHA special-interest secretary had told me earlier in 1982 that he would like me to go to Fowey, down in Cornwall. I was informed that the manager, Roger Blount (pronounced 'Blunt' – Blunt in name and Blunt in character), was not an easy man to get on with, tended to treat the place as his own and was extremely firm about who he would have to run any holiday weeks -not many hosts were invited back – and I appreciated the advice and warnings. On arrival, I parked the car and wandered across the drive to the front door of the house, then noticed someone sunbathing in the gardens so I thought I would introduce myself and ask for the manager. The sunbather was very tanned, wearing the smallest costume I'd seen, and smelt strongly of perfume. "I AM the manager", he replied. "Welcome to my home at Fowey; I suppose you're the music chap." I noticed he had a tray beside him, complete with silver pot, matching milk jug, sugar basin, biscuits, all it lacked was the servant standing by awaiting orders. "Would you care for some tea?" He asked, and promptly clapped his hands and out from the bushes came a young man, I would guess in late teens, who promptly took the order for my tea. It was incredible, like a scene from a

Somerset Maugham novel, or *Brideshead Revisited*. This was my introduction to the incredible Mr B. Later, when it was convenient to Mr B, we met up to discuss the programme for the week, and I realised that everything revolved around him. If guests wanted to hire a boat on the midweek 'off day', they did it through him; if you wanted to arrange for lunch out, Mr B. did the organising; trip round the harbour? Mr B. arranged it on "special" terms. Mr B had his hands in everything, he had been mayor of Fowey, had been on the council, and wanted everyone to know that he was a pillar of the community. Fowey couldn't function without Mr B. He told me he always showed a couple of short (!) films about his life in Fowey, and the visit of Prince Charles – one presumes just to meet Mr B, so although I had my programme already arranged I did some alterations so that the films could be shown; he had assured me that the guests each week thoroughly enjoyed it, but personally I found it a complete ego trip – The Mr B Show. After the film on Monday evening he proposed to show another one later in the week, but I had to put my foot down and make it clear that this time it would have to take place outside the programme I had already printed -- and that didn't go down very well. The excursion leaders had a hard time of it also, it was the only centre I knew where the manager took all the money for excursions (to pay for the coach) rather than the excursion leader. Later on I began to see the reasoning behind all this… The centre at Fowey overlooked the beautiful estuary, and on the midweek day off I was happy just to go down and sit on a bench watching the boats, it really was and is a beautiful place. Somehow we got through the week without coming to blows, but I returned home facing the fact that Mr B ran everything at Fowey. Some weeks later Derek Brown from CHA head office rang me to tell me that Mr B had enjoyed my visit and wanted me to go back to Fowey next summer – apparently this was a great privilege, a rare event for leaders or hosts to be invited back to Fowey for a second time.

The situation at school was going from bad to worse. Almost every term meant another inspection of my subject; I must have had three inspections in less than two years, in fact when the council music inspector put his head round the door I would automatically give him a folder – my syllabus, the timetable, exam results and so on. He admitted to me that it was a waste of his time but that if a head asked for an inspection he had to comply. My workload was very heavy, because after the departure of Judith Connet, the full-time assistant, only a part-timer was appointed, for about 1½ days a week. This replacement was worse than useless; the girls disliked him, not because he was particularly strict but they just felt uneasy about him, as did most of the staff. He made it quite clear early on that he needed no help or advice, though he had only done a little part-time work in primary schools before. On one evening the music adviser arrived at the end of a school day, but this time it wasn't for an inspection. He knew about the problems in the school, that the relationship between the head and I was pretty bad and he asked if I would go with him in to her office to try to patch things up. Naturally I was quite happy to make this effort. We went in and he told her quite frankly that he knew I wanted things to improve and that in the present state of affairs everyone was suffering; to his credit he told her that it was quite unnecessary for inspections, he was perfectly satisfied with my work, there was nothing for her to complain about in that area, as he had told her on a number of occasions. She said nothing, but quietly drummed her fingers on the desk. "Miss D***, I know that Mr Astell wants to work with you, and I would like to think that we could make a new start. Maybe we can shake hands on this, as a symbol of a happier relationship from today." he said. I stood up, held out my hand to her, but instead of shaking hands she just burst out "Get out both of you!" and swivelled her chair round to face the wall, like a petulant child. Malcolm and I looked at each other in disbelief, then quietly got up and left the room. As he closed the door he made the sign that she was crazy and shook his head, but when I challenged him to go back to the education office and repeat all this to his chief, Malcolm just said that wasn't possible – in other words he wasn't willing to get involved, and left me to face the situation alone.

This whole matter may sound as though I was wallowing in self-pity, but it was really getting me down. Teaching is always a hard, challenging, all-consuming job without the added aggro of knowing that someone wants to get rid of you for no apparent reason. During that spring term of 1983 I had to go back to the doctor on two or three occasions suffering from the most awful headaches and a numbness in my left arm, and on one occasion I let out that there would come a time when I might drive from the school and never return. He was quite alarmed by this remark – one of his own daughters had been through the school as a pupil, in earlier and happier times, and he listened to my story about the problems in my job. My blood pressure was sky-high and he was concerned about my mental state, for I was finding it very difficult to sleep, my mind would not rest, yet at seven in the morning I just wanted to sleep and stay in bed more than anything else in the world. Armed with tablets to stabilise the BP I plodded on for the rest of that term.

The holiday breaks were the only thing to look forward to, just to get away from the feeling of persecution and scared of doing anything wrong, which would give cause for the headmistress to find fault. In the Whitsun break John Buckle and I went up to Whitby to do a combined dancing and classical music week. It was the first of several visits I was to make to that lovely coastal resort. The CHA centre was at Abbey House, at the top of East Cliff, next to the ruins of the ancient abbey and was approached by walking through the tiny streets with the smell of kippers being smoked, mingled with the tantalising aroma of fish and chips – Whitby must have been the capital of the fish and chip world, they really knew how to cook them – and then climbing the 199 steps, perhaps pausing for breath at St Mary's Church halfway up the path, to finally reach the top with fantastic views of Whitby, its town and harbour lying below. During the week Prince Charles was attending a special service at St Mary's, and many of us watched as his helicopter made a very careful landing close to the church; The whole town had turned out to greet the Prince, and many of the guests at Abbey House joined in the celebrations. In those days the house still had its dormitories; I believe I slept in a dorm with about 12 others, which added to the fun of the holiday. The walking side of the holiday was fantastic; our walking leader was Terry Firth, a local man who knew the area like the back of his hand, had all the stories and anecdotes ready to tell the guests, and he certainly knew how to take us to the best, unspoilt sites; even on the C (easy) walks which I lead there were good views and good opportunities to spend lunch at a village pub. We also had the chance to go on the North York Moors Railway to Pickering, and on the 'off ' day – no organised walking – I just HAD to sample the fish and chips down in the town. I note recently that Rick Stein, an eminent TV chef, voted the Magpie Café to be the best place for fish and chips in the whole of Great Britain – certainly there were long queues of holidaymakers even in those days. In all these holidays we met up with some wonderful people, and many became friends for years after the holiday was over. Ron and Betty Simpson with their two boys became such friends. They were both very sporty types, and always won the table tennis competition – if one hadn't been set up at the beginning of the week it was only a matter of an hour or so before Betty had organised it, arranged the draw and put the list on the board. I can still remember a comedy item we did at the concert – it was something to do with people who had hurt their noses and had difficulty in speaking clearly – it was Ron's item and he was brilliant, in fact it was difficult to play our parts without bursting into laughter. We were to meet up with them on many holidays.

During the summer holiday I certainly travelled some miles. We returned to Kinfauns Castle, outside Perth, to be met by the renowned Macphersons – who once again were pleased to "Give the guests a wee haggis." and we still found ourselves hungry each day. During the walks, whenever we found a village shop open, we would raid it for bars of chocolate and biscuits to supplement the rather meagre rations doled out by the McPhersons. On this holiday were Pat, with her two boys and girl, who had been at Kinfauns the year before; they were great fun, and when I discovered that the younger boy played the French horn I'd asked him to bring it to play to the guests. Craig did bring the instrument and entertained people at the concert which was always put on near the end of the week.

As I mentioned earlier I had been requested to make a return visit to Mr B at Fowey, so after the return from Scotland, with a few days to do some washing and try to sort out the garden – it always seemed to revert to jungle when I was away on holiday – I set off down to Cornwall on a Friday, to be ready to meet the guests the following day. I was informed that the house and annexe were completely full, and I would have to sleep in the gun room for one night. I didn't mind this too much, there was a camp bed, and wash basin, and I would be given a proper room next day. On the Saturday people arrived in droves, and the house and annexe were completely full, over 60 guests – the experiment of offering classical music certainly seemed to be successful. The music sessions took place in the large hall, and on the first night I met up with a formidable, VERY serious elderly woman from Austria who took me to task – I christened her "Mrs Vienna". I had played some music connected with Vienna and she tackled me later for not playing any Richard Tauber. In her strong Austrian accent she lambasted me for leaving out one of Vienna's greatest singers. I apologised and told her that it was impossible to bring hundreds of records in the car – remember this was still the days of LPs. That night I searched in the car and, wonder of wonders, discovered a cassette with a handful of songs performed by the great man himself, so next day in the course of the programme I proudly told the guests that at great expense (!) I had found Richard Tauber – who would now perform *My Heart and I* – one of his very popular numbers. He sang away, I was feeling rather proud of my achievement, but at the end up stood Mrs Vienna: "You fool", she said, "HE IS SINGING IN ENGLISH!" I just couldn't win. I was to cross swords with her later in the week.

The big event of the week from my point of view was meeting up with Pauline Jones. She had come with her parents, I think she was getting over some affair, and I made friends with the family on the first night, after they expressed sympathy with me over the Mrs Vienna affair. Pauline was just lovely, pretty, with gorgeous eyes , no need of any makeup, with a great sense of humour, a real taste for classical music – she told me her favourite composer was Handel, so, naturally I rearranged my programme for the week to include a great deal of Mr Handel! I just fell in love with her from the first moment. The next day I joined the family on the A walk – this would be up to 12 miles -something I would never dream of attempting in normal circumstances. On our return Pauline thought it would be nice to freshen up in the sea, and I joined her in freezing water, smiling all the time. I still have the photos to prove it. The friends there who knew me realised I was a different person – they knew I NEVER did the long walks, and avoided sea bathing like the plague, and now I was getting up really early. It just had to be love. That was a glorious week in Cornwall, the two of us went off together for a boat ride on the mid-week free morning, and after lunch, with her parents we visited Llanhydrock house, the Victorian National Trust property nearby. I saw a beautiful grand piano in one of the downstairs rooms, and happened to mention to Pauline that I thought pianos were for playing rather than just being on display. The steward heard this remark and invited me to play, which I did for about 20 minutes until all the people gathering round were blocking the path for others, so I gave up at that point. This was most unusual because in my experience the stewards at NT properties generally don't let you get anywhere near the instruments, let alone play them. One of the A walks, on August bank holiday, returned to Fowey Hall along the south Cornwall footpath, and I was acting as back marker when Mrs Vienna – none other – came and told me she needed to find a toilet; I told her there was no toilet until we reached Polruan, where we were due to catch the ferry over to Fowey. She went away muttering about the stupid British, and the next thing I heard were screams and laughter – Mrs Vienna screaming from the bushes still adjusting her underwear while a group of children were laughing at the spectacle. She had decided to use the bushes, but in a very public part of the path, and when the children saw her she had fallen into the bushes and scratched herself. A couple of women guests helped her, bathing the scratches and tidying her, but she then turned on me and in an acid voice said: "I suppose now you're going to leave me behind and go off with the others."

"Definitely not", I said, "I will stay with you until we reach the very door of Fowey Hall." and I did. So she couldn't complain that she had been neglected, but I dread to think what sort of report CHA received from her at the end of the week. I do know that on these holidays there are always one or two people who you can never please, you just try to do your best.

Later in the week came my falling out with the manager, Mr B. He sidled up to me one evening to inform me that he would only charge me £10 for my night in the gun room at the beginning of the holiday; "That's fine." I replied. "As you know I can reclaim it from CHA when I send in the receipt."

Suddenly his attitude and appearance changed, "I'm not in the habit of issuing receipts" he said.

I retorted, "And I'm not in the habit of paying money without getting a receipt." He went away muttering and the suspicions I'd always had about managers and financial affairs were being realised. On the last morning I took Pauline and her parents down to the railway station and said a fond farewell, though we were determined to meet up again.

The autumn term of 1983 began as usual, but even the staff noticed that I was different. Pauline and I met up each weekend, she came to stay with me a couple of times, and I would take her back home to Sutton where she had a flat. Her parents came down to stay with her and the four of us went to the Festival Hall to a Handel concert. Everything seemed to be going well and life had taken on a new meaning. Meanwhile, I had been rather anxious about an ulcer which had gathered above my left eye, and when it started bleeding I decided to go to the doctor. He took one look and told me I should go off to hospital as soon as possible. He actually booked me in for the next weekend to a hospital in Billericay which specialised in burns and skin grafting. Pauline was coming over for the weekend, and as usual, we took the dogs for a lovely long walk in Epping Forest, the trees looking gorgeous with their red and brown leaves just beginning to fall. Then in the evening she told me that she wouldn't be seeing me again; she couldn't really give a reason though I suspect that the difference in our ages perhaps worried her, or perhaps her parents had told her to take it into consideration; perhaps it was because I had been too slow on the uptake, for I always prepared her bed in the spare room, and never discussed or invited her to sleep with me. Was I being naïve about this? Did she really want a deeper relationship at that stage? Was she expecting something more? I just don't know. We both went to church together, and were Christians, and I thought she would have been embarrassed and unhappy at any suggestion of sex. To this day I really don't know the answer. On Saturday evening I took her to the station – suddenly I couldn't be bothered to drive all the way across London to take her home. I went back to my empty house and felt shattered.

The next morning a kind member of our church drove me over to Billericay ready for an operation on the Monday. David Hatch, one of the church members, was an anaesthetist at Great Ormond Street Hospital, in fact he became professor of anaesthiology, and had contacts everywhere. He had arranged for one of his friends at Billericay who was an expert in skin grafting, to postpone his paternity leave by one day to do the operation.

Apparently I was suffering from a rodent ulcer which needed to be removed; this involved grafting skin from behind my ear on to the hole left behind by the removal of the ulcer – a fairly simple operation except that it was in rather a delicate place and required that I stay perfectly still for a good number of hours with my head completely bandaged – just a little space around the right eye so that I wasn't completely blind. Whatever pain and discomfort I had paled into insignificance compared with some of the people in the ward. There were young men who had been in the hospital for months undergoing several operations for 60% and 70% burns, requiring them to be kept still and with no bedclothes or covering on them. They were a lively bunch receiving a good number of visitors to keep their spirits up in more ways than one; at eight o'clock in the evening the place resembled a saloon bar with cans of beer and bottles of spirits, and when the visitors went home the party began. The nurses seemed to turn a blind eye, and I literally had to turn both blind eyes (!) to this situation, these patients were very much long-stay types and in pain 24 hours a day. It did mean that I couldn't sleep at night for the noise, often the radio would be on until well past midnight, yet, in true hospital tradition, we would be woken up at six o'clock in the morning. I was so grateful for a visit from my brother Allen who travelled to Billericay from London after work, and stayed for over an hour – goodness knows what time he got back home to Sible Hedingham. One of the members of my church also came to see me one afternoon, and told me he would drive me home when I was discharged at the end of the week. I was allowed to go home, still heavily bandaged over my left eye, with instructions to return after a week for its removal. Naturally I was told to take things easy and not to return to work for two weeks, and even more naturally the headmistress, on being given the news, told the school secretary that she thought I was "Swinging the lead," taking off more time than I needed. There was no sympathy in that quarter, but I was so moved to receive an enormous card from the pupils at the school wishing me well and telling me they were looking forward to my return. There was also a splendid get well card from the staff – only the headmistress had declined to sign!

The skin graft took first time and healed quickly, so that after a few weeks there was no sign of any operation. I had to go into the head on the first day of my return, and while she could not bring herself to offer a welcome or any sympathy, she did make it clear that she thought I'd taken more time off than I needed. I just could not win! So we battled on to the end of term with the usual Christmas concerts, working for the Ernest Read concert at the Festival Hall, though I confess that my heart wasn't in the work. I missed Pauline more than ever, and it was taking a long time to get over the affair. The school itself was in a state of upheaval because the headmistress appeared to be harassing other members of staff and they were calling in their union representatives to sort things out. It was almost a daily occurrence to see reps. from the National Union of Teachers (NUT), Professional Association of Teachers (PAT), and my own NAS/UWT almost passing each other in the corridors. It was around this time I received a call from the local NUT area representative to offer help if I didn't think my own union was doing enough to support me – she had heard of the persecution I was up against, was horrified by what she found at the school and the way some of the staff were treated, and that something had to be done soon.

At the end of term I was involved in the usual carol singing – members of the church would go around four or five local streets, yours truly accompanying them on the accordion, and then to warm up back at the home of David Hatch – the fellow who arranged for my operation – with lovely home-made mince pies and hot wine to warm us up; this ritual happened every year and was a sign that Christmas had really begun.

It was a busy time for my folk band, as we played at two or three parent association Christmas dances; the band had still kept me busy most Fridays and Saturdays, bringing in some useful income, though it often meant travelling many miles, getting home late and up with the lark on Sunday morning to play the organ at church. A few months earlier I had threatened to give up the folk band after doing a gig at The Blind Beggar pub in the Mile End Road. The agent had given me travel details, and I arrived there with the guitarist and a drummer. We were performing in a large hall above the pub, and as we put our stuff together I made a few remarks to the others about the rather unsavoury characters that seemed to be hanging about. To me their pockets seemed to be bulging with knives, guns and all the paraphernalia of an East End gang. The caller got a few people up to dance and things were going reasonably well for about an hour when three or four of the gang, now quite tanked up, lurched over and told me quite firmly that *they* had

had enough of this bl****** country stuff and why couldn't I play some old-time music that they could sing along to? Fortunately I always carried in the music bag a book of old-time waltzes, quick steps and sing-along songs and I rapidly put this on the stand, told the caller he would be having a rest for about half an hour, and then we gave the crowd some good old-fashioned stuff to sing. Thank heavens I had shoved in this book before leaving home otherwise I think we would have been following our instruments through the windows! Somehow we got to the end of the evening with very simple dances and waltzes, nothing complicated could be attempted as most of the crowd were fairly drunk. The organiser came over and offered me a cheque but I insisted that we NEVER took cheques and that would have been spelled out when the booking was confirmed by the agent; no way would I would take a cheque in a situation like that, it would have probably bounced all along the Mile End Road. The organiser pulled out a wad of notes and paid us, and we packed up as fast as we could. I fully expected to find all the wheels gone from my car when I got downstairs, or a few broken windows, but all seemed well and we drove off as fast as we could. When I rang the agent and made it clear that I would never go back to such a place again, how I had been scared about the whole atmosphere from start to finish… she calmly told me, "Oh Brian, didn't you know that was the pub where the Kray twins used to operate? That's where they planned many of their jobs!" had I known that I wouldn't have gone within 5 miles of the place.

Along with the folk band gigs I had also been doing some private teaching, clarinet and piano, after school at home a couple of days a week. Looking back how on earth I kept up this busy schedule I don't know.

Once again mother and I were invited to spend Christmas with Allen, youngest brother, and, bless them, they were happy to take in my two dogs and Jess, mother's Jack Russell. I'm convinced that Allen was a secret pyromaniac, for the height of his Christmas enjoyment was the annual indoor fireworks show he presented. This took place in the kitchen on Christmas night, where we watched him light – with difficulty – many so-called 'spectacular' displays. These usually turned out to be what can only be described as moving turds of brown shapes, or miniature farts of stars, all accompanied with thick smoke and foul smell; it was a gigantic show of anti-climax – never was so much expected, but so little transpired, yet it always had us laughing until we cried. It's difficult to understand in cold print, but helped along with a few drinks Allen's fireworks were an experience not to be missed. They were quite an expensive luxury and every year he vowed not to buy any more, but he would always give it another go. Brenda, his wife, always seemed to be so highly organised with meals, and everything worked so well however many she had to cater for. She also had a full-time job, so it was very good of them to open up their home to us at Christmas and let us share in their fun and games.

The spring term, 1984, started in the usual way with mock exams for O and A level students, which had to be marked quickly. The biennial Redbridge music Festival had come round again and I got down to rehearsals with the choir. Earlier on I mentioned the problems over ticket sales and how I lost £50, so when the time came to sell tickets to the pupils I informed the deputy head that I was unable to do this unless the head was willing to allow me to write a school fund cheque to pay for the whole allocation. I explained everything that had happened in '82, that I was quite willing to sell tickets but not to lose more money. She made a note of this and went away, and I thought all was forgotten, but some days later she came back and asked me very formally what I was going to do about selling tickets to the Woodford parents, and once again I had to tell her that unless circumstances changed and I was given permission to do the thing my way, with time to allocate tickets and collect money, I was left with no alternative but to refuse. She wrote every word down and, unbeknown to me, these were going to be used against me in a few months time. Eventually she sorted out the ticket allocation but it took her several days and taking children from classes to do the job – something which the head would never have allowed me to do. The evening at the Albert Hall was a great success, one of the star attractions being the item performed by the heads of various schools, but not ours – Miss D once again never even went to the festival – she certainly never supported it during my time at the school.

Many of the staff realised what I was going through and how it was affecting me. Barbara Pettit, the German teacher, was very sympathetic and asked if I would like to join the trip to Germany which she was organising for the senior girls. I made arrangements for the dogs to be cared for by mother, and off we went by coach and ferry the day after term ended to travel to Boppard, a beautiful town nestling by the Rhine, about 30km south of Koblenz in the shadow of mountains and hills – covered with vineyards. Inevitably we visited the wine cellars of Boppard – with enjoyable wine tasting; on another excursion to Birnkastel-kues we went to the site of a distillery and watched the whole process of the Riesling wine being prepared, from the collection of the grapes to the bottling – thousands upon thousands of bottles of wine. It was a sign of the times that none of the pupils under 16 were allowed to take part in the wine tasting which followed – nowadays they would be drinking it by the bottle! After a trip to the Landshut Castle high above the town, with splendid views of the Moselle Valley below we were able to look around the mediaeval town itself, naturally clutching the wine we had purchased at the factory. We also had a splendid river trip to Rudesheim, past the famous Lorelei rock, and on another morning travelled to the top of the Gedeonseck on the chairlift. On our visit to Cologne we naturally went into the cathedral after allowing the girls an opportunity to do some shopping. The cathedral was full of visitors when suddenly there was an awful cry from close to the altar of "Hilfe, hilfe" – (Help!) Everyone turned and saw one man who had stabbed himself before the main cross – it was an awful sight and I can still hear that terrible sound echoing around the cathedral to this day. There was worse to come when German police came in and pounced on the man and practically dragged him out; the last sight I had was the view of him being kicked by the police as he lay on the floor waiting for an ambulance. This was sickening, and I suppose gave me a reminder that we were in Germany, and men in uniforms had a history of cruelty. I dread to think what happened to the poor fellow who was probably mentally disturbed.

We stayed at a guesthouse, spotlessly clean – this WAS Germany, and, while not being four-star, was run by a family which took pride in its home cooking, and provided some lovely local dishes. You do get to know children much better when they're away from home, and we were able to observe some of the spoilt variety who just turned their noses up at anything they didn't recognise, in fact so much food was being left that the lady in charge was near to tears. We tried to allay her fears and stressed that the food was excellent, the problem was all about the children; most were adventurous and willing to try the food, and enjoyed every plateful. In the evenings we allowed them to go into town but staff took turns to have coffee in a bar which overlooked the mobile chippy – because we barred the girls from buying chips; if they couldn't be bothered to eat the good food that was set before them then they could go without chips – they also had to report to us personally every half an hour so that we could keep an eye on them. Other than this the group behaved very well, and it was a wonderful break from school and its problems. On the way back I can remember one of the staff telling us about the wife of our art teacher, Terry Taylor, who had just applied to retire on the grounds of ill-health; apparently she had acute pain in her neck and could not turn her head properly. There was general agreement that she would be very lucky to succeed on these grounds, you had to be quite ill to fulfil the conditions of early retirement.

The new term began – it was to be my last – with yet another visit from the music adviser to watch me teach, and once again he found no fault in my work. I can remember him breezing in holding a box containing maracas, tambourines and all kinds of percussion instruments which he was leaving with me for use in class. When he came in the girls were singing the *Bohemian Dance* from the opera *Carmen*, by Bizet, in French, and I went on to play a recording of it sung by Maria Callas. I could see Malcolm becoming uneasy and at the end he bounced up and spoke to the class – these were third form 14 year olds, most of whom would be giving up music at the end of term, not the easiest group to control and motivate. "Girls, I enjoyed your singing, but you really shouldn't be sitting at desks with a piece like this. You've got to be up and moving about with this music – it's not just for listening to; I'm going to ask Mr Astell to play the record again and I want you to get out of your seats and dance, any dance, just express yourself to the rhythm of the music," he said. They all looked rather bemused at this, but I did as I was told, the LP went on once again and Maria Callas duly obliged. There wasn't a movement – not one single girl got out of her seat, and by the second verse I decided 'if you can't beat 'em, join 'em', and did a kind of primitive 'knees- up' to the rhythm; still not a movement, though some looked at me rather pathetically. The music ended and the adviser spoke to the class, "Well girls, I am disappointed, I thought you would enjoy dancing and letting yourselves go, but I suppose I can't expect that sort of thing from the crème de la crème of Woodford County High."

That last phrase really stung them, and the girls glared back at him, I could feel the anger. Then a quiet girl who normally hardly said a word in class stood up and addressed the music adviser: "I don't know who you are or why you are here, but I think what you've asked us to do is stupid and pointless; we're not dressed for dancing and you can't dance in a space where you can hardly move for tables and chairs, and, by the way, I feel it's a privilege to be one of the so-called crème de la crème, so there." She sat down amidst great applause from the rest of the class. I watched Mr Bidgood's face and then asked if he would like to introduce anything else, but at that point he disappeared from the classroom as fast as he could. As the door closed I heard them muttering that they thought he was a complete prat... I made no comment, but inwardly realised that the man had no idea about the awkwardness and the embarrassment of the average teenage girl, who does not easily make an exhibition of herself to satisfy even a music adviser. I felt it was quite an achievement just to have 30 girls singing enthusiastically, and listening in silence to the record – but then I wasn't a music adviser, just a humble teacher who had to do the job five days a week and couldn't walk out when an experiment failed.

About three years before this event I had taken on the role of accompanist for a local amateur operatic society. This meant attending rehearsals at least once a week, playing the piano but following the conductor assiduously and, of course, being able to almost sight-read the music, for there was very little chance to work at it during the week. I remember we performed *La Traviata* and *Tales of Hoffmann*, and in 1984 we were doing *Otello*, which needed a children's chorus at the beginning of the last act. I was asked to provide some girls from the school to make up the chorus, which needed several intense rehearsals to get them up to standard. The drama department at school decided to put on the musical *Oliver* at the end of term, so I was involved in auditions for the main parts and to teach the chorus, and organise and prepare the small orchestra – this couldn't be done until the last minute because the orchestral parts were ridiculously expensive to hire – by the day – so we could only afford to have them one week before the show. All this meant rehearsals every lunchtime and most evenings after school and as if this wasn't enough there were the usual parents evenings which we were required to attend and, in the last part of May school exams. Believe me, it takes a lot of time to prepare the exam papers, and then to set about marking – this time around without Judith, my colleague, I had to mark upwards of 250 papers. According to the tradition, the marked papers are then bound up with string, a list of names and results inserted at the front and a year list of marks – all of which had to go into the head for scrutiny by a certain date. Lots of burning of midnight oil, and all this on top of the *Oliver* rehearsals kept me VERY busy. I've mentioned all this in detail because I discovered later these marks were to become evidence against me by the head.

At the beginning of June I was sent a note to see her at a particular time in her study; it seemed rather formal and I went along wondering what I had done now to invoke her anger. I was told to sit and she began, "Mr Astell you may not be surprised to know that I am filing a disciplinary charge against you, and you will report here in a week's time when a member of the education department will be present."

I was absolutely gobsmacked. "Of course I'm surprised, I don't even know what a disciplinary charge is, but it sounds rather serious, perhaps you will tell me what I've done to warrant such an action."

At that she positively leered at me. "Oh no, I'll keep you waiting for a week, it'll give you something to ponder on. You will report here at two o'clock on the 10th of June; now return to your class." I made it clear to her that I would be bringing this matter to my union's notice, and reserving the right for him to attend.

"Yes I thought you'd go running to the union", she replied. Quite incredible. I did know that disciplinary charges existed, usually for very serious matters – stealing money from the school, committing sexual acts against pupils, all that sort of thing, and I knew I wasn't guilty of anything like that. What on earth did she have against me? I reported all this to my local union representative and asked him to be present at the meeting on June 10th. So, along with the workload I've already described came the stress of wondering what on earth this was all about, and why she hadn't told me about the charges. I reported on the day; she had brought in one of the members of the education department who was also headmistress of a church school in Ilford – people later told me that Pat Dixon was probably the only friend she had among the school heads in the borough. The 'charges' against me were:

a) I had brought the school into disrepute by refusing to sell tickets to parents for the Redbridge Music Festival.

b) I had left out several names and marks on the results sheet for the fourth year music exams.

c) I had kept a parent waiting by being 10 minutes late at the fourth year parents evening.

In a way I was relieved that there was no charge of financial infringements, and that I hadn't been putting my hand down pupils' dresses!

These so-called 'charges' were so petty it was unbelievable; nevertheless I was informed that this would go into my personal folder and I would be cautioned by the education department. At this point the union man stood up and said he knew that I would ask for an appeal in the light of these ridiculous accusations and we both marched out. Howard, the rep, was equally surprised – in all his years working in the borough as a science teacher he'd never come across anything like it before, and he felt we should get someone in from the union at the very top to attend that appeal. He said it was quite obvious that she was harassing me and trying to undermine my work and it had to stop. A date was fixed for the appeal but had to be postponed when I received a letter from the department to say that they were still trying to find out the details of how such disciplinary charges and appeals worked – no one could recall such an incident happening before. Eventually the date was set and one of the top men in the NAS/UWT, in fact the assistant general secretary came down from Birmingham to represent me at the appeal. He arrived one day before the appeal, took me aside after school, having insisted despite my protests that it would mean cancelling a rehearsal, to ask me for details and questions about the situation at Woodford. "You don't worry about your rehearsals and the school at this time, you think about your own job." he said bluntly. We had a long chat, he had been made aware of the situation at school through other unions – it seems we were becoming a household word; finally he told me that he had about 50 questions to ask the head, and I retorted that she would probably walk out after the first six; "And that's exactly what we want her to do." he said, "When she loses her temper and refuses to answer questions, then we've won."

I had a sleepless night, and got up feeling like death warmed up. The staff at school knew what was going on and all of them came to wish me well and give their support – I actually had two of them waiting to be called in as witnesses if the need arose; one of the science staff had bought some champagne which was cooling in the fridge ready to celebrate my success. I wasn't too sure.

So there was Howard, the local man, with the top guns from NAS to defend me, when, 10 minutes beforehand, we discovered that Miss D had brought in the assistant head of the education department of Redbridge, to defend her, so we really were up against their big guns. At the appointed time we knocked on the door and one of the "enemy" told us that they weren't quite ready. "But it's 9.15, and we ARE ready." said the NAS man – let's call him John. We were let into the room, and it was obvious they were still moving the chairs around – I know, it sounds like the Titanic, and I felt like one of the doomed passengers. An official told us where I would be sitting and then tried to put John and Howard in a different part of the room, but once again John took the initiative: "If Mr Astell sits here, I sit next to him." he said, and the official had to allow this, though he did assert his right to put Howard a couple of seats away. I was to appear before a panel of three – the chairman was the headmaster of Beale High school, whose son had occasionally joined in with our school orchestra, then there was the principal of Loughton Polytechnic, and the third member was deputy head at Wanstead, a comprehensive school nearby, so I knew at least I had people who understood the inner workings of a school. The charges were read out and we worked through them one by one. Briefly, after I had explained that I had lost a great deal of money trying to satisfy the parents of our pupils with tickets at the 1982 Festival, I was willing to do the job only if I could be assured that I would not lose personal money, but the head had put down conditions which were impossible to meet – at no point did I **refuse** to collect money or issue tickets. At this point both the chairman and the deputy head on the panel made it clear that it was always customary to use a school fund cheque to pay for the tickets initially, that this was the procedure in all the borough schools to their knowledge and they agreed that I shouldn't have lost money in the previous festival. The chairman noted that I showed full interest and cooperation both in training the choir and taking them to the festival at the Royal Albert Hall, which he said was a long, hard day and heads were grateful that staff were willing to do this in their own time. "I don't think you've ever attended the festival, Miss D, which is a great pity." He was making the point that while we all put a great deal of time and effort into this, she couldn't even be bothered to attend.

On the matter of missing names and marks on the result sheet I had the form mistress of 4A waiting outside as a witness, if required. You see I had approached her some days before when I realised that I had possibly omitted the five music people in her class, and asked her to get back the list when she went into the head so that I could correct a genuine mistake. The form mistress came back to me with the news that the head would not return the list under any circumstances, her words to the teacher being: "That list stays here, I've got 'im now!" The panel took my word for this and didn't even ask the teacher to come in, it was so obvious that the head had been determined to find anything that she could pin on me. The chairman noted that he thought this was a ridiculous state of affairs, that mistakes were made all the time; when I also pointed out that I had at least complied with her order and sent in all my lists by the required date, but knew full well that there were at least four members of staff working on their results sheets even while this meeting was going on – nearly three weeks after the deadline, but there seemed to be no action being taken against them.

Finally came the charge that I had kept a parent waiting because I was late arriving at a parents meeting. The head insisted that the mother who had been kept waiting was Mrs Goodman, and was emphatic that I should have been meeting Mrs Goodman at 7 pm. I had kept the list of parents and the time allocated to them, and I showed this to the panel. Mrs Goodman's name wasn't even there, I was never down to meet her. To make doubly sure I had telephoned her and asked her to be willing to verify this by phone if requested. I knew her quite well, had taught three of her daughters, but knew that it was highly unlikely that she would want to see me, because her 14-year-old wasn't even doing G.C.E. music. The assistant education officer stood up and made it clear that he would not have parents brought into this affair, this was an internal matter, and I retorted that I would have the Queen Mother brought in if necessary – my career was on the line. The chairman pointed out that I had every right for Mrs Goodman to be contacted for clarification, but at this point the officer still maintained that this wasn't to happen. "If you refuse this right," the chairman said, "We are left with no alternative but to conclude that this charge has been fabricated and that the headmistress has lied." The officer agreed and told us he would accept this conclusion. Amazing. It was now the turn of my union man, John, to sum up the case and to ask her a number of questions. She was very unwilling to be questioned and had to be reminded by the chairman that she had no option – I had been questioned and now it was her turn. John did an excellent job. He asked about my school exam results, whether they were satisfactory. "Yes, I have no problem with his work at all." came the reply. I had been asked to prepare a list of GCE results going back to four years before I began at the school, and when I showed these to the panel they all agreed that these were an excellent set of results and I could be very proud of my work at Woodford. The chairman actually added that he would be more than pleased if he could get such excellent results at his own school. The head was asked about discipline, and she replied that she had no problems in that quarter, that my discipline in class was good and that I ran my lessons well. Then came the matter of the charge itself, as John put forward the case that such charges only came as a last resort, when a teacher had consistently refused to put things right, that in all cases the teacher would be told what the problem was. "I assume you called him in, told him what you wanted and he just refused to carry out your wishes, but he has consistently disobeyed you and been unwilling to do his job properly."

She came clean then that she had only told me about these charges on the day they were made. "In this particular case the head had not even told Mr Astell what he was being charged with until the very last minute." He kept putting to her this fact. "I presume you called Mr Astell in and told him about these matters and asked him to put them right; in fact you were unwilling to discuss the matter of ticket money with him, you would not let him have back the result sheet to correct the missing names, and as for the parents meeting, aside from the fact that you know these are not compulsory, that he had no requirement to attend the meeting, and as his first appointment was 7.15pm which is on this piece of paper, he never kept anyone waiting. You have fabricated this whole affair." She began to look rather glum, but he pursued the matter, asking her what problem she had with her head of music, "His work is good, his discipline is good, you have agreed on that, he does all that is required of him in out-of-school activities, he has volunteered to take school assembly on a regular basis; I don't know what your problem is. Does he get on well with the pupils and the staff?"

To which the head replied, "Yes that's the trouble, HE'S TOO POPULAR BY FAR." There was an audible gasp round the room as everybody realised where the true problem lay. I was respected and liked by most of the pupils, and I did get on well with most of the staff, and I think she was just bitter and jealous. At this point I actually felt sorry for her, she looked a pathetic figure, with nothing more to say. Her defence – the education officer also had nothing to add, and John, Howard and I were asked to wait outside while they discussed the matter. It didn't take long, John had barely lit a cigarette when we were ushered back into their presence. I was told that all charges would be dropped, that they should never have been brought in the first place. The deputy head from Wanstead wanted it put on record that this had been a complete waste of their time, he realised that I had been victimised and hounded, it was time the staff were treated professionally, and he hoped that the borough would look into this as a matter of urgency.

How did I feel? Certainly glad that the whole affair was over and that I had a clean sheet on my record, but I was worn out completely. As I thanked John for all his hard work in representing me he made two comments which I've remembered to this day, first that he had never seen a head teacher like her in all his career, and he was involved in school problems almost every day, he thought such characters only appeared in Charles Dickens; secondly he blamed the staff, "When things first began to go wrong during the first term, as a staff you should have informed the local paper that on Friday at 2 pm Woodford staff were going to march out of the school in protest." I replied that the staff as a whole would never have done this, there were always a few who would insist that it would give the school a bad name and damage the pupils, but he retorted that the whole purpose of taking action is to stop any more damage to the school and pupils, and at any rate it would never have come to a protest; the education office would have been in hot-foot to sort the matter out before bad publicity reached the public. John and Howard took their leave and I went into the staff room, where the news had already filtered through, and the glasses of champagne were waiting with my friends on the staff congratulating me on winning. For some reason school had ended at lunchtime and we had a holiday in the afternoon. I dragged myself home and just fell on the bed totally exhausted, with a raging headache and total numbness in my left arm, realising that I had won that battle but the war would go on – I'd just had enough, and wanted to get away from the whole place.

Many readers will wonder why I should spend so much time putting this appeal down in all its details –who would be interested? I just know that I had to get it all off my chest; those events are as real today as they were in 1984, and perhaps I need the therapy of going through it all, then, hopefully leaving it to be buried in time. The affair also highlights the power which heads of school wielded in the 70s and 80s. I can remember the previous head telling me once that she was quite overawed by the power vested in her. Today, I would like to think this kind of thing couldn't happen; we have parents and teachers on governing bodies who can control things rather more and have more say in election of governors, the decisions of heads and local authorities. Who knows?

The headmistress was absent the next morning, and rumour went around that she had been called to the education offices to receive a dressing down over the whole affair. The art teacher informed me that his wife had been successful in her bid for early retirement, which I mentioned earlier, and she was going at the end of term. It seemed that you had to have a medical and recommendation from your own doctor, and then appear before a doctor appointed by the department of education whose report would then go forward to the relevant authority for a decision. I set about applying immediately, and gained full support and sympathy from my own doctor, who believed that for my sanity's sake I should get right away from that school. He and others asked why I wouldn't just go for another job and I know this sounds a reasonable alternative, but at that stage I really didn't feel I could trust any head in any school. What sort of reference could I have presented from Miss D? It would also have appeared unusual to jump from the scale four post down to one or two grade. Eventually I kept the appointment to meet the doctor appointed by the Department of Education, one Dr Barnardo; I've no idea whether he was related to the great doctor who had started the children's homes which, after all, were situated just a few miles away at Barkingside. I was prepared for a thorough medical examination, but in truth I never even removed jacket or tie; he glanced at his notes and asked me to talk through the whole affair from beginning to end, and once I'd started, the whole sorry saga just poured out. He listened very attentively, asked an occasional question or made a brief comment and at the end asked me whether I had gone into the pension details to make sure I could live on what would be considerably less than a full pension. Something inside made me tell him that as a Christian I knew I would be cared for, and that faced with reasonable health or a balance in the bank I would opt for the former, at which point he thought that was very sensible and told me that he also was a Christian – in fact he was a deacon at a local Baptist church in Buckhurst Hill, so we had something in common. I kept apologising for taking up all his time, I really had talked for well over an hour, but he dismissed this by telling me that he was being very well paid for conducting this interview, so this was the least of our troubles. He ended by making it clear that officially he could not reveal his recommendation to the D of E, but shaking my hand he winked and said, "Let's say that if all goes well I wish you a very happy retirement."

There was no time to ponder on this situation, for work at school was going into overdrive as I rehearsed the main characters, the choruses and the orchestra for the production of *Oliver* which was to take place from 11th to 13th July – just 1 week before end of term. The children were marvellous in their enthusiasm, willingness to learn quickly and their sheer ability – and the tunes were going round and round in my head 24 hours a day. As always at Woodford many of the staff were involved in the production, from ticket sales, refreshments, costumes, production assistants, stage management team, scenery and props, make-up department, choreographers, house management team and so on. I had 14 pupils in the small orchestra, including the son of the headmaster at Beale School, who had been the chairman of the panel at my appeal. Dress rehearsals duly took place over the weekend and then the three nights of *Oliver* went ahead. One needs to bear in mind that every part was played by a pupil – this was a girls school, so we had to have some really good actors for Fagin, Mr Bumble, Bill Sykes, the artful dodger and Oliver himself. When the curtain came down the headmistress was called upon to thank everyone for their part in a wonderful musical; I think on the first night she thanked everyone down to the smallest program seller, but conveniently forgot the music director. Someone must have had a word because on the next two evenings she did manage to somehow bring herself to thank me as well – but it must have been a hard effort. Once *Oliver* was over she never spoke to me about it again. The whole production was a great success, as were all those produced by Jane Hall, then head of physics who went on to become deputy head some years later, and only retired in 2008. Jane had been a pupil at Woodford in the late 50s – I believe she was head girl in her last year – and, apart from a few years on the staff of St Paul's Girls School she had spent her whole career teaching at Woodford. The school really was her life, her hobby outside school was working in amateur dramatics! She put on a play or musical every single year from 1980, and was always wonderfully helped by Winifred Taylor, the art teacher who had actually retired in 1980 but still came back from her home in South Kensington to do all the stage design and props for every production – what a tremendous example of loyalty and love for the school. This is what I had noticed all the time I had been at Woodford, that we were a family, we cared about each other, the school tradition and its standing in the community, and that's why I was so gutted at the thought of being pushed out at that stage; I was leaving a job and school I loved, but I knew I couldn't go on.

The staff never even believed I would be granted my claim for early retirement, and as term came to a close, I held out little hope myself, in fact I didn't even take all my personal stuff home on the last day.

During the summer holiday I went off to run a CHA music week at Porlock down in Somerset. The house itself was a lovely old thatched affair with low eaves and veranda most of the way round, I believe it had belonged to a famous actor at one stage. It was surrounded by a splendid wild garden, with ancient footsteps down to a gate in order to reach the village or Porlock weir. The walks were quite strenuous in that area, with beautiful views over Exmoor and Lynton/Lynmouth, and certainly at the end of each day many very tired legs climbed the steps back to the house for a shower, good meal and some classical music in the evening. I particularly liked it because everything was so unspoiled and non-touristy, and as it lies virtually at the end of the A39 it still is a very quiet old village. I soon made friends with Harry, the manager, his wife and their two dogs. The dogs followed Harry everywhere and even if he wasn't around you could find Harry by following the smell of his pipe. After a couple of weeks back home, JB and I set off for Hereford. I remember the journey, once again I was allowed to drive the MG, and as we approached the city via the A438 we rounded a bend at a place called Lugwardine; I distinctly remember telling John how much I liked the scenery and I could well live in a place like that, little knowing that in nine years time that would be my home – incredible coincidence? For this holiday CHA took over the Blind College and all the halls of residence, just as well because we had nearly 100 guests who had come to dance or listen. Once again wonderful excursions and walks were in store from Hereford; one walking leader was a mature lady called Vera, rather hard of hearing who seemed to have a fascination with post offices – she was always pointing them out whether in a town, village or even by the side of the road as we drove along in our coach. It so happened that one of the friends we had made on a previous CHA holiday at Whitby had come to London with her daughter to see the sights, and as Mother was dog-minding at Woodford, I had invited Betty and her daughter Elizabeth to stay with Mother and keep her company for a few days; I had also made arrangements that if anything looking official came in the post it would be forwarded to me.

Just before we set off for the day's walk on Tuesday I was called to the telephone and Betty told me that a letter had arrived from the Department of Education, and she wondered whether she should read it to me over the phone. Briefly the letter said that my application for early retirement had been granted by the Department, and I could retire with an amended pension at any time after 31st of August. Suddenly, I had no job to go back to, my teaching career was over, what would have been another two weeks holiday was now stretching for the rest of my life, a most peculiar feeling; I spent the day walking with the guests on auto pilot, for I was deep in thought as this news sank in – in August still a teacher, but from September a pensioner – at 47. I returned from Hereford wondering what on earth the future held.

CHAPTER SIXTEEN

PICKING UP THE PIECES

"I have to inform you that Mr Astell has taken himself off!" These were the words of the headmistress, announced in her broadest Barnsley accent to the staff, meeting at the beginning of the school year; a typically vague statement which left some staff wondering whether I had died, topped myself to end it all, or just run away into the wilderness with no forwarding address. She would say no more about it, and told staff that she would prefer my name not to be mentioned again.

At that very moment I was drinking a toast to the Woodford school staff on the Glacier Express in the mountains of Switzerland. John Buckle and I had decided that we needed to get away for a few days, bought ourselves a travel ticket and a very large Swiss transport guide, and landed up at Basle at 5am after travel on the ferry and overnight train. The ticket enabled us to use trains, buses and even some ferries throughout the country, so we were plotting our route. The Swiss railway lived up to its reputation, every train departed absolutely on time and when one had to change or "Aussteigen, bitte." as the guard would announce, sure enough the next train would be standing at the platform ready to depart. We spent some days at St Johann, the nearest station to Zermatt, and used the rack and pinion train which climbed all the way from Brigg up to Zermatt itself – but Zermatt prices for a bed and food were very expensive compared to the reasonable charges in St Johann (bearing in mind that Switzerland was very expensive anyway). We met a couple of people in a car with strong American accents who wanted to find a bed for the night; I told them to look out for any notices which said 'Zimmer Frei', and it transpired that they had seen many of these signs but thought they were just names of the village! Returning from one of our trips on the train we met another elderly couple from the States who asked us, "Does this train climb the

Matterhorn?" and we reassured them that it would at least get them to the start of the line that DID climb the Matterhorn. They had European rail cards and were travelling through many countries; unfortunately when the guard came round to inspect the tickets, their very expensive cards did not cover this particular private line, whereas our travel card did. The husband told us they had a very nice room in a hotel with a small balcony and a view of the Matterhorn, but when he told us the price per night it was more expensive than our whole trip for 10 days! We told them what we were paying for our little room in St Johann, from which you could still see the Matterhorn albeit at a distance, and at this point the wife was all for moving down the line and staying in our village!

It was a very relaxing week; if the weather was poor in Lucerne, I would jump on a train down to the Italian border and in half an hour could enjoy my coffee in warm sunshine. Upon reaching Lucerne we had decided to stay in the suburbs, and caught a train to Arth-Goldau, then walked along Park Road and found a 'Zimmer-frei'. A very pleasant lady answered the door and showed us not only a large clean bedroom with two good sized beds, but a kitchen complete with stove, fridge and everything necessary to prepare meals. John was in his element, because he always prefers to do his own cooking when possible, and save money into the bargain! When I woke early the next morning I could have sworn I heard lions roaring! Now I still had much to learn about Switzerland but was fairly sure that it didn't have lions! I mentioned this to John and he'd also heard lions; later when we met the lady of the house she informed us that the zoo was just at the back of her garden, and there would indeed have been lions roaring for their food. We certainly checked carefully to see that her garden gate and wall were quite secure before we enjoyed coffee and cake on the lawn at lunchtime. On our last morning we were booking out and not very keen on carrying all our gear, because we were doing some more sightseeing before we left the Lucerne region. We were going up to Mount Pilatus, and immediately she not only volunteered to look after our bags, but when we returned in the afternoon she had coffee and cakes ready for us before we departed. A really kind, generous lady! We had no fixed itinerary and enjoyed just travelling around staying where we fancied. All in all, a holiday I badly needed at that time.

On returning home it gradually dawned on me that I had literally nothing to get up for. I would often see the children going to and from school and soon realised that I was deliberately taking the dogs for their daily walks up to Woodford Green at the very time when the pupils were coming out of school. Many would stop to speak and play with the dogs, and a good number begged me to return – they preferred me to the temporary teacher who had come in at the last minute; on two occasions a delegation of third formers actually knocked on the door and pleaded with me to go back to take them for music. One of the traditions at Woodford had been going for years. When a member of staff left, presents were always given at the end of an assembly, and the staff member was expected to make a little speech, perhaps giving a reason for leaving, wishing the school all the best in the future, etc. The head girl and prefects had collected and bought presents for me, but I was not allowed to go in or attend the assembly to collect them and say my goodbyes to the school; prefects were told they could take the presents to my house. I did go in for the school birthday celebrations, which always coincided with my own birthday, enjoyed conversation with teachers and senior pupils, and watched as the annual school birthday photograph was taken, feeling a terrible sadness that I was no longer part of it. This was so strange – for the very thing I had hoped and prayed for, to be released from that terrible tension in the school, had been granted to me, and yet now I realised how much I missed the teaching and the companionship of staff and pupils alike. On a positive note, as we had such wonderful weather right into October I decided to buy a polythene greenhouse and erect it in the garden, no mean feat for someone who was hopeless with DIY. Ironically, three years later almost to the day the Great Storm of 1987 saw trees uprooted and cars overturned; I had moved from Woodford to Cambridgeshire a year before, but neighbours told me that during the storm roofs were collapsing, chimneys falling off, windows smashing while my little polythene greenhouse apparently withstood it all undamaged, so I must have tightened all the screws in the right order!

Another tradition was that leaving heads of department were given a staff party send off – refreshments and wine included. The headmistress tried to stop this event by making it clear that I was not going into her school, but the staff committee quickly reminded her that it wasn't her school, and that they would approach the Education Department for permission. At this she relented and briefly informed them that she would not be available to attend the party, someone replied diplomatically that it was best if she didn't turn up. So on a Friday night in October I met the staff again for my official farewell, and they toasted my future life in retirement, then presented me with some gardening equipment and a recently published book on the history of Woodford, beautifully bound and signed by the author, which I still treasure to this day.

The next few months were very tough. I can quite understand why some workers go to pieces when they retire, for ideally one should move slowly into this situation. There is a lot to be said for a system whereby a successor gradually takes over one's job on a part-time basis so that the retiring person can get acclimatised to a completely different kind of life. Often I would get up in the morning, take the animals for their run, return home and just collapse in a heap on the floor in tears – poor old William the dog seemed to share my sadness and would try to lick my face, perhaps he could sense the distress I felt. I tried to work out what was wrong and came to the conclusion that it was the feeling that the rest of the world was going about its business, to work, to shop, and so on, while I felt utterly alone, with no purpose whatsoever, no work and no goal. Languishing in self-pity? It certainly didn't seem so at the time. On Fridays at lunchtime I did visit the local pub to meet up with some of the Woodford staff and catch up with the latest tales of woe and disquiet, those friends were great companions and meeting them was a lifeline. Some confessed that they envied me having all this freedom without the chore of working, an attitude which I found both heartening and confusing at the same time. I was given advice by one or two retired people and realised I had to pick up the pieces and find some new things to do with my day. Someone told me to make sure I had a goal to aim at every day. I decided to transcribe J.S. Bach's *Art of Fugue* for keyboard, picking out the use of themes and imitation in various coloured inks; it was expensive to heat the house during the day, so I became a frequent visitor at the local library; the project became quite absorbing and I was quite proud to finish this job – then realised a few weeks later that I could have gone out and bought the transcription for a few pounds. Once or twice a week I would get an all-day travel card and go to various places at the end of the line on the underground or on the bus, perhaps to Kew Gardens, have lunch in Morden, travel up to High Barnet on the Northern Line, and on one occasion went right out to Uxbridge, had a wander around for half an hour and came back on the same train to central London. I also discovered 'the land of the matinee', where one could visit the Old Vic or London theatre and watch a play or show without any booking up, often at reduced prices. I kept up the job as accompanist for the Figaro Opera Group, they were doing *La Traviata* and *Tales of Hoffmann;* indeed these evenings became a goal, where I could still use my musical talent and, most of all, not be alone. This was really the heart of the problem of retirement – I needed someone to share it with, and that feeling has never gone away over 25 years later.

The winter of 1985 was one of the worst on record; with thick snow lying for many days and plunging temperatures it was impossible to keep the house warm, and I would sit huddled in overcoat and blankets. One of my cousins was returning to Australia with his wife and two sons; George and the family were to stay overnight with me before catching an early flight from Heathrow next morning. They arrived frozen, in their Robin Reliant 'Del Boy' three wheeler car which had made the journey from Cambridgeshire over icy roads. We made valiant efforts to get warm in the house – which was never cosy at the best of times with its open plan design (what a ghastly mistake the previous owners had made in ruining the interior of a lovely pre-war house.) It snowed heavily during the night but somehow they slid their way up the road early on the following morning, and reached the airport, where George was to see them off before returning home to await the sale of his house. What a difference Brenda and her two boys must have found when they arrived in the middle of an Australian summer!

Now I had always been very wary of computers, I believe the term is a 'technophobe'; people always blamed them for anything which went wrong; in administration, banks, schools, offices, everywhere people were employed tapping away at these mindless instruments. I had never touched a computer and knew nothing about them; this was at a time when personal computers were only just coming on the market. A company called Amstrad was selling a computer package with printer for just under £400; this was one of the success stories of the entrepreneur Alan Sugar, and I bought my PCW 8256 as another goal to work on. I must say it got me hooked, soon I would be working quite late, and William or Bonnie would rub against my leg to remind me that they wanted walkies or bed, and I would gently push them away only to look at my watch and discover it might be 1am. The grey Amstrad had a tiny screen with green background and black information, hardly any memory to speak of and just one primitive game where one shot down individuals who were marching across the page... how things have changed in the PC world since those days. I bought it in January 1986 – a Christmas present to me – and it really helped get through the winter days.

I was still playing the organ regularly but not at one particular church; my time seemed to be spread between the Baptist church in South Woodford and a small ecumenical 'breakaway' church which met at Bancroft's School. Some explanation is needed about the latter. I had served as organist at a United Reformed Church for about 18 months, only leaving after the usual tension between the choir and its desire for traditional music, and rebellion among younger members for a more modern type of worship and singing. It was a great barn of a place, built in a Byzantine style of architecture, and stood in a very imposing position on Woodford Green itself. The members had made me very welcome and I tried to keep the choir going despite falling numbers – hardly a choir member below 60. One or two of the old stagers disliked the modern tunes and informed me of this in no uncertain manner; on one particular Sunday the minister asked me to play the modern tunes to two hymns, this was the last straw – *two modern tunes in one service, what was the world coming to?* and a couple rounded on me and expressed dissatisfaction, despite the fact that I made it clear that the minister had requested the tunes in question. He was slippery as an eel and always managed to avoid confrontation, I was the fall guy, and ultimately I grew tired of the whole business. I mention it in detail because it had caused problems in my work in other churches and would go on to be a problem later. This question of traditional music and what some unkind people call 'happy-clappy' choruses is a problem to this day in many congregations, and it's always the organist or director of music who bears the brunt. Problems arose within that church of a far deeper nature and as a last resort a group of members felt they must break away to form their own church. They had no premises but were fortunate in being able to use the chapel of Bancrofts School for the worship on Sunday mornings, where they began in March 1983 and continue to this day. From the start they proclaimed that they were not one denomination but were interested in having preachers from many denominations, from Catholic to Salvation Army, Jewish rabbis to London City Mission, etc. So, I divided my Sundays between the Baptist and this Ecumenical church, which had strong links with the Baptist Union (BU).

In the spring of 1985 they asked me to represent the church at the Baptist Union (BU) conference to be held at Nottingham University and I was eager to attend this function both to meet up again with fellow Baptists who I hadn't seen for many years, and get away from Woodford. On the second day at conference I bumped into Pam Neville, who worked for the BU and who I had known years before through my links with BMS summer schools where she was often the secretary. I told her briefly about my 'enforced' retirement and she answered immediately, "You should meet Michael Quicke." Apparently Michael Quicke was senior minister at St. Andrew's Street Baptist Church in Cambridge and was looking for a director of music to work at his church... low and behold while we were still talking in came... Michael Quicke – amazing when you realise there were over 300 delegates at this conference dotted all over the place, and he should just appear at that moment. Michael and I became friends from that moment; we had actually first met in August 1961 at a Bexhill summer school – indeed I am looking at his autograph in my BMS *Hymns for Today* as I write these words, though neither of us would ever realise we would meet up to work as a team 25 years later. Was this meeting up just a coincidence? Briefly, as a result of meeting Michael I was asked to spend a day at Cambridge, to play the organ for morning and evening services and meet church members over lunch in the wonderful setting of Magdalene College (Michael was quick to remind me that meals in the college dining room didn't happen every Sunday of the year). This wonderful city was already beginning to cast its spell, and I was very keen to get the job. The church voted unanimously in my favour, and asked me to become their director of music. From September I was travelling up to Cambridge each Sunday with the dogs and relying on various church members to invite me for lunch and tea, but I knew this could never be a permanent situation, for part of the job was to take the choir practice on Fridays and to get a music group organised. There was no way I could consider going up and down the M11 to Cambridge during the week as well as Sunday, especially in the winter time. Living in Woodford just a short walk from the school had spoiled me, as I realised how much time is wasted in daily travel to and from work, and I was determined not to become a commuter, so a permanent move to Cambridge would set me up for the part-time job and to be on hand for mother. Cambridge had accepted me, but I was I truly ready to consider a move from Woodford Green?

The move meant leaving many friends, the staff at school and a situation on the edge of London which was unique; I had always taken full advantage of being so close to Epping Forest, where I walked the dogs at least once a week. Woodford, still trying to maintain a village atmosphere, with cricket on the village green and grazing animals, by the side of the very busy A11 London to Cambridge road, yet within half an hour of central London with its theatres, concert halls, the West End and all the excitement of the city life. I was spoiled with such easy access to both city and countryside. At the same time came the realisation that I had to put distance between myself and the school – that part of my life was over, whether I liked it or not, and a move away would help in setting up a new life; Mother – now 77 – was living alone in St Neots, brother John was already considering a move away, so someone needed to be on hand. The house went on the market but took the best part of a year to sell, and it proved hard to buy a suitable place in Cambridge. Prices were out of this world, partly because I insisted on a detached residence – memories of noisy pop groups rehearsing next door on our council estate in the 60s had never gone away – and I wanted to be close to the city and the church where much of my time would be spent. After tramping around several houses, Michael Quicke came up with what seemed the ideal answer. Valerie and Ron Clements, two of the church members lived in a bungalow at Coton, just outside the city; their father had a bungalow close by, but was selling up to go into sheltered accommodation. So on Sunday I went over for lunch with them, had a look over Father's bungalow, as he was away for the weekend, and knew straight away it was just right. There was a pedestrian bridge from the village over the main M11 motorway, so that one could cycle into the city in 15 minutes. It seemed perfect! Then Father came home and informed his daughter that he had already promised it to someone else, so all our plans came to nothing. Had I moved to Coton, I've a feeling I might still be there; as it was the search went on!

During the winter I often travelled up to stay with Mother from Friday through to Monday, partly to make sure I could get into St Andrew's Street in good time, and also to continue house-hunting. I had parted company with the Triumph Toledo and bought a new Ford Fiesta which turned out to be a disaster, the only car I ever kept for less than two years. The Fiesta had an automatic choke, which was a thorough nuisance from day one, for the car would often refuse to start; it was never happy in very hot or very cold weather, and wasn't too reliable at other times. The garage where I had bought it had closed down and I had to pay out quite a lot of money elsewhere to get it sorted out; sadly, after paying £80, I was told they could do nothing about this choke. Mother's house had no garage, so the Fiesta stood out during some very cold weekends in early 1986; on one Sunday morning it refused to start at all, and I had to ring through to the church telling them I would not get there to play in time. On another occasion I rolled up after the first hymn, all because of this stupid choke. These were the only occasions in a long career of accompanying church services when I have been late, and I found it very embarrassing.

Eventually I bought 'Hedgehogs', a fairly new detached bungalow in a village called Abbotsley, just 3 miles from Mother's house in St Neots, but 18 miles from Cambridge along the A45, which was always a dangerous road. Now came the time of packing, a job I've always hated; as a bachelor one just hoards so many things, books, records, cassettes, the list is endless, for one can just keeps adding all these things with no wife around to keep any sense of balance. I had built up an LP collection of over 3000 by 1983, along with the bookcase full of music and scores. 1983 saw the advent of the compact disc. During that year one of my CHA holidays had been to Grasmere, where I met up with a guy called Arthur. He had quite a good knowledge of acoustics and made sensible suggestions as to where the loudspeakers should be placed to give maximum stereo effect. I discovered that he worked for the hi-fi company Akai and he was slightly surprised that I was still using LPs and turntable. I replied in a fairly light-hearted way that I was in no position to buy one of the new CD players which had just come on the market at over £400, but if he would like to give me one I would gladly use it. A few weeks later I got a message from Arthur: a brand new CD player was on its way to me via a hi-fi magazine which was going to review it and send it on, and a few days later the package arrived. Obviously I felt I had an obligation to the company to advertise this machine when I used it on holidays, and contacted Akai to ask for leaflets which I could distribute to potential customers. I was told that the model was already obsolete – it had only been out a few months – so there were no leaflets available. This put me in a quandary, and I asked whether they wanted me to send the CD player back, "No, that's all right, just enjoy it." was the reply. I must confess that despite having no CD player at home I had still gone out and bought a dozen or so of these new silver discs when they had first hit the shops in April 1983. So, I had this wonderful new machine but only a dozen CDs to play on it, hence another collection was started. I had first built up a large collection of mono LPs, from 1953 to 1961, gradually swapped them for the new stereo catalogue from 1961, and here I was faced with yet another challenge. Of course, I rose to the challenge and began what became an obsession, the result – nearly 5000 CDs purchased over the last 25 years – how I needed a wife to achieve a sense of proportion, and curb my spending, to say the least!

I moved into 'Hedgehogs' on the last Friday in August, literally left everything unopened, spent the night at my mother's and was off the next day to run another CHA holiday – this time equipped with the new CD player and discs, and I was able to show off this marvellous equipment to many guests; some, I suspect, were still enjoying the sound of '78s, indeed a few were probably still winding up the gramophone; CHA guests on music holidays were always rather old-fashioned about these 'new-fangled' gadgets.

I tried to settle down into the new routine of part-time music director, which involved attending a staff meeting on Monday mornings. Staff consisted of Michael and his new junior minister Nigel Manges, Ken Hawkins the industrial chaplain to Cambridge, Geoff Warren, a deacon with special responsibility for students –

though Geoff was involved in all sorts of activities, and me. There would be a short discussion on the previous day's services and any situations arising from them, discussion of various church members and their needs, and planning for future services. Michael was so organised – he would know his theme for the next weekend and by midweek we would have arranged the music and hymns to fit. On Wednesday evenings I went along to Cambridge to get the music group going, using what instruments were available and a group of keen singers of all ages who wanted to take some part in the services. Friday would be choir practice, rehearsing anthems with a very small group of rather elderly but keen members who were desperate to keep the choir going – it was the same old situation which had faced me in churches before. We relied on a small handful of people with good voices and if one or two were away the harmony tended to disappear and fear gripped the less confident singers.

Sadly the church routine was soon put on hold. On my 50th birthday I had an appointment with the doctor for a lump which had developed in a very sensitive area – all right, it was the penis, because that's its name – the lump had swollen and burst. I was still taken aback by the speed of events, for he asked me to go to the local hospital immediately, and within an hour I was being inspected by a specialist who wanted to keep me in for an operation there and then. I made it clear that I really had to return home to make arrangements for the dogs, whereupon the specialist reluctantly agreed that I could postpone events until the next day, "But I want you here by seven o'clock sharp in the morning, so that we can get this sorted out as soon as possible." he replied.

I was tucked up in bed at Hinchinbrook hospital in Huntingdon by eight o'clock next morning, ready for the doctors' rounds. At first I was very embarrassed by the idea of all these juniors inspecting my private parts, but it's amazing, after a while you just take it all in your stride, and you reveal all to anybody who cares or needs to see IT, whether a passing cleaner, visitor or the local vicar. The operation for circumcision and removal of this nasty lump took place. Medical people still came round to examine IT and after three days I was almost ready to set the scenario to music, with roll of drums and dramatic chords as the pyjama trousers came off – though to be honest there were no pyjama trousers involved because after the operation it was extremely painful, even the slightest movement felt like a burning poker attacking me. The specialist was brilliant, and came back with the report about the nasty lump. "Well, I'm pleased to tell you that this lump proved to be non-cancerous, so everything should heal up quickly." This brought me up with a bump, no one had even breathed the word 'cancer' before, and the specialist sensed that I had not taken it seriously. "I don't think you quite realised that if we had found cancer a whole chunk of you would have been removed – no more private parts, in other words; now you realise why this result was important." When he had moved on to the next patient I closed my eyes in a quiet prayer of grateful thanks that I had been spared what could have been a serious situation. The hospital itself was fairly new and the staff were marvellous. On Saturday morning I was in agony; apparently the painkiller had been reduced and I was feeling the full effects of the operation; bandages had been removed – to reveal a bloody mess, which also shook me up – and the pain was intense. I tried sitting in a warm bath, but the pain was still dreadful, so the sister managed to get a junior doctor – it seemed that they kept at least one on duty over the weekend – to come along and give me an injection. Of course I fell madly in love with one of the nurses, she was gorgeous and whenever she was on duty my eyes just followed her everywhere – no drifting off to sleep when she was around – and I would eventually sleep with dreams of marrying the junior nurse and living happily ever after. Naturally I was just another patient to her, but when I was finally discharged from the ward and taken home I promised myself that I would take them all back some presents, and did this after a couple of weeks when I could drive again. So a box of chocolates for the nurses on the wards, but an even better box of chocolates wrapped and addressed to my favourite nurse – adding my address and telephone number. Of course I never heard a word from her again.

I soon got to know the neighbours: Charles, living alone next door, two elderly sisters in a cottage to the front – with a large garden they desperately tried to maintain, with some help, and families who lived in half a dozen council houses on the other side of the lane. Just one family proved to be a real problem; the man had already 'served time' and was actively involved in car theft and car 'ringing'. Sometimes, with a group of youngsters watching – to learn the trade, I suppose, he and his apprentices would strip out the engine and change the ID plate quite openly in the front garden – on a large concrete strip which he had put down as soon as he moved in. Some of us wondered if there were any bodies interred in the concrete! On occasion at least 20 cars would arrive very late at night and depart at about 3am – not that I was watching, but with two keen-eared barking dogs, I would be out of bed to investigate the disturbance. Before I left that bungalow in 1993 the man in question had been back to serve another lengthy prison sentence, but the apprentices continued to run the business!

Then there was John Harding and his wife Helen who lived on a farm at the other end of the village. He was an American, had served in the USAF stationed in that area, and after the war brought his young wife over to live in Abbotsley; What characters they were, laid-back, fairly disorganised, but so charming and sincere – they would always be there to help and took a big part in maintaining village life and atmosphere. On one occasion my Peugeot let me down, stuttered to a halt in a country lane in complete darkness not too far from the Harding's farm, so I walked to their place and John came out immediately with a temporary battery and saved the day. Of course, this was in the pre-historic era before mobile phones and though I hate them – at least the way in which they are over-used, I do realise their importance in breakdowns and emergencies.

There were always large numbers of visitors at the Cambridge services, some were tourists staying in hotels (or the colleges, during vacation), and others came from overseas to hear Michael's preaching. After playing the Postlude I often found people waiting to ask questions or to have a look at the organ. I was playing the congregation out after a Sunday morning service when a quiet voice at my elbow said, "Hullo Brian, we haven't met for 44 years, but you DID share a bed with me." What a greeting! My visitor turned out to be Gillian Darvill from the time of my evacuation in Blackpoool, back in Chapter 2.When we both had chicken pox I had shared her bed, but as we recounted this episode I noticed one or two raised eyebrows from people who overheard. Gillian and her husband happened to be on holiday and she had recognised my name on the announcements sheet. It's a small Baptist world.

The work in Cambridge soon came to an end. I seemed to be driving backwards and forwards during the week and for the services all weekend. The church always treated me very well and the fellowship was a caring one, but underneath there was this age-old problem of traditional music, personified in the choir, and the move towards lighter songs, and choruses, as performed by the music group. Some of the older members did not appreciate the use of drums as an accompaniment to the worship songs, and any moves towards informal worship did not go down too well. On one Sunday evening during the summer holidays I was actually in the congregation because we had a team from another church leading the service; it was when the leader invited people to get up and dance in the aisles – no one actually took up his invitation – that dear Molly, a faithful member of the choir, whose parents and grandparents had worshipped at St Andrew's Street over many years, took umbrage. At the end of the service she went straight for Michael at the church door, and, stamping her little feet, threatened to leave the church if dancing EVER became a regular feature of the service. I stood back and watched as Michael dealt with Molly; he apologised that she felt unhappy about aspects of the service, and recognised that she found these things hard to deal with, but he made it quite clear that he would never be bullied by people threatening to withdraw their membership – this amounted to blackmail. Ultimately, Molly did leave the church after a very lively session of choruses which had produced clapping and arm raising, but she returned after a few weeks when she found some of the other churches in the area were dancing, clapping, using drums and everything down to the kitchen sink! With her tail metaphorically down, she quietly took her place back in the fellowship. This was just one illustration of the tightrope I seemed to walk musically, and it was a repeat of problems I had faced in other churches. I also had to face the fact that I was spending so much time on the A45 going between Abbotsley and Cambridge that I had very little opportunity to get to know people in the village; 'Hedgehogs' seemed to be just a place to eat and sleep. I reluctantly resigned in the summer of 1987, realising this was a big shock to Michael Quicke; a couple of months later he became quite ill with dystonia; it was so sad to visit him propped up on a settee desperately trying to concentrate for a few minutes, when you knew that this was so untypical of him, he was someone always on the go --always working. At one stage the specialist warned him that he might not be able to preach in public again. As it happened he was away from church for seven months, but, miraculously, was able to resume preaching on Easter Day, 1988. For a long time after this event I was plagued with a feeling of guilt that my decision had helped to bring on this crippling disease, and only recently when we corresponded by email – Michael these days is professor of preaching at Northern Baptist Seminary, Illinois, in the USA – that he put my mind at ease and told me that he had understood my reasons for giving up the job at Cambridge.

Yet I also found it hard to be sitting around without work, and within a short time I was doing some supply teaching in a couple of local schools; in one case I was approached by Paul, a deputy head who had been in my hospital ward a couple of years before. The doctors were investigating pains in his head. After my stint in his school I could see why he had head pains! That school was pretty awful, although I was taken on for six weeks I quit after two. Discipline hardly existed; no one seemed to have instituted any rules about going along the corridors, we were all jostled and pushed by senior boys who insisted upon going three abreast, shoving everyone out of their way. Certainly no one kept to the left or in single file, and I soon realised why most of the staff didn't use the corridor between lessons but chose to walk across the frozen playground, they had probably got tired of trying to instil any order, and were still rubbing their bruises. When I went in on the second morning I made sure I took along my large case with sharp edges and propelled it in front of me so that the gangs coming in the opposite direction had to get out of the way. A couple of days later I went into the staff room and saw a new teacher studying one of the notice boards. "Who are YOU then?" He asked, in a rather bullying tone, which I didn't take to.

"I'm the replacement head of music, so who are YOU then?"

"I'm the college principal", he said in a pompous tone, and that gave me a chance to air my views. "Well, I can understand why your head of music is away ill, I feel so sorry for her." I replied, and when he looked rather mystified I took the opportunity to 'have a go'. I asked him when he had last walked down the corridor between lessons, and added for good measure that I now could see why it was so difficult for Mother and I, along with other shoppers, to walk on the pavement in the local town without being shoved in the gutter by boys and girls who had no conception of taking others into consideration as they barged along. "Oh I'm far too busy to be thinking about details like that in the college, I'm so often away attending conferences." he replied in a lofty manner. I then pointed out with respect that at my last school we had very clear rules about keeping to the left and walking in single file, rules which we stringently kept – it worked and everybody got from A to B quickly and safely. I went on to point out the advantages of having morning assembly each day, with everyone together – community; where all pupils could share the pride of pupils who brought honour to the school in activities such as games and swimming, and share a sense of shame when individuals had let the school down outside, after all, this place proudly proclaimed itself as a *community* college. "But we don't have a large enough hall to house the whole school." he replied smugly, as if that was the final answer. I retorted that at least the school could have a junior and senior assembly, but realised I was talking a completely foreign language to this man, who obviously had no time with the nuts and bolts of running the place – this was all left to the deputy heads – he was far too busy discussing EDUCATION – much easier to be sitting in a comfortable chair around a table talking education rather than battling through a corridor or at the chalk face in front of a class. I did get in a final thrust by telling him how sorry I felt for the youngest children who had to tackle the corridors three or four times a day getting squashed in the process, and he promised he would get someone to look into the matter.

Of course the college was just a microcosm of normal society because 90% of the pupils were quite decent, hard-working kids who needed rules and basic discipline to rub along together; the other 10% were fairly hardened characters who ruled the whole place in the absence of law and order. This came home to me half way through the second week when I had a class of 14-year-olds for a double lesson of 90 minutes. Remembering the simple advice of dear old Dickie Betts back in Goldsmiths College in 1958, I set out to make them all line up in single file in silence outside the music room – for the first five minutes they didn't take a blind bit of notice, and I just waited and waited, until finally they took me seriously, and out of sheer curiosity they obeyed. Into the room they all drifted, but when I gave the order to sit down four boys took no notice whatsoever and began wandering around the room, banging on the drums, plucking the strings on the grand piano, and behaving as though I wasn't even there; the class enjoyed this entertainment – especially the girls, while I just stood at the front, helpless but getting more angry by the minute. I told them to leave the room, but, quick as a flash they informed me that it was against the school rules to send children out of the room. "Well I just changed the rules." I replied, "For I'm not doing any teaching here until you four leave." This brought them up with the question of where they should go. "Well," I suggested, "You might find the headmaster."

"We've never seen him and we don't know where his room is." they retorted.

"Well go and make yourselves known to one of the deputies, or your house tutor, or your form teacher, or one of the caretakers, or anybody, but just GET OUT!" They left and closed the door and I managed to get some teaching done with the rest of the class, although part of me was wondering whether they might actually set the school ablaze on their travels, and it did seem unbelievable that, if they were telling the truth, they didn't know who the headmaster was. After what seemed an eternity the lesson came to an end, and it was complete pandemonium as they all rushed for the doors – except that I had got there first. "No one leaves this room until you're in single file and silent." I told them, and there was immediate laughter as they all carried on talking; having informed them that I was quite happy to stay for the whole lunch hour – I had my sandwiches to hand, taking them out of my case to prove the point – but they might find themselves getting rather hungry. They became more subdued, and I duly opened the door; as she went by one of the girls whispered something to her friend, and I told them both to wait behind, and informed the one who spoke that I was not going to punish her, I just wished her to say it again. After some hesitation she told me that she had said to her friend, "He's very strict, ain't he?"

I corrected her, "What you actually said was that I was ' bloody strict', but we'll let that pass; I want to thank you, that's the best compliment I've had since I came into this school, but you probably don't understand; off you go for lunch." They both looked puzzled and as they moved away I distinctly heard one say to the other, "'E's bleeding mad!" That was one of the hardest lessons I've ever had to teach in 30 years; at one stage as the four boys – all considerably taller than me – had surrounded me in front of the class I thought they might physically assault me. I had looked out at my car in the playground, and, but for some sense of professionalism, I could have walked out and driven home. This I told Paul the deputy head when I called to his office in the dinner hour. Immediately he tapped into the computer, looked at the names of the class and informed me that, "generally they give no trouble." I reminded him that I'd been standing in front of these 30 characters, that they were flesh and blood and not just names on his monitor screen, that I had been given early retirement because of high blood pressure, there was no way I was going to let that return, and he had until the end of the week to find a replacement music teacher – I'd had enough! Paul was rather taken aback, and expressed some comment about the money I would be losing, but I had heard that one before, and quickly reminded him that one day he might realise that good health, indeed keeping sane comes before money.

It's now 20 years since that experience and as a follow-up, I can confirm that the same college is now in very good hands, with compulsory school uniform, good behaviour, very good exam results – in fact four of my brother's grandchildren have been through the school with fine results. It's yet another situation where the good school head gets a good staff around him and the place can change almost overnight – forget all these education conferences, I believe the place for the head is in his own school, insisting on the highest standards of discipline and teaching..

I then went peripatetic – not a nasty disease – it meant travelling around from school to school as a woodwind teacher working for Cambridge County Council, Huntingdon division. I only worked on two days of the week, but did a great deal of travelling. On Monday mornings I travelled to the other end of the county to teach at Ramsey in the lower secondary school, then, retracing my steps to St Neots I would go to one of the community colleges – NOT the one I have just described, thank goodness. On Fridays it was off to teach at St Ives, about 20 miles away, then west across the county to Sawtry, close to the A1, and it was back to home by about 3.30pm. This timetable meant that I was almost spending more time driving than teaching. The pupils were a fairly decent bunch, some practised quite seriously to take their grade examinations, while a few were full of promises and excuses, but their lessons were free and in some cases the clarinets had been provided, so no one worried unduly about progress. These schools or colleges, as they liked to be called, seemed very large and impersonal to me; my only point of contact was with the music teacher, I rarely had a chance to go into the staff rooms or to meet up with other colleagues, though, to be fair, this is normal in the world of peripatetic teaching – you go in, do your hour or two and then off again. In good weather the journeys around Cambridgeshire were fascinating because when it was possible I would travel on the quiet minor roads and enjoy the countryside with its large fields, fairly flat landscape and absence of traffic. Ramsey was particularly interesting, part of the school was in the ancient abbey grounds, but I taught years 7 to 9 which were housed in Ailwyn Community School. Ramsey was a lovely old town right on the edge of the Fens and the local children seemed to have a rather primitive, almost wild aspect about them, not in a bad way, but as though they were still trying to adapt to modern town life. According to my contract I had to be able to teach any woodwind instrument, and was actually presented with a young oboe player at one school. She was so keen to learn, but I did not play the oboe, and I came clean, told the truth and said we would try to learn the instrument together – someone in Huntingdon office lent me an oboe for a few weeks. The system was crazy, for I discovered that another teacher came into the same school to teach flute and clarinet, who was primarily an oboe player; she was presented with clarinettists, which was the one instrument she didn't play, so we came to an informal arrangement whereby she took on my oboist and gave me a couple of her clarinettists. It all made sense. Sadly, my work with the council came to an abrupt end after about a year all because of unfair changes in fuel expenses. We were paid a flat rate per mile for our travel around the county, but suddenly it changed without any notification; I was clocking about 160 miles a week when the council, in its infinite wisdom, decided that after 120 miles I would get a lower rate per mile. This was unfair, for I was paying the same price for a gallon of petrol regardless of any lower rate; I also discovered that the council paid a much higher rate per mile for certain of its senior officers who used large cars. I discussed this with my boss at Huntingdon Council, but he was powerless to do anything about the decision, telling me he was unable to adjust the timetable so that I did less miles so I gave up almost immediately.

I also taught the clarinet at Gamlingay Primary School near home, a delightful little school with a handful of children who were bright as buttons and so keen to learn. I did this for about 18 months because I was just not ready for full retirement – I still enjoyed teaching. In 1988 my mother celebrated her 80th birthday, and we had a party, inviting relatives and friends; for the occasion I hired the village hall at Abbotsley. My sister and the sister-in-laws organised the catering, a fine cake was made, we fixed up a PA system and made everything informal so that everyone could chat freely; mother so much enjoyed meeting up with relations, who she didn't often see these days as we had all migrated to various parts of the country. Among the guests were Gladys and Ron, who lived just a few doors from Mother and often popped in to see that she was well and to have a chat. They were an unusual pair; I think she was descended from some sort of Romany group – she certainly looked rather like a gypsy – never used the doctors, had always relied on home-made remedies of herbs, wild flowers and other concoctions which always seemed to be on the boil in her kitchen ready to heal an ailment. The house was full to bursting with furniture and all kinds of second-hand stuff which she collected, most of it was complete rubbish, covered in dust and didn't work, but she kept it there …"You never know, always comes in handy, dear". Her husband used to call in to see Mum to get away from her, and would comment on how lovely it was to sit comfortably in a chair, in a tidy room with space around and be able to see the wall on the other side; but Gladys was certainly the boss in that household. One morning she woke to find Ron had died in his sleep – had he quietly succumbed after her nagging, or had one of her herbal remedies gone wrong? We'll never know! We were all terribly upset at the sudden death of Ron, but when she talked to mother and me she expressed anger; apparently at Christmas he had hidden a bottle of whisky and box of chocolates away somewhere in the attic or the garage and died without telling her where they were. We knew that Ron had hidden them so that she couldn't drink and eat the lot before Christmas, but he died with the secret still on his lips, and she never forgave him. I'm not surprised that she couldn't find the whiskey, I'm amazed if she could find anything in that house. My brother, his wife and I had one occasion to visit Gladys and we were astounded. The front room was filled with furniture, with chairs on top of the table, just enough space for a couple of chairs to sit on and a large ashtray overflowing with cigarette ends and ash; there was a large walking stick nearby which she used to switch the TV on and off and change programmes, since there was absolutely no way of actually getting to the TV set which was definitely before the days of remote control. The hall and kitchen were exactly the same, even the stairs were packed with things, only enough space to squeeze up and down. We never got to see upstairs, Gladys admitted that those rooms were *really* crowded. If ever there had been a fire Gladys would have burnt to a cinder. So the pair of them did enjoy Mum's 80th birthday; it was probably the last time that she saw so many relatives together.

1989 brought with it various highlights, some good, some unhappy. Early in the year I went for an interview with Saga Holidays to become a music host. This event in itself should have given me some indication of the hit and miss situation that was often to occur during my years with the company. I arrived at a small London office near Victoria Station early for my midday appointment only to be told by a young man that my interviewer hadn't even left Folkestone! "She told me to send you away to have a long lunch, at Saga's expense." he said; when I told him I'd already had my sandwich lunch in St James' Park he suggested I go and ride on a bus for the next couple of hours. Around three o'clock Elsa Germaine-Bonne rushed in, quite out of breath; despite her foreign sounding name she had a very strong Geordie accent, was very pleasant and put me at ease straight away, though her opening remark as she examined the folder seemed rather strange. "My word, you seem to have walked the world!" Now anyone who knows me will be aware that I am not a great walker; on all the walking holidays I did with CHA and would do with HF later on, I was remembered as the fellow who led the C walks – 3 to 6 miles, in fact my C party walked even less if we could find a good pub for lunch, always making sure that we could arrange to get to the coach to join the other walkers for the return journey; so anyone hearing this dear lady make such a remark would have laughed very loudly. I mumbled some kind of reply, and she went on to ask me some questions about where I had been, about my teaching career and life in the army, etc. But the whole interview seemed rather weird, so at one stage I tactfully asked whether anyone else was being interviewed on that day. "Well, yes, some chap was supposed to come about music, but he obviously hasn't shown up." was the reply, and I had to respectfully ask her to look closely at the photo inside the folder to see whether she had the right person. She had picked up the wrong folder, of course it was the walking leader who hadn't turned up, so we began the interview all over again amid laughter. I was told that I had the job, but I would need to go down to Folkestone to meet the special interests manager at Saga headquarters. A few days later I caught the train and duly met the manager and Elsa, who both occupied a small corner of a room, sharing a computer, with papers all over the desks. The manager, Rosemary Willis, seemed a very grand lady, who would not have looked out of place sipping gin and tonic on the terrace of a large country house, welcomed me to Saga very briefly and that was that.

Early in March I was hosting a Saga group at a hotel on the Hagley Road, Birmingham; they were going to a concert at Symphony Hall given by the Bournemouth Symphony Orchestra (BSO), and I was there to give them a talk on the programme – though I was rather overshadowed by two members of the orchestra who turned up to demonstrate the themes and to give some background about being members of the BSO. Peter Witham, leader of the second violins, was sponsored by Saga. After our combined talk they needed lunch before rushing back for the afternoon rehearsal; there were no restaurants in the vicinity, so I took it upon myself to invite them to lunch in the hotel, and we enjoyed swapping music stories and experiences. Unfortunately I had to leave halfway through a splendid meal to go off with the customers on a sight-seeing trip round Birmingham. Later, when I came to present the invoice for this meal it caused quite a problem, and I had to justify spending a considerable amount on these two musicians. However Elsa accepted my story and just asked me to be a little more considerate in future – considerate for Saga, that is. The concert went well, and I even remember the programme: *Don Juan* by Richard Strauss and Mahler's *Symphony 4 in G*. Thus began many years of diverse holidays and opportunities to work abroad to places which I never would have visited in ordinary circumstances. More of this later!

At Whitsun I went off to Grasmere in the Lake District for a week of music/ dancing/walking; the weather was very hot and I made up my mind to drive straight home on Saturday, impatient to be reunited with my dogs, who, as usual, had stayed with my mother and her Jack Russell, Jess. As always there was a ritual of opening the gate and having three excited dogs throw themselves at you as though you had been away for years. I always had to spend time stroking them and reassuring them that I was back. Mother told me that William had been off his food, and had spent a lot of time just lying in the sun, and I should have taken this sign seriously, but we went home and on Sunday played in the garden and he seemed quite normal. That night he was panting quite a lot, but I put it down to the effects of the sun and told him to be quiet – when I went away they used to sleep in the bedroom for a couple of days until they were reassured that I was not leaving them again. He ate no food in the morning, and when he went out into the garden he seemed to be very weak on his legs. I carried him into the kitchen and laid him on the floor, rang the vet and arranged to take him in straight away, but when I went back and lifted him up he died in my arms from a sudden heart attack. Even 20 years later as I type this I find tears coming to my eyes as I recollect that awful moment when William died. I took his body to the vet and then had to go on to school, where I was doing a couple of weeks supply work, but taking lessons that day was one of the hardest experiences I've ever had; children are so observant, and at one point a girl at the front quietly said: "Mr. Astell, you seem upset today, is it because of us?" I gulped, tried to smile and told them about William, hoping desperately that I didn't break down in front of the class. William was a terrible loss because he was always the most affectionate of the two; he was so faithful and had his secret musical party piece. Soon after I had taken the dogs on I realised that William listened to the radio. The programme *Desert Island Discs* always had the theme tune *By the Sleepy Lagoon* composed by Eric Coates, and in the original version seagulls used to call in the background. Whenever he heard the seagulls, William would put his head back and bark, tail wagging vigorously. Later, a newer recording was used minus the seagulls, but William still barked. Then I happened to go into town and bought a book of famous pieces by Eric Coates, sat at the piano back home, and began to play *Sleepy Lagoon*; within seconds William rushed in from another room, head back, barking enthusiastically and wagging his tail. Whenever people came to visit me he always performed this party piece and proved he was a musical animal. If I was playing the clarinet or recorder, William would join in. Bonnie was the Philistine, she was not interested in music at all. After his death, Bonnie seemed quite lost without him – she had always been the boss, almost as a ritual every day William had stood patiently while she licked his ears with great care and detail, though she always walked away disdainfully when he tried to return the compliment, but now she seemed to wander around the bungalow looking for him. Physically she went downhill very quickly, and took to waking me to go into the garden during the middle of the night, and sometimes wetting the carpet; in normal times when I returned home, as the key turned in the lock she would have barked and come to greet me, but now she was often asleep under the bed or in a corner, and I knew she was pining for William- after all they had been together for over 12 years. Finally I took her to the vet, he announced that her kidneys were not functioning well, that there wasn't much he could do, and he felt it was probably best for her to be put to sleep. I passed her over to the vet giving her one last hug, and will never forget the look in her eyes as I said goodbye, she seemed to know what was happening, I then just broke down completely and cried my eyes out. It may seem a ridiculous thing to do over a dog, but he and his assistant were so sympathetic and understanding. "I know what it's like, the dogs become part of the family." he said, and I tearfully replied,

"It's more than that, William and Bonnie WERE my family – and now the family's gone." It took a long while to get over that loss. Coming back from working holidays, from school, and church, one would be expecting a rush to the door as the key was turned, but instead just an awful silence; this wasn't helped when, a few days later, the vet returned Bonnie's lead and collar along with his invoice; the tears came back again along with memories, and I cried like a child. Some readers may find this puzzling or even crazy, but those who are animal lovers and who live alone will understand how I felt. One of the neighbouring farmers later took on a large Alsatian as a pet, and I enjoyed taking their dog for a walk – it was a huge animal with so much energy, and enjoyed running over the fields after the ball – I had to check there were no sheep or cows around.

Having given up my work in Cambridge, I had more time to get involved in events locally. I played the organ occasionally at the parish church, and when the regular organist died I took over for a while, I also helped with the small choir which was led by Helen Harding from the village, the American lady who I talked about earlier in the chapter. She so much appreciated the help I could give, and the bass voice I offered to the singing; her husband John sang bass but always maintained that I gave him bags of extra confidence. I had also joined the St Neots Choral Society, held in Longsands, the local community college, conducted by Reg Searle, who was a housemaster and had formerly been head of music. The standard was very high and I became one of the rehearsal pianists, and occasionally took over rehearsing the men in part rehearsals which always occupied the first half of the evening. We put on at least three concerts a year plus carol concerts and the occasional 'bring and sing'. Eastern Arts Council wanted to promote modern choral music, and gave us a larger grant if we performed works by Vaughan Williams, Benjamin Britten, and, I remember, a work by Andrew Carter. So we did *Sea Symphony*, *Toward the Unknown Region*, the latter a work I hadn't performed since 1954 at school, under our enterprising music master Peter Cork; at one concert a group of us sang the early Britten work *Hymn to St Cecilia*, which we found quite difficult. Reg Searle was so enthusiastic. We engaged an ad hoc orchestra from Trinity College, London for our performances, but Reg was always keen to start up his own orchestra and he did so around 1990. The St Neots Sinfonia may have started small, but went on to do great things. In 1991 the choir performed Mozart's *Requiem* in the parish church of Eaton Socon and we had the famous tenor Philip Langridge partnered by Ann Murray, his wife, among the soloists line up. These were very famous artists who gave their services almost for nothing because Jean Searle, the conductor's wife used to design and make Ann Murray's costumes; I can remember how proud she was when she saw Ann on television wearing *her* costume for the Last Night of the Proms.

One of the big highlights of 1989 was an opportunity to attend the service of nine lessons and carols at King's College, Cambridge. As I've already mentioned, this was a service I loved to listen to on Christmas Eve, but I never dreamed that I would actually be invited to be one of the guests. Ken Hawkins, the industrial chaplain attached to St Andrew's Street Church was invited to attend as the mayor's chaplain, and there was a ticket for his wife; she worked as a nurse at

Addenbrooke's Hospital, was unable to attend, and so I became Mrs Hawkins for the event. We met at St Mary the Great Church opposite Kings, to put on our robes and get into place for the procession, and at a given signal we slowly walked over to the main gate of Kings where the provost formally met us and lead the party into the chapel and down the main aisle, to take our seats for the start of the service at 3pm. As I slowly processed to my reserved seat – just six places away from the provost himself – I felt rather sorry for the crowds who had been forced to queue since dawn. It was a magnificent experience, to be singing and listening in such a wonderful setting, no electric lights, just lines of candles, and as dusk set it became harder to read the words of the carols; the choir were excellent, and as I watched I envied them the opportunity of singing to such high standard in such marvellous acoustics, little realising that within a few years I would be doing the same thing in another cathedral on the other side of the country. At the end invited guests went back to the provost's residence for mulled wine and mince pies, and here I was able to meet Alexander Goehr, composer in residence at Cambridge University, who had composed a carol especially for the service. He came from a very musical family, his father, Walter, had been a famous conductor and composer who had left Germany in the early 1930s to work in Britain and had studied under Arnold Schoenberg. When it was all over I drove on from Cambridge on cloud nine, to spend Christmas with my brother, Allen and his wife and family and my mother; we had a wonderful time, as always, his wife Brenda was completely organised, and we all ate rather more than we should, and out came the indoor fireworks which I have mentioned previously, by now it had become a tradition – but my best remembrance of that Christmas was the service at King's College.

The folk dance scene had virtually dried up; I still had my accordion and a case full of music but very little opportunity to play. Then for New Year 1991 I was invited to Halsway Manor to provide music for their dance programme, along with Peter Boyce, the great fiddler. I always found it an inspiration to play alongside him, but the visit also brought back memories of 1979 when I had taken the two dogs there just after adopting them.

At the beginning of 1991 I took a part time job teaching clarinet at Kimbolton School, just a few miles west of St Neots. Having spent all my time in state schools where one was often treated like rubbish, to work in an independent school really opened my eyes. One was treated like a professional, the children were fairly keen, not always bright, and the staff were a great bunch to work with. Within a couple of months of doing my one day a week I was regretting that I hadn't gone into the independent sector at the beginning of my own teaching career. Quite early on I discovered Howard Chalkley on the staff who I hadn't seen for about 35 years when we had met at one of the Baptist summer schools. His wife Judy taught piano at Kimbolton and they were a great pair who I got to know in the short time I was to teach there. The Prime Minister, John Major, who lived just outside Huntingdon had his two children at Kimbolton, and I only just missed the dubious opportunity of teaching his daughter, I say dubious because apparently she was 'quite a little madam', to put it mildly. James, the boy was quite popular in the school, though I don't think he ever professed to be particularly musical. The main school is a wonderful 18th century castle, complete with very impressive archway and fantastic views as far as the eye can see. Of course the castle has its stories of ghosts and haunting. Catherine of Aragon after her divorce from Henry VIII spent her dying months at Kimbolton Castle as a prisoner, before dying of cancer in January 1536. Apparently she regularly appears in the castle, but ghosts or not, I had a great time there and was very sorry to leave in 1993.

The holidays continued for CHA, in fact it had settled into a pattern now with holidays at Whitsun and in the summer, often going from one resort to another, working at Grasmere, Whitby and return visits to Cromer where I had first started these music holidays. I remember in the summer of 1990 working at Eskdale, an amazing place; in the Lake District, it is far from the popular centres, and most guests arrived via Ravenglass on the little railway which ran along the dale and stopped right outside the guesthouse at Eskdale, on its way to Boot. The house itself was rather run down – the Association sold it not long after, so I was lucky to stay there before it closed. All guests were given a free ticket to ride on the railway at any time; if you didn't go on the official walks each day and hadn't got transport this was the only way to get around. As usual, Wednesday was the free day and I spent most of it riding up and down on the private railway. That was the last year of the 'privilege' ticket – perhaps people like me used it too much!

Saga had been giving me holidays at Sparsholt, an agricultural college just outside Winchester. In the summer vacations Saga ran inexpensive holidays in various colleges and universities around the country. They were good value for money, with excursions, single rooms and entertainment each evening. The food was fairly plain, usually self-service, but plenty of it and I knew many poor people who saved every year to go on their Saga college holiday. For the special interest guests I would give music sessions and play the keyboard in the mornings and evenings, while the afternoons gave an opportunity for short organised walks from the college; we also had a couple of excursions arranged. On one very hot day we took the guests to Alton where we boarded the 'Watercress line' – now a privately run railway, but in pre-Beeching days it had carried the watercress – a local product – up to London so that it could be sold fresh to restaurants and hotels in the capital. We went the whole journey to Alresford, and when the guests alighted we made it perfectly clear that we were returning by coach NOT train, and we showed them the exact spot where the coach would pick up, and at what time. Then they were free to explore and get lunch. It was a very hot afternoon, Wimbledon men's singles finals were taking place, and I was rather peeved that the match would begin around the time we would be returning. Sure enough the coach arrived, and within a few minutes all the passengers had boarded – except one man. We had had trouble with him earlier in the week, so I'd given him a piece of paper with the time for boarding and the exact spot – outside Barclays bank. We waited and then went on a search, I tried some of the pubs nearby, and went back to the park, but still no sign of him; the reps. and I returned to the coach, and we were about to set off without him when I had a sudden thought, "Give me five minutes." I said, and set off hot foot in the boiling heat to the station, where I saw him boarding a train about to depart! When we got him back on the coach he wouldn't even apologise to the 40 or so people who had sat there almost suffocating in the heat. I'm afraid he gave a lot of trouble to the reps and to the restaurant staff. He seemed to be very keen on stealing sugar – his pockets were full of sugar lumps, and he was quite rude to the waitresses who served him. One morning I deliberately sat at a table near him and when he insulted the waitress I stepped in and told him in no uncertain manner that he had better start behaving himself, or else… So he was one of the difficult, awkward types, but vastly outnumbered by really decent, appreciative people who enjoyed the holidays so much. I remember one lady, who I realised even from her clothes, was rather poor, and had struggled to save for her week away; at the end she came up and said she'd had such a lovely time, enjoyed the music so much, put her arms round me, gave me a big kiss and tried to offer me £1 as a thank you. I declined the tip, and told her to put it towards next year's holiday. I was also doing holidays at Newquay – a very popular resort for Saga in the days before surfers and layabouts took over and the place went downhill very rapidly. The music holidays were held in a fairly small hotel, run by the owners, Brian and his wife. They put themselves out so much for us, and made very little money; as he confessed, "These holidays at the beginning and end of the season just enable us to make sure we keep our regular staff employed, there's little profit in it." They had a lovely black Labrador who used to go walking with me every morning and evening; when I arrived in my car at the beginning of each holiday he would be running over and jumping up at me before I'd even take my case from the boot. The Saga holidays were great fun, and for the first time I was actually being paid and given expenses to host them.

After hosting again at Ambleside with John Buckle, we parted on the Saturday, he to return home ready for school, while I went to have a proper holiday just a few miles away at Scargill. This was a Christian community, run very much on the lines of Lee Abbey down in Devon, in fact Scargill had been opened as the northern counterpart to its southern partner. The house was situated just outside Kettlewell above the river Wharfe. Once you leave Skipton, the road just gets more and more narrow until you wonder whether the house exists – and then you stumble upon this beautiful set of buildings, with fine chapel, built in Scandinavian style and set into the hillside. People always confused Scargill with Arthur of the same name, who had led the NUM miners out on strike in his fight against Mrs Thatcher, but it gets its name from the stream which runs out from the cliffs on the hillside. A number of mainly young people live there in community, some for a gap year before university, others for a year or two while they find their particular job in life. This community made one feel so welcome, and so many guests expressed the feeling that they were living with the community as part of the family while they were there – a wonderful compliment to their devotion and care. I had chosen to go on a railway holiday, led by Mike Peak, who had given up his stressful job in banking, bought a lovely house in Kettlewell and worked part time at Scargill as the bursar, while Dorothy, his wife looked after the gardens and did other jobs. Mike is also a superb photographer, and he ran holidays on photography once or twice a year. It was a most enjoyable week. I remember we went on a small private line which ran just outside Skipton at a place called Embsay; it now runs to Bolton Abbey. It had a comprehensive railway bookshop, and I bought a number of souvenirs to add to the huge collection of railway books I've acquired over the years. We travelled over to York to visit the wonderful Railway Museum, and in the latter part of the week spent a day on the Keighley – Oxenhope preserved line; alighting at Haworth we made our way up through the village to the home of the Bronte sisters, and the church nearby. The real highlight for me was a day on the Settle-Carlisle route. We boarded a fairly crowded train at Hellifield; I couldn't understand one group of adults who had obviously reserved seats with tables so that they could play cards throughout the journey. Was this *really* the way to see the countryside on this incredible route? I had done some reading prior to the journey, and noted the terrible cost in lives to build this route across some of the highest parts of Britain. In several places along the line there had been whole 'towns' of navvies living and working in this desolate part of the country, and there are still graveyards where the unfortunate workers, victims of accidents, bad weather and starvation, were laid to rest. Even the construction of the many viaducts was an incredible achievement in those times and in a bleak part of the world where the names conjure up a lonely, wild terrain, places like Blea Moor, with its long tunnel, Ais Gill Moor and viaduct, where the train passes across the highest parts of its route, nearly 1700 feet above sea level. Even in late August the scenery seemed remote and threatening, so it must be quite treacherous in the height of winter, with gale force winds, drifting snow and freezing temperatures. We got off the train at Appleby-in-Westmorland (I believe it deserves its full name, and am saddened that we have lost so many of our fine county and area names) and spent some hours enjoying this very northern town, with wide main street and shops and houses huddled together against the winter weather which they experience. The return journey was fantastic; along came a huge locomotive pulling at least 10 coaches, which seemed completely empty, and we appeared to have the whole train to ourselves. Certainly this was a memorable experience, and my only regret was that I hadn't done the journey with a steam locomotive hauling the coaches… an ambition which I hope one day to achieve. The railway holiday was great fun and the following year I returned for one of the family summer weeks; I made friends with a wonderful couple, Anne Wheelwright, her husband Mick, and their daughter Rachael. He worked as a prison chaplain, was quite small, very quiet and 'deep', while Anne was tall, exuded confidence, action, and had plenty of conversation along with a wicked sense of humour. They took me in as one of their family and invited me on the trips they made to various locations in that part of Yorkshire. We went to Hawes and the market, to Fountains Abbey, across the hill to Malham. I was so grateful for their genuine friendship, for otherwise the family holiday could have been quite lonely. From 1990 I was to return to Scargill every year, sometimes twice a year, to lead music holidays. Early next year I took on some work with yet another walking organisation – HF, which at the time stood for Holiday Fellowship; in fact the CHA and HF had been one group originally, but they had each gone their separate ways. CHA was to disappear within a few years, partly because they went completely over the top with a renovation scheme in their houses. From a situation with dormitories and a few showers, there seemed a demand for ensuite rooms, and thick carpets embossed with the company's logo, I was even looking for gold taps in the bath. What with overreaching financially in this scheme, and some very bad handling of finances by the people at the top, sadly CHA would go to the wall. HF managed to cope with their modernising, partly by putting up the prices and offering very comfortable accommodation, tables bulging with food when it came to selecting a packed lunch each day before walking, potpourri on the landings, etc., but they have lasted so far. One of the first places HF sent me to was Sedbergh, staying in a small cosy, comfortable house. There were only about 20 guests, it was late in the season and the holiday pattern meant that I lectured on music in the mornings and evenings, leaving an opportunity to do some exploring in the area for lunch and afternoon. Once again I was able to make for the Settle-

Carlisle railway, and this time could see many of the viaducts from below at road level. The towns and villages are few and far between, and I got the impression of remoteness – where time had almost stood still in this part of the world, even the public school situated just outside the town seemed to be silent, although maybe the boys were all on holiday. Sedbergh is actually only 5 miles from the M6, but it could be another world away.

Mother belonged to an old folks' club which met on Friday afternoons for bingo, games and talks, an opportunity for people who lived on their own to come together and have a chat. They also organised coach trips, and I went off to keep her company on a couple of occasions. First time we went to Coventry, admired the wonderful new cathedral built right next to the ruins of the old, and enjoyed buying a lot of fresh fruit and veg in the market nearby. In the morning I remember waiting for the coach to arrive. The old folk would gather on the green with their sticks and Zimmer frames, chatting together without a care in the world, but as the time for the coach arrival drew near I sensed a movement to the pavement, and when it did come it was a case of every man for himself, sticks and frames went flying, courtesy went out of the window as everyone fought to get the front seats on the coach. Suddenly people who could hardly move were running to join the fray. It was an unbelievable sight, and I laughed about it all the way to Coventry. On another occasion we went to the Canal Museum at Stoke Bruene, and after lunch boarded a narrowboat for a trip on the canal; everyone settled down thinking they were there for the afternoon, removing top coats, but the boat only went about half a mile to the entrance of Blissworth tunnel, and then turned for home – we were not on the boat for more than 30 minutes, but at least everyone had the experience. These were good days for my mother, she made many friends, and was greatly loved by the people in the club. We had developed a routine at the weekend whereby either I took my dogs and stayed with her, or she would come over to Abbotsley with Jess and stay with me. She enjoyed cooking, had always cooked for the family, so she took great joy in preparing Saturday and Sunday dinner for two, and it was a way to make sure that she ate proper meals, for I suspected that she didn't always bother during the week when on her own, and heaven knows, eating meals alone is a boring process, best got over with as fast as possible.

During the early summer I helped to prepare the small choir of young people at Abbotsley church for a Royal School of Church music festival which took place at Ely Cathedral. I arrived early to have a look round as it was my first visit to the 'the Ship of the Fens', so-called because of its prominent shape towering above the surrounding flat and watery landscape. Driving over this flat landscape Ely is seen from miles away. I had some cross words with a rather pompous steward at the main door. Ely charged tourists to enter the cathedral, but obviously singers in the festival would not be expected to pay. This gentleman wouldn't believe I was there to sing, even when I produced the music, and informed me that, in any case, I was too early. He finally agreed to let me in on condition that I sat in the chapel on the left-hand side which was only for prayer – I WAS NOT TO GO LOOKING AROUND AT THE REST OF THE CATHEDRAL! Sarcastically, I offered to let him blindfold me so that I couldn't see the beautiful interior, and that he'd better check from time to time that I really was praying, but he finally let me go. Why do people behave in such a suspicious way? I've never ever reconciled myself fully to the need for charging for visitors. I believe the cathedral is God's house, and it is an offence to stick turnstiles at the door and make money – Overturning the Tables in the Temple from the New Testament comes to mind. Defenders of this will argue that they need the money for all the repairs, and I'm the first to agree that cathedrals cost a great deal, they just 'eat' money, I just don't think this is the only way to raise it. This festival was in honour of George Guest, who had retired from St John's College Cambridge; Arthur Wills led the choirs and it was a wonderful experience to sing with that enormous lantern shape above us.

In 1991 I had a real holiday as opposed to the working holidays for Saga and CHA. I went off on August 12th for a 10 day visit to Holland crossing over to Calais and taking a Eurolines bus through France and Belgium arriving at Breda, just over the Dutch border, in the early evening. On the bus I was intrigued by the number of Jewish men, complete with black hats, long black coats, shoulder length hair in ringlets in some cases, who all seemed to be carrying sturdy looking leather cases – many locked to their wrists. They all got off at Antwerp, and later I discovered in conversation that they would be carrying very valuable uncut jewels, and in Antwerp these jewels would be cut into various gems. This was the diamond cutting capital of Europe. At Breda I had a long walk to reach the youth hostel, and had to push on to arrive before nightfall. True to form, I was trying to have a holiday on the cheap – coaches, hostels, etc., but in all honesty I had found that travelling on public transport and staying in hostels meant I was able to meet and converse with people, and for someone travelling alone this makes a big difference. I had bought a ticket for free travel on trains and buses in the country. Holland is small but it takes great pride in its transport system, and trains were frequent and on time, bus and railway stations were side by side and timetables were co-ordinated – certainly a lesson that other countries could learn. Breda was just over the border from Belgium, amid wooded country; I hired a bicycle one day and travelled over to Tilburg, amazed to find cycle tracks everywhere, cycle lanes under busy road junctions – it was incredible, but then, Holland is the land of the bicycle. In the afternoon I rode back into Belgium, with no idea where the actual border was, and looked around one or two villages. Later in the week I moved hostel to Apeldoorn which was more in the centre of Holland and a very good place from which to get trains in every direction. I went to Arnhem to visit one of the cemeteries and the Museum at Oosterbeek in what had been the 1st Airborne Division HQ in 1944. At the top of the staircase hangs one of the few remaining parachutes that was used to drop supplies. Apparently about 20,000 of them had floated down in the area of Arnhem, almost all of them were used by soldiers and civilians as sheets or as protection against the wind and the rain, and after the war quite a few women in the area could be admired in their Sunday dresses made from the bright silk or nylon parachutes. Lines and lines of immaculate white graves in the cemetery brought back the terrible price that had been paid in trying to take and hold the bridge at Arnhem; I was completely alone in the cemetery and able to offer up my own quiet prayer of thanksgiving. Then I had time to visit the bridge and walk along each bank, to get an idea of the terrible circumstances in which men had fought in the middle of September 1944 trying to carry out Montgomery's plan. On another day I took a couple of trains north to Leeuwarden in the Friesland area, perhaps the part of Holland one always pictures – some of the people still wearing traditional costume, clogs worn not just as ornaments but for everyday work, windmills everywhere and many dikes and bridges. It was a delightful place, well away from the normal tourist trail. I went over to the coast and saw the three islands which are very popular with visitors in the summer, and then made my way down to Alkmaar, which houses one of the greatest organs in Europe, and the oldest organ in the Netherlands. I managed to arrive to hear the last 20 minutes of a lunchtime recital in a truly magnificent setting. When I came to revisit this site on the Internet recently I was dismayed to see that the church is now often used for functions and wedding receptions, but I suppose they have to raise money to keep the place going. On another day I decided to go over to the Hague and spent an hour riding on the tram down to the beach, which was packed with swimmers and sunbathers. Towards the end of the week I returned to stay at Breda overnight before catching my Euro lines coach back to Calais. The hostel was very comfortable and I actually had a room to myself; after dinner I sat on the terrace to smoke my pipe and got into conversation with a couple of Dutch teenage girls who were also on a cycling holiday. Their English was excellent, and they asked to talk to me so that they could improve it even more. One of the girls, Anne-Marie, was very interested in classical music and played the clarinet as her main instrument, so we had quite a lot to discuss. The next morning they were out front to take photographs of each other but they had run out of film – these were the days before digital cameras, of course – so I offered to take the pictures with my camera and send them over to Holland; arriving home the photos were developed and I duly sent them to Anne-Marie. This incident appears insignificant, but read on to find the incredible consequences.

Towards the end of August I did a week at Borrowdale, way up in the Lake District at a centre which the CHA regarded as its flagship; it offered opportunities for very strenuous walks and climbs so I was surprised to discover that the centre was a complete sell-out for my week of music and walking. Our main walking leader was Jack Stead, a very tall strong character who was normally a shepherd and knew the area like the back of his hand. As usual, I offered to lead the C party, those who didn't consider themselves real walkers, avoided gradients as much as possible, and just enjoyed a stroll of 4 or 5 miles in the delightful setting up there beyond Keswick. After a couple of days it was obvious that I had run out of walks for the C party – to keep on level ground one either went in one direction along the river, or in the opposite direction, and straying from those courses meant climbing. On Monday evening Jack took me aside, "Brian, you come with us tomorrow, I'll give you the most wonderful view of the area, something to remember for a long time." He explained to the C walkers that they must just organise themselves or walk up and down by the river, it was impossible to plan any further walks without climbing. So on Tuesday I joined the main party and after an hour or so WE began to climb; I puffed my way along , and when I complained to Jack he 'reassured' me that we hadn't even begun to tackle the real climb! We finally ascended High Style, which was 806m of sheer hell. The ascent seemed almost vertical and I remember clutching at the grass trying to get a hold, then scrabbling up with my legs, there was no question of standing up to walk normally. One of my great CHA friends, Derek, was in front of me, also puffing and panting – the pair of us slowly inched our way to the top and just lay on the summit desperately trying to get our breath back. "I've never felt so depressed," said Derek, "If I even dared to look down it scared me stiff and if I looked up, well, it just seemed to go on forever, so I just closed my eyes and carried on.". Of course if you knew Derek you realised at once that it was his dry, acerbic humour in action. He had enjoyed the challenge – well I think so! When we were able to breathe again we joined the rest of the party to enjoy our packed lunch seated on what appeared to be the top of the world – with fantastic views of Buttermere and Crummock Water below; it was like being in a low-flying aircraft. We savoured those views to the last minute, because I think both Derek and I knew that we would never be climbing such peaks again. Then came the descent, the latter part of which was mountain scree, so we needed to be careful of our footing to avoid breaking an ankle; eventually we all reached the bottom and continued our walk between the two lakes. When I got back, exhausted, I thanked Jack for persuading me to go, it had been so exhilarating. The next scary event came the following day when I drove over to the West Coast to Whitehaven. The place seemed dreadfully rundown, with many closed shops and young men hanging about; I reckon the unemployment figures along that West Coast were very high indeed. In the afternoon I thought I would drive back taking the scenic route, which involved going across the Honister Pass

– which looked very picturesque on the map but, in fact was quite scary; when trying to pass an oncoming vehicle it involved going too close for comfort to the very edge of the narrow track – I didn't dare look down, and then there were the sharp bends to negotiate, so I finally arrived back at Borrowdale thankful that the car and I were still in one piece.

Life had gradually assumed a regular pattern of part-time instrumental teaching, interspersed with music holidays with Saga, CHA, HF and Scargill House. Preparations for these holidays took quite a time, but it was an interesting job. My CD collection was growing by the day so that I had plenty of choice when it came to organising programmes and themes. At home my brothers and I were concerned about mother living alone, and on two occasions I had been quite scared of the situation. One morning, driving round to collect her for a shopping trip to town I turned the corner and there was a fire engine outside Mother's house. Apparently the washing machine had gone crazy, and water had just continued to fill and overflow the kitchen, resulting in a regular stream running out from the kitchen to the back door; Mum had panicked and didn't know how to switch off the water. The firemen were marvellous, took the matter in hand immediately and stayed to help clear up the mess. A couple of months later I arrived in the car to find the fire engine had returned; this time there *was* a fire, something had caught alight on the stove and flames had spread to the ceiling very quickly. The fire was put out, but it left the kitchen in a bad way and we had to redecorate. These events led us to feel that we had to try to persuade Mother to move into some kind of sheltered accommodation or old folks' home. Allen and John, with wives joined us for a meal at Mother's home, to discuss it. Now Mother was VERY hard of hearing at this stage, wore hearing aids in both ears, and one had to speak in a raised voice for her to understand, but when we *quietly* began to discuss moving she immediately turned on us and made it clear that she wasn't "going into no home, thank you." So we had to try to make her understand that we were not plotting to do anything against her will, she wouldn't be dumped in a home, but that there were some very comfortable old folks' homes which she could at least visit, without any commitment. John now lived at Whittlesey, about 10 miles from Peterborough and there was an old people's home very close to their bungalow, which had a good reputation. They took mother over to view the home, ideal because we all could visit frequently and give her the occasional weekend with us, and she would meet up with the grandchildren who all lived fairly locally. She turned down the offer, preferring to stay in her own home, so it was back to the drawing board again.

In the summer of 1992 I went to Denmark for a couple of weeks, once again by coach and staying in youth hostels. This time, with Eurolines, I set off from Victoria in a coach down to the Isle of Sheppey, to board a large ferry bound for Rotterdam and then continued up through Germany, into Jutland, disembarking at Arhus. It was a long journey; when I boarded the ferry I made for the lower decks where there were free beds and couchettes. When I later came up on deck to enjoy the sun and the sea it was packed, with no empty seats. I finally discovered an empty deckchair but the lady next to it told me it wasn't free, her friend who had gone to get some lunch would want it when she came back. I agreed that as soon as her friend returned I would vacate the seat, but I really was tired. It seemed polite to try to make conversation and 'get her on my side' – the atmosphere was rather cool, so I noticed that she had a couple of classical music cassettes and decided this would be a good opener. "It's nice to meet someone else who enjoys classical music," I said, and she took up the link, telling me that she liked classical pieces but her daughter was much more into it, and played the clarinet. "That's interesting," I replied, "I'm a clarinettist and I know at least one other young lady in Holland who plays the clarinet."

"Are you Brian Astell?" She asked, "If so you probably mean my daughter, I am Mrs Hacvoort, Anna-Marie's mother. You kindly sent the photographs to her last year!" This was unbelievable: of all the people on this crowded ferry I should be talking to that girl's mother, and we couldn't stop laughing at this amazing coincidence; we were still laughing when her friend returned, but I was encouraged to stay in my seat and we continued to chat. It's just one of those things that happen occasionally that make me realise what a small world it can be.

At Arhus I made my way to a much smaller ferry which was going over to the island of Samsø. The youth hostel was in an ideal spot; the warden and I became friends straightaway – he told me that not many English hostellers found their way to Samsø, and he could give me a room to myself, at least for the beginning of the week. This room was literally on the beach, I could open the back door and step down into the sand. My plan was to eat out at restaurants, and on the first night I found a pleasant place which was nearly deserted. The usual thing happened, I was put into the corner of the room at a single table – I felt like a naughty boy at school – and later the Danish families came in and all eyes seemed to be on me. It sounds crazy but I was embarrassed, quickly settled my bill and left. I decided then that I would get my own food in the hostel, so the following morning I went into town to do some shopping. I settled on a simple dish that I could prepare easily, it was going to be powdered potatoes, fresh tomatoes and baked beans, with spam. The girl in the shop didn't speak English, which was unusual, but with a few actions and pointers she understood what I wanted – or so I thought. Later that evening I went into the empty kitchen to prepare my primitive meal, measured out the potato powder in a saucepan, added the water and began to heat it up, while stirring. The trouble was the whole thing became terribly thick and impossible to stir, and it didn't look or smell right at all. One of the Danes came in to begin his food preparation, happened to notice my powdered potato tin, burst out laughing and ran out of the kitchen, while I still tried to stir the awful mixture in the pan, now getting thicker by the minute. His friends joined him in the kitchen and everyone seemed to be laughing their heads off except me; someone apologised and explained that the powder I was using for potatoes was actually…wallpaper paste!! Of course I then saw the joke and we all had another good laugh, and they insisted that I join them in their barbecue meal on the terrace. These Danes would spend about an hour fishing in the morning, then gut and prepare the fish for the evening, cooking it on an open fire; the results were fantastic. I think various cats and dogs ate my spam, and my 'powdered potato' went in the dustbin.

After the long journey it was glorious to spend a couple of days just lying in the sun reading and sleeping, then I explored the island on a hired bicycle, which was perfect, the island being almost flat, and visited some of the churches and villages. I returned to discover an elderly woman had taken possession of one of the other beds in my room. This seemed rather embarrassing, just two people in a room, but was perfectly accepted by the Danish people. She only stayed one night, and when I spoke to the warden, he told me she had moved out because I snored too much – that was one time when the snoring paid off. Samsø was an idyllic place, completely unspoiled, hardly any cars, and very few tourists apart from Danish families – even many Danes who I spoke to later had never heard of the place. I would love to revisit it.

Then it was off on another ferry to the island of Aero, south of Funen. The hostel was situated in the pretty town of Aeroskobing, at the top of the hill which looked down over the harbour. The houses were very small and brightly coloured with wonderfully carved doors and cast iron lamps. The streets were mostly cobblestones; one writer describes the place as a 'Lilliputian city'. One of the features pointed out to me were small mirrors outside each house, rather like wing mirrors of a car, but fixed at an angle whereby the person inside could see what was going on around without opening the window and appearing nosy! On my last morning, I paid my bill and set off with my heavy rucksack down the hill towards the ferry when a car drew up, it was the warden who had decided that I should get to the ferry in style and not have to cart my luggage – such was the generous spirit I discovered all over Denmark. This next ferry travelled north beneath the huge bridge which was being constructed to link the two main islands together. The Great Belt Bridge was finished in the middle of 1998 and is a marvellous sight. It links Zealand to Funen via a small island, Sprogø, and now means that one can get from Copenhagen right across to West Denmark by car or rail – no need for ferries any more. I must return to have another go on the train across Denmark. In this instance after my ferry landed at Roskilde, I took time out to visit the cathedral – I was staying there for a couple of days – and had a chance to go to a wonderful organ recital that evening. The music played on the Marcussen organ was splendid and sounded fantastic in that acoustic when suddenly, without warning all the lights went off and the organ came to a grinding halt. The audience sat in the darkness until a diminutive figure appeared just above the organ screen, illuminated by a torch to explain that the alarm system, obviously set so that the electrics switched off automatically, had not been adjusted to take account of the recital. We waited for about 10 minutes, the lights came back on and the organist resumed his last pieces. A group of Italians had also registered at the hostel sharing my room. After the first night they complained to me about my snoring, for which I apologised but tried to say it just couldn't be helped. The next evening they went out until late, I went to bed early and the next thing I knew the group was waking me up because of my snoring again. They seemed rather aggressive this time, but fortunately they were off at crack of dawn to get a ferry. It was slowly dawning on me that I should accept that my hostel days were coming to an end, and I ought to stay in hotels or boarding houses.

The next step of the journey involved going by train across Zealand to Copenhagen, where, after making my way out of the city on the tram I eventually found a crowded hostel – no chance of rooms to oneself here, you were just lucky to get a bed. I spent my last days in and around the crowded city and soon realised that though one had to visit the capital city, I preferred the country and island settings. On the last day I caught my Eurolines coach – a large double-decker, with my reserved seat upstairs, at around three in the afternoon, and we made our way over Zealand to catch a ferry to Funen and then to the mainland. The bus was crowded and it was difficult to sleep in such conditions. I got into conversation with the girl next to me, who I would describe as a 'beatnik' type, safety pins through the nose and elsewhere, tattoos in abundance and a *very* unusual hairstyle. Her English was quite good, but as we got nearer to the big ferry, to cross over the North Sea she seemed rather agitated. After we reached Sheppey we were instructed to make our way through customs and back onto the coach, but this girl was missing from the party. The driver went off to make enquiries, and then returned and we set off without her. Back at Victoria he told me she had been detained en route by customs, probably carrying drugs, and would be sent back to Holland. So, I had been sharing my seat with a drug dealer; I was glad that I had not volunteered to take anything through customs on her behalf, or I might have been sharing a cell.

When I arrived back home it was to find that things had moved on for Mother. My sister June and her husband had been to stay; they were planning to move to a large bungalow, and they offered to take Mother on, to live with them but to have her own room. They seem to have worked it all out – perhaps glad that I hadn't been around to ask any questions. She was glad of this opportunity, "But I've told them I will only go if are sure you can look after yourself." she said. I quickly made it clear that I had been looking after myself for at least 20 years, certainly hadn't starved in that time, and that was the last thing she should be thinking of. Everything was settled very quickly – far too quickly in my opinion – the local council was informed that she would be leaving her rented home and we began to get rid of all her furniture. Dear old Gladys, who I have referred to earlier, was in her element, very disappointed that Mum was leaving but ready and happy to take on quite a lot of bits and pieces which we didn't want. In fact her garage became full to bursting, but I heard that she was able to sell off quite a lot of the things eventually. The rent man had a word with my brother and I urging us to buy her council house, and then resell it; I think we could have bought it for about £9000, but they were saddled with mortgages and I didn't want to take on a mortgage again, which was a pity, we could have had a bargain. Fairly soon, a rather tearful Mum left her home to set up with June down at Erith, close to Bexleyheath in Kent. It was the end of an era for me, I had lost my dogs, Mother had moved and I had a premonition that I would be moving on soon. There was nothing to keep me at Abbotsley.

One of my CHA weeks was back at Hereford on a walking/music week at the blind college, the very place where I had received my letter announcing the award of early retirement, in 1984. This was always a great favourite with plenty of space, Steinway pianos and an organ to play and a good walking area. On the Wednesday I went down to the cathedral for a lunchtime recital given by the cathedral organist, Roy Massey. At the end he made his way down the aisle amid applause, I moved forward to shake his hand, thank him for the music, and said, "I would just love to sing in the choir in this cathedral."

"Well maybe you can, if you pass the audition." was his reply, and he told me to get in touch. I returned home, Hereford Cathedral would not leave my mind, and I arranged to travel over for an audition in early November. There were some awful problems on the journey however, as it had rained ceaselessly for three days, the rivers burst their banks and there was only one way out of St Neots. I thought I had allowed plenty of time for the journey, but many of the roads were impassable, flood warnings all over the place and my sense of direction seemed to leave me when I found myself at Leamington Spa; then I made for Worcester, came across more problems of flooding, and after breaking the speed limit on the almost empty M50 and going one junction too far, reached Hereford Cathedral over half an hour late. Dr. Massey was to take me to lunch, but had given up and gone on his own. I apologised to his wife and arranged to return later. We met up and I explained why I was late – I think he more or less forgave me. At my audition I had prepared a piece to sing, *The Call* from Vaughan Williams' *Five Mystical Songs*; it lay rather high for my bass register, but I could just about reach the top notes, and had practised it a few times. Dr Massey seemed surprised that I had bothered to bring two copies of the music, and, feeling rather scared, I sang. At the end he closed the piano lid rather firmly, turned to me and said, "Yes, thank you, but you wouldn't really call yourself a *singer*, would you?" I was stunned at his abruptness – later to learn that this was part of his character, and thought I'd failed. "If you mean a solo singer, then you are correct; but surely a solo singer is the last thing you want in a choir, thinking of voice blending, and so on." I replied. He grudgingly accepted this, so we moved round from his house in the cloisters to the choir school – I came to think later that 'torture chamber' might better describe it – where he showed me row upon row of music portfolios, selected a handful of pieces which I then had to sight read. The more traditional stuff wasn't too bad, but he slipped in some Benjamin Britten and Herbert Howells, which had some quite scary intervals to sing. I did my best and he seemed reasonably content with my sight reading. He went on to explain that there was no position as a 'full-time' lay clerk, the two basses were very firmly established at Hereford, but he would be delighted to have me as a supernumerary; he went on to add that there was no real money involved, he thought the ' pay' was about £10 a week; I would be involved in a full rehearsal on Friday evenings, rehearsal and Evensong on Saturday, and Eucharist, Matins and Evensong on Sunday; it would be very useful if I could deputise for one of the basses if the need arose; there was money to be had from recordings, broadcasts, etc. If I was happy with that he would welcome me into the choir. Having also made clear that there was no chance of accommodation or a job, we shook hands and I left Hereford with the task of selling 'Hedgehogs', and buying something in or near Hereford, which was to prove a difficult task.

Christmas is always a very busy time for musicians, with concerts, carol singing and services for Advent right up to Christmas day itself. Although I did not have school concerts to worry about, I was taking part in concerts and carols with the St Neots Choral Society and playing for the local church. This year I was also asked to provide some carols, along with Peter Boyce, the wizard violinist, at Lord's cricket ground. Naturally in December there was very little cricket going on, but the members liked to have carols with their dinner in the pavilion, and for 1992, Peter and I accompanied the carols and entertained them. Not being a sportsman, I had never been to Lord's to watch a match, but I was still impressed with the wonderful ground and could imagine the excitement that was often created during the matches. We actually got well paid for our troubles, which was a great bonus.

The bungalow was very slow to sell, but I did find a buyer in March of 1993, and went to Hereford three times to view properties. Having been sent to some totally unsuitable places, and some too far out for frequent journeys to the cathedral, I eventually found a suitable bungalow in Lugwardine, good size, ideal setting, an end of row, detached, with fields on one side, took morning coffee with the owner, a lady who had not long ago lost her husband and would be moving to something smaller in the city, and we came to an agreement . I departed happily to set events in motion and chased back to Abbotsley, only to discover that my buyer had pulled out, and I was back to square one! When the second buyer came along I was less optimistic, but still went off to view bungalows and houses over at Hereford, could find nothing, bought the local paper and set off to Newton Rigg, an agricultural college on the outskirts of Penrith to do my second music holiday of the year there for saga. I unpacked my cases after a long drive, and sat on the bed to have a look through the local Hereford Times, and in the property section was a picture of just the house I fancied, close to Hereford, detached and more or less at a price I could afford – but here I was stuck 200 miles away with a week to go before I had a hope of viewing the place! I contacted the agent and arranged to view on my return from Penrith. One memory stands out of this holiday and concerns one of the guests. Under the watchful eye of our walking leader on Saturday we were going to do a walk on the fells just above Kendall; there had been heavy rainfall, the grass was very wet and he urged us to wear suitable shoes, not sandals or even trainers as they wouldn't give enough grip on the wet grass. After about an hour of level walking we had to descend, and he warned us to put our weight on the soles of the feet, but, too late, one woman fell over and cried out in agony. Drama ensued as someone was sent down to the next farm to ring for the mountain rescue party as the mobile phones didn't seem to work on the fell, then I went down to wait for the mountain rescue and lead them to the injured person who was still being cared for by the walking leader and a couple of women. Within about 10 minutes I heard the police siren in the distance and was ready to praise their speed and reaction when the police car appeared; I waved it down but the police completely ignored me and sped on; behind them followed a large BBC outside broadcast van – which I learned later was on the way to do a programme on television of *One Man and His Dog!* Eventually the mountain rescue did arrive and then everything happened quickly and the injured guest was taken off to hospital at Carlisle. Within a couple of days Dorothy was back with us at the college with her leg heavily strapped. She really wanted to get back to her own home, and assured us that her loving son would drive up straight away to collect her. In fact, when we rang him, the 'loving son' showed very little care, refused to take a day from work (although I'd been given the impression that he was in banking and was the boss) and told us to pass on the message to his mother that she could use the NHS and an ambulance to take her home. When I conveyed this news she just broke down, and I felt sad that she had put so much trust in a son who obviously cared more for the money he would lose during the day than his own mother's comfort. The next morning an ambulance arrived which was really totally unsuitable, the sort of vehicle that ferried outpatients from home to their local hospital. Dorothy was strapped in and they departed the 300 miles or so to Kingston on Thames. I kept in touch with her and she did make a full recovery, but it was a slow process, as a broken ankle would be for someone approaching 80.

During the war mother had been evacuated to Rochdale with the Mills family, 'Nanny', her daughter, Edna, and granddaughter, Margaret – still at school. We had met them once since 1943, at my house at Woodford when they had come down to do some sightseeing in London, although Nanny had long since died. During the week I made a visit up to Wigton where Edna and her daughter Margaret now lived; Edna had almost lost her sight, but she and daughter still travelled all over the place – they had been to Canada and the States several times and often popped over to Europe for the sunshine. It was a grand, but brief reunion and since that time Edna has died though Margaret still does a lot of voluntary work and is involved in many community activities in Wigton. Came the final morning, and I was off very early to view the house at Hereford. It was on a small estate just three miles from the city in a place called Bartestree, and though my visit had been arranged for 4pm., I arrived about an hour early, and from the car parked outside and the sounds within I knew someone was there, but nobody answered the door. Suddenly I was really frustrated – because I had driven all the way down without stopping for any meal, I had already viewed 19 premises and it all seemed wrong that I had to hang around for an hour. I almost decided to drive away and forget the whole move, but promptly at 4pm rang the bell and was welcomed in. Somehow I knew that this was the house I wanted. It was a Barratt home, about three years old and I couldn't understand why the owners wanted to move so quickly; they informed me that three years was the longest they had ever stayed in a house and they liked to move on. I was very taken with the conservatory and south facing garden, the lounge was a good size, it was tastefully decorated, and was tucked away in a corner where I would be no trouble to anyone. There was a primary school on one side, separated from the house by a footpath, but this seemed to present no trouble. Actually the school were on summer holiday, and if I had visited the house at half past three on a day in term time with all the parents parked outside waiting for their precious children, I might have had second thoughts. This problem of parking was to become a real nuisance. We more or less agreed a price, with curtains, carpets, chandeliers and light fittings thrown in and I set off back to Abbotsley, praying that my buyers still wanted to buy. In fact my buyer wanted to move in there and then. Apparently while I was away the agent had told them to push for an early date, "He's only an old single man, rather eccentric, with no family to worry about, he can move out without any trouble." were the words quoted to me by the daughter of the couple who were buying, and when I challenged the agent she didn't deny that she had used such phrases. I was furious with her for using such language, and reminded her that she was the agent acting for me NOT for the buyers. Of course, like many agents she was acting for herself and wanted her quick 3%. The buyers were pushing and said they wanted to move in on Bank holiday weekend; I suggested that was a hopeless date because all the removal companies in the area would already be booked up, after all it was the busiest weekend of the year for moving house. Well, they did find a company in Bedford who would take my furniture in store that weekend, and my brother agreed straight away to let me stay with them until I could move to Hereford. So I had two weeks to get everything packed, say goodbye to all the friends I had made in the choral society, the orchestra, the church and in the village and move out. I worked myself into the ground doing the packing, and then on the Thursday afternoon the removal men rang to ask if they could move my main furniture out the next day – everybody was rushing to get me OUT of that bungalow, but we came to an agreement that they would do all my kitchen wrapping and packaging if I was happy with this plan. It all went ahead and on Saturday morning I said goodbye to Abbotsley, all my worldly goods were in store for the second time in my life, and I was homeless for the next two months, with just a suitcase and a couple of boxes to my name. As always when moving, I drove away with very mixed feelings, slightly excited at the prospect of a new start, but mingled with sad feelings and leaving friends behind, and always, the nagging worry as to whether I was doing the right thing – East Peckham, Woodford, Abbotsley – at each one it had been a sad farewell.

June, Dad, BA, Mum, Allen, Brenda. Mr. and Mrs.
Kirk, Alison and Valerie outside St. Martins church
Dagenham

Allen and Brenda on their wedding day August
1964

John and Jackie leaving St.
John's church, Lewisham

John Buckle and me on one of our working
holidays – note the MG in the background
and Elizabeth, who admired….the car

Rev.David Butler and Fionna at
East Peckham.

Jim, June and parents, outside the church at
Plumstead, S.E. London

Mum at my Woodford home caring
for the dogs – Bonnie, William and
Jess. August, 1984

Pauline Jones – in Cornwall, August,1983

On a Saga holiday – Pesaro

Playing my new Viscount organ –one reason for my move away

Family

St. Neots c.1981 Allen with family and Mum

311

Bonnie and William my lovely family

Holmer 2006 my 70th birthday cakes from the church

Alan Johansson, my doctor neighbour at Bartestree. We spent many hours in conversation and enjoying good wine

Pat, Alan's wife. Note the drinks cabinet well and truly open, at 5.30 p.m. Sadly Pat died in 2008

Enjoying the grand piano – publicity photo for Saga

Derek, faithful guest, great wit, happy here with his vino.He died in March 2010

in my garden at Hereford, 2000

Christmas time at
Hereford

A happy family get together: Back row: Brenda, Michael, June, Jacky ,Jim, Allen
Front Row: BA (who took the photo), Mum. John, Kirsty and James

Working for Saga

The choir at Hereford cathedral. Back row: Peter Dyke, Parry, Jeremy, BA.
Duncan, Stephen, Paul, Tim,
Colin, Stephen, Pochin, Dr. Roy Massey

Oberammergau opera holiday with Saga – with Uschi, my favourite Saga rep.
Sadly she died from breast cancer in 2009

last photo of mother, on her 90th birthday. The computer lurks in the background

CHAPTER SEVENTEEN

HAPPY YEARS IN HEREFORD

I had been made homeless once before, in 1976, and should have realised the terrible inconvenience and problems that are caused. Waiting to move into Hereford became a nightmare, with a whole load of holiday programmes to organise, no computer or printer available and only a handful of CDs from which to make up any programme. I moved on the bank holiday weekend, and by Tuesday I was on my way to Sparsholt College to do a week of music for Saga, which turned out to be a nightmare in itself. A large group of Italian students were staying at the college, and the girls' showers happened to be within a few yards of the hut where I was doing my music, while on the other side were the football pitches which the Italians used in the evenings. The weather was very hot and we had to have the windows open, so there were many occasions when the guests couldn't even hear me for the noise outside. Their favourite game was to taunt the security guards by roaming around at night and congregating beneath hostel windows – it wasn't much fun to be woken up at three in the morning by noisy Italians. A couple of our guests ended up at the hospital, having been knocked over by groups of running students, and then to crown it all, on the third night the bouncy castle arrived with loud pop music attached! This really was the limit, and I told my guests that if I was in their shoes I would be demanding my money back, it wasn't a holiday, more like a farce. I put all these details in my regular report back to Saga, and it seems for my honesty I was punished by not being given further holidays in the next couple of years. Following that holiday at Winchester I had to move off to Penrith and then to Newquay. After a few days rest and a chance to explore the Fens, with a couple of trips to Spalding I had to fulfil a further engagement at Scargill House. Meanwhile the move to Hereford seemed to be delayed. I had used a solicitor recommended by my brother, in fact the firm he had worked for over a number of years, and she told me about one particular holdup; apparently a footpath which ran across the front of my drive, and then between the shared drive with the neighbour didn't appear to have been adopted by the council. I think in the rush to build the estates at this time legal work was rather slipshod, and this particular path had slipped through the net. My solicitor had raised the matter with her counterpart in Hereford but she was not pleased. "Brian, what do you do when a solicitor tells you not to worry your pretty little head over such an insignificant item?" She was furious at his patronising manner and that he would do nothing about it. In theory someone could come along and bring out a piece of paper proving that they owned that little strip of path, which would have made me a prisoner in my own drive. She solved the matter by telephoning the Timmers (the sellers) informing them that I had waited long enough, my patience was at an end and I was going over to Hereford at the weekend to view similar properties which had become available. She also made it clear that I would not be home until Tuesday, then assured me that over the weekend the telephone would be getting red hot with them becoming anxious at losing their sale. She was right and the bluff worked, on Tuesday the solicitor got down to his job, the necessary adoption paper was received within days. I telephoned the sellers and was told that they "would rather like another couple of weeks – it was inconvenient to move while husband is away on a course;" it was my turn to be nasty, and I made it clear that I had been more than inconvenienced, I was paying a lot of money every week for furniture storage while living out of a cardboard box! I went off to play piano on the Isle of Wight for another folk week with the assurance that all would be complete within a few days. I remember Jeanne Howard, who ran the folk holiday, standing before the assembled company on Friday morning as they were about to do their last dance, to announce that she had just received a phone call from my solicitor and I was now the proud owner of 50, Barnaby Avenue, Bartestree, Hereford. I drove back to spend a quiet weekend with my brother and his wife and on Monday morning with the car filled to overflowing with boxes, pot plants and other items I had bought during my 'homeless' time, I set off for Hereford and pastures new.

318

I had arranged for furniture to arrive on the Tuesday, so it meant one more night of B&B though I did collect the keys from the agent; I parked the car outside the Cathedral School music department, opened the car door and nearly knocked someone flying – it happened to be Roy Massey, the organist and boss of the choir. He looked rather angry and was about to explode when I *think* he recognised me, "I think I know you, don't I?" he enquired, and I introduced myself as his new bass supernumerary. "Right, you'll need a couple of days to settle in and I'll see you on Friday at Evensong." he said. So I went off to get the house keys laughing inwardly at the way I had introduced myself by nearly knocking him off his feet. Back to number 50 to empty the car of its flowerpots, food and odds and ends, I wandered round the empty house reminding myself of the rooms and situation, for I hadn't seen the place since early August. It is a lovely feeling to finally stand in your new home, with all the trauma of selling, conveyancing, and moving now complete. Next morning removal men arrived bright and early, and by the afternoon the house was beginning to look like a home – a home with about 100 large boxes deposited in the rooms. As in all my moves, the first thing to set up was the hi-fi system and see how it sounded in my comfortable lounge, then to give the piano a nice welcome bash, and finally, to find out how everything worked in the kitchen so that I could prepare an evening meal. Everything went so smoothly and I did the unpacking in a steady, systematic way without tiring myself completely. On Friday when I presented myself at the cathedral, Roy suggested that I sit in on Evensong as a member of the congregation, this I was so glad to do, for I had no idea of the order of these services in cathedrals. I hadn't been to an Evensong since I'd attended King's College, Cambridge with my friend David Butler back in 1973. This first Evensong was incredible; hardly anybody was present apart from the two members of Chapter who were leading; following tradition, Friday Evensong was unaccompanied, and the whole atmosphere was one of peace and serenity. The singing was wonderful and I suddenly felt insecure about joining such a choir – even I realised I didn't have a particularly good voice, and, from day one the lay clerks reminded me of it, usually in a friendly way but sometimes they could be cruel. After the service I was introduced to the lay clerks, who were very keen to meet me because it appears that Roy had informed them,

"A new chap is joining as a supernumerary, who has a London B.Mus., could be very interesting." Maybe they saw me as some kind of threat, but they soon realised that I hadn't a clue about cathedral music, and when I did begin to sing they certainly knew I was no threat! They kept calling me 'old man', and though I was the oldest member by far I wasn't too sure that this was a compliment or not, but then heard them referring to each other as 'old men', even the youngest countertenor who was only in his 30s, so obviously it was a sign of endearment or tradition. After the introductions they very generously allowed me to lead the way into the choir school for rehearsal; I should have realised early on some of the antics lay clerks got up to (they were always acting like little boys, and I'm sure that singing in the choir gave them an excuse to return to their childhood), as I opened the door some kind of object was just hitting the wall a few feet away, apparently thrown by the director of music at one of the choristers, while he yelled out, "Come on in, you're late, we want to get started and go home for our supper! " That was my baptism into Hereford choir, and it really went on like that for the next eight years. After rehearsal I was invited to join the Friday evening ritual of visiting the local pub, discovering that the lay clerks were not only great singers but very good drinkers as well. I could never keep up with them and didn't even make the effort, so I had the occasional half while they were knocking back pints. The time came for me to buy the round of drinks, which came to about £12; I was getting £10 per weekend for singing, so membership of the choir cost me two pounds a week, but it was so enjoyable. I heard many stories about the Dean and Chapter (members of the clergy who ran the cathedral), the choir, the organist – everyone agreeing that he was a monster to sing under, and how they really didn't enjoy it at all, yet, strangely most of them had been singing there under Roy for years. The senior lay clerk, Duncan, is an educational psychologist, and if ever I've needed proof that psychologists need mental help, I see it in him. He had originally sung under Roy at Birmingham Cathedral, and when Roy moved to Hereford in 1974 Duncan followed him and had been singing bass there ever since. He was a great storyteller, loved his practical jokes, had some very unusual ideas, and was a pyromaniac – as I discovered later. Jeremy, the other bass, taught English in the Cathedral School, loved church music and singing, but would die before acknowledging it – or was claiming that he only sang for the money and was always about to resign. There were two Stephens, Mr Gowland, who lived and breathed music 24 hours a day; he travelled to various schools as a peripatetic teacher of string instruments, but he could put his hand to any instrument, and play it and teach it in a rudimentary fashion; he also composed and arranged, indeed he arranged for any kind of combination of instruments that were on offer when needed. Stephen Challenger was a tenor, wonderful voice and incredible sight reader, and always the most steady, 'feet on the ground' type of individual; with his quiet voice he never seemed to flap or panic, and with his job as bursar of the Cathedral, he seemed to know all about the politics of the place. The other tenor was Colin, who had joined the Hereford choir after leaving Liverpool Cathedral; he had been a teacher, but for various reasons was now doing supply work in schools, and was another very quiet character, always ready to show others how they should be doing their job better. Richard was the youngest member, with a wonderful countertenor voice. I believe he could have got a top job in one of London's church establishments, if he had been willing to move there and take his chance. He worked for the council, teaching with children who had learning difficulties, and they adored him for his genuine friendship and care. The daughter of one high up member of chapter had given birth to an illegitimate child, and Richard came along prepared to marry her and to take on the young boy as well; at the time of my joining the choir they also had a little girl of their own. Early on I realised that this was a very close-knit group of men, most of whom had been singing in the choir for at least 15 years, and I wondered how on earth I could ever hope to be part of that intimate group.

That weekend I took part in my first services, and was on the fastest, hardest learning curve possible. I had to learn when to kneel and when to stand, the order of events in each service – I didn't even know anything about Magnificat and Nunc Dimittis, Jubilate, Responses or any of the other terms used in the services. Hereford was particularly known for its excellent tradition of psalms, and as with all the other parts of the service, I soon understood that reading the notes correctly was only the start of the process, because one had to blend with every voice, listen intently and follow every slight action of the conductor. It wasn't just coincidence that when Priory Records had decided to make *Psalms of David,* a series on 10 CDs – using different cathedral choirs, they began with Hereford for volume 1 – that standard would always be a hard one to beat. To be honest, I did very little singing that weekend, was scrabbling around trying to find the next piece of music, watching the conductor, while silently mouthing the words, too terrified lest I come in at the wrong moment or spoil that lovely sound. I took the music home and worked hard so that I could get to know it well, in order to concentrate on all the other aspects.

Amazingly, the boys just took it all in their stride. Some were only about seven or eight but this was no handicap; and they all worked very hard, though I discovered that although most of them enjoyed their singing, there were one or two who couldn't wait until their voices changed to leave the choir. Michael, head chorister, had a fine, strong voice, with no problem on the high notes in the solos he had to perform, but when I talked to him I was saddened to hear that he hated the whole thing and couldn't wait to get away from the cathedral and the choir. Duncan, the senior lay clerk had conducted some kind of survey as part of his degree course at Exeter, into the whole question of cathedral choristers, and had found that a surprisingly high proportion not only gave up singing when they left the choir but gave up the church as well. I must admit that as I became familiar with the workings day by day and dealings with the boys I could understand such feelings. Being a member of the choir meant that parents paid a much reduced fee for their child's education in the Cathedral School, along with various other financial 'perks', and at that time even when the boy left the choir, the reduced fees continued. There can't be many professions where the child does the work and the parents reap the benefit. But Michael was vastly outweighed by many boys who were keen on their singing, wanted to do well and enjoyed the whole ethos of the choir. As I look back now I am amazed at the number of boys from Hereford who achieved great things musically. At the time of writing, John, son of the tenor lay clerk Stephen, is organ scholar at St John's, Cambridge, having been at St Georges Chapel, Windsor; John Robinson, former head chorister is assistant organist at Canterbury, and still in his early 20s, while the director of music at the Metropolitan Cathedral Liverpool, affectionately known as "Paddy's Wigwam", is Tim Noon; I think the organist and all those concerned in the education of those boys can be very proud of their achievements. I suppose I could say that gradually life took on a well ordered weekly program, but in fact, one could never say that any week was the same; so many activities and different services were involved, but at least I made myself familiar with the liturgy and routine of the choir.

At the beginning of December came the Advent service, always very popular in the cathedral; fortunately I had already learned the rather complicated job of singing while processing – I expect experience in the army band all those years ago helped a little – and then it was practicing for the big service of nine lessons and carols on 23rd of December, a service which always guaranteed a very full house at Hereford. It was almost like the fulfilment of a dream, I hadn't quite made it to sing at King's College, but this was the very same service and in an equally beautiful setting; I always loved the cathedral, where the stones seemed to change colour according to the light coming in from the great West window, and in the depths of winter with hardly anyone there, one just heard the quiet hiss of the big heating stoves situated around the nave; there was always this tremendous sense of tradition, of continuing the worship of past ages, and an atmosphere of majesty and holiness – hard to describe, but you could almost reach out and touch it. I was kept busy because mother was coming over to stay, along with brother Allen and Brenda his wife. They came down to the Christmas Day service, and I think mother was very impressed with the whole setting; I was so glad to share my first Hereford Christmas with some of the family. In early January Geraint Bowen, the assistant organist, directed a performance of Bach's *Christmas Oratorio* – sung in German, with a small, hand-picked period instrument orchestra and excellent soloists. So ended the first of many busy, happy Christmases in the choir.

A couple of months later I drove over to St Michael's School at Limpsfield in Kent. My friend John Buckle worked there as a science master, and I had been asked to adjudicate at the annual house festival. The musical standard wasn't terribly high, but it was quite a small girls' boarding school and they got great fun from their singing, which is surely what music is all about. In May the choir was back in the cathedral for three nights to make a CD for Priory Records as part of their *Te Deums and Jubilates* series. The recording process brought back memories for me of the two records I had made with the Coldstream band in the 1950s, but this time, although discipline was strict, and a great deal of patience was needed, there wasn't the terrible atmosphere of fear and terror which had existed when recording in the band. The choristers certainly showed no fear, even the boys who sang the solo parts – it was just another day's work.

Easter was the other very busy time for the cathedral choir, with important services on Maundy Thursday, when all the clergy of the diocese would gather for the consecration of holy oil; Good Friday would see the three-hour service, although the choir would only take part in the last hour. As in all services in the Anglican Church symbolism played an important part with the dramatic carrying of the cross by the dean and other members of chapter. There would be a sung version of the crucifixion story using various lay clerks and involving plainsong, while the choir took the part of 'the crowd'; one of my favourite pieces was a setting called *The Reproaches* by John Sanders, director of music at Gloucester Cathedral. At one or two of the services we also sang a haunting anthem by Edward Bairstow called *The Lamentation*, with words selected from the book of Jeremiah, which contained a refrain "Jerusalem, Jerusalem, return unto the Lord thy God." There was something about the simplicity of this chorus coupled with beautiful writing for the boy sopranos which always gave me a lump in the throat – not a good situation when you are singing! Holy Saturday would involve Evensong followed by a rehearsal for the Easter Sunday music, then slaking our thirst at the local pub – another tradition which never died – and in various states of inebriation, there would be a short rehearsal for the men before the Easter Vigil. That service would begin in the lady chapel of the cathedral and at a certain point the large Eucharist candle would be lit by the dean, the congregation then lighting their smaller candles from it, followed by a procession round a dark cathedral led by the precentor, who had to declaim various passages and we would all reply, "The Light of God," the response getting higher each time. This always caused some merriment as we tried to reach the top notes, while balancing our hymn books, music , candles and generally trying to walk in a straight line. The congregation would take their place and the men would process up to the choir stalls; now Duncan was never happier than when he could get his hands on a lighted candle, and once we had taken our places in the choir stalls he would begin to organise his own little fire in the pew. On a couple of occasions he was told off by the verger, because candle grease leaked on the carpet and took a lot of removing. At a given signal the organ would play very loud chords, all the lights being switched on at the same time, and we would all shout out our first hallelujah and greet each other with "Happy Easter". Easter Sunday in the Anglican church began after sunset. It was a most moving occasion but I'm afraid these pranks always took place, led by the lay clerks who were just a little 'puddled'. At least the choristers were not there to witness this rather silly behaviour, which went on every year; I believe Dr. Massey knew all about it, but kept well out of the way – as long as the men delivered the goods singing-wise, he felt it was OK. Easter Sunday had its three services as usual, with very large congregations – many of whom only came to these important services in the year. The choristers were very enthusiastic to get to the end of Evensong for they knew there would be a liberal distribution of Easter eggs when they returned to the choir school to disrobe -and well deserved, for they had given up a large part of their school Easter holiday.

By 1994 I reckoned I had done over 50 music holidays with various companies, and I now began work with Holiday Fellowship (HF), as a host. The first working holiday with them was back on the Isle of Wight, at Freshwater Bay, the very place where, as I pointed out in chapter 15, I had gone in 1974 as a guest. This time I was one of the leaders. With the choir commitments it was quite a job to juggle all the dates for the holidays; apart from this Freshwater Bay week I returned to Hope in the Derbyshire Dales, college holidays for Saga back at Winchester, plus the music weeks at Scargill and the enjoyable folk holidays at Whitecliff Bay, also on the Isle of Wight.

As soon as Easter was out of the way rehearsals began in earnest for the Three Choirs Festival, held in Hereford in August; it involved at least two rehearsals each week and various all-day rehearsals on Saturdays, so it was quite a commitment. On the Sunday there is the festival service with a good deal of pomp and ceremony; processions of various civic bodies slowly file in to take their place at the front. Actually at Hereford the front was the back because the big platform for chorus and orchestra was placed under the great West window, and all the seats would be reversed for the festival performances – and had to be turned yet again for Evensong each day, this 'seat-turning' chore would be done by a group of lads from the Cathedral School, earning themselves some pocket money in the process. Some of the ceremonial dress worn by the council members was a source of great amusement, with fur hats which wouldn't have looked out of place in Moscow but on a hot summer's day in Hereford Cathedral seemed quite crazy; then there were large ceremonial swords and robes of all shapes and colours. Hereford people always had a smile for Dr Massey who minced in wearing his pink and gold doctorate robes – this was his Lambeth doctorate, awarded to him by the Archbishop of Canterbury in 1991 for services to music – at least the lucky man didn't have to sit examinations to gain this award. It takes about half an hour for all the dignitaries to arrive finishing with the mayors and deans of the three cathedral cities. The festival week itself is always very hard work for the cathedral choir, for apart from the festival choir performances taking place on most nights of the week, the three cathedral choirs, Hereford, Gloucester and Worcester, also give a concert. In 1994 it was *Alexander's Feast* by Handel, conducted by Roy Goodman with his own Brandenburg Consort to accompany. At a Saturday rehearsal I reminded him of the classic Decca recording made by the King's College choir; they had recorded *Miserere* by Allegri, and young Roy had been the soloist, performing a difficult part which just seems to go higher and reaches top C. Apparently he didn't even know about the solo until he arrived late and rather out of breath from football to be told by the conductor, Sir David Willcocks, that he had five minutes to get ready for the recording. I joked with Roy that he must have made a fortune from this recording which is still going strong since it was made in 1963, when he was 12, but he assured me he only got half a crown (12½p) for his services.

I know I wore myself out during the week because I tried to attend everything I could in between rehearsals and performances. This included a marvellous orchestral concert when I first met up with Richard Hickox, who conducted Walton's 1st *Symphony*; having managed to get a free seat behind the orchestra I was able to watch at first hand his powerful, clear beat – indeed when the orchestra first came in I feared for the leading cellist, for all the world it looked as though his eye might end up on the end of Richard's baton! I also noticed that he hardly ever had to consult his score, for he had done all his work and learned it off by heart. Orchestral players and choirs always have very high regard for the conductor who has done his homework and prepared the score thoroughly before coming to rehearsal. I was to meet up with Richard in the future, singing under him and through various Saga holidays. By Friday I was shattered and knew I had a long rehearsal and performance in the evening, but I roused myself to go to a morning concert given by the National Youth Choir – a group of some 150 young people from all over the UK who met on a residential course during school holidays and then performed the works they had studied. The wonderful sound they made and the obvious enjoyment they got from singing together was an inspiration to me; so often one was hearing about teenagers who were dropouts, drug addicts, only interested in booze, yet here were a group of committed musicians whose sheer sound brought tears to the eyes – it was a memorable event. The final concert consisted of *Dream of Gerontius* by Sir Edward Elgar, led by our own festival conductor, Dr Massey. There is something unique about performing Elgar's music in Hereford. He had a long associations with the place going right back to his teenage years when he would cycle over to play the violin in an orchestral concert, including three choirs, perhaps adjourn to the local pub, and there were plenty to choose from, and if it was late he would just sleep under a tree, and cycle back to Worcester early the next morning. In all my time in Hereford I sensed the presence of dear old Elgar, and when walking the Malvern Hills I felt he might come over the horizon at any minute.

After all that hard work the choruses and cathedral choirs would attend the party held in a large marquee situated in the gardens of the Cathedral School, where there would be various speeches of thanks, lots of lovely food and plenty to drink… the lay clerks taking real advantage of the latter, with beer and wine flowing very freely. I have no idea how they ever got home. Certainly at the end of the 1994 three choirs, although I was shattered physically, musically it was one of the most outstanding weeks of my life; I thanked God that he had sent me to Hereford, and looked forward to a fairly handsome cheque for all the work.

CHAPTER EIGHTEEN

GREAT HOLIDAYS AND SAD TIMES

The hyped-up New Millennium finally arrived, with all its razzamataz and firework displays. I watched the Thames fireworks display on TV, with a brandy to hand and then went to bed. I always find New Year sad and depressing, and can never get my thoughts away from the past and those who have 'gone before.' These were busy years, with choir commitments during the term and music hosting for at least three organisations, but I still tried to get over to see my mother every few weeks. This involved either a four hour journey whether using three trains, or by car. Greetings at the door usually consisted of, "Hello Brian, so you've made it. How long will you be staying, so that I know what to take out of the freezer?" One got the feeling of not being wholeheartedly welcomed, but it was too tiring to do the return journey in one day, and would give me little time to talk to Mother who was often alone when I arrived and might have been left from 8.30 in the morning, until the children came home from school. If the truth be told, she was desperately lonely; June meant well, and cared for her as well as she could, but she and her husband both worked full-time, and Mother needed more care and company during the day. For some time she had gone to a club on one day a week, which she thoroughly enjoyed, but this opportunity seemed to have disappeared; maybe the club had disbanded. I had discussions with my brothers suggesting that we might move her to a residential home, bearing in mind the strong feelings she had about homes. At one point she had a holiday break at John's home at Whittlesey; he had found a suitable place a short distance away, and took mother to see it. She thought the home was fine, but still wanted to stay where she was. In the spring of 1998 on a beautiful morning I drove her to Horton Kirby, about 4 miles from Dartford, to visit Eglantine Villa, a BUPA Home for Senior Citizens, where I had arranged for someone to show Mother around. She was happy to go off in a wheelchair with one of the nurses, the superintendent and I stayed with her for a while, and then had a chat about finances and possibilities of Mother moving in. I thought the accommodation was excellent with spacious dining room and lounge, very cosy private room, etc. and all surrounded by acres of gardens and rolling Kentish countryside. There was even a small nursing home attached, and the whole atmosphere seemed happy and caring. I was given application forms – all it needed was Mother's agreement. She came back full of praise, and said what a lovely place it was and how kind everyone had been, but… she would rather stay with her daughter. Driving back in the car I couldn't get her to consider the move, even though she admitted she was lonely, and unhappy that she had to have the children's computer in her room; some months previously a computer desk and all the accompanying paraphernalia had been installed in HER bedroom, just like that, so that not only the grandchildren took residence, but their friends as well – Mother's last bit of privacy had been taken away.

From time to time she had to go into hospital because of breathing difficulties caused by bad chest colds, but after a few days she would be back with June. At the beginning of December 1999 I went up to see her – as usual she was sitting in an armchair, the room was freezing, and she had finished her roll and cup-a-soup for lunch. I put the electric fire on, although she protested that this would not go down very well. Next day I decided to get a late train, went shopping in the morning and cooked us both a good meal, we both sat down to liver, bacon and onions, with hot rhubarb tart and custard for dessert. She ate every mouthful, thoroughly enjoyed it, and said so, thanking me for going to all the trouble. I kissed her goodbye, and left her, waving from the window, as she always did, and as I travelled home I just wished I could have given her a happier time in her last years, with some company and the friends which she had always enjoyed. But it was too late, I never saw mother again alive. On 6th March my sister telephoned to say that Mother had gone into hospital, that it was the usual problem of a cold that had gone to her chest; she was concerned there were no beds available, Mother was on a trolley waiting for a vacant bed. To her great credit June stayed with mother for hours and visited again the next day taking in some food and drink – there seemed to be no one delivering adequate meals; only later that evening mother was given a bed. Next morning, March 9th, Jim my brother-in-law rang to tell me that Mother had died during the night. The news was awful, I was so upset that she had died alone, perhaps unable to call for help, and with all the overcrowding and shortage of nurses, she had just been forgotten and ignored. I set off immediately to Erith, and the next day we collected the death certificate, and later I was able to see Mother at the mortuary, which was another sad experience. Joyce Green hospital was very old, it had formerly been the City of London Mental Hospital, in fact it was where the poet and composer Ivor Gurney had been incarcerated and had subsequently died of TB. I don't think there was any proper mortuary for viewing relatives, we had to give sufficient notice, so that she could be laid out in what was a small Nissen hut. Someone had found a brass crucifix so tarnished it was almost black, a couple of dusty plastic flowers had been put into a jar, and there she was laid out on a pillow, with 'Property of NHS' clearly printed in large red letters – did people try to steal pillows in such circumstances? I was left for a few minutes alone with Mum – my brother had stayed outside, he couldn't face seeing her in this condition – and I just cried, partly in sorrow but also in anger that she'd been reduced to such shabby surroundings. The whole situation was completely lacking in dignity. I kissed her goodbye, and through my tears struggled to find the door and ring the bell to let the porter know that he could carry on with his dismal job.

My sister and I organised the funeral arrangements; there was no reason to stay in London so I went back home on the train trying to remember mother in happier times. The funeral was fixed for 24th March, and I was determined that the service for her cremation would be properly organised and be a credit to her. She had often gone to the local Baptist church with my sister, whose daughter was involved in the Brownies, and Bob, the minister immediately agreed to conduct the service at the crematorium; we sang *The Lord's My Shepherd* always one of mother's favourite hymns, I had put together a tribute to her, just managing to control the voice, and the final piece of music was John Rutter's *The Lord Bless You and Keep You.*" What a heart-wrenching tune. From the many times I had played at the crematorium in Hereford, I should have realised how important timing is, there is no opportunity for silence and meditation, with the next group already waiting outside you feel someone will blow a whistle if the service goes over the allotted time, and brings a kind of cheapness to the whole matter. The chapel was completely full of relations and friends who spoke so highly of her and her courage, through the war, coping with three young children, post-war times with shortages of food and money, the overcrowding in our house at Dagenham, her own fight to the end with health problems, but above all they remembered her humour. It was when I saw all the flowers laid out in the corridor that I just broke down and cried like a child. Mother had always loved flowers, had been so grateful whenever anyone gave her a bunch of flowers, and here they were looking beautiful – a final colourful tribute to our darling mother, dying at 92.

My sister had laid on a great feast of food back at their house, but I was still waiting for mother to appear and thank them all for coming, so as fast as decency would allow, I set off in the company of my nephew to catch the train home. The loss of my mother to June, and her two children was very profound, after all, they had seen her every day, had meals, and laughed and joked with her, whereas I had put some distance between myself and Mother several years earlier, and was more prepared for the loss. Nevertheless it took a long while to get over her death, and I never have returned to my sister's home – too many memories.

Another interesting holiday came along in July 2000, a chance to go back to Finland but in summertime. I had been in Helsinki the previous Christmas working for Saga. The guests were staying in a small town called Mikelli, the base for an annual festival where some of the top orchestras and conductors gather to make music in the concert hall and the ancient wooden church. We were there mainly to attend the opera festival at Savonnlina, about an hour's coach ride in a north easterly direction. The scenery in this area is quite breathtaking with so many beautiful lakes and woods. The opera is held in a mediaeval castle on a small island in the lake; the audience has to cross two bridges from the mainland to reach the castle. After the performance one evening there was quite a hold-up before we could get out, and I was amazed to see through the open doors a huge ship gliding past, the swing bridge obviously closed to pedestrian traffic. The bridge then opened and as we crossed we could follow the outline of the ship, all lit up, as it quietly made its way further north to some town at the end of the huge lake. We saw Beethoven's *Fidelio* one evening, which is set in a castle, with its dungeon, so the whole production had a very authentic and real atmosphere.

We visited a monastery which has an interesting history. The eastern border of Finland, called Karelia has suffered from disputes and fighting down the centuries, both with Sweden, and later Russia. In the Second World War the Red Army took over the Karelia section of Finland, including the orthodox monastery on the island of Valamo; the hundred or so monks were given the choice of remaining at the monastery under Russian rule, or moving. Wisely they decided to move, carrying with them as much treasure as they could manage, and built a new monastery at Heinävesi, in 1940. They also set about building another church which was finished in 1977. This area is often called New Valamo. We found it most peaceful, set in beautiful countryside, with farms and cottages where the monks live and work. Some of them formed a choir which goes round the world raising money for the upkeep of the buildings. Mikkeli itself has strong connections with the war; Marshall Mannerheim used it as a headquarters in the struggle known as the Winter War 1939-40, against the Red Army and later against the occupying Nazis. Operations were conducted from a small primary school and an underground base in the park. Both these sites are open to the public, though not many people seem to visit. Everything is well set out, and I found it fascinating to see the code books, telephones and all the emergency supplies which would be needed. I am full of admiration at the way the Finns, defeated by Sweden, by Russia, occupied by the Germans, has picked itself up and is now one of the most prosperous, crime-free countries in the world.

In the middle of 2001 my contented, happy existence in Hereford went pear shaped – indeed the world caved in. At Easter of that year Roy Massey retired as choirmaster, at the age of 67. It all happened at speed and I believe he was jumping before being pushed. Three Choirs Festival rehearsals were just beginning, our deputy organist, Peter Dyke, took charge and I agreed to be the rehearsal pianist. Some of the music was quite hard and needed a great deal of practice and sweat to get up to standard, in particular a new commission composed by David Briggs, called *Creation*. The festival was to be held at Gloucester, where David was director of music, and, though I slaved at the accompaniment which was an orchestral reduction, some of it seemed quite impossible. I rang him to ask if he had any advice, and he told me quite lightheartedly, "Oh Brian, we use two pianists for our rehearsals of the piece – one looks after the bass and the other handles the treble." I didn't have this luxury! During this period there were auditions and interviews for a replacement director of music, and Geraint Bowen was duly appointed. In the last chapter you will have read that he was deputy organist at Hereford when I joined the choir, and had then been appointed to St David's Cathedral in Wales. The lay clerks were pleased that Geraint was returning, as were the chapter. Incidentally we did not have a dean at that time, Robert Willis had moved on to become dean of Canterbury Cathedral, and Hereford was still waiting to appoint – a factor which affected this part of my story. I was also looking forward to Geraint taking over, it needed fresh blood and I knew he would organise more choir tours.

Then, in early August I received a phone call from him so devastating that I thought at first it was one of the lay clerks playing a practical joke; but I knew his voice too well. "Brian, I have some serious news to tell you; I believe you are 65 in September, so you have to leave the choir, the cathedral has strict rules about this." I just couldn't believe it, to be thrown out of the choir and via a telephone call. When I had recovered I realised there were two possibilities, "I suppose my voice is not up to standard now." I said. He reassured me that my voice was fine and well up to standard. "So, you must have a young person waiting in the wings, to step into my shoes." I added, but then received the incredible reply,

"No, Brian, we have no replacement." In fact it was two years before another bass took my place in Hereford choir. I sent letters asking for support to everyone connected with the cathedral, from the Bishop, all members of the cathedral chapter down to the lay readers. They were all supportive and pleasant but not one of them would challenge this decision! I was being sacked because of my age! I went to the precentor and threatened to tell my story to the local and national newspapers – with a suitable photo dressed in cassock and surplice, and a headline that I was ON THE SCRAPHEAP AT 65. It might create some sympathy for me but be bad publicity for the church. "Pray don't go down that route." pleaded the precentor, and quite frankly I would never have carried that threat out, though it did cross my mind. I then found the ideal solution, that I would not take the £14 a week which the cathedral paid me – I would sing for nothing. Apparently, even that was no good – it seemed it would mess up the accounts! I gave up at that point and went to Gloucester Cathedral knowing it would be my last Three Choirs as a member of the cathedral choir.

Ironically, on my actual 65th birthday I was telephoned urgently and asked to sing at Evensong; one of the bass lay clerks had fallen off his bike travelling to school, and landed up in hospital. I sang that evening, and every evening for services until mid-November (apart from a week when I had a previous Saga engagement) when Jeremy returned. I hoped this might have made the choirmaster reconsider his decision, after all, I had helped them out of a real mess. He agreed that I had done a good job, that I knew the music, but rules were rules, and I still had to leave. I finally quit the choir after the Advent service in early December; a small reception was held in the choirmaster's house, and 'weasel words' were uttered by the precentor, but I went home and wept. My whole purpose in coming to Hereford and leaving many friends behind in Cambridgeshire had been to sing in that wonderful choir. Later, I came to accept that at least I had been given a few glorious years of singing.

Christmas found me working in Solihull, with over 100 Saga guests – very hard work, with recitals, illustrated talks, and accompanying them to concerts at Birmingham Symphony Hall, Solihull Parish Church for midnight mass and Christmas Day service, and, on Boxing Day taking the guests to Warwick Castle. My rep, Dorothy and I were exhausted when the passengers went home on 27th December.

I returned to Hereford and went to the service at the cathedral as a member of the congregation, but every time I went forward to take communion, saw my empty place, and heard the choir singing some anthem which I knew well, I went back to my seat almost in tears – clearly this situation couldn't go on. After a few weeks I was asked to play the organ for a service at Holmer Parish Church, to the north of the city. The vicar, Phil Williams, was very satisfied, and asked if I would come again as one of their regular organists was unlikely to return due to ill health. I became joint organist at the church, along with Chris Embrey. Holmer was a lovely old building, with a separate bell tower in 'Black and White' pattern; a very expensive vestry and meeting room had been added at the back of the church. The organ, made by Bevington was situated in a gallery at the West end, the instrument had originally come from Hatley Park in Cambridgeshire, the very next village to where I had lived in the late '80s. It was eventually moved to Puddlestone Court, a large private house near Hereford, and was installed in Holmer parish church in the 1930s. The church had built a new hall and kitchens, and these were well used by various clubs and activities during the week. Everybody could be involved, from the over 60s' lunch club which met every other week, the men's group and a counselling service, down to the tiny toddlers – The Busy Bees. The place was a constant hive of activity, forgive the pun. The church was very outward looking, Phil, the vicar and his wife Julie always seeking new ways of attracting outsiders into the church fellowship. The worship was what is usually called low style, which I was very comfortable with, and soon I felt very much a part of Holmer. I still missed the beauty of the cathedral services and the high standard of singing, but was coming to realise that Holmer was an example of the real church, always anxious to attract newcomers and ready to experiment in worship. I recalled several occasions when I sang in the cathedral and at the end of the service someone would thank me for the singing and tell me very proudly, "Of course I come here for the music."

When I felt brave enough I would reply, "Well I come here for God and worship, the music is just to help it along." Many of the cathedral congregation drove miles past several churches where their presence would have been so important, to come to the cathedral. A few cynics would even suggest that Eucharist, Matins and Evensong were the cheapest concerts in town on a Sunday.

Around this time I decided to fulfil a wish I'd had from a boy, and bought a grand piano, going for a Yamaha, in part exchange for my faithful Knight upright, which had given me good service for over 30 years. When the piano arrived I spent every spare minute playing and revelling in the lovely deep bass which it produced – piano practice became part of everyday activity.

In the summer I had a chance to lead a new Saga holiday, at Verona in Italy, taking people to the operas performed in the great Roman arena there. *Aida* is always the main opera, and is very spectacular with a cast of hundreds, and was a production with Zeffirelli as artistic director. I stayed in one of the top four star hotels in Verona, the Accademia, and felt like a king as I came down the stairs on the deep carpet, and sauntered over for morning coffee at the bar. This was the first of at least six seasons of opera in Verona. Generally the guests were in two hotels, so I would give an hour's illustrated talk, trying to tell these very complicated opera plots so that they made sense to the guests, and then would dash across the city to repeat the talk at the other hotel. Apart from that I was free to go to the opera or just enjoy a quiet evening sitting outside a restaurant watching the world go by.

In 2004 I was with guests at a hotel in the small town of Rovigo, about one hour's drive from Verona. It was a pleasant change to be away from the crowded, noisy city and, of course it meant an opportunity to go on some different excursions. We visited Mantua with its huge castle which had been home to the Gonzaga dynasty way back in the 17th century; Monteverdi had worked there, one of many composers employed by this music loving family. I was to visit Mantua on at least three occasions hoping to go into the palace, but on the first and second attempts the place was locked up due to local strikes by the attendants; imagine anyone trying to go on strike in the days of the Gonzagas! Third time lucky and I spent a whole morning wandering around this enormous complex, once the largest palace in Europe. On another excursion we went to Padua with its ancient university, dating from 1221, and a fascinating market which the guests all enjoyed. The city became a place of pilgrimage after St Anthony died there, and most Catholics still make their way to the cathedral and queue up to see St Anthony's tongue and to kiss the large painting of him. Next door is the Baptistery, built in the 12th century, circular in design, whose walls are covered with paintings, beautiful golds, reds and blues shine out in the semi-darkness of the building. I chose a quiet time, and was able to sit and take in just some of the stories and portrayals – a place one will never forget. Our hotel was quite close to Rovigo station, and one could get anywhere in Italy from this station, so on a free Sunday I jumped on a train after lunch and headed off to Bologna on a fast, amazingly clean and almost empty express, and all for five euros return. Unfortunately the heat was too much, and

I only had energy to visit the cathedral in the square and then took refuge at one of the restaurants in the piazza, and under a large umbrella enjoyed a couple of cold beers. Later I was to visit Bologna for an all-day visit on two occasions. Of course, everyone wants to visit Venice, and Saga organised optional excursions, which involved an hour's coach ride and then a trip on the Grand Canal down to St Mark's Cathedral and square. In summertime the place is just packed and thousands of people follow their guide on the standard tour. The scene always reminds me of a flock of sheep. After two visits to Venice with the customers, I decided to get away from the crowds, hop on a vaporetto (water bus) and go over to one of the neighbouring islands such as the Lido for lunch, and then nip across to St Michael's to visit the church and go up to the tower for a magnificent view of Venice and the islands – on a hot day one was grateful for the lift. On one occasion I went just two stops past busy St Mark's on the water bus, and, walking through some invitingly cool gardens, found a completely empty street with its bridge across the canal, church and one small bar, thankfully selling ice cream. My sole companion was a mangy looking cat which followed me around. On other visits I was able to go to the Fenice Theatre, beautifully restored in 2004 after a terrible fire eight years earlier. Just across the Grand Canal I visited the Accademia Museum; as a pensioner I could go in for nothing so I spent the money on an audio guide, which was most useful. The place is packed with an incredible collection of art from early Renaissance through to late 18th century, but like many of these galleries one can only take in so much, and after a couple of hours looking at Tintoretto, Titian, and Bellini, to name but a few, the brain can take in no more. Perhaps one day I will be spared to return to see this treasure house of art. Venice is a lovely place, though the Venetians don't seem to care very much for visitors, are often quite rude, and certainly the prices are sky high. Even to take a coach to the outskirts of Venice the driver must pay a levy of about £400, so they don't do much to encourage visitors. In truth, summer is the worst time to visit, and along with my rep and the guide we always worried about getting the right number of guests back on the coach for the return journey.

Many of our Saga guests went on the sea cruises, and some suggested that I would fit in well with my talks on composers. Summer 2003 found me setting off for Dover to board the Saga Rose for a cruise to the Baltic capitals. I was classed as a guest lecturer, so did not receive any pay, in fact I had to pay £50 to park my car at the port of Dover; I did get free food and board, and a discount on any alcohol I consumed on the trip, but I was happy to have the experience of seeing some of these great cities. I was very impressed with the organisation on board ship, cases disappeared like magic, to reappear quickly in my cabin, and I was introduced to my own steward. The Saga ships employ many Philippinos because they work well, are pleasant, and, I suppose they come cheap; to be fair, I understood that the company gave them generous holidays and paid for them to go home and return to the ship, and certainly these people count themselves fortunate to have a job and to be able to send some regular money back to their families. After we waved farewell to relations and the faithful band, playing *Will ye no come back again?* It was action stations for the emergency fire drill. Despite instructions on how to put on the lifejackets and where to assemble, some people were in a terrible muddle, lifejackets on the wrong way round or still being carried, a few had even left the lifejackets behind in the cabin, and some ended up at the wrong muster station. I did worry what would happen if we had a genuine emergency but the crew were used to these mishaps, though they always insisted that we took the drill seriously. My brief was to give six lectures – I had chosen Dvořák – my first lecture wasn't until the afternoon of the second day on board ship so I felt very anonymous and found it very lonely being neither guest, nor crew member, or entertainer, just the new boy among three lecturers.

I went along to the first lecture given by Nicholas Anderson, who was a regular broadcaster on BBC Radio 3, a CD reviewer and had written a number of books, particularly about early and baroque music, he was a regular guest lecturer, so I was interested in his delivery. Entering the hall, there he was, sitting behind a table on a high stage, which seemed rather remote to me, and I made up my mind that my lectures would be given down on the floor next to the piano. He spoke about a forgotten Italian composer, and, sure enough, I've forgotten him even now. He really knew his stuff, but I felt he was talking over the heads of many in the audience, both literally and metaphorically. In the afternoon the second lecturer took the stage; Michael Geliot had been an opera producer from way back in his Cambridge days, and had then worked at Glyndebourne, for Welsh National Opera, Sadlers Wells and English National Opera and with some of the finest conductors and artists of his generation. Michael's lectures grab one's attention from the very beginning, the operatic characters he describes come to life, and his sense of humour has his audience convulsed with laughter. I imagine opera producers are fairly extrovert, and this was certainly the case with him. Whenever I was free I would attend a lecture given by Michael, and got to know him and his wife at dinner over a number of evenings. I think they felt sorry for me wandering around the ship on my own, and took me under their wings. So then it was my turn, and I launched off into my first talk on Dvořák, which seemed to go down quite well. Characteristically I added personal stories and little asides, finding, as always, that the audience enjoy being let into little secrets about one's life.

The first three days of the Baltic trip are spent at sea, and going through the Kiel Canal, and this was the lonely part. I wasn't into the entertainment part of the cruise, and certainly not into dancing, so every evening I went to the cinema and saw some great new films. On the fourth day I was standing by the rail, completely alone and looking down at the water; perhaps it seemed a suicidal picture, for one young man who I will call Philip came up and began talking. His voice and actions reminded me of Noel Coward, he was obviously quite 'gay' – no harm in that. When I told him that if I jumped overboard, no one would notice that I'd gone, he turned and laying a hand on my shoulder, firmly said, "Not for the rest of this trip, dear boy. Come down to my cabin for drinkies at 6:30." I wasn't too keen on joining him alone in his cabin, but he assured me that most of the entertainers and musicians popped in for drinks, and he shared his cabin with the pianist John. I took up his invitation and found their cabin was like a floating pub, they had bottles of every kind, some even stored in the bath! I met up with other musicians, there was a string quartet, which had been organised by Vicky Evans, who I had met on previous Saga engagements. She was an agent used by the company to find and book musicians for holidays and cruises. John was the pianist with this group, and Philip turned over the pages and was a general assistant. He had also been given his own late one man show in one of the small bars on the ship. Unfortunately for him, on the second evening one of the Saga directors, who was travelling for part of the cruise, happened to call in to watch Philip's act; he must have thought it too 'near the mark', for he summoned the entertainments director, and insisted that the show be taken off immediately. Philip was left as a page turner, but was quite happy, indeed he was always laughing and smiling, and when he and John began telling me stories about some of the clients and some of the situations on previous cruises I was just rocking with laughter. From day four we began visiting the capital cities, first calling in at Stockholm where, in the morning I hopped on and off trams, and after lunch, saw the city on a boat trip. Like all the cities and towns in Scandinavia, I was impressed with the cleanliness of each place, and the amount of green parkland, but most impressive was the scene when the Saga Rose lifted anchor and set off back to the Baltic Sea; with hundreds of islands on each side, in the early evening, the sun slowly setting, and the ship gliding along at slow speed, it made a memorable scene.

At nightfall we were into the Gulf of Finland en route to Helsinki, a capital I was getting to know quite well; this time one of the excursions took us north of the city to Järvenpää to visit Ainola the home of Sibelius. He had chosen this site, beside the lake, for its peace and quiet – nowadays a main road runs rather noisily close to the house; Ainola was built in 1904 and was to be home for him, his wife and their six daughters until his death in 1957. It is not an extravagant, expensive looking building, but rather cosy and contains his grand piano, and his drinks cabinet, possibly as important to him as the piano, for he drank and smoked far too much – it largely contributed to his death. In this house he wrote most of his famous works. After the guided tour and a chance to stand by the lake, quietly congratulating Sibelius on his good choice of home, we were on the bus with our packed lunches, heading back to the city. Finland had shown its gratitude to Sibelius in 1925 by giving him a lifelong pension, but it just happened that he hardly wrote another work from then until his death in 1957 at the age of 92; presuming that his widow continued to draw the pension, and she lived until the age of 98, the family did very well out of the Finnish government. It's only right that these days the house and land belong to the state so they get a little return for their investment. We were heading for the Sibelius Academy, the only university in Finland devoted to music, and with its 400 or so students is one of the largest in Europe. Our guests were to have a piano recital, and, sure enough onto the stage came Folke Gräsbeck, whom I'd met twice before on visits to Finland, and was to meet on two more occasions – we almost became friends. He is certainly a great pianist and has been recording all the piano music of Sibelius as part of the Bis edition. For many years he has been an accompanist and professor at the academy.

Our next port of call was St Petersburg, and everyone was at the rail as Saga Rose slowly steamed into the dockside area, curious to get a glimpse of this post-Communist country. On some occasions, because the River Neva is so wide and deep, cruise ships can actually dock in the city close to all the tourist sites. St Petersburg was the only port of call where passengers were not allowed ashore unless they were part of an official excursion, or unless you had been granted a visa; I must say the officials who stamped our passports were a grumpy, rude bunch of people who almost begrudged you coming to their country, but everyone was very glad to take your money, and it was certainly big business with at least six huge liners in port at any one time. Even as were docking I saw at least 30 buses waiting in line to take passengers disembarking from a huge Japanese liner moored alongside, off to the various sites in St Petersburg. I joined a party which was visiting Rimsky-Korsakov's house, and had a chance of a lifetime. As I was looking at the composer's piano our guide happened to mention to the lady official that I was a musician, and I was asked if I would like to play something to the guests. I sat down and played what I could remember from *Scheherazade* and then a little Tchaikovsky, and in thanking the lady for this privilege, I told her I wouldn't wash my hands for at least a week. We then headed off to lunch in the city, a meal which was reasonable, with good waiter service – they were all hoping for generous tips as they would be paid very little. I watched the people closely in the city, they seemed very serious and most looked unhappy. The condition of the buses and trams was dreadful, in our country they would never have been allowed to take on passengers; the tram lines were in an appalling condition, with great holes in the road, I wouldn't even have taken a tram ride were it possible. The guide told me that the fall of communism had just made the gap between rich and poor so much wider, and that in many ways she had preferred the Communists.

We were staying overnight, and next day guests went on the routine coach excursion, visiting all the important palaces, cathedrals and statues in a city crammed full of history and art. We stopped at the much photographed statue of Peter the Great on horseback, usually called the *Bronze Horseman*, close to St Isaacs Cathedral, though there was no time to go inside. The banks of the River Neva are full of glorious palaces, and we visited the Winter Palace and stood in the middle of the huge square, trying to imagine the days of the Revolution when the palace guard was overthrown and the Tzar and his family were captured. We crossed the river by one of the very busy bridges and on to the island where St Peter and St Paul's Fortress is located, with the cathedral and admiralty which stands out from every point in St Petersburg with its shining, golden narrow spire. A quick visit to the cruiser Aurora followed, which, of course fired on the Winter Palace at the start of the Revolution, and then we retraced our steps into the city shopping centre, travelling down the long main road called Nevsky Prospect. Our last port of call was at the Orthodox Cathedral of the Church of Resurrection, such a colourful, fairytale building with its golden 'onion' domes, and many bright colours. There was an opportunity to visit the market nearby for souvenirs followed by the usual dash back to the ship ready for sailing. Our guide told us of the huge efforts there had been to get the buildings spruced up, and to paint all the spires, etc. in gold ready for the 300th anniversary celebrations of the city's founding. She confessed that many of the poorer people were disgusted at the money that had been spent on this venture, and I admit that looking at the shining gold spires and domes one could understand their feelings. On our travels between the docks and the city along some dreadful roads I had noticed what seemed derelict factories and warehouses but which still had lights on, but when I pointed this out to our guide she assured me that these were working factories; with broken windows, parts of the roof missing and the complete air of dereliction I began to realise that working class districts of St.Petersburg were poles apart from the tourist areas. Perhaps this is true of most cities. At one stage the main road was closed and the coach was forced to do a detour into side streets, with long lines of grey, depressing flats which also looked empty and ready for demolition, except that there was washing hanging from lines and a few people talking in doorways. The guide assured me this was quite a typical block of flats in the city. I began to understand the anger of the people living in abject poverty while the government went about gilding every dome and spire they could find, and they seemed reconciled to the fact that they had exchanged one monster regime for another. So we arrived back at the ship, and for the last time our passports were checked by the serious-looking controllers, then up the gangway, with a pathetic trio of musicians trying to bring some air of celebration to the event.

Next stop was Tallin in Estonia which was a relatively new place to visit. The contrast between St Petersburg and Tallin was obvious from the moment we docked; happy, smiling people, dancing in their national costume, and a welcoming smile at customs. In the morning we were given a tour of the old part of the city, a very beautiful place with well preserved buildings; we were taken to a large hall for coffee and more national dancing and singing. The guide was obviously very proud of her country and she told us how they hated the Russians, most of whom had left, while those that remained were forced to live in just one part of Tallin. The coach then took us a little way out of town to the site of the Song Festival ground. For over 130 years Estonians had gathered each year to sing and dance their traditional music, and in 1960 a large new stand was built, with a huge acoustic arch, so that 30,000 people could be accommodated and the tradition maintained; in 1988 numbers were even larger than usual when the Estonians sang their patriotic songs in defiance of the Soviet government. In 1991 the country was granted independence and they have never looked back, fiercely proud of their new state. After lunch on the ship I joined an excursion to visit an open-air museum at Rocca al Mare, a site just a few miles down the coast from the capital. Here I must explain that normally I would pay for excursions, but if willing to act as a Saga leader then I got a free place. We were told by the excursions director that leading was "A piece of cake", one merely had to be at the coach early, direct the passengers onto the correct coach, take their tickets, introduce the guide and the driver, say a few words about the place we were visiting, and then sit back and enjoy. It wasn't always as easy as that! Sometimes there would be some anxiety about getting back to the ship in time. These cruise ships very rarely wait for anyone – there are fines of hundreds of pounds just for a delay of minutes, plus the fact that another ship may be waiting to come in to dock. On this occasion I duly arrived at the coach early, wearing my full Saga uniform and holding a large stick with a number on the end so that, hopefully, the passengers would come to the correct coach. I introduced the guide and driver, told my passengers that they would be walking over a very wide area, and hoped they were wearing comfortable shoes. One man shouted out that he wasn't doing any ****dy walking! I soon moved to the back of the coach and had a word with him and his wife, pointing out that the excursion booklet specifically allotted this excursion a number of stars to indicate that a reasonable amount of walking was involved. "We don't read all that stuff." he replied; "We paid our money so what are you going to do with us?" I quickly bit back what I would have liked to say, smiled and told them that I would find them a suitable seat, etc. On arrival I did this, saw that they were comfortable and went off with the other 38 guests and our guide. This museum consisted of many old buildings, mostly of wood, set out to make up a typical village in old Estonia – church, complete with pipe organ, which I was allowed to play, a post office, little school with two rooms containing a harmonium, which I also played, and many other interesting farm buildings, fire station etc. At one place there were performances of national dancing in progress – the Estonians do *love* their national music – and one could spend hours wandering around. After 20 minutes it was obvious that some of the 'younger' element in the party were itching to go off at a faster pace and to see more, but were held back by many who were very slow, one or two being pushed in wheelchairs. After consultation, I went against the advice of the guide, and told the party that they were free to break off and go at their own speed, but that it was absolutely vital that they were back at the entrance by four o'clock, otherwise we WOULD return to the ship without them. At four o'clock, thank God, everyone had returned. Meanwhile the couple who did not want to walk turned on me very angrily and accused me of leaving them to go off with the rest of the party, and they were going to report me and get compensation when they got back on board. Compensation is the name of the game these days! And that's what it was all about. I knew I had done the correct thing in staying with the group, and was reassured by the excursions director that my actions had been exactly right – there would be no compensation.

Anchors aweigh, and we were off to Warnemünde, an important port in north Germany; in the evening I gave another lecture to a well-filled hall, which was encouraging, word had gone round and numbers had increased, or maybe there was nothing better to do on board. Many of the passengers got up very early to travel by train to Berlin, but I didn't think it worth all the effort just for a few hours, so I decided to do my own thing in the morning, boarded a train to Rostock, and had a ride around on trams, admiring the prosperous situation of the place. Way back in the 13th century it had become one of the members of the Hanseatic league, establishing tremendous power and prosperity in that area of the world, trading with many other nations. I visited St Mary's Church, which itself goes back to the time of the Hanseatic league, we know that there was a building in 1232, and it was rebuilt in 1290. Somehow it came through the Second World War virtually undamaged. It was always the place used to convene large crowds, and in autumn 1989 they gathered on Thursdays to pray for a change in society; with lighted candles they went out into the streets to be joined by demonstrators from other churches, and this, along with similar activities in other northern cities contributed to the downfall of the Communist regime, without a shot being fired. Rostock itself has grown enormously, after being heavily bombed in the last war, it now has a number of suburbs which practically reach into the port of Warnemünde. I made my way back along the beach, close to the ancient lighthouse, and alongside the canal, with its pretty houses and colourful gardens, heaving with people on this warm August day. In the afternoon I led the Molli trip…. curious? Molli is a narrow gauge railway line which has been running since 1886 from Bad Doberan, through the main street and into the countryside until it runs parallel with the Baltic coast to Kühlingsborn. We boarded the train at its terminus and waved excitedly as the engine steamed along the street, lined with busy shops and bell ringing madly to warn pedestrians and cars, then, once out of town, we travelled close to a horse racing track which the Germans claim to be the oldest in Europe, on to a long avenue lined with lime trees, through woods and villages until we reached the Baltic coast at Heiligendamm. The Germans claim this to be the largest sea resort in the region. I was so excited on the train, with my head out, enjoying the views and smell of smoke and noise from the engine, and when I joined the guests for afternoon tea in a rather exclusive restaurant I must have looked scruffy, with all the dirt and smuts from Molli. Heiligendamm is a typical resort of that area, with very large houses and well-kept gardens to match, hotels that obviously catered for the rich, and a general air of affluence everywhere. In the 19th century it was used as a summer holiday centre for rich dukes and generals, and I'm reminded that in 1932 a certain Adolf Hitler was made an honorary citizen, the town having voted in the Nazi party that year almost unanimously. Moving on to later times, in 2007 the town was used for the G8 summit of world leaders – I don't think anyone invited Hitler to be present. After tea we boarded our coach to visit the minster just outside the town. It is a huge church which dates from the time in the 12th century when Cistercian monks built a monastery on the site, and when the town grew, one of the prosperous Mecklenburg dukes decided to extend the church.

During dinner, those of us who had led excursions talked about our successes and our anxieties. John, the pianist, and his partner had gone with the Berlin crowd, and he did agree that the whole thing was a rush. He had a rather difficult man in his party, whom we will call Harold, who was always getting lost, and John gave him a telling off when he found him urinating by the cathedral wall, pointing out that German police would have no hesitation in carting him off to prison if they caught him. "Good luck to anyone who has him in their party." muttered John, "He is a menace."

During the night the ship changed course, and we woke to find ourselves docking in Copenhagen. Our morning excursion gave us a glimpse of the beautiful city of Copenhagen from the boat, as we drifted along the canals and had the various buildings pointed out to us by the knowledgeable guide, perhaps the best way to see the city with limited time. After lunch I was selected to lead 'Copenhagen by coach', and dutifully collected tickets and ticked off names of the guests, discovering that I had drawn the short straw – I was blessed with Harold. After introducing guide and driver I sat back to enjoy the ride. We stopped at the old fish market, but only for photo shots, the guide pointing out that coaches weren't allowed to wait so we had to be quick. A few of us nipped out for some snaps, and I heard a screech of brakes as cars drew to a halt, drivers gazing with astonishment to watch Harold proudly peeing in the middle of the road. It seems that even if he didn't have a camera he was determined to leave his mark at all the sites we visited, and I had to have a quiet word with him. "But I had to go." he explained in his northern accent, so I pointed out the toilet on the bus which could be used in emergencies. This could be confession time, for perhaps I should have explained this in my introduction, but drivers aren't very keen to have everyone using the toilet, it really is for emergencies, and as soon as you mention its presence everybody suddenly wants to go. So we generally keep quiet about the coach toilet. Harold resumed his seat next to a rather well-dressed lady who had to put up with the unpleasant smell while Harold's trousers steamed in the hot coach. I was determined to keep a close eye on him, I certainly didn't want him getting lost. We made our way to the popular palace and square of Amalienborg, always milling with hundreds of tourists, and as our party consisted of over 60 people I had time to nip into a souvenir shop before catching them up as they slowly made their way down the road towards the palace. Some intuition made me look round and there in the distance was Harold moving swiftly IN THE OPPOSITE DIRECTION. I dashed back along the street to get him. "Why are you going this way Harold?" I asked. "Why couldn't you stay with the rest of the party?"

"Balls." he replied, and I told him I wasn't having that sort of language. He made it clear that he was after golf balls, he was looking for a sports shop. "Harold I didn't know you were into golf, but you won't find any suitable shop in this part of the city, and even then you don't know golf balls in Danish." I added.

"No, I don't play golf, I just fancied some golf balls!" he replied. After that incident I watched him like a hawk, I never let him out of my sight, knowing that Saga Rose would sail within 15 minutes of our scheduled return. Back on board I spoke to the excursions director who was very sympathetic, and confided that Harold was suffering from Alzheimer's, his wife had died after they had booked the cruise, but all his family had urged him to go on the cruise alone. Yes, I could almost hear them in my mind, "You go Harold, it will do you good, seeing all those places." The phrase "Out of sight, out of mind," comes to me. During my years in Saga, especially at Christmas, I met a number of these situations where people who were very frail or ill or both, and should have had a travelling companion had been left to 'go it alone'. It was always unfair to them and to the rest of the travelling party; in this case it seemed that Harold could never find his way round the ship and one of the staff always had to collect him from his cabin to take him to the restaurant, and lead him back. It was a sad time for Harold, if his wife had been spared they might at least have rattled along together on the cruise, but I did hope fervently that I wouldn't have Harold on my excursions in Oslo, our last port of call, which we would reach by morning. Like the other Scandinavian cities, I was so impressed with the cleanliness, spacious layout – no high-rise buildings and skyscrapers here – and the freshness of the whole place. Within a short walk from the ship, one could get anywhere by train, underground, tram or bus, and I spent the morning doing my own exploring, naturally having a few rides on the trams; in the afternoon I led the city coach tour which took us out of Oslo, after seeing all the usual sites, up to the ski jump at Hollmenkollen. Although it was summer, without a trace of snow, one could imagine the excitement and drama as the skiers came hurling down from the top of the jump. It was used in 1952 as part of the Winter Olympic Games, and the Norwegians are proud of this site overlooking the Oslo fjord. Before we sailed in the late afternoon, I heard from some guests about their visit to the Kon Tiki Museum, and made up my mind I would visit that if I returned to Oslo – which I did a couple of years later. So, as passengers crowded the rails both to wave goodbye to the Norwegian band and dancers and to once again watch the incredible manoeuvres as two powerful tugs turned our boat around, and we set sail for Dover and England. This was a formal dinner evening, when one was expected, not required, to dress up: black tie for the men and suitable long dresses for the ladies, a custom which I found rather pointless. I've a strong suspicion that the women thoroughly enjoyed the dressing up, but for us entertainers and lecturers, mostly sitting in our own small restaurant, it was a bit pointless; I knew that after the meal I would be either going to bed early to read, or taking in a film, and it seemed rather crazy to go to all this trouble. However, when in Rome…

During our two days returning to Dover I gave the last of my lectures, plenty of things were organised on the ship so that no one could complain of boredom. It was also the time of reckoning. On embarking one is given a plastic Saga Rose card which is used as a currency for everything on the ship, drinks, gift shop, photographs, etc. and now came the Day of Reckoning. I believe my bill came to about £10, so the company made very little out of me, while the man in front was asked for £850, and didn't turn a hair, and just wrote out a cheque. I think £500 is probably the average spend on board by a couple in a fortnight. So, with time on my hands, I stood at the rail as we sailed through a fairly placid North Sea, and asked myself whether I enjoyed cruises, and would I go on a cruise myself; it seems to be everyone's dream at retirement to go on a cruise, relax and spend lots of money. As I indicated earlier, I did find it lonely at times, though in all fairness, this was probably because I was travelling alone, most of the passengers were in couples or groups. I did find the whole thing extravagant, with far too much food on offer, one could be literally eating 24 hours a day, and we were encouraged to do so. Even after a full four course meal in the evening, we would be invited over the loudspeaker system at 10.30 or 11pm to go along and have an evening roast supper! Almost every day there were special sales on particular decks, of silver, amber, 50% off all jewellery, etc. Then there were the official photographers, always in attendance, on deck, during games, in corridors and in the restaurant, especially at the captain's table; this was a MUST for anyone sitting at his table. Quite early on in the cruise we had the usual captain's dinner, when everyone is expected to line up – in formal attire, naturally – to introduce themselves to the captain before going into dinner; the photographers take pictures of every couple, every person, indeed the captain must be the most photographed individual on board ship. I must admit these gentlemen always seemed very genuine in their greeting, and mixed with the guests a great deal, when surely they must often have been bored out of their mind having to meet such people and hear the same stories and answer the same questions on every trip. Within 12 hours all the hundreds of 'Me with the Captain' photos were ready, and the tills began to merrily ring as these essential souvenirs were purchased. The idea of exploring a new country in one day, and then returning to the security of the ship seems to appeal to many people. They like to put a toe in the water of exploration and see the scenery and customs of a different place, but happy to know that they would always be returning to their little bit of England at the end of each day. One of the Saga guests who keeps in touch went on the 'Spirit of Adventure' and a Mediterranean tour, and he summed up the feelings of him and his wife, "Much as we enjoyed the cruise I think we both decided that cruising is not our ideal way of touring, so it is back to the motorhome. I never got used to the fact that I was visiting all these different countries during the daytime but I always returned to 'England' at night."

In 2004 I went on the Saga Rose again, once again back to the Baltics, though we did visit Lithuania and Poland this time. I had a slight scare when, as before, I led the Molli excursion at Warnemünde. We had just left the ship on the coach and the guide was explaining how the afternoon would pan out, and that we would be back in time for the ship sailing at six o'clock. I had been told that the excursion finished by five o'clock, and in fact I was due to give a lecture at 5.15pm. So it meant that when we visited the minster, I had to jump in a taxi and pray that we would get through the rush hour traffic in time. I did it by the skin of my teeth, and was still putting on my tie as I walked into the lecture hall to tell people about Tchaikovsky. I never did receive the promised taxi fare of €50

In these talks, as I have indicated earlier, quite a lot of personal bits of information are given, for the listeners enjoy this sort of thing, as well as learning about music. I don't remember the context but at some point I mentioned the time when I played with the Lewisham Philharmonic Orchestra, in the production of *My Fair Lady* given by the Eldorado Opera Company, over 40 years before – the story is back in Chapter 11. At the end of my talk two men came forward and introduced themselves: Prof. Higgins and Col. Pickering, the parts they had been playing in that very same production. It's certainly a small world, and we had some laughs and reminiscences together about life in Lewisham in the 1960s. My main memory of the 2004 cruise was a storm at the end. We had left Oslo in brilliant sunshine and on Sunday morning I played the piano in the main lounge for the service, and the captain announced that we were running into some stormy weather, "Nothing to worry about, just a little movement of the ship from side to side, we'll take care of you." This must have been said to reassure people, but was the understatement of the century. By one o'clock the ship was rolling all over the place, people were staying in their cabins, indeed we had been urged not to use the corridors because of the instability of the ship. I was given conflicting advice by seasoned travellers, one group telling me to have a fizzy ginger beer, "Works like a treat every time," and another group telling me to get food inside me to stop the nausea feeling. I tried both remedies, with disastrous results. I did venture into the main restaurant, this was Sunday lunch, roast beef and all the trimmings, but only a handful of people were eating. At a table next to me were two elderly ladies tucking into everything, and muttering to each other, "There don't seem to be many people in here today, my dear; perhaps the storm is putting them off." spoken as they tucked into another roast potato. When I got back to the cabin I felt very ill, but was due to give a lecture at four o'clock, so I tried to make my way up the stairs to the entertainment's office to inform them that there was no way I could talk about Tchaikovsky. Halfway up the stairs there was a violent bang, and I ended up on the floor, and looked up to see the shiny shoes and immaculately pressed trousers of…the captain. All I could think of saying, very weakly, was, "Well if you're down here who's doing the driving?" He didn't seem to find that very funny and asked why I was out of my cabin, and when I explained the reason he told me to return to the cabin, there was no one in the entertainment's office, and there would certainly be no lecture at four o'clock. He also advised that I should have a jab because of the seasickness. No sooner had he spoken when one of the lady doctors appeared armed with her needle, but before she could use it I was sick as a dog… fizzy ginger beer and roast lunch all collided or colluded. I felt so embarrassed, heaving away into a bag while she held on to me. "Trousers down." she insisted. She wanted to inject me in the bottom, but we were in a very public place, so she relented and injected my arm. I returned to the cabin and knew no more until seven that evening when my steward came and offered me some food, as they were doing for everyone else on board. Apparently the restaurants weren't doing any trade at all, and I was rather hungry and enjoyed a good meal. The storm went on regardless and as my cabin was just over the ship's propellers, I could hear it and feel it all night long. We were due to land in Dover at eight o'clock the next morning, but we were running about three hours late, so coffee and biscuits were served, and then at lunchtime we were given a full meal because we still couldn't get into the dock because of the huge waves. Eventually we disembarked at three o'clock – the ship was due to sail again at five, so it was a fast turn around, and I felt very sorry for passengers who were not disembarking, but had booked to do the next part of the cruise. They were going to have to face the Bay of Biscay in a few hours! With my case, I practically ran down the gangway, anxious lest the next lecturers had not turned up and I would be asked to go back on board… no way. It put me off sea cruising for the next two years.

2005 was a typical year of travelling, lecturing and playing the organ. Looking at the diary I know that I gave six lectures for the WEA, played folk music on the Isle of Wight after Easter, returned to Croatia and after my return had just two days before driving up to Scargill House in the Yorkshire Dales to present a music programme. This was to be the last of about 20 visits I had made to that unique centre. A couple of years before, Keith Knight, the warden, had retired and been replaced by a woman who seemed to have rather different ideas about how the place should be run, who should be on community, in fact the whole ethos seemed to change, and rather too quickly. Formerly the guests had always commented on the wonderful personal approach they found from the moment they arrived; staff were interested in them, talked to them, and from the moment one entered there was a feeling of care and REAL fellowship. On subsequent visits I noticed that the various rooms were turned into offices, with managerial names on the door and someone inside who seemed to be glued to a computer screen. The welcoming approach gradually fizzled out; on arrival one gave one's name to a member of staff behind a glass partition, and received a room number and the instruction that tea was at 4.30 then the partition closed. I prided myself on the fact that every holiday I had done brought in a full house of guests, sometimes people even willing to stay down in the village of Kettlewell on a bed and breakfast basis in order to come to the various sessions. To that effect while I was there, they usually gave me a choice of dates for the next visit so that some of the guests could book before going home. This time on 6th May I drove home with no future date, merely a promise that the warden would be in touch, which didn't happen, and when I contacted them I was informed that my type of holiday was not really wanted in the New Scargill venture. "In our vision, we are not really catering for Christians and their enjoyment." I was told. So that was it. Subsequently the place ran heavily into debt, many of the former guests (called partners) who had given money regularly over many years changed their mind and withdrew from Scargill. Something had obviously clouded their "Vision for the Future" for in 2008 it closed with huge debts; but so many people had good memories of Scargill and people from all over the world who had heard it was to close gathered together determined to re-open it. At the moment the house and land have been re-purchased and staff are already employed to open this centre again in safe hands. Great news.

Then one of my real dreams came true: the diary says 'Thursday, May 12 Norway for six days'. On the cruise ship we had visited Oslo for one day, but now came the opportunity to spend a week in one of the loveliest parts of that beautiful country, for we were bound for the Hardanger Festival. The guests, tour manager and I flew to Bergen where we stayed overnight in a very modern hotel. After supper I slipped out for some exercise and saw the rows of houses crowded together, rising in tiers above the harbour, their lights twinkling. It was around 10.30 but still light enough to pick out houses and shops by the harbour, brightly coloured and all made of wood; I discovered that there used to be many fires in this area, so that houses, hotels and shops were always being rebuilt. Next morning we were given a coach tour of Bergen with a knowledgeable guide, very proud of Norway. This included a visit to the house of the composer Edvard Grieg, at Troldhaugen where his original manuscripts could be studied, his pianos seen – unfortunately they were strict in the house and would not let me play – and many mementos of his life and work. Grieg had engaged an architect to build the house overlooking the fjord in 1885, he was in his early 40s, but this was to be the first permanent home of the Grieg's, for since their marriage in 1867 the couple had rented homes and spent much time travelling around. I found the house fascinating, and tried to imagine the wonderful view Edvard had each day over the fjord, before trees, houses and roads gradually obscured the view during the 20th century. After bidding farewell to the house we boarded the coach for the four hour journey, which included a ferry crossing, until we reached our hotel at Ullensvang. The first sight of Hardanger Fjord and our hotel at the water's edge just took our breath away, it was so beautiful and majestic; whenever I had a free moment during that holiday I would sit by the water and take in the wonderful views because, whatever time of day or night, it remained magical. The Utne family have owned the hotel for several generations, and they all live on the premises. Every day Mr Utne would check with the guests that they were happy with their meals and rooms, and he would speak to the rep to ensure that people were enjoying their holiday. This was despite the fact that the hotel was bursting to the seams with guests, with important musicians, with visits from the queen, who often popped in just to listen to a concert and quietly disappear again. I gave some illustrated talks on Norwegian Music, and gave a recital –first ensuring that Vladimir Ashkenazy was NOT within hearing distance. With all this top musical talent about, I suddenly felt like a beginner. I enjoyed telling them how Grieg had built a hut for privacy, which contained just a piano, table and chair higher up the mountain, but village folk still listened outside so he found 50 strong men who picked up the hut, moved it to a new location and were rewarded with a barrel of ale and food. When I came to this part of Grieg's story I could just point outside the window for there was the HUT standing in the grounds! During the ten years Grieg and his wife spent at Hardanger they mostly stayed at the guest house run by the Utne family – who wore their national costume proudly every day – and this is now the Ullensvang hotel, rebuilt and extended. The Utnes still put on their costume for special days of the festival. We attended concerts every day, morning and evening in the hall which had been built at the side of the hotel, or in the local church situated up the road, giving yet another fantastic view of Hardanger Fjord. The musicians mixed with the hotel guests, and at lunch one day I found myself at the salad bar next to Vladimir Ashkenazy. I complimented him on his wonderful CD set of Sibelius symphonies, and went to move away, but he asked me to bring my food over to the table he was sharing with his wife and son, to continue our conversation. Such a humble but incredibly fine musician. The first concert took place after the Queen of Norway had opened the festival. During that interval I saw that one could buy a glass of champagne or white wine, but it was incredibly expensive, so I nipped up to my bedroom to get my carton of blackcurrant juice, but on the way down in the lift I pressed the wrong button and landed up in the basement. As I emerged from the lift I almost fell over the Queen of Norway who was chatting to the hotel staff. I was so shocked I just stood there stunned, but she turned and smiled when I apologised for my intrusion. The queen then asked a few questions about the group I had brought to the festival and then we all dispersed for the second half of the concert. I could never get over the informality of these occasions. On our excursion day we visited the folk museum in the national park and went on to see one of Norway's glaciers at Folgefonn, and nearby the hydro-electric power station at Sima. We made our way back to the hotel to arrive at about four o'clock, and noticed that the staff were lined up at the entrance; I made a joke that we were indeed honoured to have the staff formally waiting to welcome us, but as we got off the coach the hotel manager asked me to arrange for our party to just stand on one side for a few moments. The queen emerged from reception, carrying her own case, had a few words with the members of the staff who were lined up, then got into a waiting car and departed, presumably back to Oslo, with just one person accompanying her and one escorting car. Our group couldn't believe the sheer informality of the occasion; one guest said that it was as though a member of the family was booking out. In the UK none of us would have been allowed within a mile of that hotel, and there would be a cavalcade of cars and motorcycles and police escorts with sirens screaming out. Probably we would have all have been vetted before being allowed to stay in the hotel. What a pity we can't go some way towards following the informal customs of the Scandinavians with respect to their royal families. I was truly sorry when that holiday came to an end; I wanted to stay there forever, enjoying the views, the peace and quiet of the whole place, but we had to make our way back to Bergen for the flight home. A holiday I will never forget, it has never been repeated by Saga probably because profits, if any, would have been very small, after paying for us to stay at one of the best hotels in the country and at one of the busiest times. This had to be the most enjoyable Saga holiday out of the 60+ assignments I've worked on over 20 years. As I listen to Norwegian music these days I have authentic scenes in my head of the enchanting countryside.

CHAPTER NINETEEN

SAD EXODUS FROM ENGLAND

In chapter 13 I spoke of Rev David Butler, who was minister of the Methodist church at East Peckham, my first home, in 1970. I had stayed in touch with David; after he and his wife realised they could have no children they adopted two boys, who have grown into fine young men. David became a doctor of theology, and eventually worked as lecturer in church history at Queens College, Birmingham. Sadly the marriage did not work out, and he remarried, and as the time for his retirement drew near he came over to Hereford with Rosemary, his second wife. I must say they seemed to suit each other and were a very happy couple. He was quite taken with the city and the prospect of offering his services to the cathedral and the Methodist church; they eventually bought an oldish detached house just within the city, close to trains and coaches, and we looked forward to many get-togethers, both musically and socially. He quickly took on some work in the cathedral, which was much appreciated, and he preached there a couple of times; strangely, the Methodist church never seemed to appreciate the help he could have given, and he was rather pushed out.

I discussed with David my idea of starting a music club in the city, and he was keen to be involved. In the winter of 2005 they came over for a meal, and Rosemary reminded him of his appointment with the doctor, for he had been suffering with some pain and kept putting off the visit, and mainly because he had a serious diabetic problem she had nagged him to get some help. Within a couple of weeks we knew he had pancreatic cancer, and he was in hospital for some time. When he was discharged he asked me to visit him and I found a terrible change in his appearance, very thin and haggard, this wasn't the David I had known all my life, and I realised he was slowly dying. He had been putting the finishing touches to another book – he had already written one published in 1996, this was *Dying to Be One* – a well researched discussion on the ecumenical movement of the church in England, though the title now seem to take on a much sadder aspect. He insisted that he needed a new computer to print his manuscript, we ordered it and I went over to set it up for him. Sadly he never ever used it, he went into a hospice for a short time, but cried out to return home until the time of his death when he reluctantly returned, for it was becoming impossible for Rosemary to cope without help. David died in St Michael's Hospice, and I attended his funeral on 17th June. The cathedral was packed with people who had known him during his all too short life: friends who knew him on the mission field, members from his various churches, and many from Queens College, both staff and students. He had chosen his service with great care, especially the hymns, but I had such a lump in my throat and tears in my eyes I could not sing a note – inside I heard him urging me to sing: "Come on Brian, I chose these hymns so that you can belt them out." but my inward reply was, "You shouldn't have died on me, then I would have shown you how to sing." Only members of the family went with the coffin to a beautiful, quiet churchyard at Burghill just outside Hereford, where he was buried; meanwhile I went into College Hall for refreshments and to meet some of the other people; as I wandered around I seemed to hear people just talking about mundane things, the weather, the state of the church, the cathedral building, and I just wanted to shout in a loud voice, "Our best friend David has died; is this all you can talk about?" Looking back, of course I don't blame them, life moves on, and I suppose they were remembering him in their own way, but I couldn't stay and went out into the cloisters, with the birds singing and water quietly gurgling from the fountain, I remembered David and just cried. We had been going to do so much together and now it was denied us, and, to be honest, I did ask God why he was so hard on David, and couldn't he have given him a few years of happy retirement after a long life of Christian service? Hereford changed for me after that sad event, and perhaps, subconsciously I began to look for an escape.

Throughout my life I have had a mission to try to spread my love of music to others; I feel it has so much to say, it doesn't need any special intelligence or talent, and people who come into classical music discover a wonderful Aladdin's cave to suit all moods. To this end I'd always wanted to begin a music club, for it was at one such club in Chadwell Heath Library that I had discovered wonderful music as a boy of 15. There is something special about enjoying musical works together as a group; although of course one is silent, there is a happy atmosphere of sharing something wonderful at a deep level. After some preparation I decided to begin a music club in Hereford. At the beginning of September the Music Circle had its first meeting at the small church of St Mary's and over 40 people attended. During that year I prepared a programme for two hours each Monday, with some refreshments at half-time to enable people to socialise. I'm pleased that five years later it is still going from strength to strength in the hands of a small committee, although, sadly I can no longer be part of the scene.

I was fortunate to be free in the latter part of September. On 25th, after Evensong the new statue of Elgar was unveiled by Dame Janet Baker. It is a very striking statue, showing him in plus fours, leaning against his bicycle, on the grass of the cathedral close, looking towards the tower. As a young man he would have cycled over to earn some much-needed cash by playing in the orchestra for various festivals, including Three Choirs, and later, as a successful composer he returned to conduct his oratorios and cantatas, some of which had been commissioned by the festival committee. I will always associate Elgar with Hereford, and this statue has become very popular. Well over 300 people had gathered for this simple ceremony, and as I moved around having conversation I realised that I knew over a hundred of them as friends, a consideration I should have remembered a few months later, it might have prevented me from making a bad decision.

I travelled out to Prague at Christmas as a music host for Saga. We were fortunate to be staying at the Hotel Bohemia right in the centre of the city –next to the Powder Tower, for those who know their Prague – I looked onto the tower from my bedroom. Our guide for the city tour was very proud of her country and extremely knowledgeable. Many of us attended midnight mass at one of the large churches nearby; we were warned to get there early for a seat, useful information because long before the service began the place was packed with people sitting on the floor all around. I'm glad I went to the service; although I didn't understand one word it was still a good way to begin Christmas celebrations. On Christmas

Day itself a few of us found a service in English at an Anglican church just a short walk from the hotel. Many English people live and work in Prague and their church is vital. The hotel was justly proud of its ballroom. Everything was in gold and red baroque style, with huge chandeliers and boxes from which people could look down on the dance or concert being given below. Sadly the floor had been affected by bad floods at the beginning of the year, but they had painstakingly restored every panel of wood. Later I found out a little about the history of the hotel. During the Communist era it officially did not exist; no one could book or stay there, it wasn't on any city map; in fact it was for people at the top of the Communist party so that they could gamble, entertain their women and live like lords without the rest of the public knowing. Security for anyone trying to enter the Hotel Bohemia was very strict, but with the downfall of the communists the hotel re-opened, back to its former glory, and it very much deserved its five-star label. I gave talks and recitals in the large ballroom, our 36 guests seemed a very small party in that large space. The hotel was very proud of the piano, but the more I played it the harder it became, and more notes decided not to respond.

In the afternoon we had been booked to go to the state opera but this proved to be a musical disappointment, on the whole. The Czechs love the *Mass* by Jacob Ryba, it is part of their tradition; unfortunately large chunks consist of narratives in the home tongue and no translation is given, so we felt left out of the story. I mentioned this in my report to Saga and suggested that if the holiday was repeated Saga should book for any one of a dozen classical concerts which are put on during Christmas Day. On Boxing Day we visited the castle on the other side of the river, with the huge cathedral of St Vitus. Next morning guests had a treat when we visited the Mozart Museum. Mozart and his wife loved Prague, and when Vienna shunned him musically in the last three or four years of his life, he turned to Prague and wrote his opera *Don Giovanni* and his *Prague Symphony* for the Czech people. In the museum we had our own private performance from a string quartet, and, naturally they played some Dvořák – a delightful experience. As we left the museum snow began to fall. I spent my free afternoon riding on trams, and going out to the suburbs of the city. This was a Christmas to remember.

Before you come to the conclusion that all these Saga music events are just one big holiday for me, I must stress that often there are problems which have to be overcome quickly. One might have been assured that CD players are on hand in a hotel, but then discover that none exist. Often I have had to give illustrated talks but without the use of a piano – a difficult task. On a few occasions no room would have been booked – at least that would be the hotel's claim, and there would be phone calls to make and contracts to study to prove that the hotel had agreed to provide a room. Some rooms prove very unsatisfactory; I remember in Salzburg having to give a talk in a beer-keller....type of basement bar/café, which was just about bearable until a large family sat down a few yards away to celebrate someone's birthday! In Vienna at the Renaissance Hotel I was forced to give my talk in the restaurant itself, after the guests had eaten. While a hundred or so other people were enjoying their meal they had a background of extracts and story of *Die Fledermaus* as an accompaniment. At one stage there was a round of applause behind me, and I discovered a large party of Japansese listeners who had eavesdropped thinking this was all part of a Viennese dinner! The two most basic requirements for music talks are a room which is quiet and has comfortable chairs...not *too* comfortable I hasten to add, because the listeners tend to snooze; the addition of a keyboard is a luxury but rarely to hand. In 2002 I was sent to Boringdon Hall, near Plympton in Devon. It was a very old manor house on the edge of Exmoor and various other buildings had been added. In those days we did not have the luxury of a Saga representative for UK venues, so I was always kept very busy. At the beginning one had to meet various trains at Plymouth Station and direct guests into taxis which would take them up to Boringdon Hall; waiting for hours on the station platform can be very cold and depressing, and I was still waiting for two more guests who were not on their appointed train, so I gave it another half hour. Still no guests so I jumped into a taxi and got myself back to the hotel and discovered at reception that these two guests had cancelled their booking a week before, but neither Saga nor the hotel had informed me. This often happened and it was infuriating. The guests' rooms were scattered all over the hotel complex and I was doing a great deal of walking especially when the quartet arrived. They were giving recitals in the middle of the week and I was doing music programmes at the beginning and end, when the quartet had departed. While being a friendly group of four women they obviously thought I was their personal slave; I was told to bring coffee and biscuits exactly halfway through their rehearsals, and they wanted me to deliver it personally. I did this every time, and even moved the chairs around the hall to their satisfaction. This was alright but I was already looking after 45 guests. I had brought my own keyboard for this holiday – as usual no piano was around – and had set it up in the corner along with my own hi-fi system; one of the quartet felt that it was "not quite the right thing to have them visible when we perform," and wanted me to dismantle the whole thing, but this I refused to do and we compromised by covering it all up with a sheet. To my mind this looked even more grotesque, and guests thought it looked rather like a ghost, but the quartet had to have their way. With all the walking involved in and around the hotel and the excursions to Plymouth and the Eden Project with the guests, my feet were in a terrible condition and for one of my own recitals at the keyboard my feet had swollen so much that I couldn't get my shoes on so I had to wear slippers. A week later, holiday over, reports sent in, and I received a call from my Saga boss thanking me for my hard work BUT one guest had thought it "In rather bad taste for Brian to be wearing slippers for his recital." Well, the guests are *always* right – says he, through gritted teeth – and I apologised.

In 2006 two events were to lead to a radical change in my life. The church at Holmer decided to buy a Makin electronic organ, which was duly installed and dedicated in the early part of the year. I made up my mind to buy an organ for my own home, and went for a Viscount organ. Jeremy Meager, the consultant, came over to discuss the organ and assured me it could be installed in my spare room upstairs; however when the organ arrived it was obvious that a mistake had been made, "No chance of getting it up those stairs, gov'nor." said the organ man immediately he saw the situation, so the organ had to live in my lounge along with the grand piano. Needless to say the room became very overcrowded.

Meanwhile in February my brother John and his wife returned from Ireland to meet up for a family reunion. They had moved from the UK a year before; after a lifetime of fishing in Ireland, it had always been John's intention to retire there, and after taking Jackie for one or two exploratory holidays, they had bought a bungalow and moved in 2005. I went up to the reunion at Peterborough and listened as John talked of the peace and quiet of the countryside where he now lived, the complete absence of traffic and a rather laid-back simple attitude to life in their rural part of the country. As a consequence I went out to see them in May, flying over to the small airport at Knock. John's description was absolutely right. It was warm and sunny for the whole five days – very deceptive – and though we were travelling on one of Ireland's main roads we hardly ever met another vehicle, and this was at 2 o'clock on a weekday afternoon. The countryside seemed harsh and less developed than in England yet it had a beauty all its own. I gathered that there were hundreds of bungalows and houses up for sale in the area because Ireland was at the height of the Celtic Tiger and developers and builders had been putting up property as fast as they could, though all this was to change within 18 months when the money ran out. In the same area now are hundreds of new, empty properties with no takers, despite reductions of up to 50%. Within 24 hours I had found a new four bedroom bungalow set in a field of about an acre, with garage, for sale at under half the price of its equivalent in England. I came home ready to put down a deposit on my new bungalow in Ireland, partly spurred on by the realisation that I needed a room for the organ. In fact I had to part with the grand piano, and begin the process of getting rid of furniture and a great amount of clutter which one gathers after a long time in one house. Looking back, I know that I made a tremendous mistake and rushed into the purchase without looking at all the pros and cons. I should have realised that it is one thing to spend five happy days on holiday but quite different to move everything and live in another country. I had reckoned on the house taking quite a while to sell but in fact it sold to the second couple to view it, two days after it went on the market; they then informed me that their own house was going to be rented out so... in short, when was I going to move? Suddenly I felt I was being propelled along in my actions and decisions, unable to stop things and give thought to the outcome.

In the middle of the preparations for moving I also had holidays to fulfil – yet again I had been booked to go to the Verona Festival, this time staying at Vicenza. About one hour's drive from Verona, this is a wonderful city, the home of Palladio, with some fine examples of his architectural style, including the Olympic Theatre, the oldest surviving example in the world. Our hotel was quite close to the railway station, so once again I had opportunities to explore the area by train. Apart from the usual trip to Venice with all the crowds, we went to Sirmione, at the southern tip of Lake Garda, and had a boat ride to see the old castle and the grand villas of the rich and famous, including one which had been owned by Maria Callas.

The dreadful storm I had encountered on Saga Rose in 2004 had rather put me off cruises, but I did agree to give some lectures on the smaller ship, Saga Ruby, which sailed in August, once again back to the Baltic capitals. I was in the company of two other lecturers, one whose name I have forgotten came at the last minute to replace John Amis, famous for his part in the TV show *Face the Music*, when he would often display his ability at whistling. He was indisposed for this cruise. The other lecturer was a young man called Simon Dunbavand, an extremely talented musician who goes to great lengths in presenting his music with illustrations on computer PowerPoint. His talks were always interesting and packed with information, and, indeed he was a very hard act to follow. I had arranged to do my six talks on Tchaikovsky, but, I was let down by the PA system which always seemed to be breaking down in the middle of a lecture. At one time I just gave up completely when the CD player failed and the microphone – at least the piano was still in working order. I made known my feelings to the entertainment's manager, and will probably not be invited again. In spite of this it was the most successful of the three cruises I have done; I made friends with many of the entertainers and felt much more at home in the more intimate atmosphere of a small ship. The talk at dinner table was very much centred around my move to Ireland, I seemed to want others to justify and support my action.

I made a brief trip to Ireland at the end of August to see how work was progressing on the bungalow; it had been left in what is called 'builder's finish', meaning that it is really a shell waiting for fireplaces, bathroom accessories, tiling, etc to be added. The builder was there and seemed very jovial as he put his arm across my shoulder and told me he would put everything right and have it all ready for moving in: "I'll look after you, there'll be no problems, I can sort everything out." were his reassuring words and like a fool, I was taken in. I went off to order carpets for the bungalow, to be ready and fitted for my arrival.

September and October were months for saying goodbye to many friends. The Music Circle which I had started one year before was going to continue, but I was so sad to be leaving. I celebrated my 70th birthday at the end of September but didn't have a party this time. My sister came over from Dartford – alone – and Allen and his wife, along with my dear friends and neighbours, Pat and Alan, all joined me in a celebratory meal at a local restaurant. Someone had informed the church at Holmer, and a little party was held at the end of morning service complete with birthday cake. They were such lovely people and I was so sad to say goodbye after five years as their organist. Allen and Brenda stayed on over several days to help with the packing, an enormous job, but I then had about a week putting stuff into boxes all day and every day until I was exhausted. Along with physical exhaustion came grave doubts about moving – I had finally faced up to the fact that I didn't want to move, but decisions had gone so far down the line that it seemed impossible to reverse. Pickfords came along to view the situation and summed it up in one sentence: "Blimey governor, this isn't a house move, you've got a bleedin' library!" And he was only seeing the books, music and CDs *after* I'd given away a third of them! The organ was the biggest item to handle and at £10,000 it was the most expensive. They worked for two whole days packing and loading on to the biggest Pickfords van they possessed, and on Wednesday afternoon they departed for Ireland, via their depot in Gloucester. I had arranged to stay overnight with my neighbours, Pat and Alan, and had a final walk around the empty rooms and the garden, already with tears in my eyes at leaving my lovely house in the loveliest county in England.

Next morning, 25th October, I began my long journey to Holyhead and the ferry, after saying goodbye to Pat and Alan – Pat subsequently died in 2008. Somehow the trip seemed long and lonely, as though I didn't really belong anywhere at that particular time; it wasn't helped by the rain which began as I left Hereford and more or less continued all day and the following night. As the ferry sailed away, through my tears, I got a last glimpse of a dismal looking England – but dismal or not I would have given anything to turn round and go home.

Inevitably I arrived at Dun Laoghaire in the middle of the rush hour and had to somehow negotiate my way across the city and find the N4 Dublin – Sligo Road.

I pulled in to ask directions at a bicycle shop and was told it was crazy to try to find a way in all the busy traffic. "You'd do better to call in at the pub along the way and have a wee drink and a rest till the traffic dies down." I was advised. I followed the suggestion and found a pub which was already very busy, and it was only 5.30 in the evening; there was a dramatic silence and all eyes were on me as I ordered tea and biscuits, and even the man who served me seemed rather taken aback. "To be sure, I think we can find some tea if we look hard, so take a seat and I'll bring it over." After 10 minutes or so he arrived, beaming, with a pot of tea. "Here you are sir, lovely hot cup of tea for yourself, enjoy it". But something was wrong.

"Thank you very much, but there's no lid on the teapot," I replied.

"Ah yes sir, very sorry about that, but the lid, it did go missing some time ago"... I knew then that I had reached Ireland.

The 'rush hour' in that part of the world is more like three hours, and I battled my way through heavy rain and miles of road works, noticing at one stage that signs for the N4 and the West had just disappeared. I was complimenting myself on the fact that at least Ireland seemed to have a good number of hospitals, I had passed three in 15 minutes, but then realised I was going round in a circle and it was the same hospital each time. In pouring rain I reached my brother's house at around nine o'clock.

Fortunately the sun shone next day and, sure enough the Pickfords lads were waiting at the gate to unload. My brother then informed me that it had been touch and go whether we could have unloaded, for the 'reassuring' builder had held onto the keys until the day before my arrival, so the carpets had only been laid the day before. Had I but known, this was just the first of endless troubles with the bungalow, but the men got to work, the van was emptied, while they consumed many cups of tea and biscuits, and with a handsome tip they wished me good luck leaving 103 large boxes I had to open.

Many things were wrong with the bungalow, mainly to do with the electrics and the plumbing. This builder had titled himself as an electrical engineer, but I came to the conclusion that I wouldn't even have trusted him to change a light bulb. He had employed young unskilled lads to do much of the work in the bungalow, who were quite lazy and had done jobs badly – if a door hinge needed 4 screws you could bet your life that there would only be two or maybe three fitted, half the electric sockets had not been wired correctly, and, when I did get in a qualified electrician – an Englishman as it happened – he showed me one or two dreadful bits of wiring which could have been lethal. I realised in time that this is one of the weaknesses of workers in Ireland, there seems to be no such thing as a foreman or inspector. In my case neither the builder nor any other qualified person had been round to inspect the work in the bungalow, even the two showers were left hanging on the wall for someone else to screw in. In the lounges wrong carpets had been fitted; apparently the assistant who had taken the order found that one colour was not available, so he had quietly substituted another, without even consulting me. The list could go on and become boring, but the last straw was when the Eircom engineer came to connect up my telephone. What should have been a 15 minute job took over two hours, and the patience and determination of this man at least began to restore my faith in Irish workmanship. We opened up the small box outside to find the telephone lead ready for connection, but there was no lead. It should have come in from the road via an underground concrete channel to the connection box. We dug a hole to discover that the end of the concrete channel had itself been cemented up, so the engineer had to go through the whole process. After I had made a very angry, threatening phone call the builder did send his assistant, *after* we had dug the hole, but it was obvious that he hadn't a clue about what to do. That was the last time I spoke to the builder, from then on he never even answered my calls. When I made enquiries around I discovered he had a very poor reputation, no one trusted him and it seems, only English mugs like me were taken in. Like most of the builders in Ireland he was greedy, overreached himself financially and when the recession came along he was bankrupt. Not many tears have been shed for such people over here.

You may be getting some idea of the mood I was in and a feeling of complete disillusionment. At one stage I put this all on paper, and below I have reproduced my feelings about the move six months after it happened; at one point you will notice that I was going to put the book completely aside for ever.

In the summer of 2006 the book came to a standstill. I went out to visit my brother in Ireland and made a very hasty, ill-considered decision to move out

366

from England and to live in Ireland. All the gory details will be set out, if and when I reach that point in the book, but it led to a time of depression, and, on occasions, almost breakdown. When you go to bed at night and just pray that the whole thing is a dream and you will wake up once again in your old house in Hereford, things have to be pretty bad. Trouble was, every time I woke up I was still in my bungalow and still in Ireland, with no hope of returning to my old life again, unless I went through all the trauma of moving yet again. The prospects of doing this depressed me even more; Pickfords had left me on 26th October with the furniture installed and 103 large boxes of books, CDs, kitchen utensils and other things, which had to be unpacked and sorted out. The task took weeks, the weather turned bad, with intense rain and the most frightening gales – the winds almost blew one over, and whistled around the bungalow all the time. Though I tried on several occasions to get on with writing this book I just couldn't find any energy or motivation; perhaps I couldn't cope with the idea of projecting my mind back to life in England in the '70s and '80s, I had just lost interest in the whole thing and was living from day to day, hoping and praying that things would get better. After 16 months out here things have improved; I am adjusting to a completely different life and feel the urge to write again; so, just read on for the Ireland episode and all its sad details. I was encouraged yesterday when I read an extract from the 8th edition of *Lonely Planet Guide to Ireland*. While it is damning about Ireland's efforts to protect the environment it goes on to say, "The six central northern counties – Roscommon, Cavan, Monaghan, Leitrim, Longford and Westmeath might be a long way from the country's coveted coast (in Irish terms, at least) but with the mighty River Shannon surging through the wooded countryside interspersed with trout-teeming lakes, there's no shortage of water in these parts. There is a refreshing lack of tourists. That's not to say there's nothing here for visitors to see. It has some significant Celtic sites… the central North's abundance of water, the vast tracts of bog, unfolding fields and mist-shrouded forests means it remains, perhaps, Ireland's final frontier and the perfect place to retreat." So, perhaps I have retreated and this is the place where everyone wants to live, but if I could turn the clock back I would have gladly stayed in England, and were I to be given one wish, it would be to close my eyes and be back in that lovely house in Hereford, with all my friends…

The last phrase really says it all, I left behind so many friends in musical circles – indeed in the Music Circle itself, and in church and cathedral context, and my own family; not that one was for ever rushing out to meet people but at least they were on hand, just a car drive away. During my first few days here I had to go and register with the doctor in the village, and when he discovered where I was living his words were, "Why are you living up there? You are living among savages, those people wouldn't know a book if they tripped over it." This seemed a harsh statement but Dr Hardiman was absolutely right. The people are mainly 'small' farmers, they have a day job and do their farming in the evening and at weekends so they have to work hard. Many have lived here in a very simple fashion for generations, and there is no culture or desire for it. As I said to a friend back home in a recent telephone conversation, the most dramatic thing to happen during the week is when the dustbin men call, or there may be high drama if one or two cows get out of the field onto the road. Having just typed this sentence I looked out of the window to see just that… a calf prancing around in my garden; it had jumped over the wire from the field next door. Now, to inform the farmer and get it re-united with its mother.

Obviously when I considered moving here it would have made sense to live near a town or city, to take in concerts and other activities; but, in England I had had more than enough of cities, crowds, traffic jams and noise and this rural backwater of Ireland provided the answer.

I was looking forward to a return to Prague for the Christmas holiday; it would get me away from Ireland for a few days and I would spend time with friends and have some interesting conversations and exchange of ideas, but unfortunately the holiday proved to be a nightmare. Just at the time when everyone was flying away to be with relations and friends a very dense fog came down over England and refused to go away, affecting flights badly. I was able to take off from Dublin, heading for Heathrow, and the Aer Lingus desk kindly took my luggage, telling me I needn't bother about it until I reached Prague. As we approached Heathrow to land we could see that the fog had thickened, and suddenly the engines roared to a high pitch as we shot up into the air at a steep angle; the pilot later apologised and told us that a previous plane had overshot the runway and had to line up to land again, so all other planes were scattered. There was a big cheer and a sigh of relief when we did hit the tarmac. I discovered that my flight to Prague with British Airways had been cancelled, and then came the problem of reclaiming my suitcase; after much haggling and producing passport and flight ticket I was allowed to go into a huge warehouse stacked from floor to ceiling with at least 2,000 items of luggage, and there was no way of identifying my black bag among all the rest – a completely useless task. I was in touch with Saga head office and eventually was put on a coach to Manchester to book in at a hotel for just a few hours sleep before reporting back to the airport and getting a flight out to Amsterdam, and from there to Prague, in business class, where I arrived at about six in the evening, just 24 hours late and minus my luggage. I had to go and buy some clothes, but the biggest loss were my CDs, piano music and all my information and notes for the music talks; Prague is a very musical city with several music shops, so I spent the morning of Christmas Eve buying replacement CDs and reorganising my programme. To add to the misery I discovered that the Saga rep was a fellow I couldn't get on with, in fact the ONLY one I ever had problems with; having worked with him in Italy I had told Saga that I would not do a holiday with him again. He had so many hangups about the holidays and the guests, and had told me point blank that he saw no reason for music hosts – he could equally well do the job himself. But I had to work with Derek somehow, though I always made sure I sat with other guests at mealtimes. On the previous Prague Christmas holiday I had mentioned in my report that it was pointless going to the usual traditional Christmas mass by Ryba as none of us understood the Czech language. Instead we were going to a lovely old church in the city centre called St Nicholas; guests relaxed in their places and I passed around some programmes only to discover that the main item was...*Christmas Mass* by Ryba. What a pity no one from Saga had checked this out before the tickets were bought. I had a very early return flight, and, my luggage mysteriously appeared at the hotel just a few hours before I checked out. In spite of all these problems my love for Prague had not diminished and it's on the list of places for a revisit if I'm spared.

On my first Sunday in Ireland I went to the local Catholic church in the village, and looked around expectantly for the hand of friendship and some sort of welcome. Instead I sat in a pew on my own and at the end quietly filed out, no one even looked at me let alone spoke, so I got in the car drove home and sat over coffee wondering what was wrong with me. I came to accept that basically the Irish are rather shy and lacking in confidence, they don't push themselves forward to speak to strangers, though this characteristic changes fast when a few drops of Guinness or whiskey have been drunk. Eventually I joined the Methodist church in Longford, the nearest town about 20km away. The minister, Andrew Dougherty and wife Joyce were a delightful couple, and welcomed me into their home, always a lively place with their three children, Matthew, Patrick and Charlotte. There was nothing posh about them, you just dropped in any time and took them as they were. Sadly, as part of the Methodist custom they were being moved on to a church at Bray in the summer, so our friendship was short lived.

After about a year I wanted to get to know more people and thought I could do it through my music and was able to persuade Longford and Carrick-on-Shannon councils to allow me to do some evening classes. I never got more than ten to a dozen people at any one class, which seemed disappointing to me, but the arts officers seemed quite satisfied with this number. Those who attended were very keen but pointed out that they knew nothing about classical music. The classes went on for one term, but Carrick encouraged me to repeat it a year later. I still had this missionary urge to offer music to the local community, so in 2008 I found a suitable venue – the old school in Roosky where various adult activities took place – and put many leaflets around the village. I had bought an expensive projector and screen and a large number of opera DVDs and planned to use these in my musical endeavours. On the first night I was there punctually at seven, but no one else arrived, but then, this was Ireland and people always came late. Soon a mother turned up with a little boy aged about 10; it turned out that she was Polish and was not planning to stay, but was leaving the little boy and would pick him up at nine o'clock. He told me his name and I said how pleased I was that someone so young was interested in music. "I don't really like music," he replied, "But on Tuesdays Mummy's boyfriend comes round." So, at 2 euros a session, I had become the cheapest child minder in Roosky. A man appeared 10 minutes later assuring me that the football on television was bl*** rubbish so he thought he'd give me a try. Not very encouraging, but with a class of two we listened to a lively overture after some illustrations about its construction. Halfway through a tiny man banged his way into the class, slammed the door and immediately began telling me how much he loved classical music, and he went on telling me all through the overture and afterwards, in fact he never stopped talking. We listened to one or two more pieces, and I kept glancing at my watch, feeling it was the longest and most embarrassing two hours in my whole career. At the end the boyfriend came to collect his charge, and the two men went away, the little man still telling me how much he loved classical music. There was no further meeting of the Music Club, and I still haven't the heart to try again.

About a year after arriving in Ireland I was asked to take on a rescue dog. As a puppy she had been abandoned with her brother in a bag which was left hanging on a gatepost by the road side. Fortunately someone found the dogs, but one of the puppies ran across the road and was killed. The bitch was taken to the ISPCA centre and eventually found a home, but the elderly woman couldn't cope with a young dog, and it had been shunted back to the centre, rescued by a gentleman who also changed his mind and returned the dog. One of my English friends over here works for the ISPCA, took pity on it, but when she took it home it wasn't accepted by the three dogs she already had, and that's when I came into the picture. She appealed to me to give the dog a home otherwise it would have to go back to the ISPCA pound yet again. I went along to see Badger – as I later named her – and we both took to each other immediately. She jumped all over me and licked me to death. How could I refuse? I took her in and Badger has been great company ever since. Twice a day she insists on taking me for a walk, so I do get some exercise. Of course she's a terrible tie when I have to go away and she ends up in the kennels, but at least Badger has been given a permanent home.

At about the same time I contacted the local school and discovered that there was no music at all offered there, so I volunteered to go down and do one session each week. This has been successful, the children are grateful and enjoy singing and music listening, we have even started to learn how to write music. The village school is over 120 years old, still using the original building. There are just two classes, an infants class of five to seven-year-olds, and the junior class with ages ranging from eight to twelve, which is the class I take. It is hard to teach to such a wide age range, where even basic reading cannot always be taken for granted, but because the numbers are small, only 13 children, the teacher is able to do almost one-to-one tuition. There are no computers for the children in the school so one wonders what happens when they get to the second grade of education and discover that children from larger town schools are already computer literate. It must also be hard to adapt to a secondary school with over 1000 pupils after four years in the same class in a tiny village environment. Somehow they seem to cope.

Despite problems in travel, the Saga holidays have proved to be a lifeline, something I can look forward to, and prepare for, each year. In 2008 I returned to Italy to do a second year at the Puccini Opera Festival . The year before guests had stayed at a large hotel called *Il Ciocco* which was situated high up the mountain side, a few miles from the ancient walled city of Lucca, birthplace of Giacomo Puccini. Views from the hotel were fantastic at any time of the day and we were looked after, but felt very much like prisoners – without a car one was totally isolated. On one of the two trips to the Puccini opera we visited his house – Villa Museo Puccini and actually met his granddaughter Simonetta who owns the building. She is an elderly woman but still very much in charge of the Puccini situation. She refuses to have the Puccini birthplace in Lucca restored, which is a great pity for Lucca itself is a big tourist attraction. The open air theatre at Torre del Lago is new – only opened in 2008, and for our 2007 visit they were still using the old one, while the new theatre was taking shape next door. The setting is very beautiful with the lake nearby – it had also been owned by Puccini, who loved to shoot everything with wings.

When I returned for the Puccini Festival in 2008 it was to stay in another hotel at Montecatini Terme; as its name implies, it is a town full of thermal spas; in fact people come from all over the world to take advantage of treatment in the baths and spas. I nearly missed the whole experience and came closer to death than at any time in my life. I had flown direct from Dublin to Pisa, arriving at the airport close to midnight, and eventually found a taxi with an elderly driver who seemed very tired before we even set out on the hour's journey. The trip to Montecatini meant driving on the motorway for a considerable distance and like all Italian taxis this one was driven at top speed. We were on the motorway in the overtaking lane and a very large lorry came out to overtake, but my driver didn't seem to be reducing speed. As we were getting very close I glanced towards him and saw that he was fast asleep – the taxi was driving itself at 100 miles an hour straight for the lorry! I shouted to wake him up and, thank God, he didn't swerve the taxi but braked hard – we were only a few feet from the lorry's tail lights. "Dormi [sleeping]." he said, smiling, but I was furious, we could have both been killed, and I told him not to try any more *"dormi"* again. He spoke no English but I just kept chatting to him in my 'pidgin' Italian to keep him awake. Had I been on a normal road the sensible thing would have been to stop the taxi and find another, but this is very difficult on a motorway at one o'clock in the morning. When we finally reached the hotel the driver helped to carry my luggage in and I told the reception clerk what had happened. He turned on the driver and obviously told him off and even mentioned the police, and suddenly the driver stopped smiling – to think I even gave him a generous tip! That incident stayed with me all through the holiday and I am so relieved that I was sitting in the front and noticed him asleep otherwise, no Puccini holiday.

On my free day I went off by train to Viareggio and spent the morning and afternoon on the beach, remembering that the last time I had been in that seaside resort was in the summer of 1964 on holiday with a group led by the incorrigible deputy head of Northbrook School, Mrs Kirby.

When the recession came along in 2008 Saga holidays suffered badly. Many retired people paid for their holidays on the interest from personal savings, but suddenly this interest was down to zero. What an indictment that a government penalises those who are thrifty and have regularly saved yet encourages everyone to take on large debts with credit cards. Surely this was one reason why we have gone through a recession – the whole world spending money it doesn't actually have. Another factor was that in many cases grandparents were now helping to pay the mortgage, if their own children were unemployed. In former years I had done at least eight holidays each year for the company but now it was reduced to just two. The situation hasn't been helped by my removing to Ireland, for the company has to pay my air fare to get me back to do UK holidays.

I look back in a situation of *real* retirement and realise how busy I was in earlier years. At the height of my career, with all the demands of time and energy made by teaching, I still managed to find time to be organist, to lead a folk band, attend concerts and operas in London, often taking school parties with me, and go off to host music holidays and play for the Isle of Wight Folk Festival. Suddenly that's all come to an end and I suppose my mixed up feelings and depression could be a refusal to admit that at some stage one just retires, gives up all that work and responsibility, to enjoy a simple life and an empty diary. At least I'm NEVER bored, there may be no concerts to attend but I do have my CD collection to keep me going and the Proms on BBC TV and radio, there are so many books I want to read, and get frustrated that I will 'Pop my clogs' before I have read them all. While wrists and fingers are still fairly flexible, I try to play the piano or organ most days of the week, staving off the onset of arthritis which has afflicted so many of my musical friends – there are a variety of ways to spend this spare time, only hindered by the fact that once I settle in a comfortable armchair with a book or CD on the go I inevitably fall asleep within minutes. At the back of my mind I must accept that I will never be a real member of the community here in Ireland. The nearest village, Roosky, with shops, post office and a doctor is situated by the River Shannon; on the other bank are the boundaries of two counties, Longford and Leitrim, while on this side of the river we have County Roscommon. My colleague at the village school tells me of people who have lived for years on the other side of the Shannon Bridge not being fully accepted by the locals on this side, so what chance do I have? The Irish are different in so many ways and I have to keep telling myself that I must not criticise or compare them with my English counterparts; if I'm here to stay then I must accept Ireland with all its customs and differences. The thought still haunts me that I would not want to die and be buried in Ireland, for a whole part of me yearns for England every day. But who knows?

At the time of writing (December 2010) Ireland is facing financial ruin, the Celtic tiger has well and truly died leaving the evidence of greedy, unscrupulous property developers and bankers, egged on by a corrupt government. The country is bankrupt. In my own county there are nearly 2,000 new houses which have never been sold; despite reductions of up to 50% there are few takers. In this financial climate it is all but impossible for me to sell my bungalow and relocate back in the UK. I am a prisoner here in Ireland, literally praying for a way out; the homesickness does not go away, even after four years.

I trust you have enjoyed reading about my life in music. Five years ago I began this story, "It all started in Islington", and as I conclude, I often pause and wonder, where will the journey end?